OLD AGE IN
THE OLD REGIME

OLD AGE IN THE OLD REGIME

Image and Experience in Eighteenth-Century France

David G. Troyansky

Cornell University Press

Ithaca and London

First published 1989 by Cornell University Press.

International Standard Book Number 0-8014-2299-X
Library of Congress Catalog Card Number 88-43286

Printed in the United States of America

Librarians: Library of Congress cataloging information appears on the last page of the book.

The paper in this book is acid-free and meets the guidelines for permanence and durability of the Committee on Production Guidelines for Book Longevity of the Council on Library Resources.

*For Anna and Aaron, in honor of their
grandparents and great-grandparents*

Everyone treats me as an old man. I laugh about it. Why?
Because an old man never feels like an old man. I understand
from others what old age implies for those who see it from
without, but I do not feel my old age. Thus my old age is not a
thing that in itself teaches me something. What teaches me
something is the attitude of others toward me. To put it
another way, the fact that I am old for others is to be
profoundly old. Old age is for me a reality that others feel,
they see me and say, "This nice old man," and they are kind
because I will die soon, and afterwards they are respectful, etc.:
it is other people who are my old age.

Jean-Paul Sartre

Contents

Illustrations, Figures, and Tables

TABLES

Acknowledgments

It is a pleasure to acknowledge the advice, assistance, criticism, and encouragement I have received during the making of this book. The inspired teaching of Carl Weiner at Carleton College first drew me into French history. In the graduate program in comparative history at Brandeis University the critical sense, attention to detail, and friendship of Rudolph Binion mattered most.

In France I had the good fortune to receive generous attention from two scholars whose work has profoundly influenced contemporary historiography. The late Philippe Ariès welcomed me into his seminar and his home and suggested several important paths of research. Michel Vovelle encouraged me to work in Provence, gave me the opportunity to speak to his seminar, and helped solve several historiographical and practical difficulties. I also thank Jean-Pierre Bardet, Christoph Conrad, Françoise Cribier, Denis Crouzet, and Jean-Pierre Goubert for their friendship and good services.

My colleagues at Texas Tech University have acted as intellectual sounding boards, particularly James Brink, John Howe, Catherine Miller, Ronald Rainger, and Edward Steinhart. Joan Weldon typed the manuscript with speed and accuracy. The History Department, the College of Arts and Sciences, and the Graduate School provided institutional and financial support. Other support came in the form of a 1979–80 Sachar Travel Grant from Brandeis University, a 1980 Camargo Foundation Grant, and a 1986 National Endowment for the Humanities Summer Stipend.

Thanks are also due Robert Aldrich, Eugene Black, Steven Clay, Thomas Cole, Mark Cummings, John Demos, Robert Duplessis, Cissie

Fairchilds, David Hackett Fischer, Robert Heckenroth (*maire d'Eguilles*), Arthur Imhof, Frank Kafker, Colin Kaiser, Emmet Kennedy, James Leith, Frank Manuel, Richard Menkis, Frederik Ohles, Jean-Claude Perrot, Janet Polasky, Michael Pretina, Steven Saba, Ellery Schalk, Simon Schama, Antoine Schnapper, Robert Schneider, John Schrecker, Theda Shapiro, Peter Stearns, and Russell Young, as well as archivists and librarians in Paris, Aix, Marseille, Amiens, Caen, Carpentras, Avignon, and elsewhere. I thank John Ackerman, editor-in-chief of Cornell University Press, for his enthusiastic encouragement of this project and the anonymous readers for the Press who made important suggestions for revision.

Finally, I turn to family. My parents, Howard and Leila Troyansky, have provided all kinds of support, reminding me of the impossibility of separating the personal from the professional. I thank also my grandparents, who introduced me to things European and helped bring the past alive in my childhood. My sister Valerie made important criticisms of the chapter on art. My in-laws, Albert and Nancy Anderson, contributed their enthusiasm. Amy, my wife, a better wordsmith than I, might be able to find the language suitable for expressing a partner's gratitude and esteem, but I cannot. I thank her for everything, including Anna and Aaron, to whom this book is dedicated.

D.G.T.

Lubbock, Texas

Abbreviations

The following short forms are used throughout the footnotes and in the Selected Bibliography.

A.D.	Archives Départementales
A.M.	Archives Municipales
A.N.	Archives Nationales, Paris
A.P.	Archives de l'Assistance Publique, Paris
A.T.P.	Musée des Arts et Traditions Populaires, Paris
B.H.V.P.	Bibliothèque Historique de la Ville de Paris
B.M.	Bibliothèque Municipale
B.N. MS	Bibliothèque Nationale, Paris, Salle des Manuscrits
B.N. Estampes	Bibliothèque Nationale, Paris, Cabinet des Estampes
Deloynes	Collection Deloynes, B.N. Estampes
De Vinck	Collection De Vinck, B.N. Estampes
Duvillard	Collection Duvillard, B.N. MS
F.F.	Fonds Français, B.N. MS
J.F.	Collection Joly de Fleury, B.N. MS
M.C.	Minutier Central des Notaires Parisiens, A.N.
N.A.F.	Nouvelles Acquisitions Françaises, B.N. MS
Opéra	Bibliothèque de l'Opéra, Paris
Soleinne	Collection de Soleinne, B.N. MS
Widener	Widener Library, Harvard University, Cambridge, Mass.

OLD AGE IN
THE OLD REGIME

Introduction

Old age is no longer the "new" topic it was just a few years ago, but it is a subject that will not go away. As Western populations continue to age, fears arise that their declining productivity and reproductivity threaten the solvency of social security systems. Alarmists speak resentfully of the aged as sapping the "vitality" of nations. The elderly themselves—backed by those who appreciate that they too will be among that number—demand their due as contributors to the well-being of societies. The aged are the objects of investigation after investigation into their housing, work, leisure, and physical and mental health. A new science of gerontology has arisen; demographers, political scientists, and economists are among its practitioners.

The scope of inquiry into old age has transcended questions of social policy. The subject belongs equally to the humanities and the social sciences. Classical and biblical scholars, historians of art and literature, historical anthropologists and sociologists have all addressed questions of old age in other times and other places. If nothing else, they have demonstrated that its meaning has been far from constant.[1]

---

1. See, among others, the collections by Stuart F. Spicker et al., eds., *Aging and the Elderly: Humanistic Perspectives in Gerontology* (Atlantic Highlands, N.J., 1978), and David D. Van Tassel, ed., *Aging, Death, and the Completion of Being* (Philadelphia, 1979); the volumes of anthropological essays by Christine L. Fry et al., *Aging in Culture and Society: Comparative Viewpoints and Strategies* (New York, 1980), and Pamela T. Amoss and Stevan Harrell, eds., *Other Ways of Growing Old: Anthropological Perspectives* (Stanford, Calif., 1981); the study of the Aliyah Senior Citizens' Center by Barbara Myerhoff, *Number Our Days* (New York, 1978); the English oral histories in Ronald Blythe, *The View in Winter: Reflections on Old Age* (New York, 1979); and the occasional older work of interest such as Bessie Richardson, *Old Age among the Ancient Greeks* (Baltimore, Md., 1933).

Simone de Beauvoir tried to cover the entire history of old age in one volume. She concluded that despite scattered expressions of respect, veneration, and even affection, the aged have always had a difficult time. She cited the behavior of "primitive" peoples, described in all its variety in 1945 by Leo Simmons,[2] as evidence of the abysmal way the aged have been treated by us all. If she communicated any sense of historical change, it was that the situation of the aged should have improved but had probably worsened. As old age became less a rarity, it became less a privilege.[3]

The literary approach does not preclude historical analysis or cross-cultural comparison. Some belletristic writing is more daring than the anthropological work that seeks merely to describe cultures without addressing change or difference. V. S. Pritchett observed, "It has often been said that the British venerate old age," and he suggested a contrast with France, "where old age is often publicly derided."[4] Perhaps there is something to Pritchett's stricture against the French. A traditional French derision of old age may explain Beauvoir's ambivalence with respect to her own subject. But it would be rash to assume that a nation has any consistent "attitude" toward anything. A little history is in order, particularly when one comes across a comment such as Etienne de Jouy's early nineteenth-century lament on "the little respect that old age gets today": "It will be said that I am preaching in my interest; but it is certain that I remember a time when society would have demanded equal justice for an insult done to a woman and an old man; when our young people, Athenians in all other ways, were true Spartans on this issue."[5] But when were those good old days in which the old were respected? In the mid-eighteenth century Jean-Jacques Rousseau had offered the same complaint.[6] It is as if each generation looked back to a golden age that was fast receding. An almost mythic memory provided a standard by which to judge the present.

That present-minded attitude also characterized the first American

2. Leo Simmons, *The Role of the Aged in Primitive Society* (New Haven, Conn., 1945).

3. Simone de Beauvoir, *La vieillesse* (Paris, 1970).

4. V. S. Pritchett, "E. M. Forster: The Private Voice," in *The Tale Bearers* (New York, 1980), p. 64.

5. Etienne de Jouy, *L'hermite de la Chaussée-d'Antin*, vol. 1 (Paris, 1813), pp. 28–29.

6. Jean-Jacques Rousseau, *A M. D'Alembert* (1758), in *Oeuvres complètes*, vol. 3 (Paris, 1852), p. 135.

histories of old age. A consensus quickly emerged that in a premodern time the aged had ruled over a respectful and deferential society. The pressures of "modernization" were said to have destroyed the patriarchal basis of traditional society, raising youth to equality and, eventually, predominance. The dating varied from one historian to the next: David Hackett Fischer argued that the period 1780–1820 witnessed a "deep change" in mentalities that proved detrimental to the status of the aged, whereas W. Andrew Achenbaum and Daniel Scott Smith found that gerontocracy survived until after the Civil War. All agreed that changes in attitudes preceded the most dramatic demographic changes of the modern world and that in general the status of the aged had declined. Lawrence Stone did argue, to the contrary, that things had improved from a material standpoint, but even he accepted the prevailing view that a single great change had occurred.[7]

For the gerontologists, "traditional" and "modern" were assumed categories. As the first "old age historians" too had been debating "modernization theory"—whether by that was meant the rise of capitalism, the growth of cities, the division of labor, the coming of industry, or all of these—the temptation to adopt sociological periodization was almost irresistible. Alone among the first American historians in the field, John Demos departed somewhat from this consecrated formulation and wondered about the psychological state of the aged in the "premodern" era. If old age conferred respect then, did it guarantee security? He thought not: "The position of the elderly . . . was sociologically advantageous but psychologically disadvantageous."[8] It was not a question of simple upgrading or downgrading. Since then, American historians have addressed more limited populations or professions, and English and European scholars have expanded our knowl-

7. David Hackett Fischer, *Growing Old in America* (Oxford, 1978); W. Andrew Achenbaum, *Old Age in the New Land* (Baltimore, Md., 1978); Daniel Scott Smith, "Old Age and the 'Great Transformation': A New England Case Study," in Spicker et al., *Aging and the Elderly*, pp. 285–302; Lawrence Stone, "Walking over Grandma," in *New York Review of Books*, 24, no. 8 (1978). Fischer does propose a second great historical change, but he locates it in the present and near future; hence, as far as the past is concerned, there was only one.

8. Donald Cowgill and L. D. Holmes, *Aging and Modernization* (New York, 1972); W. Andrew Achenbaum and Peter N. Stearns, "Old Age and Modernization," *Gerontologist*, 18, no. 3 (1978), 307–312; John Demos, "Old Age in Early New England," in Van Tassel, *Aging*, p. 155, and in Demos and Sarane Spence Boocock, eds., *Turning Points: Historical and Sociological Essays on the Family*, supplement to *American Journal of Sociology*, 84 (1978), 282.

edge about aging in the past, painting a more complex picture. The field has moved well into adolescence.[9]

In France, the historical demographers led the way but focused attention on the modern aging of populations rather than on the aged themselves. Their sights fixed on contemporary concerns, they also tended to ignore pre-nineteenth-century trends.[10] It was left to Philippe Ariès (though he was not researching old age as an issue separate from the family or private life) to suggest that if the chronology were extended, more than one change would emerge. It was insufficient to speak only of "premodern" and "modern." On the whole, he said, old age was ridiculed in the seventeenth century and honored throughout the eighteenth. The image of the honorable old man lasted until the end of the nineteenth century, when, according to Ariès, old age, like death, became taboo. Whatever the merits of such a chronology—derived as it was from a limited number of elite sources—the point that there is more to social history than the inevitable coming of modernity was well taken. Just as Ariès's formulations of the history of childhood and family life and of attitudes toward death sparked a whole series of monographs that deepened our knowledge, his suggestion about the history of old age requires examination.[11]

9. William Graebner, *A History of Retirement: The Meaning and Function of an American Institution, 1885–1978* (New Haven, Conn., 1980); Carole Haber, *Beyond Sixty-Five: Old Age in Nineteenth-Century America* (Cambridge, 1983); Richard Wall et al., eds., *Family Forms in Historic Europe* (Cambridge, 1983); *Ageing and Society,* 4, no. 4 (1984); Christoph Conrad and Hans-Joachim von Kondratowitz, *Gerontologie und Sozialgeschichte: Wege zu einer historischen Betrachtung des Alters* (Berlin, 1983); David Gaunt, "The Property and Kin Relationships of Retired Farmers in Northern and Central Europe," in Wall et al., *Family Forms,* pp. 249–280; Reinhard Sieder and Michael Mitterauer, "The Reconstruction of the Family Life Course: Theoretical Problems and Empirical Results," in Wall et al., *Family Forms,* pp. 309–346.

10. Arthur Imhof et al., eds., *Le vieillissement: Implications et conséquences de l'allongement de la vie humaine depuis le XVIIIe siècle* (Lyon, 1982); INED, *Les âges de la vie,* 2 vols. (Paris, 1982–83); Peter N. Stearns, *Old Age in European Society: The Case of France* (New York, 1976); *Annales de démographie historique 1985: Vieillir autrefois* (Paris, 1986); *Pénélope: Pour l'histoire des femmes,* vol. 13, *Vieillesses des femmes* (Paris, 1985).

11. Philippe Ariès made reference to aging in *Centuries of Childhood: A Social History of Family Life* (New York, 1962); in *L'homme devant la mort* (Paris, 1977); and in his review in *New Republic,* July 2, 1977, of Fischer's *Growing Old in America.* But he first suggested a history of old age in 1948; see his *Histoire des populations françaises et de leurs attitudes devant la vie depuis le XVIIIe siècle,* rev. ed. (Paris, 1971), pp. 375–381. Georges Minois, *Histoire de la vieillesse: De l'antiquité à la renaissance* (Paris, 1987), which appeared when my work on this book was virtually completed, suggests that the early modern antipathy toward old age which I link to the Counter-Reformation has important sources in the Renaissance revival of classical thought.

This book explores changes in French attitudes toward aging and the aged in the eighteenth century. The changes are many because old age is not a self-contained category but something to be sought in a variety of sources—in demography, the family, work, retirement, folklore, philosophy, medicine, and literature. One might write an entire book on the place of old age in each of these fields. A more fruitful approach is to take into account as many perspectives as possible, using each of them to illuminate the others. A history of attitudes must consider social phenomena (see Chapters 6 and 7) as well as images and ideas (Chapters 2–5). One can build up a portrait of an era by drawing connections between demographic and domestic phenomena on the one hand and economic literature on the other; between the realities of work, retirement, and death and the prescriptions of religion, philosophy, and science; between the view of old age communicated by the poor seeking public assistance and that imparted by writers of plays and novels.

Seeking connections between ideas and social reality is a historical exercise that itself has a history. In the past, one might have chosen—in gross caricature of Marx or Weber—to explain ideas exclusively by class relationships or, conversely, social structure by ideology alone. More recently, practitioners of *l'histoire des mentalités* have offered a more complex view of these questions. Studies that juxtapose mortality rates and attitudes toward death, household structure and familial sentiment, agrarian economy and religious heresy have demonstrated that complexity.[12]

The richness of source materials for a history of old age in the French eighteenth century makes it possible to study such connections between ideas and reality. Moreover, the historiography of the period has already raised a broad variety of related questions: the *crise de conscience* of the intellectual elite at the beginning of the century, the general decline in piety by midcentury, the changing views of the family and of death, the growth of bureaucracy, and the perennial problem of the relationship between Enlightenment and Revolution.[13] Each of these issues had consequences for the aged.

12. François Lebrun, *Les hommes et la mort en Anjou aux XVIIe et XVIIIe siècles* (Paris, 1971); Jean-Louis Flandrin, *Familles: Parenté, maison, sexualité dans l'ancienne société* (Paris, 1976); Carlo Ginzburg, *The Cheese and the Worms: The Cosmos of a Sixteenth-Century Miller* (Baltimore, Md., 1980).

13. Paul Hazard, *The European Mind, 1680–1715* (New York, 1963); Michel Vovelle, *Piété baroque et déchristianisation en Provence au XVIIIe siècle* (Paris, 1973), and *Mourir autrefois: Attitudes collectives devant la mort aux XVIIe et XVIIIe siècles* (Paris, 1974); J. F. Bosher, *French Finances, 1770–1795: From Business to Bureaucracy*

This book combines social and cultural history to explore a major shift in French attitudes toward aging and the aged in the eighteenth century from one extreme of ridicule and neglect to another of respect and care. It describes the emergence of a new view of old age at a time when demographic, socioeconomic, cultural, and political factors challenged existing institutions and stimulated a remarkable concern for the problems of the elderly. Perhaps most important, it finds the discovery of a modern social problem in a period that antedates the dramatic aging of Western populations in the nineteenth and twentieth centuries. The modernist might argue that this view ignores such recent phenomena as the political mobilization of the aged and the invention of industries and bureaucracies catering to them[14]—but those trends are all foreshadowed in the Enlightenment and the French Revolution.

The discussion begins with a demographic and anthropological overview of old age in the old regime (Chapter 1), then traces the evolution of thought about old age throughout French culture. Art focused less upon the iconographical meaning of aged characters as representatives of metaphysical qualities than upon the division of the life course and the situation of the widowed and the infirm (Chapter 2). Graphic images reflected changes in literary treatment of the elderly as novels, poems, and, above all, plays replaced a stereotype of resentment with one of respect (Chapter 3). At the heart of the eighteenth-century shift lay a process of Enlightenment secularization, which downplayed the role of the afterlife, freeing old age from the hands of baroque religion and death and permitting the elaboration of philosophical ideas for coping with longevity (Chapter 4). Scientific study focused on the diseases and ailments of the aged, as specialization took hold of medical thinking; doctors explained the physiological roots of retreat from the world but proposed ways of permitting the elderly to participate as active members of society (Chapter 5).

Subsequent chapters attempt to explain the cultural shift in attitudes by placing it in the context of the demographic, domestic, social, economic, and legal situation of the aged. An increase in life expectancy for

(Cambridge, 1970); François Furet, *Livre et société dans la France du XVIIIe siècle* (Paris, 1965); Daniel Roche, *Le siècle des lumières en province: Académies et académiciens provinciaux* (Paris, 1978).

14. While there are no equivalent political movements in France as visible as the American Gray Panthers, there are very visible *clubs du troisième âge* and regular columns on old age in the press.

adults, lengthening the period of overlap of adult generations, posed the "problem" of old age at the level of household and parish. Chapter 6 explores the consequences for rural society, using notarial records and the registers of parish, municipal council, and hospital in two sample villages in Provence and Picardy. Chapter 7 examines the problems of aging in urban society by means of hospital records and notarial archives for Paris, Amiens, and Marseille.

Finally, Chapter 8 combines ideas and reality. It examines social policy and political rhetoric in the last decade of the ancien régime and in the Revolutionary period. Social thinkers became aware of the plight of the aged, and political discourse inherited this concern, youthful authorities claiming the tacit approval of their elders. Revolutionary legislators attempted to institute an unprecedented social policy of old age insurance and assistance; their attempt set the agenda for old age policy in the following two centuries. It constituted the practical analogue to the new view of age, crystallized in the French Revolutionary festival of old age.

Despite the remarkable eighteenth-century French experience of aging and the aged, all would not be well. For as the population aged in the nineteenth and twentieth centuries, the bugbear of "depopulation" was periodically blamed for French economic difficulties.[15] The aged were visible; children were not. Consequently, the aged were looked on as somehow alien; they even came to look upon themselves as "other." In an interview published just before his death, Jean-Paul Sartre reflected upon his old age. Echoing his famous line about hell, he said, "*Ce sont les autres qui sont ma vieillesse.*"[16]

What follows includes some testimony about the subjective experiences of aging. Memoirs, letters, and philosophical treatises recount the perspectives of their aging authors. But even those introspective souls express themselves in terms used commonly by their culture. In this sense it is true, in this book as in Sartre's world, that the image of the aged left us is one imposed by *les autres*.

15. The theme appears in many of the demographic works of Alfred Sauvy, perhaps most stridently in *La montée des jeunes* (Paris, 1959). For a survey of the problem, see J. J. Spengler, *France Faces Depopulation* (Durham, N.C., 1979).

16. "It is other people who are my old age": Jean-Paul Sartre, *Le Nouvel Observateur*, 800 (March 10, 1980), 102.

1   The Aged in the French Population: Numbers and Meanings

Looking back at the population of France in the eighteenth century, as at virtually any preindustrial population, we are struck by its relative youth. Mean life expectancy at birth remained under thirty years for most of the century. Roughly 40 percent of the population was under the age of twenty, less than 10 percent over sixty. French age structure has evolved as shown in Table 1. Consequently, an age pyramid for the ancien régime is much broader at the base and narrower at the top than a pyramid representing a twentieth-century population (see Figure 1).

Demographers interested in aging have directly related the broadening of the top to a dramatic narrowing of the bottom. Awareness that falling natality has been the primary cause of the aging of populations, however, has led students of demographic aging to focus almost exclusively on the nineteenth and twentieth centuries. Patrice Bourdelais's history of the aging of the French population begins its analysis only in 1851.[1] Some historical demographers who have explored the Old Regime have done so to find the origins of the modern fall in fertility and of the population explosion that brought on the industrial revolution, but most have preferred to describe the "homeostatic" nature of the *ancien régime démographique* and its survival to the end of the century. Theirs is a demographic history that, compared with more recent times, stands still.[2] Old patterns persisted. The aged continued to die from respiratory

---

1. Alfred Sauvy, "Le vieillissement démographique," UNESCO, *Revue Internationale des Sciences Sociales,* 15, no. 3 (1963), *Le troisième âge,* p. 374; Patrice Bourdelais, "La population française de 1851 à 1975: L'histoire d'un vieillissement" (thesis, forthcoming).

2. Michael W. Flinn, *The European Demographic System, 1500–1820* (Baltimore, Md., 1981); Jacques Dupâquier, *La population française aux XVIIe et XVIIIe siècles*

Age structure in France, 1776–1973

Age	1776	1801	1906	1951	1973
0–19	42.8%	42.0%	34.2%	29.9%	32.5%
20–59	50.0	49.3	53.2	53.9	49.4
60+	7.2	8.7	12.6	16.2	18.1

Sources: J. Bourgeois-Pichat, "The General Development of the Population of France since the Eighteenth Century," in D. V. Glass and D. E. C. Eversley, eds., *Population in History: Essays in Historical Demography* (London, 1965), pp. 498–499; Roland Pressat, "Evolution générale de la population française," *Population,* 29 (1974), p. 11.

diseases in winter and infants from intestinal disorders in summer.[3] Mortality still fluctuated wildly (if less so), and birth and death rates continued to achieve balance (and growth), as early modern populations stabilized through adjustments in rates of marriage and fertility.[4]

We might be tempted to assume that the cultural change examined in Chapters 2–5 could have had nothing to do with population. But upon closer inspection, the eighteenth-century population reveals some fascinating characteristics. Whether they alone induced cultural change is an unanswerable question. Most probably they played a role. In important ways, the old "self-regulating" structure was breaking down. Lim-

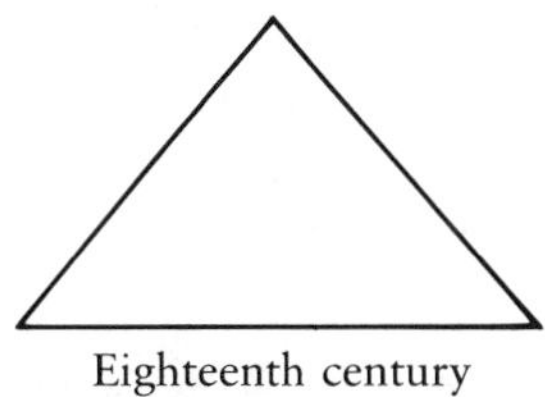

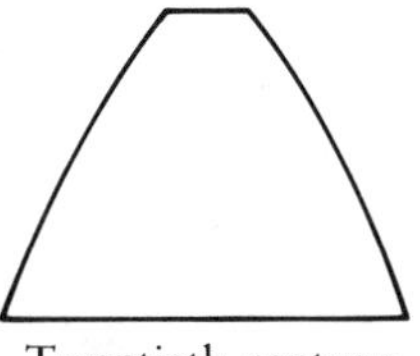

Sources: See Table 1.

FIGURE 1. Population pyramids

(Paris, 1979). For the notion of *l'histoire immobile,* see Emmanuel Le Roy Ladurie, "History That Stands Still," in *The Mind and Method of the Historian* (Chicago, 1978).

3. See, e.g., Thomas F. Sheppard, *Lourmarin in the Eighteenth Century: A Study of a French Village* (Baltimore, Md., 1971), p. 43; Pierre Goubert, *Beauvais et le Beauvaisis de 1600 à 1730* (Paris, 1960), pp. 69–70; Maurice Garden, *Lyon et les lyonnais au XVIIIe siècle* (Paris, 1970), p. 142.

4. Dupâquier refers to marriage as "the most social of demographic phenomena": *La population rurale du bassin parisien à l'époque de Louis XIV* (Paris, 1979), p. 387. E. A. Wrigley and R. Schofield, *The Population History of England, 1541–1871* (London, 1981), also emphasizes marriage.

its to growth were being tested. Population grew from 21 to 29 million over the course of the century. In certain places fertility fell in ways that announced a premature Malthusianism.[5] Throughout France, especially in the second half of the century, mortality was in retreat.[6] All these trends would become more dramatic in the nineteenth century in France and elsewhere and, to be sure, were mitigated by setbacks in the 1740s and 1780s, but they were already significant in old regime terms, the only ones imaginable to most people.

We should not be fooled by the low life expectancy at birth; there were old people in France. High infant and juvenile mortality render life expectancy figures at birth misleading. Even so, those figures increased throughout most of the century; significant advances were characteristic at most ages; and advances for adults occurred from a base figure much higher than one might have guessed from the figure at birth (see Table 2).

If we consider the aged as a component of the adult population rather than of the total population, we get a clearer notion of their importance. Throughout the second half of the eighteenth century, national estimates suggest that 13 to 15 percent of the French population twenty years of age and up was sixty or older.[7] Jean-Claude Perrot has argued that the 1798 "census" of adults in Caen revealed an incorrectly low figure of 12.5 percent; national figures in 1796 and 1801 were 14.9 percent and 15.1 percent.[8] Etienne Gautier and Louis Henry found the ratio of 60+/20+ in the Norman town of Crulai to be 13.7 percent.[9] Some local studies have discovered even larger proportions of the aged: Pierre Valmary found 18.7 percent among peasants of Bas-Quercy in

5. Dupâquier, *La population française;* Louis Henry, "The Population of France in the Eighteenth Century," in Glass and Eversley, *Population in History,* pp. 434–473. Jean-Pierre Bardet, *Rouen aux XVIIe et XVIIIe siècles: Les mutations d'un espace social* (Paris, 1983), has the most useful recent discussion of fertility.

6. Pierre Chaunu, *La civilisation de l'Europe des lumières* (Paris, 1971), pp. 151–162; Yves Blayo, "La mortalité en France de 1740 à 1829," *Population,* 30 (special issue, 1975), 123–142. On drawing conclusions about attitudes from this demographic change, see John McManners, *Death and the Enlightenment: Changing Attitudes to Death among Christians and Unbelievers in Eighteenth-Century France* (Oxford, 1981), esp. pp. 93–94.

7. Louis Henry and Yves Blayo, "La population de la France de 1740 à 1860," *Population,* 30 (1975), 100.

8. Jean-Claude Perrot, *Genèse d'une ville moderne: Caen au XVIIIe siècle* (Paris, 1975), p. 138.

9. Etienne Gautier and Louis Henry, *La population de Crulai, paroisse normande: Etude historique* (Paris, 1958), p. 202.

TABLE 2
Female life expectancy, 1740–1830

	At birth	*At age 5*	*At age 20*
1740–49	25.7	41.2	34.2
1750–59	28.7	45.2	37.3
1760–69	29.0	44.8	37.0
1770–79	29.6	45.6	37.8
1780–89	28.1	44.3	36.6
1790–99	32.1	47.2	38.6
1800–1809	34.9	47.2	38.0
1810–19	37.5	49.2	39.8
1820–29	39.3	49.8	40.2

Source: Yves Blayo, "La mortalité en France de 1740 à 1829," *Population,* 30 (1975), 141.

the later seventeenth and eighteenth centuries; Hubert Charbonneau found 18.3 percent in Tourouvre au Perche in 1801; and Jean Ibanès found 16 percent in the Place des Vosges in Paris in 1791.[10] Of course, if we consider age thirty a more meaningful measure of adulthood—the practice of late marriage throughout the early modern period would recommend such a decision[11]—we find ratios of 60+/30+ considerably higher: 19.1 percent for Crulai, 20 percent for the Place des Vosges, and 25.3 percent for Bas-Quercy.[12] In Crulai, 39.3 percent of the twenty-seven-year-old men would survive to sixty; half of the twenty-five-year-old women would survive to fifty-five.[13] Clearly the aged were a significant proportion of adults.

Another useful indicator is age at death. Higher rates of mortality in old age, of course, indicate higher rates of survival to old age. Hence, increasing mortality rates in advanced age are a paradoxical indication

10. Pierre Valmary, *Familles paysannes au XVIIIe siècle en Bas-Quercy: Etude démographique* (Paris, 1965), pp. 60–61; Hubert Charbonneau, *Tourouvre au Perche aux XVIIe et XVIIIe siècles: Etude de démographie historique* (Paris, 1970), p. 212; Jean Ibanès, "La population de la Place des Vosges et de ses environs en 1791," in Marcel Reinhard, ed., *Contributions à l'histoire démographique de la révolution française,* vol. 1 (Paris, 1962), p. 88.

11. Late marriage has been recognized as crucial since the publication of J. Hajnal, "European Marriage Patterns in Perspective," in Glass and Eversley, *Population in History,* pp. 101–143.

12. Gautier and Henry, *La population de Crulai,* p. 202; Ibanès, "La population de la Place des Vosges," p. 86; Valmary, *Familles paysannes,* p. 60.

13. Gautier and Henry, *La population de Crulai,* p. 185.

of a triumph of life.[14] A privileged group like the bishops of France lived to fifty-two in the sixteenth century, fifty-eight in the early seventeenth, sixty-six in the late seventeenth, and seventy-four a century later.[15] Some less privileged folk too died at a more advanced age.[16] Pierre Goubert offers figures for selected parishes in the Beauvaisis, and shows that important, if less dramatic, advances occurred also in the Saumurois (see Table 3).

Most regional studies have confirmed this "aging" and linked it to a decline in mortality. In his 1979 lectures on early modern European demography, Michael W. Flinn remarked: "Oddly enough, demographic historians have given rather less attention to the measurement of mortality trends in the eighteenth century than to the question of fertility."[17] Since that time, despite the continued emphasis on fertility and nuptiality, more attention has been paid to mortality. Yet historians still disagree about precisely what happened in the eighteenth century and what changes were most important: a leveling out of the peaks of mortality, a fall in the frequency of subsistence crises, or a decrease in base rates in unexceptional years.[18] Jacques Dupâquier has denied any significant mortality decline before the nineteenth century, much as Michel Morineau denied any agricultural revolution in eighteenth-century France.[19] Dupâquier exaggerates in order to make the point that mortality decline in the eighteenth century is better understood in terms of ancien régime demography than in terms of a Vital Revolution. He is more interested, in this case, in what did not happen than in what did. It

14. See Hervé Le Bras, "Lois de mortalité et âge limite," *Population*, 31 (1976), 655–692, on this and other paradoxes and problems of mortality and the life span.

15. Michel Peronnet, *Les évêques de l'ancienne France* (Lille, 1977), vol. 1, pp. 444–445.

16. Alfred Perrenoud finds the working classes in eighteenth-century Geneva making more significant gains at all ages beyond infancy than their social superiors, but the final result is still shorter life expectancy; Maurice Garden finds greater persistence in differential mortality rates by class in eighteenth-century Lyon. See Perrenoud, "Le recul de la mort: Structure par âges et facteurs sociaux," in Imhof et al., *Le vieillissement*, pp. 43–76; Garden, *Lyon*, pp. 144–145.

17. Flinn, *European Demographic System*, p. 91. The lectures were given in 1979 and published in 1981.

18. Dupâquier, *La population française*; Blayo, "La mortalité"; Alfred Perrenoud, "Le biologique et l'humain dans le déclin séculaire de la mortalité," *Annales: E.S.C.*, 40 (1985), 113–135.

19. Dupâquier, *La population française*, p. 102; Michel Morineau, *Les faux-semblants d'un démarrage économique: Agriculture et démographie en France au XVIIIe siècle* (Paris, 1970).

Table 3

Proportion of adults dying at 60+ and 70+ years, seventeenth century and 1771–90

	60 years		70 years	
Parish	*17th century*	*1771–90*	*17th century*	*1771–90*
Beauvaisis				
Auneuil	28.3%	52.1%	17.1%	37.3%
Clermont	39.5	55.1	21.9	35.5
Crèvecoeur	36.3	55.7	20.5	35.6
Senantes	33.8	56.2	16.9	31.2
Mouy	40.9	60.3	23.3	41.1
Beauvais, Saint-André	41.7	60.9	24.7	33.6
Beauvais, Saint Quentin	40.0	43.5	20.0	31.7
Beauvais, Saint-Sauveur	?	51.8	?	28.7
Saumurois				
Saint-Lambert-des-Levées	35.1	47.2	19.5	29.0
Fontevrault	38.3	47.5	21.1	28.5

Source: Pierre Goubert, *Beauvais et le Beauvaisis de 1600 à 1730* (Paris, 1960), p. 63.

is true that changes occurring in the 1790s and early 1800s were more dramatic than those over the course of the eighteenth century. We are not yet in the contemporary world, but, to paraphrase Fernand Braudel, conjunctural change too is important.[20] Such was the retreat of death, perhaps best symbolized by the virtual disappearance of plague in western Europe after 1720–21. Some scholars account for the decline in mortality by pointing to improvements in diet and hygiene; others, to advances in communication and the spread of markets.[21] Not all follow Morineau completely on the economy, but few find an agricultural revolution in France. Yet somehow the French economy was feeding 38 percent more people, and the average life span had grown by ten years. Alfred Perrenoud's consideration of the decline in French mortality in an international context suggests that none of these particular factors explains everything. He opts for climatic change and even evokes alteration in the appearance of sunspots.[22]

We do not know exactly why the life span changed, but we know that it did. People lived longer. Indeed, Pierre Chaunu has called the length-

20. Fernand Braudel, "Histoire et sciences sociales: La longue durée," *Annales: E.S.C.*, 13 (1958), 725–753.
21. Perrenoud, "Le biologique et l'humain."
22. Ibid., pp. 132–133.

ening of human life "the only great event of the eighteenth century."[23] There was clearly greater competition for resources between generations and between individuals. If we can understand people's expectations of life and of nature in the early modern period, we can imagine the consequences of added longevity in the eighteenth century. How longevity affected lives qualitatively is not self-evident. We need to consider relations between people of the same and different generations. We need to discover how individuals reflected upon their own lives and destinies.

Historical demographers who have sought meaning in their graphs and curves have contrasted a new sense of control over life, derived from falling fertility and mortality, with the traditional fatalism that had long reconciled people to the mysteries of Providence.[24] As the French population grew and approached the limits of preindustrial demographic expansion, individuals recognized their own abilities of beating the old demographic odds. They were still largely limited by old expectations, but they could imagine essentially new ones. As Michel Vovelle has observed, the meaning of death was changing even before the pattern had been completely transformed.[25] It is almost as if the change in meaning had prepared the way for changes in experience. The change in discourse during the century of Enlightenment was quite radical. Old baroque practices and gestures went into decline, yet the demographic revolution had hardly begun. Perhaps this teaches us most of all to understand the period as one of demographic transition rather than demographic revolution.[26]

Arthur Imhof has suggested an alternative way of regarding attitudes or beliefs about the life course. His sources are German, but they are more complete than most found in France, and the lessons they teach apply broadly across the Rhine. After reporting that his Berlin sample

23. Chaunu, *La civilisation de l'Europe des lumières*, p. 158.

24. See, e.g., the discussion of old age in Alain Molinier, *Stagnations et croissance: Le Vivarais aux XVIIe–XVIIIe siècles* (Paris, 1985), pp. 329–330. Also on old age, see McManners, *Death and the Enlightenment*, pp. 84–88; on birth control, André Burguière, "De Malthus à Max Weber: Le mariage tardif et l'esprit d'entreprise," *Annales: E.S.C.*, 27 (1972), 1128–1138.

25. Michel Vovelle, *La mort et l'Occident de 1300 à nos jours* (Paris, 1983), pp. 380–381.

26. Jacques Dupâquier makes this point in his chapter on population in Peter Burke, ed., *The New Cambridge Modern History*, XIII, *Companion Volume* (Cambridge, 1979), p. 90. The elusive idea of "demographic transition" was addressed at the fall 1987 colloquium of the Société de Démographie Historique.

points to 1875 as the great divide in the transition from old to new mortality patterns, he suggests that we pay closer attention to changes in *mentalités*. Accordingly, he presents life expectancy as having been considered infinitely great in premodern populations: death merely brought on passage to the afterlife. Hence, the crisis of belief was more important than the demographic transition itself in "imagining" the life course. Once life was seen as limited, the last years became that much more important, and their meaning changed. Indeed, a whole system of meaning was changing.[27] Earthly life attained a new value or urgency. To a certain extent that new value was felt even by those who still clung to Christian assurances of an afterlife, but in old age the old beliefs survived and provided a sense of serenity. Those in religious orders in the eighteenth century benefited more than the lay population from falling mortality until the age of fifty. Thereafter, they seem to have lost interest in delaying the final passage, as their rates of mortality rose to the level of the laity.[28]

Demography alone cannot tell us everything, but we dare not ignore it. We should understand the demographic system of the era in its own terms. And we must understand the potential significance of seemingly slight incremental changes in the population. For example, in a society whose property was transferred at the "moment" when one generation was dying and the next reaching maturity, small increases in longevity may have had a very significant impact on relations between generations. Indeed, that moment was highly elastic. In eighteenth-century France, 84 percent of children had at least one grandparent at birth, 62 percent at age ten, 27 percent by age twenty-one. Sixty-two percent of twenty-one-year-olds still had a living father. Two-thirds of all orphans still had grandparents at age five, 60 percent at ten, and 36 percent at fifteen.[29] The overlap of generations was nothing like what often hap-

27. Arthur E. Imhof, "Von der unsicheren zur sicheren Lebenszeit: Ein folgenschwerer Wandel im Verlaufe der Neuzeit," *Vierteljahrschrift für Sozial- und Wirtschaftsgeschichte*, 71 (1984), 175–198; "From the Old Mortality Pattern to the Twentieth Century," *Bulletin of the History of Medicine*, 59 (1985), 1–29.

28. Hervé Le Bras and Dominique Dinet, "Mortalité des laïcs et mortalité des religieux: Les Bénédictins de St-Maur aux XVIIe et XVIIIe siècles," *Population*, 35 (1980), 347–384.

29. Hervé Le Bras, "Parents, grands-parents, bisaïeux," *Population*, 28 (1973), 9–38. Le Bras's figures are derived from a computer simulation of the national norm; in particularly unhealthy settings, these rates would obviously not be achieved. See, e.g., Gérard Bouchard, *Le village immobile: Sennely-en-Sologne au XVIIIe siècle* (Paris, 1972), p. 275.

pens today in the world of the "empty nest," but it could be important. And looking at other sorts of kin, one finds a greater range in ages in the eighteenth century.[30] Isolation was not as common a phenomenon as one might expect from the high rates of mortality of the ancien régime.

Still, in the context of a system of relatively rapid transmission of authority, where marriage of children tended to coincide with death of parents, eighteenth-century adults might find themselves in conflict whenever longevity increased. In much of France, age at marriage rose in the second half of the eighteenth century—the traditional brake on excess natality was in operation—as paths of advancement were temporarily blocked. However, that increase could not keep up with the increase in survival for adults. The old system was trying to make the usual adjustments, but the system itself was being challenged—not only by falling mortality but by a decline in the age at which mothers gave birth to their last children. Even when married at twenty-six instead of twenty-four, many women experienced childbirth for the last time at thirty-five rather than forty, saw their children reach maturity before they themselves were sixty, and died in more advanced age. The overlap of adult generations was especially long in elite families. In the seventeenth century, men and women of the aristocracy married at 25.5 and 18.5 years of age respectively; by the end of the ancien régime those ages had fallen to 21.3 and 17.7. Such parents typically had only two children, down from 6.1. And those women who married before the age of twenty had their last children at twenty-five, down from thirty-one.[31] Bourgeois families also reduced fertility, if not as radically. Bardet provides figures for Rouen (see Table 4).

More parents were living past the age of child rearing and of establishing their children in the adult world. In some regions, as long as the parents were still active, their adult children remained in what Jacques Dupâquier has called a "matrimonial purgatory" and constituted a "reserve army of old bachelors and spinsters."[32] Their patience and filial piety would be tested, and their parents would confront the challenges of old age; indeed, wherever aged parents did not block the advance of their heirs, they ran the risk of abandonment—unless at

30. Hervé Le Bras, "Evolution des liens de famille au cours de l'existence: Une comparaison entre la France actuelle et la France du XVIIIe siècle," in INED, *Les âges de la vie,* vol. 1, pp. 27–39.

31. Dupâquier, *La population française,* p. 118.

32. Dupâquier, *La population rurale,* pp. 390–391. Dupâquier's comments refer to the rural population near Paris, but they apply to other (though not all) regions as well.

Table 4
Age at birth of last child, Rouen, 1670–1789

	Notables	Shopkeepers	Artisans	Workers
Mean age, women married before 30				
1670–1699	37.1	38.1	40.3	39.0
1700–1729	35.8	37.0	39.0	39.5
1730–1759	36.3	36.1	37.9	37.7
1760–1789	33.5	33.9	36.6	37.4
Last birth before age 35				
1670–1699	30%	25%	11%	4%
1700–1729	32	28	19	15
1730–1759	31	32	27	24
1760–1789	59	53	31	28

Source: Jean-Pierre Bardet, *Rouen aux XVIIe et XVIIIe siècles* (Paris, 1983), p. 282.

some point parents and children came to understand the interest of the household that transcended their own. To appreciate the importance of the longer period of overlap of adult generations, we must look closely at the experience of individuals in particular local settings. And we need to understand the "meaning" of aging and the life course. From historical demography, then, we turn to historical anthropology.

It is difficult to discuss biological aging in historical terms: the traditional age of crisis or climacteric—unlike baptism, marriage, and burial—never found its way into the parish register. Creighton Gilbert estimates that Renaissance artists reached old age at forty-five to fifty. François Lebrun opts for sixty for the privileged, fifty and younger for others in the ancien régime. Robert Favre suggests that old age came much later for writers of the Enlightenment, and Frank Kafker demonstrates the Encyclopedists' great productivity in their later years, indicating perhaps that personal experience was responsible for their interest in the aging process.[33] But Arthur Young's encounter with a peasant woman who "at no great distance, might have been taken for sixty or seventy, her figure was so bent, and her face so furrowed and hardened

33. Creighton Gilbert, "When Did a Man in the Renaissance Grow Old?" *Studies in the Renaissance*, 14 (1967), 7–32; François Lebrun, *Se soigner autrefois: Médecins, saints, et sorciers aux 17e et 18e siècles* (Paris, 1983), p. 152; Robert Favre, *La mort dans la littérature et la pensée françaises au siècle des lumières* (Lyon, 1978); Frank Kafker, "La vieillesse et la productivité intellectuelle chez les encyclopédistes," *Revue d'Histoire Moderne et Contemporaine*, 28 (1981), 304–327.

by labour—but she said she was only twenty-eight" forcefully attests to class differences that complicate any statements about biological aging in an entire society.[34] By age fifty, eighteenth-century textile workers had gone blind and farm laborers were virtually broken. Artisans were commonly poisoned by the very materials required by their crafts.[35] Eighteenth-century medical and economic literature recognized that people of different occupations fell apart at different ages.[36]

If more precise data on physiological aging are beyond the historian's scope, however, one ought to consider other ways in which people of the eighteenth century defined old age. There was, for example, a long tradition of dividing the life course into idealized periods. Dictionaries frequently defined old age as that period that came after adulthood and before death. An eighteenth-century ballet called *Les âges* was composed of four parts: youth, virile age or coquettish love, rival ages, and old age or mad love.[37]

Further subdivisions were proposed, both earlier and later. Vincent of Beauvais in the thirteenth century had suggested six ages: *infantia* to seven years, *pueritia* to fourteen, *adolescentia* to twenty-eight, *juventus* to fifty, *gravitas* to seventy-two, and *senium* to death.[38] A French woodcut of 1826 proposed eleven ages, one more than those enameled on a glass jar in Germany in the sixteenth century (see Table 5).[39] Like Jaques's seven ages of man in *As You Like It,* there is something universal here and yet, in most lives, against nature: lives long enough to fit the model are rare even in the twentieth century.

Yet one should not be taken in by the pose of mathematical specificity. People who were vague about their numerical age were nonetheless aware of aging. A peasant might decide he was old and therefore call himself sixty, sixty-five, eighty-five, or even one hundred. Parish regis-

---

34. Arthur Young, *Travels during the Years 1787, 1788, and 1789 . . .* (Bury St. Edmunds, 1792), p. 134.

35. Jeffry Kaplow, *The Names of Kings* (New York, 1972), p. 88; Olwen H. Hufton, *The Poor of Eighteenth-Century France, 1750–1789* (Oxford, 1974), p. 111; Georges Lefebvre, *Les paysans du Nord pendant la revolution française* (Bari, 1959), p. 302.

36. Perrot, *Genèse,* p. 828.

37. A. Campra, "Les Ages" (ballet), MS, Opéra, A 99.

38. *Vincentius Bellovacensis, Speculum naturale* (Graz, 1964), bk. 31, chap. 75, pp. 2348–49, "De gradibus aetatum," cited in David Herlihy, "Vieillir à Florence au quattrocento," *Annales: E.S.C.,* 24 (1969), 1339 n.2.

39. Both objects are on display at A.T.P. Another example of the German jar is at the Art Institute of Chicago. The list can be translated "child, youth, man, well-made, stands still, grows old, gray-haired, never wise, scorn of children, straight to God."

TABLE 5

Divisions of the life cycle in France, 1826, and Germany,
sixteenth-century

Age	France, 1826	Germany, sixteenth century
4	âge de puérilité	
10	adolescence	Kindt
20	jeunesse	Iungling
30	âge viril	Man
40	âge de maturité	Wölgethan
50	âge de discrétion	Stille Stan
60	âge déclinant	Geht Alter An
70	âge de décadence	Greis
80	âge caduc	Nimmerweis
90	âge de décrépitude	Kinder Spot
100	âge d'imbécilité ou d'enfance	Geradt Dir Gott

ters are filled with inflated and rounded-off ages. It was said that a resident of the Morvan (western Burgundy) decided precisely at sixty that he would pass on the patrimony and retire.[40] But did he know he was sixty by checking the parish register or by saying to himself that he felt old?

When death did come, the life cycle was still not complete. In a sense, death pushed the aged to another generation; ethnographic study of Brittany shows that the deceased were counted in the ages of life.[41] This should not be surprising in a world steeped in the supernatural, a world whose elite depicted dead relations in family portraits, read religious guidebooks that recommended a good death over a decrepit life, and wrote classical tragedies that found old age unacceptable when compared with the glories of a tragic death at the height of one's powers.[42]

Such a view of human life could be pictured as a straight line or a regular curve along which one traveled to death and beyond. For people of different classes those paths were surely different as well, but age

40. Emile Blin, *Le Morvan, moeurs, coutumes, langage, historiettes, légendes, croyances populaires, topographie, histoire, monuments* (Château-Chinon, 1902), pp. 65–67, cited in Michel Philibert, *Les échelles d'âge dans la philosophie, la science et la société: De leur renversement et des conditions de leur redressement* (Paris, 1968), pp. 114–115.

41. Anatole Le Braz, *La légende de la mort* (Paris, 1928), cited in Philibert, *Les échelles d'âge*, p. 115; Perrot, *Genèse*, p. 565.

42. Ariès, *L'homme;* Orest Ranum, *Paris in the Age of Absolutism* (New York, 1968), pp. 144–145.

brought experience and some authority at all levels of society.[43] In a Catholic society of subtle class distinctions, death was seen as the great equalizer, and the dead were depicted as equal—dancing in a circle, the king with the pauper, the priest with the merchant, the man with the woman. The *danse macabre* was an image of simplicity: death leveling all.

In the fifteenth and sixteenth centuries the art of dying had required training, and guidebooks proliferated. The *ars moriendi,* holding out a vision of successful death for all, reached a peak in the early sixteenth century. From the mid-sixteenth century, however, it went into decline, reflecting perhaps the recognition that death was inseparable from life and that people were unequal in the face of death.[44] In the heightened religious atmosphere of the Counter-Reformation, the sorting out of those who would find salvation, damnation, or a lengthy stay in Purgatory became quite urgent.[45] And it had become clear that different classes had different life expectancies.

Life began to take on a new shape. While village life continued to be seen in simple linear fashion—until and beyond death—urban life and elite life found a new image. The ages of life were regarded as forming a stepladder, the *degrés des âges,* rising from the left in ten-year intervals to a peak at age fifty and descending to the right until age one hundred.[46] During the course of their popularity from the sixteenth to the nineteenth century, representations of the *degrés des âges* underwent some historical change. At first the ladder rose and fell above a depiction of the Last Judgment; hellish flames were prominent in the sixteenth and early seventeenth centuries. Devils carried old men to hell; angels bore young women to heaven. During the eighteenth century, however, the emphasis on final judgment dwindled; the flames subsided. In the

43. Perrot, *Genèse,* pp. 826–832. In early modern England, the higher up in society, the earlier one advanced to positions of authority in one's class; see Keith Thomas, *Age and Authority in Early Modern England* (London, 1976).

44. Johan Huizinga, *The Waning of the Middle Ages* (New York, 1954); Roger Chartier, "Les arts de mourir, 1450–1600," *Annales: E.S.C.,* 31 (1976), 51–75; and in the same issue, Daniel Roche, " 'La mémoire de la mort': Recherches sur la place des arts de mourir dans la librairie et la lecture en France aux XVIIe et XVIIIe siècles," pp. 76–119.

45. Gaby and Michel Vovelle, *Vision de la mort et de l'au-delà en Provence d'après les autels des âmes du purgatoire XVe–XXe siècles, Cahiers des Annales,* 29 (1970).

46. B.N. Estampes, Td. 24, T. XI; Jean Avalon, "Les âges de la vie dans l'imagerie populaire," *Passiflora,* 4, no. 10 (1934); Champfleury, *Histoire de l'imagerie populaire* (Paris, 1869).

A natural cycle. *The Four Seasons: Winter*, print. Phot. Bibl. Nat. Paris.

A typical early modern depiction of the *degrés des âges*. *The Human Life Course*, print. Phot. Bibl. Nat. Paris.

nineteenth century the supernatural elements disappeared, and the life cycle was rendered as a tame natural process. Nevertheless, as has been suggested by one ethnographer, it still had more to do with culture than with nature.[47]

Despite important changes over time, there does seem to have been an almost timeless natural or cosmic view in which ages corresponded to seasons: white-bearded winter and infant spring. Sowing and reaping, the work of peasants everywhere, were depicted in medieval books of hours and nineteenth-century popular prints. Old men represented death, time, gods, winter, night. Old women, less happily, represented decay and avarice.[48]

The use of the aged as symbols, though, does not explain when old age was thought to begin. In 1512 Octavien de Saint Gelais described himself as old at thirty-six. His contemporary Erasmus chose thirty-seven. Ariès suggested forty as the seventeenth-century benchmark.[49] But does old age come at a particular year? Should it be measured biologically, psychologically, or economically? Does it have to do with an internal clock, an alteration of one's self-image, or the decline brought on by long labors?

Elite culture provided a range of answers, to which I will turn shortly. Popular culture often defined old age by estranging the aged; folk practices in Provence caused Fernand Benoît to remark that "rare were the elderly who received respect."[50] On such traditional occasions as the *expulsion de la mauvaise saison,* the *vieille de la Sainte-Agathe* (February 5), and other days of *la vieille* (late February and early March), the aged represented bad times, bad seasons, bad harvests. In a symbolic way they were what stood in the path of progress and prosperity. Only their symbolic death could bring good weather, a good harvest, prosperity. Spring brought that death—and a rebirth.

Perhaps ridicule was greatest in the region of Roman law (see Chapter 6), where the classically comic contradiction between legal and physical

47. Alain Charraud, "Analyse de la représentation des âges de la vie humaine dans les estampes populaires du XIXe siècle," *Ethnologie française,* 1 (1971), 59–78.

48. B.N. Estampes, Td 23–24; Hubert-François Bourguignon, dit Gravelot, and Charles-Nicolas Cochin, *L'iconologie ou traité de la science des allégories à l'usage des artistes en 350 figures* (Paris, n.d. [late eighteenth century]).

49. Ariès, "Growing Old in America."

50. Fernand Benoît, *La Provence et le Comtat Venaissin: Arts et traditions populaires* (Avignon, 1975), pp. 226–228, 248.

force was most extreme. But proverbs from all over France and songs from throughout Europe attest to the same contradiction.[51]

Folklore, moreover, did not present only the ugly side of old age, the resentment that maturing children felt toward their elders. It expressed also a certain wonder at those who had beaten the demographic odds, perhaps even a recognition of the changing of the odds. When the aged were viewed outside the family, resentments were not quite so keen; the elderly became local heroes. Thus, Annibal Camous, *le Socrate marseillais,* who died at the reported age of 121 years, 3 months, and 13 days but was actually only ninety at his death in 1759, became the subject of local legend.[52] In reality he was born in Nice in 1669, came to Marseille in his youth, and spent most of his life as a laborer, residing in the *quartier* of Notre-Dame-de-la-Garde. It was said that he was born in 1638, labored on the construction of the Fort Saint-Nicolas (1660–65), learned the use of herbs from the naturalist Joseph Pitton de Tournefort (1656–1708) in the Pyrenees in 1681, and used this knowledge to his own benefit and that of the duchesse de Parme, daughter of Louis XV, whom he was alleged to have healed in Marseille in 1756.

Camous's legend has remained famous in Marseille to this day and, in an example of the cross-fertilization of elite and popular culture, spread to the rest of France in Joseph Vernet's 1751 painting of the port of Marseille. Camous was also painted by Louis René de Vialy, Henry d'Arles, and Michel-Honoré Bounieu, and prints from the paintings offered explanatory information about their subject. A print after Henry's painting which served as frontispiece to the anonymous book *Le Socrate marseillois* (1773) was captioned: "Do you want a happy life? Take him for your model."[53] The author of that caption assumed that a

51. Proverbs and songs are mentioned in Eugen Weber, *Peasants into Frenchmen: The Modernization of Rural France, 1870–1914* (Stanford, Calif., 1976); and Lutz K. Berkner, "The Stem Family and the Developmental Cycle of the Peasant Household: An Eighteenth-Century Austrian Example," *American Historical Review,* 77 (1972), 398–418. For more proverbs, see Françoise Loux and Philippe Richard, *Sagesses du corps: La santé et la maladie dans les proverbs français* (Paris, 1978). Most of these proverbs were gathered in the nineteenth century, and their age is difficult to guess—of course, that is one reason they are proverbs.

52. I thank M. Régis Bertrand for the reference. A.M., Marseille, *registre* 306 f. 13v, and 341 f. 80v. See Louis Thibaux, "Le faux centenaire marseillais Annibal Camoux (1638!) 1669–1759," *Bulletin de l'Institut Historique de Provence,* 34, no. 2 (1957), 49–50.

53. *Le Socrate marseillois, ou Particularitiés instructives et intéressantes pour l' humanité: Au sujet du fameux Annibal Camoux de Marseille . . .* (Marseille, 1773). An

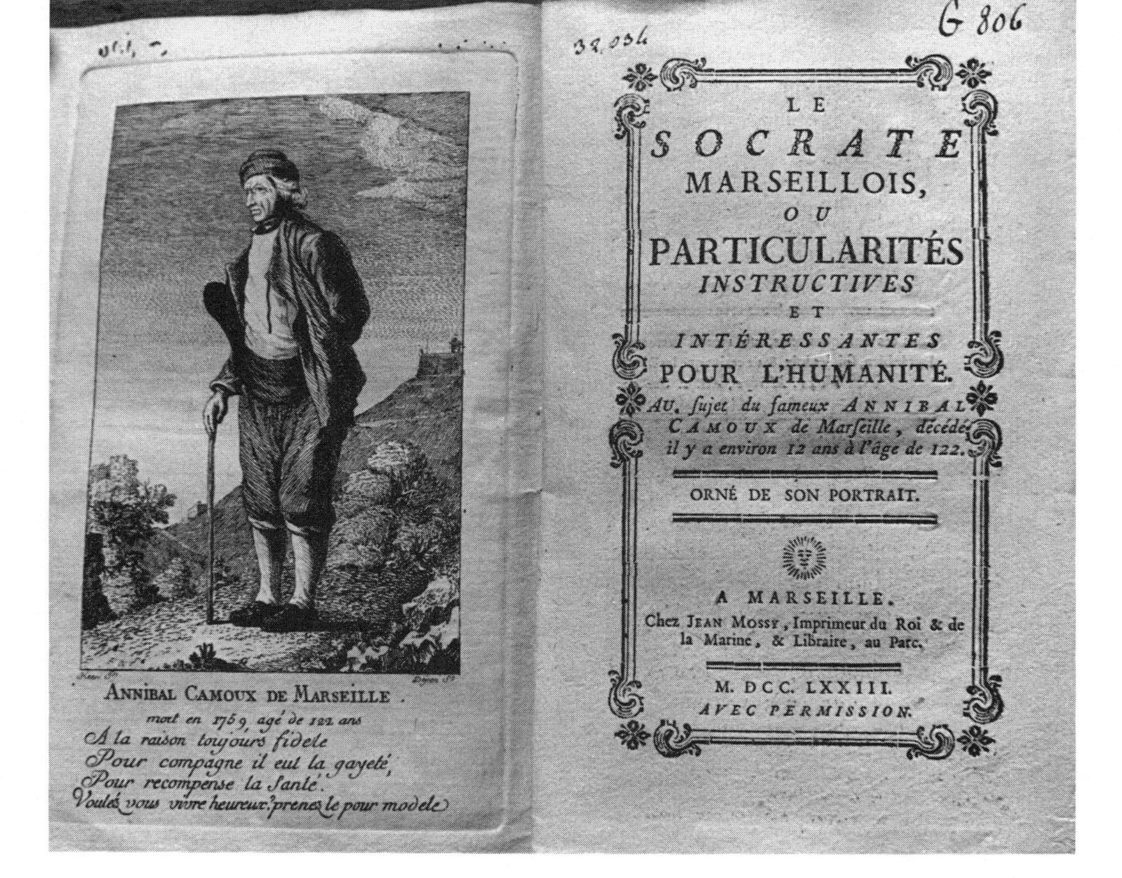

Tales of longevity. *The Marseille Socrates,* print, 1773. Bibliothèque Méjanes, Aix-en-Provence.

long life was a happy one, but whether longevity was desirable was a question open to debate in the early modern period.

Social historians have long recognized the difficulties of using such images and discourse as historical evidence and, until recently, almost automatically distrusted "qualitative" sources. Some have begun to understand, though, that "scientific" standards may unreasonably rule out some very rich source materials. It is true that the ways in which people choose to depict and describe reality have as much to do with cultural traditions and rhetoric as with "reality." They are intertwined.[54] The trick in surveying images and ideas is to learn how to read them, how to accept them not at face value but as cultural stereotypes that have evolved over time. Once we have done that, we can ask why they evolved as they did and what relationship they bore to social reality.

alert old man is said, in Provençal, to resemble "paire Niba." See display at the Musée des Arts et Traditions Populaires du Terroir Marseillais (Musée de Château-Gombert).

54. For a trenchant discussion of this historiographical issue, see Dominick LaCapra, *History and Criticism* (Ithaca, 1985).

2 A New Presence: Images of the Aged in Art

A walk through a gallery of French eighteenth-century art leaves the impression that artists discovered old age at midcentury. This impression is reinforced when one sees these paintings falling into two broad categories, products of two major periods of artistic production: the rococo of the first half of the century, and the neoclassicism of the second, with the realism of Jean-Baptiste Chardin or Françoise Duparc and the sentimentality of Jean-Baptiste Greuze sandwiched between them. Art historians have commonly identified a certain mentality appropriate to each of these styles: frivolity in the first half, austerity in the second.[1] In general, a shift in the depiction of aged characters fits the pattern: the aged are marginal at most (if not totally absent) in the first half and seriously present in the second.

One must search assiduously to find elderly subjects amid the youthful lovers and theatrically dressed characters of the *fêtes galantes* in the early part of the century.[2] Some of the mythological and religious characters of the seventeenth century continue to appear in the eighteenth, but in general the paintings of Antoine Watteau, Nicolas Lancret, Jean-Baptiste Pater, and François Boucher depict the pleasures of youth in a world of exuberant color and rather stagy nature. Whether expressing the liberation from academic preference for line over color, the pleasure-seeking aristocratic style of the Regency, or freedom of painterly qualities from the constraints of text, the art of the early

1. Or, as Denys Sutton has written, "Frivolity and Reason," in Royal Academy of Arts, *France in the Eighteenth Century* (London, 1968); he quibbles with such terms but cannot avoid them.
2. Charles Blanc, *Les peintres des fêtes galantes* (Paris, 1854).

eighteenth century seems to have pushed youth to the center of the canvas and kept the aged confined to the edge. Even though the young Watteau was employed in printing multiple editions of the popular Gerrit Dou, *Old Woman Reading,* his adult work is filled with young lovers and children in pastoral settings. The old doctor in *Le chat malade,* the piper in *Les bergers,* the peasant father serving *Le repas de campagne,* and the old servant in *L'occupation selon l'âge* are notable exceptions.[3] The elderly commedia dell'arte characters are shunted to the side in *Les comédiens italiens.*[4] The Savoyards he drew on several occasions were socially marginal and his pilgrim rather exotic.[5] In Boucher, too, love and frivolity are central, and age appears only to illustrate the mocking themes so common in seventeenth-century literature: thus a print of his *L'avare* appeared in an edition of Molière, and of *Le calandrier des vieillards* in the tales of La Fontaine.[6] Even Chardin, the great painter of the mundane, as Pierre Rosenberg has noted, "prefers women to men, adolescents and children to adults."[7] At least such is the case until the last pastels of the painter and his wife.

One awaits the *têtes d'expression* of Jean Honoré Fragonard and the academic painters educated under the authority of the comte de Caylus, the gushy domestic scenes of Greuze, and the neoclassical deathbed scenes of the end of the ancien régime for the aged to find their place in eighteenth-century art. Old age was not "discovered" in midcentury, but viewers recognized a new presence. Aged subjects were emerging as a way of celebrating human dignity. It was a far cry from an earlier complaint that the subject of old age was ugly and demeaning.[8]

The relative scarcity of elderly subjects in the first half of the century, however, should not lead to any hasty conclusions about early modern painting in general, for extending the chronology back into the seven-

3. See plates in Hélène Adhémar, *Watteau—sa vie—son oeuvre* (Paris, 1950).

4. "Thus Pantalone and the Doctor, stable props of any Commedia performance, make only a brief appearance on the extreme edge of Watteau's pictures": Anita Brookner, *Watteau* (London, 1967), p. 8.

5. *The Old Savoyard,* in Art Institute of Chicago, *Selected Works of 18th Century French Art in the Collection of the A.I.C.* (Chicago, 1976), no. 30.

6. Musée du Louvre, *François Boucher: Gravures et dessins provenant du Cabinet des Dessins et de la collection Edmond de Rothschild au Musée du Louvre* (Paris, 1971), nos. 43, 78.

7. Pierre Rosenberg, *Chardin, 1699–1779* (Cleveland, Ohio, 1979), p. 55.

8. See the comment on Ribera's Saint Bartholomew in Jean-Baptiste Boyer d'Aguilles, *Recueil d'estampes d'après les tableaux des peintres les plus célèbres d'Italie, des Pays-Bas et de France . . .* (Paris, 1744).

teenth century discloses a plethora of elderly characters. There is no dating the first appearance of the aged in French art. The twelfth century saw the depiction of the twenty-four old men of the apocalypse; the thirteenth brought sculptures of individual old men and depictions of aged saints; the end of the Middle Ages had the elderly dancing the *danse macabre;* and the early modern period depicted old people in death and life.[9] Among imports to France one also encounters all manner of old people, from Ghirlandaio's rhinosclerotic old man with his grandson (in the Louvre) through the portrait of an old man by Quinten Metsijs (in the Musée Jacquemart-André) to any number of northern moral pieces such as David Rickaert's *L'avarice* (Musée des Beaux-Arts, Lyon), in which an old woman weighs her gold and silver before an erect pig.[10]

In prints as well as paintings the aged had their accustomed roles. A perusal of early French collections reveals depictions of old people approaching death, warming themselves by the hearth, and even participating in the life of the street and the market.[11] Prints frequently illustrated moral themes and appeared beside proverbs. The earliest example of the *degrés des âges,* depicting all the ages of life, is a fifteenth-century German print, but the theme was quickly internationalized, appearing in multilingual editions, and Paris became an important center for the production of these images.[12] Some of Jacques Callot's victims of the Thirty Years War were elderly, and similar characters appeared in prints as victims of age and poverty as much as of war.[13] Scenes based on street life, cabaret life, and the various trades showed the aged at work and at leisure.[14]

9. Emile Mâle, *L'art religieux du xiie siècle en France: Etude sur les origines de l'iconographie du moyen âge* (Paris, 1924), *L'art religieux du xiiie siècle en France* (Paris, 1925), *L'art religieux de la fin du moyen âge* (Paris, 1925), and *L'art religieux après le concile de Trente* (Paris, 1932).

10. The Ghirlandaio dates from the late fifteenth century; the Metsijs *Portrait posthume d'un vieillard* dates from 1516. The Rickaert is in the Musée des Beaux-Arts, Lyon; the artist lived from 1612 to 1661.

11. See the first two (of four) volumes of François Courboin, *Histoire illustrée de la gravure en France* (Paris, 1923–29). See also B.N. Estampes, B6C. In addition, Marguerite Pitsch, *Essai de catalogue sur l'iconographie de la vie populaire à Paris au XVIIIe siècle* (Paris, 1952).

12. Jean Mistler et al., *Epinal et l'imagerie populaire* (Paris, 1961).

13. Jacques Callot, *Les misères de la guerre; Les gueux.*

14. Bouchardon, *Etudes prises dans le bas peuple, ou Les cris de Paris* (Paris, 1737–42), in B.N. Estampes, Oa 132; Poisson, *Cris de Paris* (Paris, 1774); Balthazar-Antoine

In short, old people were not newcomers to the cast of characters in French art. Their relative absence in the early eighteenth century stands out as an exception rather than the rule and might be explained in stylistic terms as a consequence of a growing emphasis on luxuriant, youthful color and pleasing scenery, or in semiotic terms as a consequence of greater interest in image as image than in image as symbolizing a deeper textual significance. As one historian of the period has recently argued, applying the argot of semiotics to his own discipline, early eighteenth-century artists favored figure over discourse and focused their attention on the "signifier," whereas their predecessors and successors exhibited a greater interest in the "signified."[15] If our interest lies in the attitude underlying the image of the old person, then we ought to ask how the signified (attitude or meaning) evolved as the signifier (old person on canvas or paper) recurred over time. In other words, what did the old person represent? And how did that representation change?

Throughout the early modern period, certain allegorical and mythological figures and themes had commonly been represented by the aged. Gods, Fates, death, time, winter, night, rivers, and wind are among them.[16] The late eighteenth-century *Iconologie* of H.-F. Bourguignon, dit Gravelot and Charles-Nicolas Cochin brought together 350 representative figures that had served in Western art.[17] The date of publication does not indicate when these themes were commonly employed. Rather it was in the eighteenth century, when one was freer to explore alternative figures, that one could look back on an entire allegorical language of graphic representation that had held in the past.[18] Gravelot and Cochin gathered together the allegorical figures for arts, sciences, continents, months, virtues, and vices. Virtues were generally younger

---

Dunker, *Esquisses pour les artistes et amateurs des arts, sur Paris,* 96 illustrations for Louis-Sébastien Mercier, *Tableau de Paris* (Amsterdam, 1783–88).

15. This is the approach of Norman Bryson, *Word and Image: French Painting of the Ancien Régime* (Cambridge, 1981). As Michael Levey remarks, without recourse to semiotic jargon, in Wend Graf Kalnein and Michael Levey, *Art and Architecture of the Eighteenth Century in France* (Harmondsworth, 1972), p. 106: "The growth of public interest in painting in France in the middle years of the century—an interest which was really more literary than visually artistic—introduced a new social factor. Style became less important than subject matter."

16. B.N., Estampes, Td 24.

17. Gravelot et Cochin, *L'iconologie.*

18. For an alternative version of the Fates, where two of three would be younger than Atropos, see ibid., vol. 4, no. 77.

than vices. Vice was more ugly than old, though, and some virtues were clearly the province of the elderly. Old men represented grief, suspicion, overscrupulousness, evil genius ("old man having a frightful look, long beard, hair standing on end"), insanity (playing like a child), chastisement, and zeal—but they also stood for courage, time, and thought. Old women fared rather poorly, representing malice ("old woman, hideous, with a wild look and menacing attitude, having both hands armed with daggers"), winter, severity, excessive assiduity, parsimony, prejudice, adversity, calamity, and punishment. In their favor, however, they personified experience, medicine, penitence, and Christian Reason. As elsewhere in Western culture, the woman represented the worst and the best, and aged women shared in both extremes.

In painting as in prints, the aged appeared in predictable roles: Old Testament patriarchs, Sara, priests and prophets, Elias, Tobias, saints, the gods of wind and sea, satyrs, Philemon and Baucis, Anchises, Charon, Chronos, the accusers of Susannah, the father in Roman Charity, and Belisarius. These appear among the baroque themes catalogued by A. Pigler, and the list, though not complete, does indicate the kinds of roles the aged filled.[19] Some were allegorical characters, but most were particular individuals from the great Western sources: biblical, classical, and historical. As individuals they could not be taken to represent a view of old age per se.

In the seventeenth century, biblical and classical characters gave the aged an otherworldly look. The kneeling magus in Georges Lallemant's *L'adoration des mages* (Lille); *Abraham,* as painted by Antoine Coypel (Valenciennes); the aged apostles in *The Last Supper* of J.-B. de Champaigne; *Moses* of Philippe de Champaigne; the Saint Jeromes of Gaspard Dughet, Nicolas Poussin, Simon Vouet, Moïse Le Valentin, and Claude Vignon the elder; the Josephs of Guy François, Eustache Le Sueur, and Reynaud Levieux; Georges De La Tour's *Peter,* Vignon's *Ambrose,* Vouet's *Chronos,* an anonymous *Matthew,* La Tour's *Philip,* and Le Maître du Jugement de Salomon's *Les philosophes* all present spiritual old men.[20] None of them is just anyone's grandfather.

The traditional genres of historical and religious painting did not die

19. A. Pigler, *Barockthemen: Eine Auswahl von Verzeichnissen zur Ikonographie des 17. und 18. Jahrunderts,* 3 vols. (Budapest, 1974).

20. These paintings were included in an exhibition in the series Trésors des Musées du Nord de la France: *La peinture française aux XVIIe et XVIIIe siècles* (Dunkerque, 1980); and in Pierre Rosenberg, *France in the Golden Age: Seventeenth-Century French Paintings in American Collections* (New York, 1982).

out in the eighteenth century. The aged continued to play traditional roles, such as the mourners in Jean Jouvenet's *Déposition* and Sébastien II Le Clerc's *Mort de Saphire* or Antoine Coypel's God in *Adam and Eve* (1704) and Anchises carried by Aeneas (Montpellier).[21] Nevertheless, while such painters as Jean-François de Troy continued to depict the lascivious old harassers of Susannah and an elderly King David ogling Bathsheba, the prime purpose in appropriating these themes was simply to paint the female nude. The old men are incidental; their voyeurism is less important than that of the viewer of the painting. And in Jean-Baptiste Santerre's 1704 *Suzanne* the old men are absent.[22]

Religious painting in France too survived the amorality of the Regency. The reign of Louis XV saw a revival of religious painting, with canvases that included the usual old people seen in the art of France and Italy in the seventeenth century: Joseph in Boucher's *Nativity* (1750), Jean-Baptiste Pierre's *St. Thomas-à-Becket,* Jean Restout's *St. Andrew* (1748), Jean-Baptiste Deshays's *Andrew* (1758), Carle Van Loo's bishop listening to *Augustine* (1755), Joseph Marie Vien's *Denis* (1767), the poor old man whose feet are washed by Louis-Jacques Durameau's *St. Louis,* and others.[23] Religious and historical subjects, in contrast to the *fêtes galantes,* kept certain aged figures at the center of the canvas.

Still, we might wonder how contemporaries viewed these subjects. When people of the seventeenth century looked at a Saint Jerome, what did they see? A particular saint? Saintliness in general? Old age? Certainly they saw all these things, but Jerome as a representative of the aged was eclipsed by a complex iconographical tradition in which characters and objects of the material world point to scripture and legend rather than simply back to the material world. So too for the countless other elderly figures of the baroque. Even those characters who benefited from a Caravaggist realism signified something more metaphysical than age, particularly to an educated audience. They had spiritual qualities that took precedence over details of baldness and wrinkles, no matter how much care an artist put into representation of a particular individual's physiognomy. Characteristics of youth and age

21. See plates in Pierre Rosenberg, *The Age of Louis XV: French Painting, 1710–1774* (Toledo, Ohio, 1975).

22. Michael Levey, *Rococo to Revolution: Major Trends in Eighteenth-Century Painting* (New York, 1966), p. 32, fig. 14.

23. See plates in chapter on religious painting in Philip Conisbee, *Painting in Eighteenth-Century France* (Ithaca, 1981).

appear in seventeenth and early eighteenth-century treatises on physiognomy. They follow the guidelines of Cartesian human development, but as with the old people described by Gravelot and Cochin, they represent qualities independent of age. A wrinkled face bespeaks years of life, but it may also refer the viewer to moods of rage and fury.[24]

If the use of the aged to signify metaphysical or emotional categories suggests that the depiction of the aged was not a direct expression of attitudes toward age, we still must consider the stark realism of genre paintings by such seventeenth-century masters as the brothers Le Nain, Philippe de Champaigne, and Georges de La Tour.[25] Standing before their views of peasant families and individuals, we feel that we are looking directly into the seventeenth century. Even the stiffness of many of the characters, their air of expectation, reminds us of the uncomfortable look of the subjects of early portrait photography. This is a realism that looks lifelike yet also posed. In outdoor scenes the seated old women are frozen into landscapes whose tranquility is disturbed only by the games of children. In peasant interiors the individuality of particular persons is somehow reduced to the coherence of the family as a whole; members of the peasant family are hardly individuated. And there is something quite foreign about those portrayed.[26] Perhaps it is a reflection of the occupational distance or class tension between painter and sitter or the historical barrier between viewer and subject. Maybe the fact that there is little action—that these are people defined by their work and yet we see them in repose—causes the uneasiness. Or maybe it is the difficulty of accepting them as individuals. Viewing them in their rural milieu, we see them as part of the landscape or of the interior. All ages blend into the household unit and its material and natural surroundings.

There is certainly a moral component to these paintings. In Georges de La Tour's *Musicians' Brawl* the particular message is unclear, though Pierre Rosenberg suggests that it might be "Wretched is he who can find

24. Bryson, *Word and Image,* has an excellent discussion of physiognomy. Facial expression is central to John Montgomery Wilson, *The Painting of the Passions in Theory, Practice, and Criticism in Later Eighteenth-Century France* (New York, 1981).

25. On these painters, see Rosenberg, *France in the Golden Age;* Benedict Nicolson and Christopher Wright, *Georges de la Tour* (London, 1974); S. M. M. Furness, *Georges de la Tour of Lorraine, 1593–1652* (London, 1949); Orangerie des Tuileries, *Georges de la Tour* (Paris, 1972); Grand Palais, *Les frères Le Nain* (Paris, 1978).

26. See John Berger's essays, "The Suit and the Photograph" and "La Tour and Humanism," in *About Looking* (New York, 1980).

Louis Le Nain, *Landscape with Peasants*, canvas, c. 1640. National Gallery of Art, Washington, D.C., Samuel H. Kress Collection.

no one more wretched than himself."[27] Rosenberg marvels at the toothless old woman who stares out of the canvas, but again her significance is unclear. The La Tour *Old Man* and *Old Woman* that serve as pendants to each other evidently depict characters of the theater in poses from the stage.[28] The old man cringes from the abuse of his wife. But what of the La Tour and Le Nain peasants?[29] Can we distinguish between those that express dignity and those that do not?[30] Such difficulties have not prevented some art historians from reaching grand conclusions, but we might better simply assert only that there is a realist strain in French painting running fitfully from the Le Nain brothers to the realists and naturalists of the nineteenth century.

But surely realism in one period is not realism in another. The northern genre paintings that influenced seventeenth- and eighteenth-century France had clear moral content, which survived to one degree or another. The seventeenth-century Lorraine painters were illustrating texts. The genre paintings of the eighteenth century illustrated new themes. For a time, however, there seems to have been a concern for simply capturing reality.[31] The work of Chardin and Duparc depicts the surface of the material world with little moralizing baggage. Chardin's portraits of himself and his wife bring the elderly to the foreground and dispense with text. The portraits of working-class figures by Duparc do the same.[32] Her old woman is remarkable for her dignity. The subject's simplicity and directness are heightened by Duparc's white palette.[33]

27. Rosenberg, *France in the Golden Age*, p. 255.

28. Ibid., p. 254; Martha Kellogg Smith, "Georges de la Tour's 'Old Man' and 'Old Woman' in San Francisco," *Burlington Magazine*, 121 (1979), 288–294.

29. For example, Louis Le Nain, *Peasants before their House* and *Peasants in a Landscape*, and Mathieu Le Nain, *Peasant Interior*, in Rosenberg, *France in the Golden Age*.

30. Berger, "La Tour," has attempted to do this. Robert Wheaton has also tried to go beyond questions of household size and regional family types in "Ariès and the Development of French Family History: The Iconography of the Family Portrait" (paper delivered at the 1980 meeting of the American Historical Association; I thank him for sending me a copy).

31. For an important recent discussion of "mere" description in painting, see Svetlana Alpers, *The Act of Describing: Dutch Art in the Seventeenth Century* (Chicago, 1983); cf. Simon Schama, "The Unruly Realm: Appetite and Restraint in Seventeenth-Century Holland," *Daedalus*, 108, no. 3 (1979), 103–123.

32. Duparc's four known paintings—*La vieille dame*, *L'homme à la besace (Le vieillard)*, *La marchande de tisane*, and *Jeune femme à l'ouvrage*—hang in the Musée des Beaux Arts, Marseille.

33. See also the appreciation of *la vieille dame* in Rosenberg, *France in the Golden Age*, no. 32, p. 85.

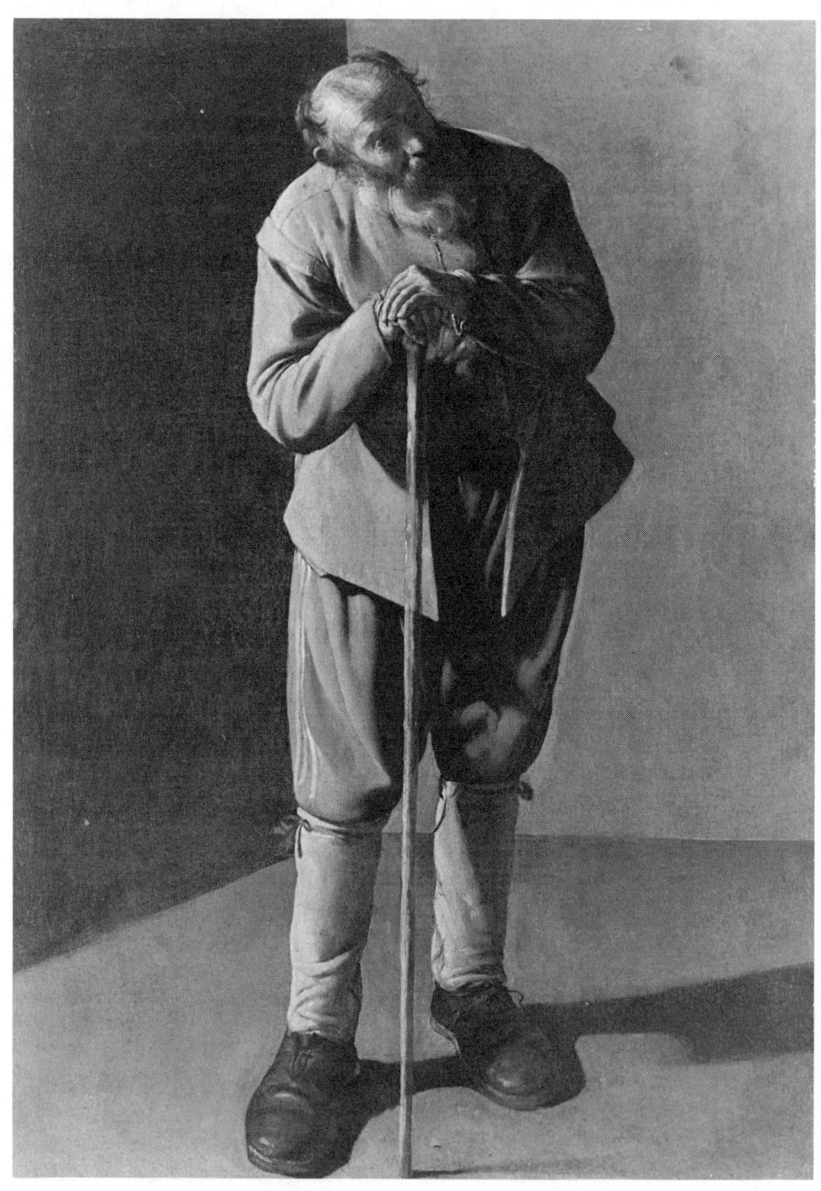

Georges de La Tour, *Old Man*, canvas, ca. 1618–19. By permission of The Fine Arts Museums of San Francisco, Roscoe and Margaret Oakes Collection.

The old man has been identified as Annibal Camous, the figure of Marseillais folkore discussed earlier.[34] Whether or not the connection is valid, he too projects an image of simple dignity and practical wisdom. Both paintings pose beautifully the problem of the Enlightenment depiction of old persons. They are called old but look quite strong; one might argue that therefore they are not old at all. But this was one solution to the problem of depicting age and dignity simultaneously. By the turn of the century some saw strength and beauty in wrinkled faces.[35] At midcentury the Académie des beaux-arts, in training young painters, encouraged the exercise of depicting expressive and, frequently, old faces—the various *têtes d'expression*.[36] Most were *têtes de vieillard*. We have examples of these studies from those who matured at midcentury. Even Fragonard, who remained apart from the Academy, produced a plethora of them: for example, the Jacquemart-André, Amiens, and Strasbourg paintings.[37]

Such surface description contrasts markedly with the bourgeois moralizing of Greuze. The unreal situations of his paintings—the dramatic entrances and exits perfectly timed to the rhythms of the life cycle—have a clearer meaning for us.[38] They explore the fragility of the domestic unit, the distinctiveness of generations, and the melodrama inherent in everyday life. By now, Greuze's meaning is banal, but in the eighteenth century it was original. His characters tell us about age as well as virtue. They may insult us by belaboring the obvious, but what is obvious now was evidently a revelation then.[39]

Although Greuze fell rather quickly into personal obscurity when the extraordinary initial enthusiasm over his work subsided under attacks on stylistic grounds, painting throughout the rest of the century continued in his thematic vein—as have mass-produced greeting cards of

34. See the article on Camous in Paul Masson, *Les Bouches-du-Rhône: Encyclopédie départementale* (Marseille, 1913–37).

35. J. H. Meister, *Lettres sur la vieillesse* (Paris, 1810), pp. 5–6.

36. See Wilson, *The Painting of the Passions*.

37. Jacques Thuillier, *Fragonard* (Geneva, 1967); Georges Wildenstein, *The Paintings of Fragonard* (Garden City, N.Y., 1960), especially cat. nos. 190–208.

38. Bryson, *Word and Image,* points out quite correctly, though, that while the call to honor old age is easily recognizable today, the twentieth-century viewer's reaction also involves a sense of guilt due to an awareness of the difficult position of the aged in the contemporary world.

39. Anita Brookner, *Greuze: The Rise and Fall of an Eighteenth-Century Phenomenon* (London, 1972), emphasizes the celebrity of Greuze in the eighteenth century as well as the literary character of his work.

Françoise Duparc, *Old Woman,* canvas. Musée des Beaux-Arts, Palais Longchamp,
Marseille. Phot. Giraudon.

Françoise Duparc, *L'homme à la besace* (*Old Man*), canvas. Musée des Beaux-Arts, Palais Longchamp, Marseille. Phot. Ville de Marseille.

Jean-Honoré Fragonard, *Head of an Old Man*, canvas. Musée de Picardie, Amiens.

the last two hundred years—finding a constantly appreciative market. The mysterious realism of the seventeenth-century Lorraine painters and the descriptive detail of Chardin and Duparc were inappropriate for mid-eighteenth-century artists who had more obvious textual meanings to communicate. They did not want merely to show the life of the peasants, to provide an undifferentiated view of rural space and time. They wanted to comment upon the lives they were depicting.[40] Greuze's paintings touted domestic virtues. Repeatedly they depicted both conflicts within the household and, more often, solidarity among family members. Despite his failure to attain the rank of history painter, Greuze's themes of private virtue joined with themes of public virtue in the work of established artists—especially history painters—in the later eighteenth century.

The ages of life became an essential theme. The ambiguity of two adult generations in a society that was really prepared to deal with only one was masked by sentiment. There are no simple *vieillards* in Greuze, as there were in the Le Nain. There are *vieillards respectables* or, in one case, a *vieillard dénaturé*.[41] They do not live in the fullness of time; rather, they are depicted at critical junctures. An aged patriarch hands his daughter over in marriage. The prodigal son quits the home of his aged father and returns to find him dead. Those paintings and prints that do not depict the critical moments nevertheless argue a point: they favor filial piety, charity, and virtue. They show how an old father ought to read the Bible to his children. They show how charity ought to be given. Or, in contrast, they show how people should not behave toward the old: the blind old husband should not be cheated.[42]

Greuze's subjects were emotionally charged and ideologically pointed. While his themes may have reflected his own psychological makeup—the brothers Goncourt report suspicions of his wife and fear of old women—they accord with the concerns of the period.[43] Greuze told stories, and his critics reported them, debating the precise ages and motivations of the various characters.[44] For example, the aged father in

40. On discourse vs. figures, see Bryson, *Word and Image*.

41. *La mort d'un père dénaturé* (sketch) appeared in the 1769 *Salon*.

42. This theme is derived from Dutch painting; see Anita Brookner, "Jean-Baptiste Greuze," Part I, *Burlington Magazine*, 98 (1956), 158, referring to *L'aveugle trompé*.

43. Edmond and Jules de Goncourt, *French Eighteenth-Century Painters* (Ithaca, 1981), p. 256.

44. On what occurs in these paintings, see the criticism in Deloynes, now available on microfiche. On the theatricality of the painting, see Michael Fried, *Absorption and Theatricality: Painting and Beholder in the Age of Diderot* (Berkeley, Calif., 1980).

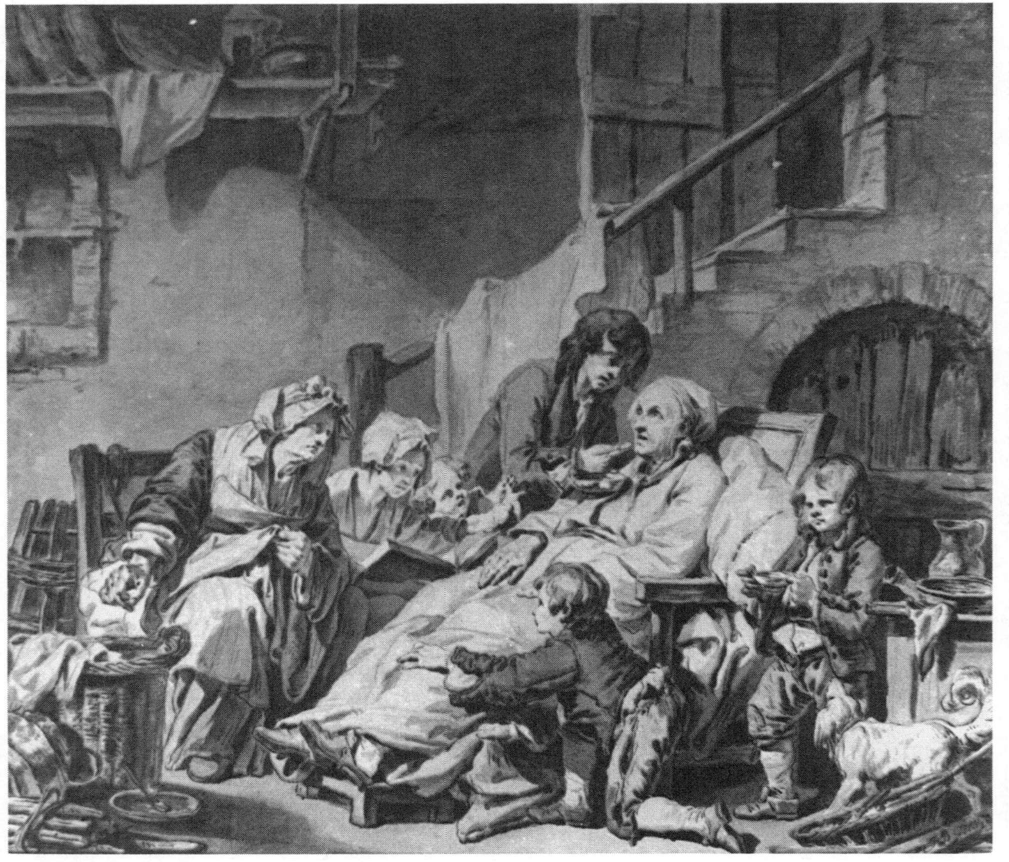

Jean-Baptiste Greuze, *The Paralytic*, sketch, 1761. Phot. Musée des Beaux-Arts, Le Havre.

L'accordée de village was described by one critic as "an old man with an open face and all the nobility of his state. One notices that what has furrowed his face is less the decrepitude of age than work and the elements. The brush speaks through this old man."[45] Of the same character, Diderot remarked: "He has a pleasing air of bonhomie."[46]

The painting of *Piété filiale* drew this comment from Mathon de la Cour: "This old man, decrepit and stricken with paralysis, turns his languishing eye upon his son and thanks him for his care. One sees on his brow those respectable wrinkles that the years imprint and which have not been hastened by any excess."[47] The same critic reacted violently to the drawings of *Le fils ingrat* and *Le fils puni:* "One suffers too much in seeing them. They poison the soul with a sentiment so profound and so terrible that one is forced to avert his eyes."[48] Throughout his criticism, Mathon referred to the depiction of age. Commenting on Louis Lagrenée's *Aurore et Titon,* Mathon noted that "the contrasts of youth with advanced age have a great effect in this painting."[49] He compared the bald old man with the pretty young woman painted by Deshays.[50] In Van Loo's sketches for the Chapelle des Invalides, illustrating the life of Saint Gregory, Mathon noticed the aging of the saint from one picture to the next.[51] Elsewhere he discussed art criticism in general and raised the question of the changing taste of the aging viewer.[52]

The new literary genre of art criticism placed a premium on storytelling. Diderot's *Salons* told stories and judged paintings by the effect they had on viewer and reader. Since his words were accompanied by no prints, he was obliged to describe paintings, in effect narrating them. The narration expressed an appreciation for a certain kind of art, corresponding to his own notion of the *drame* on stage. Even religious painting was described in terms of physical types designed to move the

45. *Observations d'une société d'amateurs; sur les tableaux exposés au salon cette année 1761: Tirées de l'Observateur littéraire de M. l'abbé (Joseph) de la Porte* (Paris, 1761), in Deloynes, vol. 7, p. 48.

46. Denis Diderot, *Salons,* vol. 1 (Oxford, 1957), p. 142 (1761).

47. Charles-Joseph Mathon de la Cour, *Lettre à Madame * * *, sur les peintures, les sculptures, et les gravures exposées dans le sallon du Louvre cette année* (Paris, 1763), p. 64.

48. Idem, *Lettres à Monsieur * * * . . . 1765* (Paris, 1765), pp. 12–13.

49. Idem, *Lettre à Madame,* pp. 20–21.

50. Idem, *Seconde lettre à Madame * * ** (Paris, 1763), p. 9.

51. Idem, *Lettres à Monsieur,* pp. 5–6.

52. Ibid., p. 22.

public. Thus, of Deshays's *Martyre de St. André,* Diderot wrote: "The entire upper part of his body is nude in front: these are quite the flesh, the wrinkles, the stiff and dry muscles, all the traces of old age. It is impossible to look for long without terror upon this scene of inhumanity and furor." And, moving to sculpture and here discussing the Etiennne-Maurice Falconet head of Dr. Camille Falconet, Diderot commented: "It is bald. A great nose; heavy wrinkles quite deep; a large forehead; long plaits of old age stretching from beneath the jaw, the length of the neck, to the chest; a mouth of a special and very agreeable form. Serenity, ingenuity, vivacity, bonhomie; everything that makes of an old person of ninety years a very interesting and amiable man."[53]

Diderot remarked upon the beauty of several painted heads of old people: Greuze's *Paralytique,* the artist's father-in-law *Babuti,* the old man spying on Lagrenée's *Susanne,* the old man in *La piété filiale.* On the other hand, he did not care for Fragonard's old men. Age alone was not sufficient to gain Diderot's approval. In commenting on *La chaste Susanne* and *Charité romaine,* he suggested changes. The old man in Lagrenée's *La Charité romaine* was deemed too strong: he "is handsome, certainly too handsome; he is too fit, plumper than if he had had two cows at his service: he has none of the look of having suffered for a moment; and if this young woman is not careful, he will end up by making her pregnant." In Bachelier's version of the story, according to Diderot, the old man is hideous. In Lagrenée's *La chaste Susanne,* the old men just do not seem a threat.[54] By the 1760s it was necessary to pay attention to the old men, for the theme was not just an excuse for painting a woman in her bath. Reflecting on the theme in general, Diderot found the moral content of the tale unconvincing: "I look at *Suzanne;* and far from feeling horror for the old men, perhaps I have desired to be in their place."[55]

Both these themes, so popular with baroque and rococo painters, presented problems for the sentimental middle of the century and earnest neoclassicism of the end. Referring to the new view of the neoclassicist, Hugh Honour has examined the transformation of Roman Charity with particular emphasis on a German version of about 1800: "The subject had been treated by innumerable Baroque and Rococo painters,

53. Denis Diderot, *Salons* (Oxford, 1957–67), vol. 1 (1761), pp. 121, 137.
54. Ibid., pp. 97, 135, 234; vol. 2, pp. 95, 104–106; vol. 3, pp. 94–97, 280.
55. The remark comes from Denis Diderot, *Pensées détachées* (1798), in *Oeuvres complètes,* vol. 12 (Paris, 1876), p. 84. A footnote in *Oeuvres esthétiques* (Paris, 1959), p. 767 n.2, suggests that Diderot may have been thinking of the Sébastien Bourdon painting owned by Baron d'Holbach.

Jean-Jacques Bachelier, *Roman Charity*, canvas, 1765. Ecole Nationale Supérieure des Beaux-Arts, Paris.

sometimes as an allegory of youth and age, often with lascivious over-tones, generally as an exercise in painterly ability. But Gottlieb Schick painted it simply and starkly as an example of filial piety."[56]

Filial piety and civic virtue were better communicated in other ways. Such domestic scenes as Etienne Aubry's *L'amour paternel* or Marguerite Gérard's *Le premier pas de l'enfance* would suggest as much piety as did Greuze—but with somewhat less sentimentality.[57] Civic virtue was communicated by the worthy actions of some heroic old men; for example, François-André Vincent's *Président Molé* of 1779 portrayed, according to Kalnein and Levey, the "brave hero, aged, unarmed, fearless, and morally indignant before mob rule."[58] Jacques-Louis David also represented it many times by classical themes. But while the death of Socrates, the oath of the Horatii, and the begging Belisarius were depictions of events long past, they had an air of contemporaneity about them. Civic life could be democratized and repre-sented within any kind of family. With the emphasis on deathbed scenes and virtuous widows, the serious virtues and models for behavior could be exemplified by all people for all people.[59] The historical setting for virtuous acts simply universalized the acts. This was the key to neo-classicism.[60] David's *Bélisaire* may have had contemporary significance in the light of the restoration of the reputation of the comte de Lally-Tollendal, but the old general—in painting as in literature—stood for all old people and all victims of the state.[61] And while Belisarius and Oedipus at Colonus might represent aristocratic exiles during the Directory, in general they were merely poor old people, victims of time:

> Qu'importe sa naissance, ou comment on le nomme?
> C'est un père, un vieillard, un malheureux, un homme.[62]

56. Hugh Honour, *Neo-classicism* (Harmondsworth, 1968), p. 144. For earlier versions of Roman Charity and charity in general, see Musée des Beaux Arts de Caen, *L'allégorie dans la peinture: La représentation de la charité au XVIIe siècle* (Caen, 1986).

57. For the Aubry, see Kalnein and Levey, *Art and Architecture*, p. 188; for the Gérard, Réunion des Musées Nationaux, Paris, *French Painting 1774–1830: The Age of Revolution* (Detroit, Mich., 1975), no. 71.

58. Kalnein and Levey, *Art and Architecture*, p. 190.

59. Robert Rosenblum, *Transformations in Late Eighteenth-Century Art* (Princeton, N.J., 1967).

60. Rémy G. Saisselin, "Neo-classicism: Virtue, Reason and Nature," in Henry Hawley, *Neo-Classicism: Style and Motif* (Cleveland, Ohio, 1964), pp. 1–8.

61. Réunion des Musées, *French Painting*, no. 30.

62. James Henry Rubin, "Oedipus, Antigone, and Exiles in Post-Revolutionary French Painting," *Art Quarterly*, 36, no. 3 (1973), 141–171.

Jacques-Louis David, *Belisarius,* canvas, 1781. Musée des Beaux-Arts, Lille. Phot. Giraudon.

Whether one was arguing for the dignity of the poor in the ancien régime or for the aristocracy in the Directory, the humanity of all victims of biological, economic, and political forces was affirmed. This was particularly true, says Cummings, in "those last, significant years of the Ancien Régime, when French painting was dedicated to one principal theme: the human condition and the regeneration of society."[63]

The philosophical point made at the end of the ancien régime required a realism that had force, not the simple realism of the seventeenth century. While one may now look back on it and contrast it, as a bourgeois realism, to the naturalism and photographic realism that would come later, at the time it was an art with a certain urgency engaged in a search for the proper style. It might go beyond the bounds of contemporary taste in Jean-Baptiste Pigalle's nude sculpture of the aged Voltaire. But even where it did not overstep those bounds, from the 1770s on, in the sculpture of Jean-Antoine Houdon and in countless prints, it contributed to a stereotypical view of *le vieillard de Ferney*, a good old man worthy of apotheosis.[64]

How can one explain the earnestness with which artists turned their attention to old age and other such problems? It is really the same question as that of the shift in mood which characterized both sentimental painting and neoclassicism. One explanation is easy: that mainstream artistic institutions were demanding a new kind of artistic expression. The Academy itself, in reasserting its predominance, required art that made a clear point and took something from the classic past. It required serious historical subjects but also impressive facial expression and a visualization of the passions. From a theoretical point of view, the didacticism of art and its value as propaganda reigned supreme.[65]

But that explanation does not go far enough; moreover, it cannot stand alone, because the rule of Academic officials was not as authoritarian as it had been under Charles Le Brun. And even those who produced the big history paintings also produced portraits and genre

63. Frederick J. Cummings, "Painting under Louis XVI, 1774–1789," in Réunion de Musées, *French Painting,* p. 43.

64. See Honour, *Neo-classicism,* p. 120, and H. H. Arnason, *The Sculptures of Houdon* (New York, 1975), pp. 7–9, on the statues. On depictions of Voltaire, see Garry Apgar, *Charges et caricatures de Voltaire: Essai sur les images d'un Monsieur Multiforme,* Mémoire de Maîtrise de Lettres Modernes, University of Paris, IV (Sorbonne) (1979); on the Pigalle, Dena Goodman, "Pigalle's *Voltaire nu:* The Republic of Letters Represents Itself to the World," *Representations,* 16 (1986), 86–109.

65. James A. Leith, *The Idea of Art as Propaganda in France, 1750–1799* (Toronto, 1965).

paintings. Taste was not determined simply by state authorities. In the eighteenth century, taste was democratized, and public opinion grew. Art came to be judged not simply as the visual means of transmitting noble sentiments of the spirit but also as a way of reflecting on nature. In the seventeenth century, art corrected nature, and although the eighteenth century certainly saw no good in presenting a random nature and found considerable benefit in pleasing the eye, it wanted to depict something that the growing public would see as true. The canvas could be held up to nature.[66]

Why, then, did eighteenth-century artists not produce the same sorts of paintings as the Caravaggist and Lorraine realists of the previous century? The answer may lie in the realm of ideas. Nature, for the eighteenth century, had an ethical aspect and served as the measure of virtue for the Enlightenment. It could not be separated from the world of teaching, of moralizing, and of text. It would teach, and it would do so by obvious, seemingly natural images. It would depict good and bad families, noble and (rarely) ignoble old people—not the blank families of the Le Nain. A new stereotype was emerging in painting; it was even more evident in literature.[67]

66. André Fontaine, *Les doctrines d'art en France—peintres—amateurs—critiques de Poussin à Diderot* (Paris, 1909), pp. 217–218. On the development of an art public, see Thomas E. Crow, *Painters and Public Life in Eighteenth-Century Paris* (New Haven, Conn., 1985).

67. On their connection, see Warren Roberts, *Morality and Social Class in Eighteenth-Century French Literature and Painting* (Toronto, 1974).

3 From Ridicule to Respect: Literary Discourses on Old Age

The new literary image of old age that developed in the eighteenth century is the more noticeable when seen against traditionally gerontophobic expressions. In previous centuries a certain constancy of roles for the aged had emerged in French literature, offering a mocking view of decline, ugliness, and vanity.[1] There were exceptions, to be sure: the Latin literature of Europe from Roman times to the seventeenth century included the recurrent topic of the *puer senex,* the boy wise beyond his years, and the equivalent young girl–old woman; during the Renaissance, Petrarch wrote penetratingly and sympathetically about growing old.[2] But more common in the vernacular was a less charitable view. A sixteenth-century history of wars between Christians and Turks referred to "poor old men, and aged women and other imbecilic creatures."[3] In literature, the most common traits of the old person were lechery and avarice. The old crones of medieval *fabliaux*[4] and the equally perverse fools of the early modern period, wrinkled yet vain old women and jealous old men beaten and cuckolded by younger wives,[5] suffered from excessive attachment to people and things.

1. Beauvoir, *La vieillesse.* For a similar treatment across the Channel, see Richard Freedman, "Sufficiently Decayed: Gerontophobia in English Literature," in Spicker et al., *Aging and the Elderly,* pp. 49–61.

2. Ernst Robert Curtius, *European Literature and the Latin Middle Ages* (Princeton, N.J., 1967), pp. 98–105; James D. Folts, Jr., "Senescence and Renascence: Petrarch's Thoughts on Growing Old," *Journal of Medieval and Renaissance Studies,* 10, no. 2 (1980), 207–237.

3. Guillaume Aubert de Poitiers, *L'histoire des guerres faites par les chrétiens contre les turcs* (N.p., 1559), p. 59. I thank Denis Crouzet for the reference.

4. Joseph Bédier, *Les fabliaux: Etudes de littérature populaire et d'histoire littéraire du moyen âge* (Paris, 1964).

5. In an anonymous text of 1618, a jealous old man dreams of having grown horns and considers all the other horned animals in nature; see *Le vieillard jaloux tombé en*

Many were the tales, plays, and poems titled *Le vieillard amoureux* and *La vieille amoureuse*. One of the former from 1718 recounted the story of a jurist, addressed as *Monsieur le Docteur,* who would have seemed distinguished and respectable if judged only by "his austere look, his long beard, and his white hair."[6] But his old age consisted of one attempted seduction after another, which exposed him to the trickery of servants, shame within the community, and the embarrassment of failing to perform even when his efforts appeared headed for success. The character of *la vieille amoureuse* was generally even more grotesque, a reminder of the ephemeral nature of beauty and of the unavoidable approach of death. In one version her lips were of a morbid blue, her breath full of contagion, her smile the grimace of a monkey, her demeanor that of a werewolf.[7] Common scatological passages suggested that it was impossible to distinguish between her mouth and other orifices.[8]

Even in more elevated literature the aged tended to fare poorly. A poem used as the legend of a seventeenth-century academic portrait noted that the exceptional subject "was old and gallant, without being ridiculous,"[9] whereas ridicule had been the common lot of the aged in literature. Whether in the commedia dell'arte imported from Italy or in indigenous French theater and poetry (if one can speak in national terms where perhaps only continental ones will do), the old man was commonly presented as a *barbon,* an old fogy. He was avaricious and amorous; for his faults he was mistreated, abused, and robbed. His strength lay in his money and his consequent control of his heirs' destinies, but time and most other characters were against him. Whether dressed as Pantalon, the caricature of the old Venetian merchant, or as his relative the doctor, or simply in the style of his youth, he was the butt of laughter even before opening his mouth.[10] Jean de La Bruyère called the loving old man a great deformity in nature, and Molière likewise ridiculed the amorous aged.[11]

---

rêveries à la louange des Cornes: Avec une expresse d'effence aux femmes de ne plus battre leurs maris . . . (Paris, 1618).

6. "Le vieillard amoureux: Histoire nouvelle" (The Hague, 1718).

7. "La vieille amoureuse: Stances," B.N. Ye 4797.

8. E.g., ibid., pp. 17–18.

9. Description of Isaac de Benserade in *Théâtre françois,* vol. 7 (Lyon, 1781), p. 19.

10. Léon and Frédéric Saisset, "Un type de l'ancienne comédie: Le barbon," *Mercure de France,* 183 (1925). Gustave Attinger, *L'esprit de la commedia dell'arte dans le théâtre français* (Paris, 1950), esp. chap. 3, "Le type."

11. Cited in Louis Fiaux, *La femme, le mariage, et le divorce: Etude de physiologie et de sociologie* (Paris, 1880), p. 47.

The exception that proves the rule is the libertine literature and life of the seventeenth century, particularly as exemplified by the aging circle of Ninon de Lenclos. The members of this Parisian coterie of scientists, writers, and courtesans, including Bernard Le Bovier de Fontenelle and Charles de Saint-Denis de Saint-Evrémond, grew extremely old together and, through their letters, left a record of the process. Complaints of the infirmities of age and the loss of friends darkened the atmosphere of this band of libertines, but they still managed to affirm their friendship, maintain a busy social life, and express their mutual admiration. The marquis D'Argenson wrote of Fontenelle at eighty that his desire to live to a hundred led him to the single-minded occupation of preserving his health: "He is regarded as one of those masterworks of art, produced with care and delicacy, that one must beware of destroying, because no equals are made." And the Chevalier de Solignac remarked, "Even his final old age had something handsome and virile."[12] Indeed, he nearly reached the goal of a hundred years.

Ninon de Lenclos lived almost a century and had long been renowned for her life as a libertine—having taken countless lovers, including three generations of one family. Her reputation gave rise to such characterizations as the following song:

> Il ne faut pas qu'on s'étonne
> Si souvent elle raisonne
> De la sublime vertu
> Dont Platon fut revêtu
> Car, à bien compter son âge,
> Elle doit avoir f . . .
> Avec ce grand personnage.[13]

Not all commentaries were so racy. For Ninon was known as a woman who had aged gracefully. In *Epitre à Ninon l'Enclos* André Pétrovich Chouvalov wrote:

12. D'Argenson quoted in Louis Maigron, *Fontenelle: L'homme, l'oeuvre, l'influence* (Paris, 1906), p. 77; Le Chevalier de Solignac, *Eloge historique de M. de Fontenelle prononcé à la séance publique de la société royale des sciences et belles-lettres de Nancy le 8 mai 1757* (Nancy, 1757), p. 23.

13. "One must not be astonished / If she often reasons / With the sublime virtue / With which Plato was endowed, / For, considering her age, / She ought to have fucked / That great fellow." (All translations are mine unless otherwise indicated.) Attributed to Claude Emmanuel Luillier, dit Chapelle, in Voltaire, *Oeuvres complètes*, vol. 32, *Appendice* (Paris, 1880), p. 533. In a letter "Sur Mlle. de Lenclos à M***" (1751), Voltaire reports her reaction: "She responded that she would have liked much more to sleep with

> Heureux qui, comme toi, dans une paix profonde,
> Sur l'emploi de la vie a sainement pensé![14]

The anonymous epitaph of another aged woman, who died in 1694, presented Ninon as a moral authority among the Parisian elite; this woman, aside from retaining a light and charming spirit in "frigid old age," also had "the estime of Lenclos."[15]

As libertinage ceased to shock, Ninon, Fontenelle, and Saint-Evrémond came to serve as models of longevity for the eighteenth century. Literary roles changed. Comedy still centered on family wealth and problems of succession, but generational conflict seemed less troublesome, and aged characters were spoken of with less of the old malice. In the theater, aristocratic characters were still ridiculed,[16] but as playwrights responded more and more to bourgeois aspirations, the family was presented as a place of minor troubles and major sentiments.[17]

The novel evolved similarly: fictional *mémoires* looked back over the course of a lifetime, frequently from the perspective of the retired narrator.[18] There may have remained a frivolous veneer, but beneath it lay serious bourgeois virtues of long marriage and filial piety.[19] Retreating from the attacks of critics who saw the novel as unrealistic and immoral, novelists managed to create a genre that combined realism with moralism.[20] Good old characters satisfied both requirements. In

---

Plato than with Chapelle" (*Mélanges,* vol. 2 in *Oeuvres complètes,* vol. 23 [Paris, 1879], p. 511).

14. "Happy is one who, like you, in profound peace, / Has soundly thought about the use of life." Comte André Pétrovich Chouvalov, *Epître à Ninon L'Enclos* (Geneva, 1774), p. 6. For a supposed response, see Claude-Joseph Dorat, *Réponse,* printed with his *Anacréon citoyen* (Amsterdam, 1774), pp. 18–19.

15. "Epitaphe, par un anonyme, de Madame Cornuel, morte en février 1694," in Ninon de Lenclos, *Correspondance authentique* (Paris, 1886), p. 258.

16. On ridicule, see Frederick Charles Green, *La peinture des moeurs de la bonne société dans le roman français de 1715 à 1761* (Paris, 1924), p. 52. Even when, in the 1790s, it had become unfashionable to ridicule the aged on stage, it was still permissible if the old characters had ancien régime aristocratic pretensions. In one comic opera two sickly old misers dress for a duel; each hopes the other will die of fright. When they do come to blows, they barely touch each other. One of them cries: "Is he approaching or am I retreating?" J. A. Ségur, *Les vieux fous, ou Plus de peur que de mal* (Paris, 1796).

17. Félix Gaiffe, *Le drame en France au XVIIIe siècle* (Paris, 1971).

18. Henri Coulet, *Le roman jusqu'à la révolution,* vol. 1 (Paris, 1967), p. 320.

19. Edmond Pilon, *La vie de famille au XVIIIe siècle* (Paris, 1941).

20. On the effect of criticism, see Georges May, *Le dilemme du roman au XVIIIe siècle: Etude sur les rapports du roman et de la critique (1715–1761)* (New Haven, Conn., 1963). On the realistic pose in the novel, see Philip Stewart, *Imitation and Illusion*

poetry as well the other-worldly deathwatch gave way to an earthly one that accepted old age and an ever longer reprieve before death.[21] And although some translations and imitations of Anacreon's odes approved of the continued sensuality of the aged, in general the *vieillard amoureux* learned to control his instincts, becoming *amoureux et raisonnable*.[22] The *aimable vieillard* or *heureux vieillard* dispensed with the avarice and vanity of his predecessor.[23] J. F. Ducis evokes the new *vieillard heureux* in a typically pastoral setting:

> Dans un clos peuplé d'arbres verts,
> Libre et caché sous des couverts,
> Je goûte, dans un calme extrême,
> Et la nature, et les beaux vers,
> Et l'amitié, ce bien suprême.[24]

The old man is happy without wealth: "Few needs make my ease." In an anonymous poem nature provides solace even for an old man who is going blind. He urges a younger one to look at the beauties of nature; the old man can no longer see them, but he has memories.[25]

He also has friends. Friendship survived the cooling of passions late in life. The focus on friendship rather than love permitted a more sympathetic view of the aged. The abbé Morellet, in his *Senectutis Encomium*, shows a ninety-year-old man, surrounded by his friends, praising old age and the continued ability to participate in society—to eat, drink, and converse.[26] In dealing with the loss of friends that brings loneliness

---

in the French Memoir-Novel, 1700–1750: The Art of Make-Believe (New Haven, Conn., 1969).

21. E.g., l'abbé de Villiers, *Dernières stances sur ma vieillesse* (Paris, 1727). Several typical late-eighteenth-century poems on old age were entered in a Norman poetry contest, *le palinod de Caen*. For example, "Le vieillard donnant à son petit-fils l'exemple de la bienfaisance," in G.-A.-N. Audet, *Poésies latines et françaises qui ont obtenu des Prix . . .* (Caen, *an II* [1793]), pp. 19–22; "La mort d'un vieillard vertueux" (D496); "Le triomphe du sage" (D498); "La retraite du sage" (D1261)—all in A.D. Calvados.

22. N. Neveux, "Le vieillard amoureux et raisonnable" (Paris, *an XI* [1802–3]). For Anacreon, see e.g., Dorat, *Anacréon citoyen;* Charles-Joseph Mathon de la Cour, "Traduction de la 34e Ode d'Anacréon," in *Almanach des muses* (Paris, 1767), p. 50.

23. Philippe-Néricault Destouches, *Scènes de l'aimable vieillard* (1745), in *Oeuvres dramatiques de N. Destouches,* vol. 5 (Paris, 1811), pp. 155–187.

24. "In an orchard filled with green trees, / Free and hidden in the shade, / I taste, in perfect calm, / Nature, and beautiful poetry, / And friendship, that supreme blessing": J. F. Ducis, "Le vieillard heureux," in *Oeuvres* (Paris, 1839), p. 297.

25. A. M., *Le vieillard devenu aveugle: Stances,* B.N. Ye 53929.

26. André Morellet, *Senectutis encomium: La vieillesse,* B.N. 8° Ye Pièce 4438, p. 14.

and a reminder of one's own mortality, eighteenth-century poetry examined the spiritual pain of aging. Bernard-Joseph Saurin, regretting the loss of his friend the intendant Daniel-Charles Trudaine, wrote:

> O Trudaine! l'Etat te retrouve en ton fils;
> Mais, qui pourra jamais consoler tes amis?[27]

In another *épître* he mourned the death of Helvétius:

> O douleur impuissante! ô regrets superflus!
> Je vis, hélas! je vis, et mon ami n'est plus![28]

One's own death, however, could be faced stoically not because of a heavenly afterlife but because of earthly posterity. The old person's good works remain, his legacy survives in his children and grandchildren. The good death is part of the good life, one more stage in the family cycle. The "ages of life" became a common organizing principle for poems, stories, and plays. The four stories in Pierre-Jean-Baptiste Nougaret's *Les passions des différens âges,* the three volumes of plays addressed to different age groups in Guillaume Mouslier de Moissy's *L'école dramatique de l'homme,* and the *Fables* of Mancini-Nivernois were didactic works that taught morality for all ages.[29] Some poems dealt with the fear of being abandoned by adult children, others with the cyclical nature of life and the special intimacy that may exist between grandparents and grandchildren. Chamfort juxtaposed the growth of the grandchild with the death of the grandfather: the child serves as a symbol of earthly immortality and, for a few years, the happiness of his

27. "Oh Trudaine! the State recognizes you in your son; / But who will ever be able to console your friends?" Bernard-Joseph Saurin, "Epître sur les malheurs attachés à la vieillesse," in *Epîtres sur la vieillesse et sur la vérité* (Paris, 1772).

28. "Oh unavailing grief! oh useless regrets! / I live alas! I live, and my friend is no more!" Saurin, "Aux mânes de mon ami," quoted in Louis Petit de Bachaumont, *Mémoires secrets,* vol. 6 (London, 1777), p. 83 (January 7, 1772).

29. Pierre-Jean-Baptiste Nougaret, *Les passions des différens âges, ou Tableau des folies du siècle* (Utrecht, 1766), p. 67; Alexandre Guillaume Mouslier de Moissy, *Ecole dramatique de l'homme,* 3 vols. (Amsterdam, 1769–70). The proverbs illustrated by the five plays of old age may be translated as follows: "He who chases two hares catches none"; "What a woman wants, God wants"; "The Devil is not always at the door of a poor man"; "Such a life, such an end"; "The end crowns the Work." Louis-Jules Barbon Mancini-Mazarini, duc de Nivernois, *Fables,* 2 vols. (Paris, 1796–97). Following La Fontaine, Mancini-Nivernois published 243 fables: some included wise old crows and foxes; a great many others, sympathetic old people.

grandfather. But the old man insists on signaling his imminent death, suggesting that just as he has taught his son how to live, he will teach him how to die.[30]

Deathbed scenes, so common in the literature and painting of the second half of the eighteenth century, provided the opportunity to portray all the ages of life, as friends, neighbors, and family gathered around the dying patriarch. *L'heureux vieillard,* a *drame pastoral* by Gaspard Guillard de Beaurieu, crystallizes the themes of the good death (the original title was *La mort naturelle*), friendship in old age, and earthly immortality in one's posterity. Testimony by friends and relations to the noble character of Ariste, the happy old man, and Ariste's own preparations for death make up the body of the play. The old man is clearly in charge of things, orchestrating his death as if directing the play on stage and preparing the final tableau. Upon his deathbed he announces a double immortality: "I am going, then, to finish in the arms of this nascent People, of whom each individual is another 'myself'; in whom I see myself live again, and who assure me down here of an immortality, symbol of that to which I aspire."[31]

It is particularly the sensitive alliance of age with youth that permits an enlightened death. *Les quatre âges de l'homme* of Alix points out the sympathy between old and young: in the eyes of children the aged are truly heroic, and the natural sympathy between childhood and old age closes the circle of life. The elderly see themselves through children's eyes; with their own they gaze upon death, but its terror is relieved by the thought that the newly deceased, joining the remains of the great, will become part of the same posterity.[32] Thoughts of the final return to nature bring pleasing repose. A sense of earthly progress overcomes individual mortality. The old person's legacy is in knowledge and wisdom rather than in property. The resented old *propriétaire* gives way to the beloved old teacher.

The various aged characters of the second half of the eighteenth century seem to have produced a composite type of the respectable old man. Thus, the Wandering Jew (a character of Christian creation), who had scorned Jesus and was sentenced to wander the face of the earth forever, appears in the eighteenth century not as a villain deserving

30. Sébastien-Roch-Nicolas Chamfort, "Epître d'un père à son fils, sur la naissance d'un petit fils" (Paris, 1764).

31. Gaspard Guillard de Beaurieu, *L'heureux vieillard* (Amsterdam, 1768), p. 26.

32. Alix, *avocat, Les quatre âges de l'homme: Poëme* (Paris, 1782), p. 49.

punishment but as a blameless and honored old expert in geography and history.[33] Wherever he goes in Europe he is welcomed, listened to, and offered more hospitality than he will accept. Even older is the Old Man of the Mountain, observing four thousand years of history from a peak in Lebanon.[34]

Elderly teachers are legion in the literature of the period. The eighteenth-century *Bildungsroman*, whether *Candide* or *La vie de mon père*, offered many glimpses of elderly teachers and companions who contributed to the education of the maturing hero.[35] Some texts took longer looks at venerable characters. For example, Mésophée, the antiphilosophic, benevolent Christian landowner and entrepreneur of the abbé Crillon's *Mémoires philosophiques*, instructs the young narrator and dies in the presence of the people of the countryside, who are led by their elders.[36]

Similarly, in *Le vieillard abyssin*, the young prince Amlac travels throughout his kingdom and meets the quintessential old sage: "His walk was majestic; his brow glistened with the purity of the immortals; his lips appeared to be the font of wisdom. Though curved beneath the weight of years, he still had a freshness that one could not fail to admire. Everything about him announced the satisfaction of a good conscience, and the victories that he reaped over his senses and his passions."[37] The modest old man had retired thirty years before, seeking the proper solitude in which to philosophize. He offers Amlac the fruit of his reflections in a three-hundred-page monologue on morality, nature, physiocratism, enlightened monarchy, justice, honesty, and the family.

33. George Anderson, *The Legend of the Wandering Jew* (Providence, R.I., 1965), esp. chap. 6, "Ahasuerus the Eighteenth-Century Traveler"; Roland Auguet, *Le juif errant* (Paris, 1977), esp. pp. 103–107. On a 1749 sighting, see *Histoire admirable du juif-errant . . .* (Rouen, 1751).

34. Jean-Baptiste Claude Izouard Delisle de Sales, *Le vieux de la montagne* (Paris, 1799).

35. Rétif de la Bretonne, *La vie de mon père* (Paris, 1970), is not without irony. Consider the following exchange concerning the old priest at Saint-Roch: "He is a dignified man . . . a venerable old man, great, majestic; with white hair . . . he inspires respect . . . his speech has unction . . . you ought to know him.—No; I recognize no one of the parish in this portrait" (pp. 100–101). On Rétif's own old age, see Maurice Heine, "La vieillesse de Rétif de la Bretone (1794–1806)," *Hippocrate: Revue d'humanisme médical*, 1934, pp. 605–633.

36. Louis-Athanase Des Balbes de Berton, l'abbé de Crillon, *Mémoires philosophiques du Baron de **** (Vienna, 1777).

37. *Le vieillard abyssin rencontré par Amlac, empereur d'Ethiopie* (London, 1779), p. 13.

He laments the disrespect that sons show their fathers: "You believe you are receiving a friend, another 'yourself,' in your house, and you are only receiving your enemy."[38] Amlac, moved by the speech, departs at sunset with thoughts of the inevitable and peaceful death of the sage. From the prince's point of view the old man has communicated his wisdom and may now die. But the sage still has reason to prolong his enlightened, patriotic, and Christian retirement:

> The old man continues to live separated from the hustle and bustle; he meditates upon eternal years, saves for bad days, adds more and more to his glory and to his treasures; he makes of his soul a sanctuary inaccessible to fragile honors, to passing riches, to the foolish hopes of the children of men; he familiarizes himself with the remembrance of death so dreaded by the sensual and the imprudent, sets himself up as inexorable judge of his own weaknesses, shudders only at the idea of the nothingness with which the impious shamelessly contents himself.[39]

Among the most commonly depicted old men in the period was Belisarius. The sixth-century Byzantine general, blinded by Emperor Justinian, was protagonist of play, novel, poem, and painting. In the famous 1767 novel by Jean-François Marmontel, old age is at least as important a theme as loyalty, patriotism, and duty.[40] Belisarius demonstrates his loyalty to a misguided ruler by refusing the overtures of the Bulgars, who despite their barbarism are scandalized by Justinian's cruel and disrespectful act. When the old man encounters one of his former soldiers living on the family farm and supporting his father's old age, the meeting serves as an object lesson in patriotism. The younger man derides his country and regrets having brought children into a world where so great a general could be so abused, but Belisarius teaches him that there is no place in the world where the just are not victimized. All one can do is not deserve the evils that befall one in life. When Tiberius, the spy of Justinian, arrives on the scene, he tells Belisarius that he would like to study with him. For the moment Belisarius prefers solitude, but he looks forward to the role of distinguished instructor, a position that will give him pleasure and fulfill the duty of the aged. He praises the natural ties of neighborliness and the sympathetic and em-

---

38. Ibid., p. 97.

39. Ibid., p. 322.

40. For the ideal of *l'obscurité tranquille*, see Jean-François Marmontel, *Bélisaire*, vol. 1 (Brussels, 1792), p. 908. For the controversy surrounding the Sorbonne's censoring of the novel, see Marmontel et al., *Pièces relatives à Bélisaire* (Amsterdam, 1767).

pathic bonds of youth and age. When Tiberius reports to Justinian, the emperor decides to disguise himself as the young man's father and visit the old general himself. Belisarius teaches the contrite emperor about virtue and government, playing the "natural" role of elderly adviser.

Bélisaire was brought to the stage by six different playwrights between 1641 and 1795, and the evolution of the character is instructive. The two seventeenth-century versions, the 1641 tragicomedy of Nicolas-Marc Desfontaines and the 1643 tragedy of Jean de Rotrou, concern a younger Belisarius, victimized by a jealous empress.[41] In these the general is a great warrior, a noble and altruistic character, and the plays trace his downfall from most honored and respected soldier to imprisoned and, in the Rotrou version, blinded and murdered victim, but the plays are not really his; in classical terms, the tragedy belongs to the emperor. The tragic element is the emperor's mistake in not recognizing his general's loyalty, and his final realization provides the cathartic moment. The Rotrou tragedy uses light and dark imagery to foreshadow the general's blinding and the emperor's subsequent enlightenment:

> O funeste disgrace! ô douleur non prévue!
> De quel aveuglement dessillez-vous ma vue?
> Bélisaire n'est plus! Hélas! il paroît bien
> Que mon aveuglement a précédé le sien.[42]

The eighteenth-century versions, inspired by Marmontel's novel, depict an aged Belisarius returning from long exile, seeking a peaceful retirement and death in the arms of his family. The 1769 *drame* of D'Ozicourt focuses upon Belisarius's forgiveness of Justinian. A soldier who meets the old general wants revenge for "the lamentable state in which injustice has placed your august old age." But Belisarius calms him, saying, "For a dying old man, your zeal is useless." The soldier's desire for revenge anticipates that of the general's wife, Antonine, whom Belisarius tries to comfort by likening his situation to that of any old man: "They have only anticipated what old age would have done in depriving me of light."[43]

41. Desfontaines, *Bélisaire* (Paris, 1641); Jean de Rotrou, *Bélisaire* (1643), in *Recueil des meilleures pièces dramatiques,* vol. 7 (Lyon, 1781), pp. 457–572.

42. "Oh fatal disgrace! Oh unforeseen grief! / From what blindness do you deliver me? / Belisarius is no more! Alas! It seems indeed / That my blindness has preceded his": Rotrou, *Bélisaire,* final scene.

43. D'Ozicourt, *Bélisaire* (Paris, 1769), pp. 18, 26.

The lover of Belisarius's daughter Eudoxe thinks the emperor should at least know of his mistake, but the old general does not want to trouble Justinian's old age:

> N'y pensons plus. Hélas! Tibère, c'en est fait.
> Il ne faut point ouvrir ses yeux sur un forfait
> Qui feroit le tourment de sa triste vieillesse.[44]

Nevertheless, Justinian does learn of Belisarius's loyalty and is moved to demand his general's pardon. All is forgiven, Eudoxe marries her love Tibère, and Antonine dies happy.

In the same year Alexandre Guillaume Mouslier de Moissy offered a *comédie héroïque* that gave the story *un coloris de gaieté* by keeping Antonine alive and offstage.[45] Again, revenge and forgiveness are highlighted, but the overarching theme is retirement and making peace with one's past. It is not only Belisarius and Justinian who seek solace in old age; even Gélimer, king of the Vandals, has retired to the countryside, where—in the company of his wife, Hortense—he rises early in the morning to enjoy the beauties of nature and to atone for a life of violence.

The 1781 tragedy of Jean-Baptiste Claude Izouard Delisle de Sales has something in common with the seventeenth-century tragedies—Justinian still thinks of Belisarius as a threat until the general quells a popular disturbance—but even this play takes place during its characters' old age and involves the restoration of the general as well as the catharsis of the emperor.[46] The Desfontaines and Rotrou tragedies were concerned with the immediate consequences of the palace intrigue.

Most sentimental is the 1795 opera of Auguste-Louis Bertin d'Antilly. Again the action has occurred before the curtain goes up. Onstage the actors emote, create tableaux, and sing the praises of Belisarius, old age, the republic, liberty, and patriotism.[47] One art historian has interpreted the story as a plea for the amnesty of returned aristocratic exiles,[48] but here we are concerned with a republican exile. After Justi-

44. "Let us think no more of it. Alas! Tiberius, it is done. / You must not open his eyes to a heinous crime / That would torment his sad old age": ibid., p. 29.

45. Alexandre Guillaume Mouslier de Moissy, *Bélisaire* (Paris, 1769), p. 3.

46. Jean-Baptiste Claude Izouard Delisle de Sales, *Bélisaire,* in *Recueil des meilleures pièces* (Paris, 1781).

47. Auguste-Louis Bertin d'Antilly, *Bélisaire* (1795), B.N. MS F.F. 9286, Soleinne 45:92–109.

48. The same argument is made for the aged Oedipus in Rubin, "Oedipus, Antigone, and Exiles."

nian's death Belisarius joins Antonine at the head of a column of soldiers. The aged are of use as leaders of the republic, even in the military.

The Belisarius of the Revolutionary period, in a scene of the opera or in paintings depicting the blind old hero, can easily be taken for a model of old age, the sentimental old man victimized by society rather than the special imperial general wrongly disgraced. One ought to believe him when he says (in more than one play), "In depriving me of my eyes my enemies have only done that which old age or death was going to do."[49] Either theatrical or painted portraits of the hero remind one of the problems of old age generally and the pleas for the aged that were common in the literature of the period.

Representations of Belisarius in literature and painting can also be confused with those of Oedipus at Colonus—another blind old man who wishes to end his wanderings and find repose[50]—or with the various versions of King Lear, who raises the additional problem of the risks inherent in the premature transmission of property. Moreover, it was not only kings who experienced such difficulties; Louis-Sébastien Mercier offered a commoner Lear in *Le vieillard et ses trois filles*.[51]

An appreciation of the tragic plight of Shakespeare's character once prompted George Steiner to note that "the destiny of Lear cannot be resolved by the establishment of adequate homes for the aged."[52] And yet for the eighteenth century that was one proposed solution. Late eighteenth-century writers blurred the distinction between literature and reality and displayed a concern for social issues that took on a political hue during the Revolution.

One genre that combines and confuses the social with the fictive is that of *mémoires*. Madame de Genlis delivered herself of some insightful observations about the aged; in her own *Mémoires inédits* she described many touching domestic scenes, particularly those surrounding a death-bed. She drew attention to the problems of old age—"one does not think enough that old age is the longest state of life, it can last forty years"[53]— and reflected upon the good old age that is the reward of the pious. Similar reflections accompanied by real-life examples occur throughout

49. Bertin d'Antilly, *Bélisaire*, scene xx.

50. See, e.g., the *Oedipes* of Ducis and Chénier and the paintings in Réunion des Musées, *French Painting*.

51. Louis-Sébastien Mercier, *Le vieillard et ses trois filles* (Paris, 1792).

52. George Steiner, *The Death of Tragedy* (New York, 1980), p. 128.

53. Madame de Genlis, *Mémoires inédits de Madame la comtesse de Genlis . . .* (Brussels, 1825), vol. 3, p. 267.

the fictional *Souvenirs de Félicie L**** as well. She described the old grandmother of a deaf-mute, the pleasant qualities of an old face, the feeling of age among courtiers upon the death of Louis XV, the old age of the comte de Maurepas enlisted out of retirement, and several death scenes. She marveled at the sociability of the elderly—"I love the society of lively old persons who do not speak of themselves and who, at the same time, are pleased to recount anecdotes of past time"—and described the storytelling ability of the Marquise de Rochambeau and the monomaniacal love of opera of Monsieur d'Etréhan.[54] She emphasized the importance of piety in old age and offered the example of the admirable Maréchal de Balincour, who had maintained health, teeth, eyesight, and memory. She marveled at his conversation with his old comrade at arms, the Marquis de Canillac:

> These two respectable warriors told each other stories of sieges and of battles whose antiquity gave us a thrill: one thought one was hearing History speak; their conversations resembled also those dialogues of the dead between characters of another century. Finally, I admired the evenness of humour, the sweet gaiety of this old man; all his preparations were done, nothing worried him, and one saw by his perfect serenity, that he had ended all his affairs. He enjoyed the leisure and the repose of a virtuous old age. How that age is interesting and venerable, when it has purified life.[55]

Piety was the preferred condition of the old age of women, and Madame de Genlis contrasted the pious old age of Madame de Puisieux with the modern excesses of Madame du Deffand.[56] In each case, the plight of the elderly was sympathetically drawn.

In the same volume Madame de Genlis recalled a trip to the Pyrenees and described rural *rites de passage* and the prescribed roles of generations there. Boys from eight to fifteen served as shepherds under the tutelage of their elders; from fifteen to seventy they turned their attention to farming and other labors; and at seventy they entered a second childhood as shepherds once more. Blindness was overcome by memories of childhood duties. Each day the young people brought refreshments to the elders. Madame de Genlis focused her gaze on a particular family in which the father retired from heavy labors at seventy just as his

54. Madame de Genlis, *Les souvenirs de Félicie L**** (Paris, *an XII* [1804]), pp. 21–22, 41–43, 92, 100–101, 170–175.
55. Ibid., pp. 335–336.
56. Ibid., pp. 342–359.

son Tobie reached fifteen. The father joined the grandfather of Tobie's fiancée and the other elders in a peaceful and natural old age, and both men lived to see the young couple joined in marriage.[57]

The *Mémoires de Mlle. Clairon* offered the perspective of an old woman, this time a retired actress, looking back at the eighteenth century from the end of the ancien régime. She had endured imprisonment and other ills and complained of a weak constitution, but age evidently strengthened her will to persevere: "The sagging of my body does not yet influence my spirit and my head; I have all the sensitivity, all the activity of my first age. My taste for reading has happily grown; it is useful to me to surround myself daily with the great characters of all times and all places; I learn with them to compare, to reflect, to bear the void and the pains of life, to prove to myself that it is necessary that everything passes and becomes as nothing, and that it is without impatience and without regret that I ought to await my turn."[58]

A similar sentiment marks the two volumes of Marmontel's *Mémoires d'un père*, written in old age in the wake of the Terror. Attempting to sum up an entire lifetime for the edification of his children, he began with memories of the old people who inhabited his childhood: the aged priest who tutored him, the impressive father of a childhood friend ("this good old man with white hair"), the maternal grandmother who presided over the household, and the great-grandmothers who sat in the corner by the fire drinking wine and recalling events of the distant past. He described a Jesuit teacher who found himself abandoned by his order in old age, his great-grandmothers teaching him special recipes before Christmas, and his old aunts spying good-naturedly upon his first romantic adventures. He claimed to have included in an examination for entry to the *collège* at Clermont a dialogue in which a young man promises his father to be "the consolation, the support, the honor of his old age." He recalled a visit to the aged Jean-Baptiste Massillon and a discussion with the *recteur* at Clermont of a plan for a Jesuit old age home. He reflected upon the hopes that motivated a hard-working muleteer named Pierre: "It is a tranquil and calm old age that he is working to procure for himself, and this repose, which he enjoys in expectation, lightens the burden of his fatigues."[59]

57. Ibid., pp. 371–392.

58. *Mémoires de Mlle Clairon*, in *Bibliothèque des mémoires relatifs à l'histoire de France pendant le 18e siècle*, vol. 6 (Paris, 1846), p. 45.

59. Jean-François Marmontel, *Mémoires d'un père pour servir à l'instruction de ses enfants*, vol. 1 (Paris, 1827), pp. 4–8, 15, 33, 40, 50, 56, 79, 85.

He wrote of a prudent old age and an Epicurean one. His comments concerned aged writers (Prosper Jolyot de Crébillon and the abbé Raynal), the retirement of an old soldier (M. de la Sablière of Béziers), and the demanding old age of a lady of the salon (the Marquise du Deffand). Age was a factor in his assessment of the ministries of the comte de Maurepas, who held a long-term grudge against Jacques Necker, and Etienne de Loménie de Brienne, of whom Marmontel wrote, "This old child was a foreigner to his century." The Terror found Marmontel seeking refuge with an old ecclesiastic, and the Directory found him devoting the rest of his old age to the instruction of his children.[60]

All genres can help us reconstruct the literary discourse on old age, but theater provides the widest window on the representation of the aged in various stereotypical forms. Tragedy of the seventeenth century had demonstrated the weakness of the old man—Corneille's aged knight in *Le Cid* finds himself in the ridiculous condition of being unable to wield his own sword[61]—but comedy displays the richest collection of old characters and most neatly expresses the transition from the ridiculous oldster of the seventeenth and early eighteenth centuries to the honored patriarch of the later eighteenth.

The *barbon*, a classical type in Greek and Roman comedy and a popular character on the European stage, was typically avaricious, libidinous, and obstructive with regard to the other characters; physically weak, generally repulsive, and ridiculous in the eyes of the audience. He played an essential role in the most common dramatic problem: courtship and marriage. When parents tried to force a daughter into a profitable match with a wealthy old man, the young person—with the aid and trickery of domestic servants—was able to marry for love and, with the eventual consent of parents, money; the aged were left out in the cold. Typical is the anonymous *Le vieillard supplanté,* described as a "little comedy," in which the heroine's mother is particularly eager for her daughter's match with an old *barbon*.[62] The audience is treated to the foolishness of the doddering suitor as well as the servants' resentful comments about mean old masters. In a sense, the tension between master and servant is translated into a less revolutionary tension between age and youth. The "natural" order of age was

---

60. Ibid., pp. 207–215, 236, 253, 345, 411–412, 464–467.

61. Pierre Corneille, *Le Cid* I.v: Don Diègue: "O rage, ô désespoir! ô vieillesse ennemie!" In *Oeuvres complètes,* vol. 1 (Paris, 1980), p. 718. Elsewhere, Corneille transcended the traditional stereotype of the old character. See Joseph Marthan, *Le vieillard amoureux dans l'oeuvre cornélienne* (Paris, 1979).

62. *Le vieillard supplanté,* B.N. MS F.F. 9428, Soleinne 7:341–373.

evidently safer to attack than the more political orders of class or wealth.

As late as 1733 Parisian audiences could see the stereotypical Italian comedy in *Les vieillards dupes de leur amour* of Joseph Dominique Biancolelli. The end of the play is the marriage of young lovers, but two aged fathers must first be shamed and beaten.[63] Their shame is similar to that which the *charivari* stimulated in society. It is a sign of resentment at the "unfair advantage" that the older suitor has over his younger competitor.

Emmanuel Le Roy Ladurie has provided a diagram for the dramatic structure of Provençal comedy:

> the opponent or rival   the girl's father
> the hero   the girl
>
> ──────────────────────────────────────→
>
> hero and (wealthy/old) rival compete
>   to marry girl

It holds for much northern theater as well, in which the young resented the sexuality and wealth of the old, and French society lampooned these characters, especially their vanity and avarice. But the eighteenth century was more interested in dignified old characters. Old persons are now allied with the young lovers, facilitating the happy ending; their love is that of the friend and teacher, not the vain lechery encountered before. If any character is avaricious, it is the parent. Middle age is the new opponent:

> the old allies   the girl's parents   the rival
> the hero   the girl
>
> ──────────────────────────────────────→
>
> elderly characters help hero
>   to marry girl; rival is shut out

Avarice, considered the chief sin of the elderly in the traditional model, was expressed in the economic relations between generations. The

---

63. Joseph Dominique Biancolelli, *Les vieillards dupes de leur amour* (1733), in T. S. Gueullette, *Manuscrit autographe de l'histoire du théâtre italien*, vol. 2 (Paris, ca. 1760), Opéra, Réserve 625 (2).

youthful desire that the aged pass on their wealth matched the religious prescription to think of death.[64]

That link is also present in the treatment of vanity. In theater and in religious thought (see Chapter 4), the aged were indecently concerned with time, money, and sex. Vanity was expressed in the search for rejuvenation and love. Whether in actual pursuit of the fountain of youth or in attempts to disguise the signs of age, the old person would be taught a lesson at his own expense—thus the fountain of youth theme in *Geronée ou le vieillard rajeuni* (1696; performed again in 1701 as *La fontaine de jouvence*) and *Les vieillards rajeunis* (1738), and the lecherous old men of *Le calendrier des vieillards* (1753) and *Le vieillard amoureux*.[65]

But even in these plays, a change can be detected. The vain old man or woman is less subject to shame than before, and in some plays younger characters who have assumed the worst of their elders learn that the stereotypes are exaggerated. The Thomas Laffichard *vieillard amoureux* "is always a dupe of love," but the extreme generational tension is missing, and one of the characters is a respectable old man throughout the play. The usual problem of wealth and arranged marriage is treated in Michel Guyot de Merville's *Le dédit inutile ou les vieillards intéressés* of 1742, but there is little need for ridicule, as the old men are not terribly powerful.[66] In De Vilorié's *Les vieux garçons* of 1761 the plight of aged bachelors is viewed sympathetically, and we learn that Parisian ways, rather than transformations inherent in the aging process, are responsible for diverting respectable old people from honorable provincial habits.[67]

Traditional stereotypes persist, but they are open to question. They are presented in extremely farcical manner, and the aged characters prove themselves much more sympathetic. Filial piety becomes more and more evident on stage in such works as *La comtoise à Paris ou le vieillard dupé* (1770), *Le vieillard coquet* (1786), *Agathe ou le vieillard*

64. Emmanuel Le Roy Ladurie, *L'argent, l'amour, et la mort en pays d'Oc* (Paris, 1980), for the first diagram; the second is mine.

65. *Geronée, ou Le vieillard rajeuni* (Paris, 1696); *La fontaine de jouvence* (1701), B.N. Réserve Yf 2694–2695; Alain-René Lesage and Nicolas Fromaget, *Les vieillards rajeunis* (1738), B.N. MS F.F. 9314; Antoine Bret and I. V. Guillot de la Chassagne, *Le calendrier des vieillards* (Paris, 1753); Thomas Laffichard, *Le vieillard amoureux*, B.N. MS F.F. 9321.

66. Michel Guyot de Merville, *Le dédit inutile, ou Les vieillards intéressés* (Paris, 1742), p. 78.

67. De Vilorié, *Les vieux garçons* (Paris, 1761).

trompé (1787), and *Le vieillard crédule* (1772).[68] There is no doubt about the wisdom of age and the foolishness of youth in Alexis Piron's *L'école des pères* (1733), and both generations are sympathetic and caring in Elbée's *Léandre ou le bon père.*[69]

The change in aged characters was gradual and, in many instances, probably unconscious. Still, writers demonstrated an awareness of the cruelty of earlier literary conventions and a desire for a new way of presenting the aged. That self-consciousness is most evident in critical writing about the theater. As Rousseau observed in his letter to D'Alembert: "Who can doubt that the habit of always seeing odious characters in the old men of the theater aids in rebuffing them in society, and that in accustoming oneself to confound those that one sees in the world with the *radoteurs* and *Gérontes* of comedy, one scorns them all equally?"[70] Rousseau's solution for Geneva was to ban the theater outright.

This solution—and the generally illiberal and antimodern thrust of the letter—marks a break between Rousseau and the other philosophes, and D'Alembert's reply chastised him for confusing the comedic ridicule of vice with mere ridicule.[71] But in refusing to tolerate mockery of the aged, Rousseau was not alone. Critics and playwrights who were not at all in favor of censorship agreed that old stereotypes had to go and that there ought to be a conscious change in the way dramatists depicted the aged. Such a solution was elaborated by Mercier in *Du théâtre* as part of a general attack on outmoded conventions, themes, and characters. Mercier's position occupies a space between the "realistic" depiction of bourgeois and country life on the one hand and Enlightenment propa-

68. Alexandre-Louis-Bertrand Robineau, dit Beaunoir, *La comtoise à Paris, ou Le vieillard dupé* (1770, 1783), B.N. MS N.A.F. 2890; Cléronome, *Le vieillard coquet* (1786), B.N. MS F.F. 9266; Abraham Nicolas Lesueur, *Agathe, ou Le vieillard trompé* (1787), B.N. MS F.F. 9278; Benoît-Joseph Morsollier de Vivetières, "Le vieillard créd- ule," *Mercure de France*, April 1772, p. 54.

69. Alexis Piron, *L'école des pères* (1733) (same play as *Les fils ingrats*), in *Oeuvres*, vol. 1 (Paris, 1758). Piron himself became the subject of J. N. Bouilly and J. Pain's *La vieillesse de Piron* (Paris, 1810). The selfish protagonist's nastiness has less to do with his being aged than with his being Piron. He keeps his niece, Annette, locked up so that she will care for him in his old age: "You are so necessary to the blind old man: think then that you are his support, his consolation, his tutelary guide; and history, Mademoiselle, does not say that Antigone ever took a husband." She replies that he is referring to the wrong characters: "Oh! what a difference! although you may have made ungrateful sons [reference to *les fils ingrats*], you are not Oedipus." See also, Elbée, *Léandre, ou Le bon père*, B.N. MS F.F. 9269.

70. Rousseau, *A M. D'Alembert*, in *Oeuvres complètes*, vol. 3, p. 135.

71. Jean Le Rond D'Alembert, "Lettre à J.-J. Rousseau," in *Oeuvres de D'Alembert*, vol. 4 (Paris, 1822), pp. 432–458.

ganda on the other. He blamed Molière for the *barbon* and preferred a
new type in which a moral would be implicit:

> Destouches has sketched a play whose subject makes me laugh a great
> deal; it is the *vieillard aimable*. What could be more moral than to teach
> men that there are pleasures for them in all ages of life, if they apply
> themselves to calling them forth; to teach them that old age, which
> appears dreadful, can be adorned with flowers, if it makes itself the friend
> and not the inflexible censor of youth. It would be beautiful to prove to
> these downcast old men that the order of nature will not be upset if they
> present themselves with this sweet joy which suits the man who has
> known and tasted life; and that it is not the honorable whiteness of their
> head that makes young people flee but the evil humor which devours
> them and which they spread imprudently about them. A play thus han-
> dled would be cheerful and philosophic; it would offer the most satisfying
> of spectacles, an old man content with his past life, because he is without
> remorse, surrounded by young people whom he surpasses in gaiety,
> mixing now and then with his instructions the diverting salt of the
> epigram, deploying his acquired knowledge to temper the ardor of an
> indiscreet youth, speaking of the past without scoffing at the present,
> looking at death without fearing it, and smiling, as La Fontaine said, *in
> the evening of a beautiful day.*

He appended a note: "Someone has said of a beautiful and honorable
old age that it was the childhood of immortality. This line is sublime."[72]

As if following the critics' advice, playwrights began to create sympathetic old characters. An analysis of French titles of plays written from
1700 to 1789 reveals a far greater number of references to the aged in
the second half of the century than in the first.[73] And a reading of those
and other plays suggests the adoption of new ways of thinking—both in
the new genre of the *drame,* where virtue was taught by example and
declamation, and in the revised sort of comedy, with its lesser degree of
vice less baldly ridiculed.

It would be foolhardy to conclude from the observation of such a stylistic evolution that assumptions and behavior had radically changed.
Conflict between generations, abandonment of the elderly, and ridicule
of the decrepit may have remained constant or even increased. The
change in discourse may mask an entirely different sort of social alter-

72. Louis-Sébastien Mercier, *Du théâtre, ou Nouvel essai sur l'art dramatique* (Amsterdam, 1773), pp. 121–122.

73. Clarence D. Brenner, *A Bibliographical List of Plays in the French Language,
1700–1789* (Berkeley, Calif., 1947).

ation or none at all. But before making the leap from culture to society, one must continue to draw out the various elements in the new discourse.

In more and more plays at the end of the ancien régime, the aged are depicted as repositories of wisdom and sources of advice, not as obstacles to progress. In a Spanish play translated into French and performed in 1782, a wise old farm laborer of the country who had always shunned the city is brought to court as an honored adviser, his family ennobled.[74] The old man offers wisdom in return for respect and a good deal of sentiment.

A sentimental domestic ideal came to include new sorts of individuals, for in the same year *Le vieux garçon* of Paul Ulric Dubuisson broached the subject of bastardy. Still central, though, was the predicament evoked by the title. The old bachelor is Gercour, whose situation is introduced in a conversation between his nephew Dorval and Dorval's wife, Lucile:

Dorval

Oui, Lucile, c'est là le triste caractère
D'un Garçon suranné, d'un vieux célibataire
Qui commence à sentir qu'un systême trompeur
Ne peut, à soixante ans, faire que son malheur.

Lucile

Sans femme, sans enfans, et ne tenant à rien
A quoi lui servira d'avoir beaucoup de bien?
Sa vieillesse livrée à des mains mercenaires
Manquera bien souvent des secours nécessaires.[75]

In fact, the servants do rob him, and his nurse warns that even Dorval and Lucile only want his wealth. Publicly, Gercour derides marriage; it is not for him. But privately, he is lonely, and the sight of the young lovers Sacrifar and Sophie makes him wistful. The plot takes a twist when Sacrifar says that because of his parentage he cannot marry. Meanwhile, Dorval has been telling his uncle of the joys of family life, especially in preparation for old age:

74. Juan de Matos-Fragoso, *Le sage dans sa retraite* (The Hague, 1782).

75. Dorval: "Yes, Lucile, that is the sad disposition / Of a superannuated chap, of an old bachelor / Who begins to sense that a deceptive system / Can, at sixty years, only be his ruin." Lucile: "Without wife, without children, and attached to no one, / What's the use of having a large estate? / His old age committed to hired hands / Will quite often run out of needed relief." Paul Ulric Dubuisson, *Le vieux garçon* (Paris, 1783), I.i.

> Regardez un vieillard au sein de sa famille,
> Appuyé sur son fils, consolé par sa fille;
> Malgré le froid des ans, il aime, il est aimé!
> Si des feux du plaisir, il n'est plus animé,
> L'amitié paternelle échaufe au moins son âme;[76]

Gercour surprises everyone by suggesting that if Sacrifar will not marry Sophie, he will. As Gercour informs his friend Dorimon:

> Mon cher ami, l'on change.
> Le célibat convient tant que l'on n'est pas vieux,
> Dans l'arrière saison il devient ennuyeux.
> L'attrait d'un tel état passe avec la jeunesse.
> De quoi la liberté sert-elle à la vieillesse?[77]

But such a match does not occur: Gercour recognizes Sacrifar as his illegitimate son and makes Sophie his heir. As the lovers marry, Gercour tenderly looks on and asks them for the support the aged ought to receive from their children: "Supportez-moi, c'est tout ce que je veux."[78] In reciprocal fashion it is the old man's action that makes the marriage possible, while the marriage secures his retirement.

The problem of marriage is still a key plot element, but the elderly have become active characters instrumental in bringing about the happy ending. In the anonymous *Les vieux pensionnaires,* the *maître de pension* is pestered by Babet, a servant who wishes to become his wife, and he refuses to allow his daughter to marry her love. But the people who engineer the happy ending are the elderly residents of the *pension,* a *chevalier,* a deaf woman, and a blind musician. Their easy sociability (they entertain each other with extraordinary tales of woe) stands in marked contrast to the pedestrian marital conflicts.[79]

One way of reviving the issue of marriage was to permit the aged to indulge their desires. In César Ribié's *Le vieillard amoureux* of 1788, an old man, Copandre, wants to marry a young widow, Isabelle. Co-

---

76. "Consider an old man in the bosom of his family, / Supported by his son, consoled by his daughter; / Despite the cold of the years, he loves, he is loved! / If he is no longer inflamed by the fires of pleasure, / At least paternal love heats his soul." Ibid., III.v.

77. "My dear friend, people change. / Bachelorhood is suitable so long as one is not old, / In the evening of life it becomes boring. / The attraction of such a condition passes with youth. / What's the use of liberty in old age?" Ibid., III.vii.

78. "Support me, that's all I wish." Ibid., final scene.

79. *Les vieux pensionnaires,* B.N. MS F.F. 9247, Soleinne 6:152–167.

pandre's valet, Polichinelle, wonders about the wisdom of the marriage, but the sixty-year-old argues that with his health and wealth he is more like a man of forty. When Isabelle hears of the amorous sexagenarian, she immediately thinks of the stereotype: "But he's doubtless an old *barbon*, jealous, scolding, miserly." No, replies her valet (another Polichinelle), he is very easygoing. After a little negotiation in which Copandre promises to be not Isabelle's master but her slave—again the rhetoric plays on a classic ridiculous pose—the match is made.[80]

The French Revolution brought a whole series of kind, virtuous, and patriotic old people to the stage.[81] In *L'hospitalité, ou Le bonheur du vieux père,* performed in *an II* (1793–94) and published the next year, L. A. Dorvigny created a good old mayor named Candor, whose six sons serve in the army and whose two daughters sit home sewing uniforms. Candor promotes civic virtue by example, having adopted a boy named, of all things, Décadi (the tenth day of the Revolutionary week). During the course of the play the big, happy, patriotic family grows bigger, happier, and more patriotic.[82]

A happy old couple is the subject of *Les vieux époux* of F. G. Desfontaines, a propaganda piece demonstrating the importance for household and country of a good domestic life. The central events are the feeding of a poor old man, the repetition of marriage vows after fifty years of marriage, and the return of the old couple's long-lost cousin, a deaf-mute. Most of the characters are elderly (the younger people are off fighting for the republic), but they manage to sing, dance, and preach the usual Revolutionary sentiments. The old husband comments on the wisdom of the new divorce law for those less fortunate than he and his wife, and the mayor presides over the repetition of (secular) marriage vows and remarks that the old couple will set an example for generations of patriots to come.[83]

Not all Revolutionary theater was so programmatic. *Le jeune sage et*

80. César Ribié, *Le vieillard amoureux, ou Les deux Polichinelles* (1788), B.N. MS N.A.F. 3014:190–204, scene v. Another Parisian play of the 1780s in which an old man marries was L. A. Dorvigny's aptly named *Les noces du Père Duchesne* (Paris, 1789).

81. As one student of the serious Revolutionary theater observed, fraternity took the place of Christian charity, uniting people who had previously been divided by politics or religion. Loyalty to family and country were mutually reinforcing (though called into question by Brutus and other classical figures); see Jean-Alexis Rivoire, *Le patriotisme dans le théâtre sérieux de la révolution (1789–1799)* (Paris, 1950), pp. 141–160.

82. L. A. Dorvigny, *L'hospitalité, ou Le bonheur du vieux père* (Paris, *an III* [1794–95]).

83. F. G. Desfontaines, *Les vieux époux* (Paris, *an III* [1795]).

le vieux fou of F. B. Hoffman, first performed in 1793, utterly confused the roles of age and youth. Merval is a pleasure-loving sexagenarian who stays out all night; Cliton, his son, is old at sixteen. Father and son court the widow Elise and her niece Rose—or, to be precise, Merval does most of the courting while Cliton stays home and studies. The problem of the play is to decide who should marry whom: should the young niece marry the old father and the old aunt the young son, or the other way around? In the end, age marries age and youth youth, but only after it is made clear that ironclad rules of behavior are unrealistic and that a mixture of wisdom and folly characterizes all ages.[84]

In a later play, *La femme de quarante-cinq ans,* Hoffman offered a picture of vindictive middle age. Camille is the forty-five-year-old widow who, out of jealousy of her niece Agathine's lover Victor, banishes the young man from the house and promises Agathine to old Monsieur Roch. The elderly servant Catherine saves the day by sleeping in the girl's bed the night of an expected tryst with Roch. The old man is a pathetic type, but old age itself is no target, as Catherine is clearly the cleverest and most charming character in the play.[85]

Where an old bachelor uncle stands in the way of his nephew's fortune in *Le vieux célibataire* by Jean-François Collin d'Harleville, the problem is due not to any flaw in the old man's character but to the selfish designs of a servant and to an old misunderstanding. Dubriage, the uncle, is understandably worried about his old age and is considering marriage as the answer to his insecurity. In the end, uncle and nephew are reconciled, Dubriage is called *père,* and there is no need for a marriage of his own.[86]

Collin d'Harleville brought a particularly virtuous old man to the stage in *Le vieillard et les jeunes gens.* Again it is a tale of marriage. The adolescent sons of Madame Merville look up to their debauched friend Lorsan, twenty-five, and want him to marry their sister, Euphrasie. Madame Merville first asks the advice of Naudé, the sixty-two-year-old friend of her late husband. Naudé advises against such a marriage. Lorsan accuses Naudé of wanting Euphrasie for himself, and the old man, to everyone's consternation, does play the suitor and even seems likely to succeed. But then we discover that Naudé has all along been

---

84. F. B. Hoffman, *Le jeune sage et le vieux fou* (1793; Paris, *an X* [1801–2]), pp. 37–38.

85. F. B. Hoffman, *La femme de quarante-cing ans* (Paris, *an VII* [1798–99]).

86. Jean-François Collin d'Harleville, *Le vieux célibataire* (1792; Paris, 1801).

courting the girl on behalf of her serious, virtuous, and exceedingly poor cousin Olivier. Naudé will see to their material needs, just as he has seen to the establishment of a compatible marriage. Of his own action he declares:

> Ah! mes amis . . . je viens de vous prouver
> Qu'un vieillard à son but peut encore arriver.[87]

A seeming case of senility in F. P. A. Léger and R. C. G. Pixerécourt's *Le vieux major* (1800–01) is not so serious as to upset the family; in fact, it is rather charming. Herman, a retired army officer, is still waging war in his garden; he has transformed his ballroom into a hospital, his living room into an arsenal. Herman's mania has a beneficial side, though, for while he strikes his Napoleonic poses, he has provided much-needed training and work for the poor people of his region. The problem of the play is that Herman's daughter Adèle wishes to marry Edouard, whose father, a former friend of Herman, is quarreling with the old major. Adèle's aunt effects a rapprochement between the families, but it takes place in a military fashion: Edouard lays siege to the garden, is captured by Herman, and—upon the arrival of a letter from the aunt—united with Adèle. There is sanity beneath Herman's game; in the end he declares that the lovers' punishment will be to be bound together.[88]

Elderly characters of the Napoleonic period were rarely so daft, and depiction of the wisdom of the elderly continued to hold the stage into the nineteenth century. Some of the noblest and most humane old people in the theater of the period appear in two plays of L. B. Picard. *La vieille tante* is the story of a rich old widow, Madame Sinclair, who is surrounded by greedy relatives waiting impatiently for her death. But she is not ready to think of dying and is amused by the way her relatives cater to her. She seems to enjoy her old age, and she is not the only good elderly character. Her friend the old clerk Dorigny is the most admirable of men; having in his youth married an orphan, he is still working yet finding time to read classic literature and to compose Latin verse and songs for his wife. Madame Sinclair admires him but prefers a more

---

87. "Ah! my friends . . . I have just proven to you / That an old man can still reach his goal": Jean-François Collin d'Harleville, *Le vieillard et les jeunes gens* (Paris, 1803), V.viii.

88. F. P. A. Léger and R. C. G. Pixerécourt, *Le vieux major* (Paris, *an IX* [1801]).

sociable old age for herself: "I still love gambling, walking, music, theater, even dance."[89] The friends learn that Dorigny's son Ernest and Madame Sinclair's grandniece Louise are in love and decide that the young people ought to marry. But the aunt's other relatives, protective of their own interests, object and propose alternative matches. When Dorigny sees how selfish and unvirtuous they are, he refuses to allow his son to marry into such a family. Madame Sinclair saves the day, first by suggesting that she will marry Ernest herself and then, to allay the even more strenuous objections of her relatives, by convincing everyone to permit the original marriage. The play concludes as the aunt tells her nieces and nephews to leave, that the young couple will provide quite happily all her needs in old age.

Picard's *Le vieux comédien* features an active old couple, modeled from real life. Floridor is a retired Parisian actor who resides with his wife in Senlis. There he advises the local theatrical troupe and occasionally plays his old roles. He has a small grudge against his cousins, a doctor and a lawyer, because in his youth they convinced his father to disinherit him for entering an ignoble profession. When Auguste, son of the lawyer, and Lise, daughter of the doctor, seek refuge with the old couple because their fathers wish to prevent their marriage, Floridor finds a way to settle old scores while providing for the happiness of the young lovers.[90]

The real-life model for Picard's Floridor was the actor Préville, who had retired in 1786 only to return to the stage five years later. But age had taken its toll; he had grown weaker, his memory and eyesight failing him. After losing his place on stage, he decided to retire for good. He had never saved for old age, and his pension was reduced by the Revolution, but fortunately, he had been such a good father and uncle that his children supported him in his final years.[91] He died at seventy-nine in the first year of the new century.

Literature in the early nineteenth century continued to play upon themes of old age developed throughout the eighteenth. The aged Indian in Chateaubriand's *René* continued an Enlightenment tradition of wise old men, and Chateaubriand memorialized the old age of his grand-

---

89. L. B. Picard, *La vieille tante, ou Les collatéraux* (Paris, 1811), I.vii.

90. L. B. Picard, *Le vieux comédien* (1803), in *Fin du répertoire du théâtre français*, vol. 21 (Paris, 1824).

91. Henri-Alexis Cahaisse, *Mémoires de Préville* (Paris, 1812). Contrast the late eighteenth-century ideal of Floridor/Préville with his ridiculous late seventeenth-century counterpart Tiberio Fiorilli, the elderly Scaramouche; see Emile Campardon and Auguste Longnon *La vieillesse de Scaramouche, 1690–1694* (Paris, 1875).

mother in his own memoirs, which served to recall a long-lost past: the irretrievable political past of the ancien régime and the personal past of his dead friends.[92] The latter problem had already haunted Goethe and would become a commonplace in European literature in the nineteenth century. The quest for rejuvenation was revived in Balzac's *L'élixir de longue vie,* and Balzac invented many other old people: the dried-up, mysterious, wise, godly, devilish, and professorial types in *La peau de chagrin;* the amorous and avaricious Nucingen in *Les splendeurs et misères des courtisanes.*[93] Theater continued to deal with problems of old age in such plays as Casimir Delavigne's *L'école des vieillards,* in which a sixty-year-old husband and his young wife undergo a crisis after moving from Le Havre to Paris and solve it simply by returning to provincial retirement.[94]

Poets took up the theme of aging, particularly the question of the passage of time, treated frequently by both Lamartine and Musset.[95] Victor Hugo wrote in a more recognizable Enlightenment tradition, singing the praises of wise, experienced old people. Support for the aged was seen by him to be part of the role of the poet. In the preface to *Les rayons et les ombres* (1840) he urged fellow writers to inspire "veneration for old age, in showing old age always to be great" and quoted from one of his own poems in *Les voix intérieures* (1837):

> Pierre à pierre, en songeant aux vieilles moeurs éteintes,
> Sous la société qui chancelle à tous vents,
> Le penseur reconstruit ces deux colonnes saintes,
> Le respect des vieillards et l'amour des enfants.[96]

The literary treatment of the aged in the nineteenth and twentieth centuries surely has sources in the eighteenth. But except in the natural-

92. François-René de Chateaubriand, *René,* in *Atala et René* (Paris, 1805); Marie-Jeanne Durry, *La vieillesse de Chateaubriand 1830–1848* (Paris, 1933), pp. 9–15.

93. Honoré de Balzac, *L'élixir de longue vie* (1830), in *Oeuvres,* vol. 15 (Paris, 1845); *La peau de chagrin* (Paris: Gallimard, 1974); *Splendeurs et misères des courtisanes,* in *Oeuvres,* vol. 11 (Paris, 1844).

94. Casimir Delavigne, *L'école des vieillards* (1823), in *Oeuvres,* vol. 2 (Brussels, 1832).

95. On the passage of time, see Alphonse de Lamartine, "Le lac" (1817), and "Souvenir" (1819), in *Méditations poétiques* (Paris, 1973); Alfred de Musset, "La nuit de Décembre" (1835), in *Pages choisies, I: Poésie* (Paris, 1959).

96. "Stone by stone, in thinking of the faded old morals, / Beneath the society that bends to all winds, / The thinker rebuilds these two holy columns, / Respect of old people and love of children": Victor Hugo, *Les chants du crépuscule, suivi de Les voix intérieures et de Les rayons et les ombres* (Paris, 1964), pp. 235, 238.

ism of Zola and his heirs it seems to have lost the political urgency of Enlightenment and Revolutionary literature, which considered the social problems of economy and society, of riches and poverty, of childhood and old age. The solutions suggested in those writings were elaborated and proposed more formally in a literature of economics and social science that never divorced itself completely from the sentiment of contemporary belles lettres. Before examining that sentimental but extraordinarily progressive social science (see Chapter 8), we must explore the religious and philosophical views that underlay all literary treatment of the aged. Implicit in changing French literary and graphic images—evolving from one provoking distaste and ridicule to another treated with almost saccharine honor and affection—were profound changes in ideas concerning the meaning of old age, retirement from an active life, and preparation for death.

4 From Augustinian Retreat to Ciceronian Retirement: Religious and Secular Views

How a person of the ancien régime reacted to the onset of old age was largely an individual matter. Then, as now, it depended partly on each one's particular experience of life. But it also depended on the dictates of the culture. We can know how people were told to understand old age, for certain texts dispensed wisdom on the subject; they borrowed from ancient and modern sources, repeated old saws and invented new ones. They brought the contradictory messages of Western culture down to the lived reality of the aged individual.

The wisdom of the past presented old age as good and bad, strong and feeble, happy and sad, honored and resented. Opinions were gathered from the Greeks and Romans, Old Testament and New, Church fathers and modern commentators. In his *Comes senectutis* of 1709 Claude Le Pelletier brought together scripture, patristic literature, ancient orations, philosophy, and poetry.[1] Such a compendium argued no explicit thesis. Turn to one page and find an honorable age and a hoary head; turn to another and find physical decline and preoccupation with death. It was a book intended to occupy the reflective retiree. Appropriately, it was published by a man of state who had retired from government service. Le Pelletier, born in 1630, had become *prévôt des marchands*, chief municipal officer of Paris, in 1668 and later councilor of state. He replaced Jean-Baptiste Colbert as comptroller general of finances, then retired from the post after six undistinguished years, remaining a minister of state. In 1691 he took the place of the marquis de Louvois as *surintendant des postes*, a combined position of postmaster general, minister of transport, and interior minister. He retired definitively,

1. Claude Le Pelletier, *Comes senectutis* (Paris, 1709).

though against the wishes of Louis XIV, in 1697. His book on old age appeared in 1709, two years before his death—two years in which he may or may not have sorted out the opinions he had transmitted.

The storehouse of knowledge about aging was certainly varied. If for Le Pelletier it consisted simply of proverbs and sententious pronouncements, for others there were fuller arguments to be made. Philosophical and medical remnants from antiquity provided the sources for an anonymous manuscript *Traitté de la vieillesse,* of the late sixteenth or early seventeenth century. Beginning with the observation "It is a strange thing that all men desire to become old, and almost all, when they have reached old age, impugn it and complain of it," the text promoted a Hippocratic view of things—four ages of man, with corresponding humours—and suggested that a good old age was indeed possible: the last age saw the "perfection of man" because it was then that his reason, the quality separating him from the beasts, reached its pinnacle; spiritual improvement and a decline in worldly ambition yielded a "safe, judicious, and constant disposition."[2]

Nowhere is the complexity of opinion so obvious as in a 1677 text, *Considérations sur les avantages de la vieillesse dans la vie chrestienne, politique, civile, économique et solitaire.* The author, Pierre Poncet de la Rivière, Baron de Prelle, searched everywhere for knowledge of the aging process and the "sweet things" to be found in old age. He repeated the familiar identification of old age with winter, delved into the Hippocratic tradition, and explored the phenomenon of the climacteric, remarking that both Saint Bernard and Martin Luther died at age sixty-three. He paraphrased Augustine on old age as preparation for death and emphasized the importance of breaking off exceedingly close ties with other people, beginning a process of social death which he called "euthanasia."[3] But he also borrowed from Cicero on public life and retirement, discussed the family as the basis of economic life, and urged patience upon maturing children. He warned against completely solitary retreat and urged a stoical attitude toward death.

Furthermore, he attempted to typify various kinds of old age: "extreme" or "decrepit," "premature," and "common or ordinary" old age. In the first, survival is uncomfortable; "one can say that man ceases

---

2. "Traitté de la vieillesse," B.N. MS F.F. 4822, fol. 58–70.

3. Pierre Poncet de la Rivière, *Considérations sur les avantages de la vieillesse dans la vie chrestienne, politique, civile, économique, et solitaire. Ouvrage du Baron de Prelle, édité par Dominique Bouhours, Jésuite* (Paris, 1677), pp. 84, 162.

to live before dying." In the second, the aging process is speeded up. In the third, events follow a normative course with signs of aging appearing at sixty, infirmities at seventy, and weakness at eighty, after which "the body suffers and the spirit pains."[4]

The second type, premature old age, most interested the author. He imagined three possible causes: a dissolute life, a weak constitution, or the practice of a religious life. While the rest of the book offers no such clue, the discussion of religious life unmasks his true sympathies: "The third sort of premature old age proceeds by a holy and free will. It is contracted by those who pledge themselves to God, who in this state banish the thoughtlessness of the first age, subdue the passions of the second, avoid the embarrassments of the third, and enter abruptly into the fourth and last age . . . like Samuel, David, Solomon, Jeremiah, Tobias, Daniel, and others who by their wisdom have in their youth deserved to be called *Vieillards*." Age is treated as a metaphysical state divorced from biological experience, a variation on the Latin *puer senex*, the old man in the young body. Echoing the earlier remark that extreme old age was the cessation of life before death, Poncet suggested that "in religious life one dies before finishing life; it is in this condition that one is more capable of taking advantage of the benefits of old age than in any other."[5] The religious life would be pushed harder in other texts; here it was only recommended.

A variety of themes was taken up throughout the early modern period. Many derived from Renaissance texts. The Italian humanist Poggio Bracciolini wrote a dialogue on the question of marrying at advanced age.[6] After outlining positions pro and contra, he decided in favor of marriage and, at age fifty-five in 1435, proceeded to marry a much younger woman from a rich Florentine family. Both sides of the issue, though, would be argued in the centuries that followed. Books of advice in the tradition of Luigi Cornaro's treatise on longevity were printed and reprinted.[7] Texts on aging and the loss of beauty were commonplace. The old person who tried to hide wrinkles or white hair was the butt of much ridicule, though one writer argued sympathetically in 1690 that the elderly dyed their hair only because age was so ill-

4. Ibid., pp. 17, 50.
5. Ibid., pp. 40–41, 49.
6. Poggio Bracciolini [Pogge, Florentin], *Un vieillard doit-il se marier?* (1435; Paris, 1877).
7. Luigi Cornaro, *Conseils pour vivre long-tems* (Paris, 1701).

treated that they had no alternative.[8] Love and vanity were the themes of this literature, which was appropriate at the dandified court in Versailles or in Parisian high society. The same themes would recur in middle-class guides to proper behavior in the nineteenth century; in 1877 Bracciolini's text appeared in French translation.

All was not courtly frivolity in the seventeenth century, however. A stoic literature, following upon the revival of stoicism in the sixteenth century, also treated questions of aging and the aged.[9] Marin Le Roy, sieur de Gomberville, outlined a battle between virtue and nature. As a child of fourteen he had made his literary debut with an *éloge* that preferred tranquil age to tumultuous youth. At forty-six, in *La doctrine des moeurs,* he presented life as an opportunity to learn virtue in order to repress passion. Life was to be spent well, and death was not to be feared. Gomberville offered a series of proverbs, each illustrated with a print and elaborated in poetry and prose. In order to teach the lesson "Do not regret time past," a white-bearded and winged Father Time, carrying a scythe and balancing an hourglass on his head, appears at the door of an old man who walks calmly out of his home to face death. "To philosophize is to learn how to die," he preached, and piety "does not retard either old age or death; on the contrary, it hastens their coming." The great evil of old age is avarice, an excessive attachment to things of this world.[10] "Old age has its pleasures," but they are not earthly. "The old man ought to think only of dying":

> Que te sert vieil Ambitieux,
> De voler toutes nos Provinces
> Pour élever en mille lieux,
> Des Palais dignes de nos Princes?
> Ignore tu que les destins,
> Après quelques facheux matins,
> Vont borner le cours de ta vie?
> Déjà tes plus beaux jours ont éteint leur flambeau,
> Pense donc à la Mort. Ton Ame t'y convie;
> Et si tu veux bâtir, va bâtir un tombeau.[11]

8. Laurent Bordelon, *Remarques, ou Réflexions critiques, morales et historiques, sur les plus belles et les plus agréables pensées, qui se trouvent dans les ouvrages des auteurs anciens et modernes* (Paris, 1690), p. 333.

9. On the revival of stoicism, see Michel Spanneut, *Permanence du stoïcisme: De Zénon à Malraux* (Gembloux, Belgium, 1973).

10. Marin Le Roy, sieur de Gomberville, *La doctrine des moeurs, qui représente en cent tableaux, la différence des passions, et enseigne la manière de parvenir à la sagesse universelle* (Paris, 1685), pp. 347, 358, 376, 204.

11. "What is the use, old go-getter, / Of robbing all our Provinces / To erect in a thousand places, / Palaces worthy of our Princes? / Don't you know that the fates, / After

The concern with death in stoical literature bears some resemblance to the teachings of Christian philosophy. But all heavens are not Christian. The 1644 letter *De la vieillesse* by François de La Mothe Le Vayer concludes with an evocation of heaven: "Let us show that we have arrived in this last season not by way of a storm and in spite of ourselves, but voluntarily and as in a port where we happily conclude our commerce, to see soon the dear country that is heaven." The bulk of the letter concerns itself with old age on earth, with memory, experience, and wisdom. Then, after devoting twenty pages to physical infirmity, it argues that metaphysical factors yield a good old age. Material factors "hardly merit being considered," since old age has "so many other spiritual and incorruptible advantages."[12]

Seventeenth-century discussions of old age suffer from the same ambiguities and complexities as all philosophical themes of the period. François de La Mothe Le Vayer, who sometimes hid behind a mask of "Christian skepticism," blended stoicism, Christianity, and libertinism.[13] Stoics and Christians shared a dislike of Epicureanism, but because they diverged on questions of Providence, the subject of death and old age posed irreconcilable differences; there was no agreement even among stoics themselves on the matter of immortality. And while Christians and stoics alike recommended retreat from the world, they did so with different ends in mind. For the stoic, retreat could bring a time of reflection on past deeds, free of material intrusion but untroubled also by the Christian demand for repentance.

It was precisely the material difficulties of old age, however, that made the promise of Christian salvation so attractive. Stoic resignation was not enough. The consolation of old age, the title of a 1626 text of Nicolas Bertin, would be found in thoughts of piety and death. Physical changes induced such thoughts. "Old age gives us the grace of God in making us resemble him." The Hippocratic cosmology is eminently suited to this approach: "And just as out of the West ordinarily rises a sweet rain that, running in the veins of the earth, makes the trees flower and bear fruit, so old age, which is the true West and the setting of

---

some sad mornings, / Are going to limit the course of your life? / Already your most beautiful days have extinguished their torch. / Think then about Death. Your soul invites you to; / And if you want to build, go build a tomb": ibid., pp. 362, 378, 379.

12. François de La Mothe Le Vayer, *De la vieillesse, lettre VII,* in *Opuscules ou petits traictez,* vol. 2 (Paris, 1644), pp. 393, 357–358.

13. Julien-Eymard d'Angers, "Stoïcisme et 'libertinage' dans l'oeuvre de François La Mothe Le Vayer," *Revue des Sciences Humaines,* 75 (1954), 259–284; René Pintard, *Le libertinage érudit dans la première moitié du XVIIe siècle* (Paris, 1943).

human life, produces a certain humidity that flows through all the members of the human body, and after having drowned the perturbations and passions which incessantly excite and traverse the person, it endangers a peace and a repose which makes virtues sprout in man." Physical decline makes the elderly ready targets for both God and the Devil. It is for the old person to choose. If he chooses properly, old age can serve as the ladder of Jacob, aiding him in his climb to heaven. Age brings him closer to the next world, whose attractions are greater than those of this one. When death approaches, the old man may begin to miss his wife, children, and closest friends and relations, but he will soon find himself in the "desirable company" of parents, grandparents, and deceased children and friends.[14]

The discomforts of age make an attitude of contempt for the world all the more appropriate. The Christian literature of old age lays great emphasis on that scorn, a theme in the poetic literature of the late sixteenth and early seventeenth centuries.[15] The flesh is painfully unattractive, and one yearns for death. As Charles Aubert, *avocat et prêtre,* argued in his *Discours consolatif de la vieillesse* of 1643, the weakening of the body "fortifies the spirit and renders it capable of carrying vigorously the greatest charges." The soul "finds new forces in malady and even in infirmity."[16] As the soul begins to free itself from the body, a peaceful port is spied at the end of the storm. The world is described variously as a storm or temporary shelter; old age is the gateway to permanent repose.

It is a joyful death that is proposed in these books. Their authors had no need to threaten the reader—life could do that by itself—but could simply point out the advantages of old age and death. A seventeenth-century manuscript in Carpentras, *Du bonheur et des avantages de la vieillesse,* called the first happiness of old age the decline of passion, the second the accumulation of experience, the third the learning of prudence, the fourth the approach of death, and the fifth the gaining of respect. The author, P. de Montereul, found old age a time permitting

14. Nicolas Bertin, *La consolation de la vieillesse* (Paris, 1626), pp. 3, 29–30, 62, 107.

15. E.g., Jean-Baptiste Chassignet, *Le mespris de la vie et consolation contre la mort* (1594; Geneva, 1967). On correspondence between art and literature, see Marc Bensimon, "La porte étroite: Essai sur le maniérisme (Le Greco, Saint Jean de la Croix, Sponde, Chassignet, d'Aubigné, Montaigne)," *Journal of Medieval and Renaissance Studies,* 10, no. 2 (Fall 1980), 255–280.

16. Charles Aubert, *Discours consolatif de la vieillesse* (Le Mans, 1643), pp. 4, 106.

the attainment of Christian perfection, based upon "the horror of sin and the pursuit of virtue." He asserted that because Christians have their eyes on heaven, they find greater peace and tranquility in old age than do pagans—an opinion contradicted by the many seventeenth-century religious tracts that presented old age as frightfully ugly and by eighteenth-century texts that found a better, more natural old age among the pagans.[17]

Montereul's tone is one of calm conviction. Like Cicero, he dismissed common complaints against old age. Saint Ambrose had argued that a long life meant more sins, but Montereul saw it as an opportunity for "penitence, prayers, and good works." To those who complained of the impossibility of fasting or making pilgrimages, he replied that the heart is more important than the stomach or limbs. Against those who called old age choleric, he argued that energy must be channeled properly: "If we have passed our life in the tempest, let us finish it in the port."

The tone of books of piety urging retreat in old age was not always so calm. That of the abbé de la Chétardie, a preacher of Saint Sulpice in Paris much admired by Pope Clement XI, was shrill. For him the alternative to salvation was indeed frightful. In paraphrase of Augustine he presented old age as one of the consequences of the fall of man; the tree of life had been "preservative, not only against sickness and death, but also against old age, which is after all only death begun." Adam and Eve "committed a crime for which old age and death were the punishment." And in the weakened condition of old age, one's enemies could get the better of one's soul. One might be tempted to say, "Let us eat and be merry . . . because tomorrow we die," but Augustine said, "On the contrary, let us fast and pray today, because tomorrow we die." In old age there is still a chance, according to Chétardie, to accept the Lord's Supper, "the last refection of the day, after which there remains nothing but to lie down."[18]

As late as 1757 the abbé Clément, canon of Saint-Louis-du-Louvre, offered an equally negative assessment of old age, "a gift that nature makes us under such hard conditions that I do not know why anyone wants to have any part of it." In a variation on the maritime image that

17. P. de Montereul, *Du bonheur et des avantages de la vieillesse,* B.M. Carpentras, MS 254 fol. 543–548.

18. Joachim Trotti de La Chétardie, *Homélie XXVIII pour le dimanche dans l'octave du Saint Sacrement sur la vieillesse,* in *Homélies de M. de S. Sulpice,* vol. 2 (Paris, 1708), pp. 6, 26, 27, 29.

had served La Mothe Le Vayer's stoical philosophy, Clément presented life as a storm at sea, from which old age is a haven—but one that permits little peace, only the assessment of much damage: "Old age is a port where one arrives only after having run up against many reefs. Oh! how does one arrive there? The riggings are broken; the sails are torn by the force of fighting against the waves, the crew is exhausted, the vessel leaks water from all parts; only the handling of the pilot has saved it from shipwreck. . . . Old age is a time of sterility and want." In other words, be pious in youth in order to be prepared, for "in old age, everything fails us; but God remains for us. We have lost everything; but we are rich if we have ensured our salvation. Let us learn to become old before we are old. . . . In the successive decline that an old man experiences, what will support him, what will console him if he has neither morals nor religion?"[19]

Religion had to be practiced habitually. Old age was a warning, perhaps a bit tardy, but it was a message from the body calling the soul to repentance. Other messages might precede it; widowhood, for example, also offered an opportunity to retreat from the world. The author of one popular guidebook suggested Saint Anne—working in the Temple at age eighty-four—as a model for the aged widow. For those to whom widowhood came much earlier, Judith served as a younger model. The pious retreat of the young was even more welcome than that of the old, for in youth one could mortify the flesh before time took its toll. "One sees in scripture and in sacred history that ordinarily all those who have undertaken penance and who have worked seriously at mortifying and crucifying their old man [the body] have fled the greater world and sought solitude."[20]

The physical, said the guidebook, was unseemly. Thought of it would at best force one to ponder the spiritual, at worst lead to despair. Widowhood was a circumstance that permitted one to separate oneself from the world of the flesh. One did not need to worry about old age. Money was not important; with business out of the way, piety remained. The loss of family simply made retreat the simpler. As Saint John Chrysostom had argued, upon losing a child do not say you have lost your only support in old age but trust in Providence. And as Saint

19. L'abbé Clément, *Réflexions sur la vieillesse, Mercure de France,* August 1757, pp. 81–82, 87–89.

20. Girard de Villethierry, *La vie des veuves, ou Les devoirs et les obligations des veuves chrétiennes* (Paris, 1719), pp. 140–141.

Ambrose remarked, if widowed, do not remarry, for "it is a sort of shame."[21]

Consolation in old age in the religious seventeenth-century world came from pious acts that filled a lifetime and assured salvation. It was one's own responsibility and was quite opposed to the *consolation de la vieillesse* represented in the later eighteenth century by children. Where judgment was important, individuals could rely on no one else. Their thoughts must run to heaven and not to earth. Such was the argument of a much reprinted text of the seventeenth century called *La trompette du ciel*. It reminded earthly sinners of their dependence upon God: "Life and death are equally in the power of God." All one could do was repent, but repentance would bring a joyful death. And it was death that seemed to be the goal of life; old age certainly was not. The author, Antoine Yvan, called it the worst time of life: "Alas! You give your youth and the best time of your life to the devil, to the flesh, to the world, and to your foulness, and you reserve the worst for God. . . . If you do so, what can you expect but to be abandoned by God, and to die in sin; and whatever you will do in your old age will not be received by God, and will not draw his mercy upon you."[22] It is too late to mortify what is already dead.

In his preference for an early death, Yvan resembles the classical tragedians. For him, penitent, joyful death replaces the heroic death of the military leader, but old age is miserable in both genres. In some ways it is difficult to speak of a Christian view of old age in the seventeenth century, for it is not a view of old age per se; it is a view of death. And the literature on how to die religiously indicates a relative disdain for old age. Yvan recounts the infirmities of old age and posits sure damnation: "Alas! it is impossible for old people to be able to escape or to deliver themselves from the miseries, pains, troubles, and other incommodities of life. Thus it is not really the time to think of a true conversion when one has neglected it; it is necessary to have provided for it early. Actions follow the temperament of ages; those of youth are ardent and vital; in adulthood they are strong and robust; but the actions of old people are cowardly, negligent, slothful, frigid, coarse, defective, trembling, accompanied by sorrow and *ennui*."[23]

21. Ibid., pp. 221–222, 347–348, 369–370.
22. Antoine Yvan, *La trompette du ciel, qui réveille les pécheurs, et qui les excite puissamment à se convertir à Dieu* (Rouen, n.d.), pp. 119, 336–338.
23. Ibid., pp. 466–467.

The stoical approach to the life cycle permitted some dignity in a vital old age. By contrast, Christian piety recommended a longing for death. As another text, designed for those on retreat, argued: "It is good to die from time to time while you are alive; that is to say, to perform all the duties of a sick person and of one who is dying while you still have all the strength of body and spirit."[24] Longevity was vanity.[25] Jacques Noüet argued in 1679 that existence on earth detracted from eternal life. There was something suicidal in this sort of pious behavior: "Mortification is a voluntary death," or, as Bishop Bossuet put it, "Mortification is an essay, an apprenticeship, a commencement of death."[26]

The relationship between life and death was complicated by the problem of body and soul. The death of one freed the other. One popular guide to thoughts on death—written by Pierre Lallemant, *recteur* and *chancelier* of the Université de Paris who took time between those appointments for a retreat at St. Vincent de Senlis—distinguished four kinds of Christians: those who live by life (exterior and interior), die by death (exterior and interior), die by life (life of the body), and live by death (eternal life of the soul). The saints—John Chrysostom, Jerome, Gregory, and Bernard—were enlisted to instill disgust with life and desire for death. Old age was seen as a great obstacle: "What advantage will we find in living longer? Do not old age and the infirmities that accompany it render us insupportable for others and for ourselves? Consider an old man overburdened with years, his spirit dejected, his body exhausted, his face lined with wrinkles, his eyes half closed, his voice trembling, his head bent toward the earth as if seeking a sepulcher in which to throw himself: is not this a kind of monster in nature?"[27]

If Lallemant's aim was to get people to desire death, François Nepveu's was to teach people how to prepare themselves for it. Like anything else, death required practice; Nepveu recommended a retreat of eight days and monthly practice sessions (he suggested the last day of

24. Jacques Noüet, *Retraite pour se préparer à la Mort, prise des dernières paroles et actions de Jésus-Christ, depuis son retour dans la Judée jusques à sa Passion* (1679; Paris, 1694), p. ii.

25. See Philippe Ariès, *L'homme devant la mort* (Paris, 1977), p. 17.

26. Noüet, *Retraite,* p. 44; Jacques Bénigne Bossuet, "Oraison funèbre de Marie-Thérèse d'Autriche," (1683), in *Oeuvres* (Paris, 1961), p. 130.

27. Pierre Lallemant, *Les saints désirs de la mort, ou Recueil de quelques Pensées des Pères de L'Eglise, pour montrer comment les Chrétiens doivent mépriser la vie, et souhaiter la mort* (1673), 5th ed. (Brussels, 1713), pp. 38–40, 46–47.

the month) during which one ought to say the proper prayers, repent, meditate, and go to one's bed as if it were a tomb. He argued that not only is it necessary to die, but "it is necessary to die soon"; more people die before age twenty-five than after. His readership was apparently of all ages.[28]

For those who were already ill, Antoine Blanchard wrote a guide to dying and the administration of the last rites. He emphasized the brevity of life, "only an instant when compared with eternity." There is no medicine for the "incurable malady" of old age. More than mere acceptance, he urged a life of retreat in which one would be "completely occupied with one's salvation. . . . Prudence requires you to prepare yourself for every eventuality, and to detach yourself entirely from the world, regarding yourself as a victim who will soon perhaps be immolated."[29]

Preparation for death overshadowed old age. In a sermon that brings to mind the *Pensées* of Pascal and other texts that reveled in man's pettiness, Bossuet remarked upon that brevity of life: "Man is such a little thing, and everything that is finite is such a little thing. . . . How I occupy such a small place in this great abyss of time! I am nothing; this little interval is incapable of distinguishing me from the nothingness where I must go."[30] In a paraphrase of Corinthians II, he concludes a sermon on death: "O soul, console yourself: if this divine architect, who has undertaken to repair you, allows this old building of your body to fall apart piece by piece, it is because he wants to render you in a better state; it is that he wishes to rebuild you in a better order."[31] Death should be preferred to life; old age merely impedes the soul's progress. In a funeral oration, Bossuet wondered at the good qualities of a person who had lived a long life, but he still felt compelled to refer to old age as "ordinarily . . . soiled with the filth of avarice."[32] And while he could contemplate the good one old person might have contributed to the

28. François Nepveu, *La manière de se préparer à la mort pendant la vie* (Paris, 1713), p. 56.

29. Antoine Blanchard, *Nouvel essay d'exhortations pour les états différens des maladies où l'on trouvera un grand nombre d'exhortations pour l'administration du viatique et de l'extrême-onction*, vol. 1 (Paris, 1718), pp. 38–39; vol. 2, p. 158.

30. Jacques Bossuet, "Méditation sur la brièveté de la vie" (1648), in *Oeuvres* (Paris, 1961), p. 1035.

31. Bossuet, "Sermon sur la mort" (1662), in *Oeuvres*, pp. 1083–1084.

32. Bossuet, "Oraison funèbre de Madame Yolande de Monterby" (1656), in *Oeuvres*, p. 15.

world had he survived, he nevertheless concluded that death was welcome: "His old age, however heavy, was not without action: his example and his words animated others. He has died too soon. No; because death never comes too suddenly when one prepares for it by a good life."[33]

Books specifically written about the end of life had curiously little to do with age; rather their topics were death, judgment, paradise, and hell. The reader was reminded that such were the ends of life for all, king and subject, the scholarly and the uneducated, rich and poor, young and old. The cause of death was not illness or accident but original sin. Under such circumstances, longevity was beside the point. But for L. Rouault, the author of *Les quatres fins de l'homme*, that it was beside the point was itself a point worth making: "What good does it do Adam, Methuselah, or Noah to have lived each nearly a thousand years: are they any less dead? What difference is there between their life, long as it might have been, and that of those who have only lived forty or fifty years? For there remains for the ones and the others only the thought of having been." It is better to die poor than rich, better to die than to live. If one is "advanced in age, what remains for him but misery? If he is young, he still has more to suffer."[34]

Even in the shadow of death, old age takes a back seat. Resurrection will occur "in the force of age," as for Jesus at thirty-three. Eternal life will be lived in strength. Rouault argued that his lesson needed to be learned because people in the countryside were ignorant; they did not understand Christianity or death but thought that with death everything came to an end, that there was no judgment.[35] Perhaps his complaint should be taken as one more contribution to the history of scorn for the idiot peasantry. Maybe they did need constant reminders of Gospel truth, like the refrain of *Pensez-y-bien*, which appeared on virtually every page of another book on *les quatres fins dernières*. However, Rouault may have detected some alteration in the popular mentality as a result of the dechristianization movement brought to light by recent historical studies.[36]

33. Bossuet, "Oraison funèbre de Messire Henri de Gornay" (1658), in *Oeuvres*, p. 22.

34. L. Rouault, *Les quatres fins de l'homme, avec des réflexions capables de toucher les pécheurs les plus endurcis, et de les ramener dans la voye du salut* (Paris, 1734), p. 58.

35. Ibid., pp. 169, 232–233.

36. Paul de Barry, *Pensez-y-bien, ou Réflexions sur les quatres fins dernières* (Paris, 1737); Vovelle, *Piété baroque*.

What were the consequences of secularization for attitudes toward old age in the eighteenth century? The most immediate consequence was plain disregard for Christian notions of retreat. The next was the rise of a secular doctrine. A reading of secular books of advice suggests that some things undoubtedly did not change. Whether Christian or stoic or even philosophic, the book of advice to the aged had a consistent role: it was a book of reflection, of piety; it recommended retreat and meditation. But it pointed to alternative traditions. On the one hand, the Augustinian tradition of religious retreat from the world emphasized thoughts of death; on the other hand, the Ciceronian tradition of honorable retirement from public office emphasized reflection on past actions and guidance for youth. Renaissance humanists would have been comfortable in either tradition, but from the Counter-Reformation to the French Revolution, sides had to be chosen. We can view Augustinian retreat and Ciceronian retirement as ideal types to explain the religious view of old age in the seventeenth century and the philosophical view in the eighteenth. There are overlaps, regressions, and counterrevolutions, but in general the latter period is one of secularization or dechristianization. And so the devoutly religious retreat that might be encountered on the eve of the Revolution or in its wake must be considered a relatively exceptional resistance to change.

The Augustinian tradition recommended separating oneself from the world and pondering death. In effect, the unseemliness and decay of old age forced upon one a refusal to face earthly reality, a commonplace attitude in the Middle Ages when such practices were the specialty of monks of all ages. For them retreat began early and lasted a lifetime. But as the Reformation gripped Europe and the Counter-Reformation transformed France, the idea of retreat had to be considered by people who still had to operate in the world. Salvation became one's own business, one's individual responsibility. Retreat was not just for the monk. The period of the Reformation saw more than a reaction to ecclesiastical abuses: it brought about a change in the religious view of Europeans.[37]

The Ciceronian tradition also recommended a separation—indeed, Cicero's text provided inspiration for Christian humanists and neo-

37. Lucien Febvre, "Une question mal posée: Les origines de la réforme française et le problème des causes de la réforme," in *Au coeur religieux du XVIe siècle* (Paris, 1968); John Bossy, "The Counter-Reformation and the People of Catholic Europe," *Past and Present*, 47 (1970), 51–70.

stoics alike—but its version of *retraite* was closer to a secular notion of retirement than a religious one of retreat. Written in the form of a dialogue between Cato the Elder and his younger admirers Scipio and Laelius, it gave Cicero a chance to put into Cato's mouth the words he himself wanted to believe about his own old age in forced retirement from political life.[38] Cato responds to four kinds of arguments against old age—that it necessitates inactivity, weakens the body, deprives one of pleasure, and announces the coming of death—and indicates that it can still be a good time of life, not merely the last chance to think of death. He reminds his listeners of elderly people who have continued to participate in political and intellectual life, agriculture, and education. He recalls examples of hearty old people, lists the ways in which they can still lead pleasurable lives, and concludes with a stoical discussion of death.

It is unclear whether Cicero himself believed the ideal he was offering in the words of Cato. A letter to Atticus, written in the year of the dialogue's composition, demonstrates that Cicero was rereading his book to fight off despondency.[39] Nevertheless, subsequent editions of the book not only transmitted ancient attitudes toward aging but also offered an ideal about the life of the aged. As divisions between secular and religious practice became deeper in the early modern period, it served as an alternative to the Christian ideal. Christians might make use of Cicero's argument, and he was a favorite of sixteenth-century humanists in his practical wisdom. But his legacy was seen differently as France moved into a period of religious regimentation. Where the Latin text expressed a pagan attitude toward death or the world, it was sometimes altered in French translation. Thus, the Latin "Et si qui deus . . ." is rendered, "When it please God . . ." rather than, "And if some god . . ." The Latin "turbulent world" becomes in seventeenth-century French "a crowd of people so low, so naughty, and so importunate." And where the Latin speaks of nature's fixing the limit of all things, the seventeenth-century translation refers to the limits of "all things created."[40] Such alterations were unnecessary in the eighteenth century.

38. A useful edition of Cicero's *Cato Maior (De Senectute)* is that of P. Wuilleumier: Cicéron, *Caton l'ancien (De la vieillesse)* (Paris, 1940).

39. Emile Krantz, "Sur le *Traité de la vieillesse* de Cicéron," *Annales de l'Est,* 1894, 1–31, esp. 6–7.

40. For the Latin, see the Wuilleumier edition, pp. 182–184; for the seventeenth-century French translation, Cicéron, *Dialogues de la vieillesse et de l'amitié* (Paris, 1640), Widener, ML 216.38.3.

The rise of a Ciceronian approach to old age occurred differently at different levels of society. A philosophy originally intended for an officer class, by the eighteenth century it reached further down in society. What appears to be the first French translation of the text, a fifteenth-century manuscript of Laurent de Premierfait, is addressed to the royal aged. It is bound with *Le régime des princes,* and its first page is illustrated with a scene of a throned monarch surrounded by clergy and courtiers. The royal personage is being presented with a book, presumably the one in hand. The text is dedicated to the "very excellent glorious and noble prince Louis uncle of the King of France" and mentions his descent from Saint Louis. It presents *la dame philosophie* as a connection between things divine and human, between heavenly and earthly kingdoms.[41]

Cicero's ideal of old age applied to anyone with sufficient wealth to retire. His passages about the military or political adviser's retirement to a country estate were appropriate to the aristocracy of the ancien régime and, more and more, to the bourgeoisie—but certainly not to poor aged Christians on retreat. The life of Etienne Pasquier provides a perfect example of old age in an urban elite family in the old regime. His testament and letters and the letters of his son Nicolas reveal occasionally tense but generally amiable relations. Pasquier retired from the Cour des Comptes in 1604 at age seventy-six to pass on his office to his son and establish the other children. His friends had already dissuaded him several times from retiring, but he finally did leave his post and retreat to his study. He explained quite eloquently in a letter to Achille de Houlay, who would himself soon retire from the presidency of the Parlement de Paris, that he had decided to heed the advice of his doctor and family. He turned domestic affairs over to his son and, according to the son's letters, lived a very good old age indeed—*une verte vieillesse.* Not only did Pasquier see to the establishment of his sons in offices of the robe nobility, but he also dedicated himself to the education of his grandchildren. It was for their use that he intended his manuscript on the *Institutes* of Justinian. In a conflict involving the marriage of his granddaughter, he took her side against her parents.[42]

<hr>

41. Cicero, *De Senectute ou "Livre de Viellesse," de "Tulle," traduction de "Laurent" (de Premierfait)*, 15th-century MS in B.N., MS F.F. 126 fol. 121.

42. Etienne Pasquier, *Oeuvres choisies* (Paris, 1849), pp. 417–424; *Testament olographe d'Etienne Pasquier (12 décembre 1614)*, in M. Jurgens and J. Mesnard, "Quelques pièces exceptionnelles découvertes au Minutier central des notaires de Paris (1600–1670)," *Revue d'histoire littéraire de la France*, 79, no. 5 (1979).

Pasquier's was the ideal old age of his class and very much in line with the recommendations of Cicero. Retirement from public office, after all, could only occur to those in office. One can similarly point to Montaigne, retiring to his library, or to Montesquieu, in the eighteenth century, leaving the Parlement de Bordeaux for his own studies. In the early modern period the nobility was evolving in its own eyes into an aristocracy of service, honor, culture, and, eventually, merit.[43] And with this evolution came the Ciceronian philosophy of old age.

Cicero's ideal old age, a reward for past deeds and services, was maintained in an aristocratic and courtly milieu but held out a certain attraction for the middling orders as well. Retirement, in the sense that presupposed a working career, was most commonly associated with the middle classes, those people who filled the ranks of the liberal professions. By saving (which the laborer could hardly do), the bourgeois might retire and, by retiring, live out his days as if he were ennobled. A businessman might retire from his profession, passing on the trade to his son, and buy a judicial position; he would live from his property and have the prestige of a judge. A doctor, upon attaining an important position in a hospital, could afford to leave the actual practice of medicine to others.[44] An innkeeper or *cabaretier* too might retire. When the son of Jean Ramponeaux, owner of the famed Parisian cabaret Au Tambour Royal, was old enough to run the business himself, the father bought another establishment, La Grand'Pinte; nevertheless, after marrying for the third time in 1795 at age seventy, he retired to a private clinic until his death in 1802.[45]

Husbands and wives who had worked together might retire together. Wealthy widows may have enjoyed the best old age: if they had married older men (and the wealthier the couple, the greater the usual difference in their ages), they could become quite powerful, veritable *chefs de*

43. That philosophy was appropriate for the nobility described in Franklin L. Ford, *Robe and Sword* (Cambridge, Mass., 1953); and in Guy Chaussinand-Nogaret, *The French Nobility in the Eighteenth Century: From Feudalism to Enlightenment* (Cambridge, 1985; original French ed., 1976).

44. On bourgeois retirement in general, see Elinor G. Barber, *The Bourgeoisie in 18th-Century France* (Princeton, N.J., 1955), pp. 89–90; for specific examples, Olwen H. Hufton, *Bayeux in the Late Eighteenth Century: A Social Study* (Oxford, 1967), pp. 60–61, 70.

45. C. Ver Heyden de Lancey, "Coup d'oeil sur deux figures curieuses de la vie parisienne au XVIIIe siècle," *édition de la Revue des Indépendants* (Paris, n.d.). For a less fortunate innkeeper ("a couple of elderly people living alone in an inn would be the easiest of all targets in eighteenth—and early nineteenth—century conditions"), see Richard Cobb, "L'Affaire Perken: A Double Murder on the Franco-Dutch Border, 1809," in *A Sense of Place* (London, 1975), p. 68.

famille. But women who had never married could expect nothing in old age. They lived on the margin of society; as Adeline Daumard has said, they were considered a "bother, useless, and scorned." Women of all classes required marriage to ensure a good old age, for the plight of the unmarried old woman was generally dreadful.[46]

Infirmity might force retirement regardless of age, but without a pension or traditional alms, withdrawal from the workplace was difficult to negotiate. In the prebureaucratic rural world, various manifestations of village solidarity or sociability informally protected individual patriarchs. Artisanal corporations were supposed to provide for their members' retirement, and there were some homes for retired priests.[47] Among minority groups a similar solidarity protected the aged; Jews and Protestants in France supported needy elders as well as the widowed and orphaned. The Portuguese Jews of Bordeaux, Narbonne, and Perpignan maintained funds in Amsterdam for the support of their needy, and Protestants in Grenoble who made charitable bequests in the seventeenth century kept them in their community.[48]

If priests retired, they did so by hiring successors to their posts, and a notarized act of retirement was sent to Rome. Or a *curé* simply appointed a *pro-curé* to fulfill his duties. But because the replacement had rights to most of his salary, commonly leaving too little for the old priest to live on, priests from various parts of France lobbied for a pension system at the end of the ancien régime and in the early years of the Revolution. Without an effective pension the *curé* would probably die while still at his post,[49] though some found aid with relatives, and a lucky few took up new posts that were less demanding.[50]

46. Adeline Daumard, *La bourgeoisie parisienne de 1815 à 1848* (Paris, 1963), pp. 357, 375; Perrot, *Genèse*, p. 316; Roderick Phillips, "Women's Emancipation, the Family, and Social Change in Eighteenth-Century France," *Journal of Social History*, 12, no. 4 (1979), 553–567.

47. William H. Sewell, Jr., *Work and Revolution in France: The Language of Labor from the Old Regime to 1848* (Cambridge, 1980); A.P., F.F. MS 19.

48. Léon Kahn, *Histoire de la communauté israélite de Paris: Quatrième partie— Les sociétés de secours mutuels philanthropiques et de prévoyance* (Paris, 1887), p. 30; Gérard Nahon, "Les rapports des communautés judéo-portugaises de France avec celle d'Amsterdam au XVIIe et au XVIIIe siècles," *Studia Rosenthaliana*, 10, no. 1 (1976). I thank Richard Menkis for the reference. On Protestant and Catholic charity in Grenoble, see Kathryn Norberg, *Rich and Poor in Grenoble, 1600–1814* (Berkeley, Calif., 1985).

49. Timothy Tackett, *Priest and Parish in Eighteenth-Century France* (Princeton, N.J., 1977), p. 106. The replacement received 60 percent of the *portion congrue* and the *casuel* (p. 141). In the Dauphiné, two-thirds of priests died in office (p. 142).

50. John McManners, *French Ecclesiastical Society under the Ancien Régime: A Study of Angers in the Eighteenth Century* (Manchester, 1960), p. 6; Hufton, *Bayeux*, p. 31.

The practice of seeking an assistant who would be promised the position upon the elder's retirement, though particularly important for the celibate, was the method not only of priests but of secular workers as well. In 1791 the mayor of Paris received a letter commenting upon the advanced age of the chief locksmith of the hospital of Bicêtre; the writer offered himself as a potential assistant or even a full-fledged replacement if it were deemed necessary to retire the old man.[51]

Finding a successor was of course irrelevant for members of the nobility, of whom no work had been required in the first place. Once nobility was no longer identified with a military profession, the sense of a career was different: adult life was passed in constant retirement, interrupted occasionally by state service. Cardinal de Fleury was appointed to a ministry under Louis XV at the age of seventy-three. And retired or not, members of the first two estates lived in greater physical comfort than their neighbors in the third, whether in city or country. Whereas riding on horseback had been an important symbol for the old nobility of the sword, for the new elite of sword and robe a carriage (with improved suspension) was perfectly adequate for travel.[52]

In the eighteenth century a variety of practices demonstrates that a modern sort of retirement, based upon bureaucratic arrangements, was beginning to appear. The military provided the first regular pensions. The seventeenth century saw the creation of many pensions for the wounded, but not until the eighteenth century could one expect a given reward for a certain period of service; the "old soldier" of the Invalides was a creation of the eighteenth century.[53] Nonmilitary pensions were also won in another state office, the *fermiers-généraux*.[54] It is indicative of national economic priorities that while dock workers in the customs service received the first nonmilitary pensions in England,[55] tax-farmers (who paid for the privilege of collecting taxes—and retaining a goodly share) should receive the first in France.

51. A.N. F[15] 247 no. 486 (August 6, 1791).

52. Ariès emphasizes improvement in carriages in his review of Fischer ("Growing Old in America"). On the movement away from nobility as profession, see Ellery Schalk, *From Valor to Pedigree: Ideas of Nobility in France in the Sixteenth and Seventeenth Centuries* (Princeton, N.J., 1986).

53. André Corvisier, *L'armée française de la fin du XVIIe siècle au ministère de Choiseul: Le soldat* (Paris, 1964), p. 983; Jean-Pierre Bois, "Une politique de la vieillesse: La retraite des vieux soldats, 1762–1790," *Annales de démographie historique*, 1985, pp. 7–20.

54. Yves Durand, *Les fermiers généraux au XVIIIe siècle* (Paris, 1971), p. 56.

55. Marios Raphael, *Pensions and Public Servants: A Study of the Origins of the British System* (Paris, 1964).

Retraite, then, came to apply to secular retirement, and repose became an ideal of privileged life. The life of the chateau required wealth, but repose at a level of *médiocrité* increasingly became a topic for philosophical treatment and approval. In his history of the idea of *bonheur*, Robert Mauzi summarized eighteenth-century opinion on leisure by defining the good life as that which begins in the world and ends in repose—but this sort of repose was contrary to Christian ideals of asceticism and solitude. The new *retraite* was characterized by sociability, by continued contact with family and friends.[56]

And if Cicero was the classical expert on old age, he was equally expert on questions of friendship. One eighteenth-century commentator argued that the Roman orator deserved a revival. He observed in 1732 that while Cicero had been relegated to the *collèges*, two hundred years before he had been the favorite of the best minds of France among the Robe and the Clergy. He added that as he himself had aged, Cicero had grown on him.[57] Apparently others thought the same. A letter of Vincent Mignot to his sister Madame Denis (nephew and niece of Voltaire), introducing his translation of the *De senectute* and the *De amicitia*, offered quite an Enlightened view: "Friendship, my dear sister, is the charm of all ages and the consolation of old age: I feel it as I am acutely pleased to grow old with you. Full of the desire to pass more peacefully the time that it remains for me to live than that which is past, I have reread with avidity the ancient philosophers. The two treatises of Cicero on old age and on friendship have made more of an impression upon me than all the rest."[58]

The connection between aging and friendship was crucial in Cicero, as in other Roman writers, and the two themes underwent a parallel development. Revived by such humanists as Montaigne, they were denied in the seventeenth century by the bearers of both the Counter-Reformation and neo-stoicism, for whom earthly ties bespoke vanity on the one hand and unreality on the other.[59] But those same ties were lauded in the eighteenth century. Madame Du Deffand wrote Voltaire about the importance of long-term friendship in old age; S. R. N.

56. Robert Mauzi, *L'idée du bonheur dans la littérature et la pensée françaises au XVIIIe siècle* (Paris, 1960), pp. 40, 177, chap. 9, pp. 351, 591, 593.

57. Cicero, *Tusculane . . . sur le Mepris de la Mort, Traduite par M. l'abbé d'Olivet, de l'Académie Française, avec des Remarques de M. le Président Bouhier, de la même Académie, sur le texte de Cicéron; On y a joint le Songe de Scipion* (Paris, 1732), pp. 7–8, 28–29.

58. Vincent Mignot, *Traités de Cicéron sur l'amitié et la vieillesse* (Paris, 1780).

59. Frédérick Gerson, *L'amitié au XVIIIe siècle* (Paris, 1974).

Chamfort remarked that the aged also require new friends to replace the old ones.[60] Even when philosophers continued to write about living well and dying well, the emphasis was on the living. As Saint-Evrémond had observed at the turn of the century, "Better a week of life, than a week of fame after you are dead."[61]

The revaluation of life on earth presented a challenge to the Church, for it diverted attention from the business of salvation. Cicero's Cato scorns death, argued one Catholic critic, but one should scorn life instead; ecclesiastical authorities continued to demand that the old person anticipate his demise and, consequently, detach himself from the world.[62] While Church law had not prohibited marriages involving the aged, it had certainly cast suspicion upon them: in canonic and medical tradition, impotence could prevent marriage or force annulment, because marriage was invalid where conjugal duties could never be fulfilled. One theologian argued that the aged "ought to be judged unable to contract marriage. . . . The cold winter . . . has extinguished any natural vigor, and their blood, half frozen in their veins, is no longer capable of warmth." Another considered old men eunuchs and their wives widows. And a third wrote that "old age seems to be also a sort of frigidity and impotence."[63]

Eighteenth-century prescriptive literature on aging exhibits a view of life similar to that observed in the movement from *contemptus mundi* to a new worldliness in eighteenth-century eulogies.[64] The new attitude permitted expectations of a vital old age and even suggested the need for some planning, whether for pleasant diversions in retirement or simply for the financial wherewithal to retire.[65] Beneath this evolution lay a transformation from a Catholic ethic to a bourgeois one.[66] That trans-

60. Cited in Mauzi, *L'idée du bonheur*, p. 111, and in Gerson, *L'amitié*, pp. 104–105.

61. Quoted in Hazard, *European Mind*, p. 125.

62. *Le discernement de la vraye et de la fausse morale; Où l'on fait voir le faux des Offices de Cicéron, et des Livres de l'Amitié, de la Vieillesse, et des Paradoxes* (Paris, 1695), p. 232; Ariès, *L'homme*, pp. 294–295.

63. Quoted in Pierre Darmon, *Le tribunal de l'impuissance: Virilité et défaillances conjugales dans l'ancienne France* (Paris, 1979), pp. 66, 68.

64. George Armstrong Kelly, "The History of the New Hero: Eulogy and Its Sources in Eighteenth-Century France," *Eighteenth Century: Theory and Interpretation*, 21, no. 1 (1980), 13.

65. For a letter in which Madame Roland expresses hope to read Plutarch in old age, see Harold T. Parker, *The Cult of Antiquity and the French Revolution* (New York, 1965), p. 59.

66. Bernard Groethuysen, *The Bourgeois: Catholicism vs. Capitalism in Eighteenth-Century France* (New York, 1968).

formation also involved a separation of the living from the dead, reflected in the movement to wall up or close cemeteries in the eighteenth century.[67] Philosophical and medical opinion would permit no more of the religious promiscuity with death. While the long-term effect was a submerged concern with mortality that eventually sprang up in a Romantic cult of the dead, divorced from earlier Christian doctrine though certainly influential in nineteenth-century Christian practice, the short-term effect was a refusal to look at death at all.[68] And once death became hidden, old age stood revealed.

As attention turned to the life of the aged, the difficulties for which Christianity had held out some solace were not shunned. The same Saint-Evrémond who preferred life over posthumous fame also advised retirement in a passage quoted in a dictionary of 1769: "The end of the pleasures of life ought to be the beginning of retirement."[69] In the same book a poem on old age, attributed to Voltaire, offered a secular version of the traditional death in life:

> C'est l'âge où les humains sont morts pour les plaisirs,
> Où le coeur est surpris de se voir sans désirs.
> > Dans cet état il ne nous reste
> Qu'un assemblage vain de sentimens confus,
> Un présent douloureux, un avenir funeste,
> Un triste souvenir d'un bonheur qui n'est plus.
> Pour comble de malheurs, on sent de la pensée
> > Se déranger tous les ressorts:
> L'esprit nous abandonne; et notre âme éclipsée
> Perd en nous de son être, et meurt avant le corps.[70]

A popular dictionary of 1768 offered a similarly negative assessment of old age as a "state that pleases no one, and where one arrives at a gallop

67. Madeleine Foisil, "Les attitudes devant la mort au XVIIIe siècle: Sépultures et suppressions de sépultures dans le cimetière parisien des Saints-Innocents," *Revue Historique*, 510 (1974), 303–330; Françoise Zonabend, "Les morts et les vivants: Le cimetière de Minot en Châtillonnais," *Etudes Rurales*, 52 (1973), 7–23.

68. Michel Bée, "La société traditionnelle et la mort," *XVIIe Siècle*, 106–107 (1975), 81–111.

69. Antoine Sabatier de Castres, *Dictionnaire des passions, des vertus, et des vices, ou Recueil des meilleurs morceaux de morale pratique, tirés des auteurs anciens et modernes, étrangers et nationaux*, vol. 2 (Paris, 1769), pp. 531–532.

70. "This is the age when men are dead for pleasures, / When the heart is surprised to see itself without desires. / In this state there remains for us / Only a vain assemblage of confused impressions, / An agonizing present, a deadly future, / A sad memory of a happiness that is no more. / To crown the misfortunes, it dawns on us / That we are becoming completely deranged: / The spirit abandons us; and our soul eclipsed / Loses in us its being, and dies before the body": ibid., p. 532.

without even perceiving it."[71] But it had shed the Christian baggage of the next life. Even La Mettrie suggested retirement for the age when pleasure would be beyond reach and urged reading, meditation, and writing in order to offer something to future generations. What alternative was there for one who suggested that the reason for existence is existence itself?[72]

Nevertheless, at a time when the proper study of mankind was man, the proper study of old age had ceased to be death. In his articles on old age in the *Encyclopédie,* the chevalier de Jaucourt dealt primarily with the biology of senescence.[73] The entries on medicine and physiology took up most of the space; those having to do with moral philosophy reviewed the classical literature on the difficulties of aging and the possibility of enjoying a happy retirement. Almanacs and journals of the period turned not only to classical literature but also to contemporary examples of longevity. Reports of vigorous and extreme old age were common in the second half of the eighteenth century, and from 1764 to 1771 one almanac was devoted specifically to reporting cases of centenarians.[74]

The turn toward the quotidian involved some anthropological research. From Montesquieu to Holbach and Helvétius, the study of other cultures indicated the variability of treatment of the aged. In a lengthy description of the response to the problem among hunting peoples, Helvétius argued that parricide could be committed in the name of humanity, for although it made the eighteenth-century Frenchman recoil in horror, it saved the old tribesman from a far more cruel fate in the forest.[75] More commonly, observation of other societies permitted the elaboration of a theory of natural aging. As Jean Ehrard has pointed

71. Louis-Antoine de Caraccioli, *Dictionnaire critique, pittoresque, et sentencieux, propre à faire connoître les usages du siècle, ainsi que ses bisarreries,* vol. 3 (Lyon, 1768), p. 309.

72. Julien-Offray de La Mettrie, *L'homme machine* (1748; Paris, 1966), pp. 42, 111.

73. See Jaucourt's articles "Vie," "Vieil," "Vieillard," "Vieillesse," in Denis Diderot, *Encyclopédie, ou Dictionnaire raisonné des sciences, des arts, et des métiers, par une société de gens de lettres,* vol. 17 (Neufchastel, 1765), pp. 249–260.

74. See the themes listed in Geneviève Bollème, *Les almanachs populaires aux XVIIe et XVIIIe siècles: Essai d'histoire sociale* (Paris, 1969), p. 103; Augustin-Martin Lottin, *Almanach des centenaires, ou Durée de la vie humaine au-delà de cent ans, démontrée par des exemples sans nombre, tant anciens que modernes, avec le calendrier de l'année,* 10 vols. (Paris, 1764–71).

75. Claude-Adrien Helvétius, *De l'esprit* (1758), in *Oeuvres,* vol. 1 (Paris, 1793), pp. 211–212.

out, nature occupied for the Enlightenment a capital though ambiguous position of normative behavior and transcendent goal.[76] For Diderot the old age of the Tahitians, a settled people, offered one ideal of strength and community support.[77]

A theory of natural aging provided a way of assessing the place of old age in contemporary French society. Physiological views (investigated more fully in the next chapter) combined the Hippocratic system as modified by Descartes and a sensualist philosophy adopted from Locke. The system of humours expressed the slowing down of bodily functions, the cooling of the spirit of life, and the hardening of the body in general. Sensualist philosophy, based upon the principle that there are no innate ideas, presented the old person as a creature of habit: as the senses are deadened and the passions grow weak, one survives on memory and reflex. The avaricious adult, for example, grows more grasping in old age. In a maritime metaphor that departs substantially from both stoic and Christian traditions, Helvétius wrote: "Similar to the vessels that the waves still carry on the coast of the Midi even when the north winds no longer swell the seas, men follow in old age the direction that passions have given them in youth."[78]

Holbach, while repeating the view of a spirit of life—phlogiston or inflammable matter—which is diminished in old age, also argued that man's goal was "to preserve himself and to render his existence happy." On the one hand, "in old age, man fades entirely, his fibers and his nerves stiffen, his senses become dull, his eyesight gets cloudy, his ears become callous, his ideas become disjointed, his memory disappears, his imagination is muffled; what then becomes of his soul? Alas! it gives way at the same time as his body." But on the other, man does not want to die. He is used to life, "the only life that he knows."[79] Christian books of consolation urge the elderly not to mourn excessively the death of friends and relatives.[80] But Holbach saw no realistic alternative: the death of a spouse, a child (who could have provided for his parents' old

76. Jean Ehrard, *L'idée de nature en France à l'aube des lumières* (Paris, 1970), pp. 394–395.

77. Denis Diderot, *Supplément au voyage de Bougainville* (Paris, 1935), esp. "Les adieux du vieillard," pp. 117–132, and specif. the old man's strength at age ninety, p. 123.

78. Helvétius, *De l'esprit*, p. 45.

79. Le Baron d'Holbach, *Système de la nature, ou Des lois du monde physique et du monde moral*, vol. 1 (Paris, 1821), pp. 150–152, 160, 306, 324.

80. Mourning, nevertheless, provided some income for the Church.

age), or a friend was too deeply felt. He contrasted the ways of nature with the ways of religion: "Nature tells children to honor, to love, to heed their parents, to support them in old age; religion says to prefer the oracles of their god and to spurn father and mother when it is a matter of divine interest." The voice of nature speaks: "Under the eyes of united and virtuous parents let your children learn virtue, that after having occupied your maturity, they may render to your old age the cares that you will have given to their weak childhood."[81] As Le Maître de Claville had similarly observed, "The good father makes the good son. . . . What a torrent of delights for this son . . . to render to his father in his old days the same cares that he received from him in his youth."[82]

The sense of the reciprocity of generations marks Enlightenment texts above all. Mirabeau's *Hommes à célébrer,* a biography of France's economic ministers, offers perhaps the best statement of this position: "Each day adds to the forces of the son and diminishes those of the father: thus the primitive tie, based upon the advance from father to son, is removed and apparently weakened; but the duty of the son, which is to return his father's advance, draws near and is reinforced proportionately. Thus the good father, supported by his son, is soon going to taste the sweetness of the object of the design of nature, which meanwhile prepares for the just son the same happiness in his children." In another passage, Mirabeau's treatment transcends the basic exchange of authority and respect to project an image of divine old age: "that happy age, sweet, honorable and tranquil, attains goodness, tolerance, the full bloom of the soul, the wisdom that, in a word, consists in placing his spirit and his heart between God and the children of men, to draw the light from on high, to pour feeling on the dusty course of human agitations, to possess if he can a ray of the divine essence, which sees, which aids, which cherishes and which pardons: there is the sage, there is the happy old man."[83]

Mirabeau's philosophizing strikes one as ironic, considering the battles that raged in his own family, but the view was common enough that even he could appropriate it. More remarkable is the ability of other

81. Holbach, *Système de la nature,* 2, pp. 259, 411.

82. Charles-François-Nicolas Lemaître de Claville, *Traité du vrai mérite de l'homme considéré dans tous les âges et dans toutes les conditions: Avec des principes d'éducation, propres à former les jeunes gens à la vertu* (Paris, 1734), p. 388.

83. Victor Riqueti, Marquis de Mirabeau, *Hommes à célébrer* (Paris, 1789), vol. 1, pp. 86, 136; vol. 2, pp. 267–268.

writers to address serious questions of family strife in the eighteenth century. Gabriel Sénac de Meilhan, another public official, wrote of the problems faced by the aging individual: "Boredom is the painful sentiment of his existence." He addressed the problem of the woman who loses her beauty, suggesting that at a certain age more women of the *grand monde* die than those of the *bourgeoisie* or *peuple*. These women are no longer loved and face a veritable midlife crisis, *"la maladie de quarante ans."*[84] In *La femme de trente ans,* Balzac would describe it as occurring earlier,[85] though Helvétius had put the same phenomenon at the age of forty-five or fifty: "They fall into an unbearable *ennui.* What to do to withdraw from it? Substitute new occupations for the old, make themselves devout, create for themselves pious duties, go every day to mass, to vespers, to the sermon, on a visit to a spiritual guide, to do penance. They prefer mortifying themselves to being bored."[86] But Sénac, going beyond boredom, looked head on into households irreversibly riven with generational strife. He told a story of four generations occupying the same house. He offered a cross-section of a Parisian building stratified not by class but by age, the occupant of each floor awaiting the death of the elder beneath his feet.[87]

Less contemporary but no less important were the countless references to the honor shown old age in ancient Sparta. By the time it had become a subject of the addresses of the Revolutionary festivals, the role of age in ruling Sparta and in governing its families had long been commonly alluded to. Giving up one's seat in the stadium to one's elder was an act frequently mentioned. Even an academic paper addressing the question of the change and disappearance of the laws of Lycurgus praised the Spartan attitude toward old age.[88]

The Spartan system became an important model in the Revolutionary catechisms intended to replace the Catholic ones of the ancien régime. In a section on the rights of man, one such catechism asked what the rights of the aged would be. The answer read as follows: "At the age

84. Gabriel Sénac de Meilhan, *Considérations sur l'esprit et les moeurs* (London, 1787), pp. 172–173, 251, 259.

85. Balzac, however, gave different timetables in different books; see Philibert, *Les échelles d'âge,* p. 18.

86. Helvétius, *De l'homme* (1772), in *Oeuvres,* vol. 4 (Paris, 1793), p. 264.

87. Sénac de Meilhan, *Considérations,* pp. 307–309.

88. Charles-Joseph Mathon de la Cour, *Par quelles causes et par quels degrés les loix de Lycurgue se sont altérées chez les Lacédémoniens jusqu'à ce qu'elles ayent été anéanties* (Lyon, 1767).

where the Senators will quit their employ, they will quit all work or will continue it only for their recreation; they will be better lodged, better clothed, and better nourished than the young people, and if it is possible to indemnify them for the loss of their strength by songs that recall their services, one will employ them, and they will see their fellow citizens eager to serve them, distract them, and console them."[89]

Less sober treatments of old age also appeared in the eighteenth century. One book of 1755 recounted the stories of people who had died laughing; it repeated the familiar saws about the pains of growing old—the wrinkles, the coldness—but its Epicurean attitude toward death was new.[90] In avoiding the tormented seventeenth-century approach, it permitted a sympathetic view of old age as well. And when the younger Mirabeau surveyed the sexual life of men and women of all ages (complete with illustrations; the book may be read only in the reserve room of the Bibliothèque Nationale), he called the period from age sixty to the tomb the age of regrets but still pointed to some individuals who were capable of continuing their sexual activities at an age when most other commentators had declared sex absolutely disgusting.[91] In a similar vein, Diderot remarked that the story of Susannah with the elders who tried to seduce and then blackmail her had shown him the merits of the elders' position.[92]

There was a tendency toward exaggeration and selective evidence, but some eighteenth-century texts that contradicted old wisdom permitted greater subtlety. It was possible to reject the hysterical tone of seventeenth-century discourse without opting for pure sentimentality. An unpublished academic essay of 1757 argued for a secular and social view of old age while also criticizing new forms of orthodoxy. A Monsieur Bocquet du Hautbosc, addressing the Académie Royale des Belles-Lettres de Caen on December 1, 1757, claimed that the aged were owed respect precisely because of their usefulness to society. Yet having made social utility the measure of all things, he elaborated on an observation of Alexander Pope that the aged tend to be stuck in their generation's way of thinking; they criticize their own elders as well as their suc-

89. Rilliet de Livron, *Catéchisme sans superstition* (Geneva, 1791), pp. 29–30.

90. André-François Boureau-Deslandes, *Réflexions sur les grands hommes qui sont morts en plaisantant, avec des poësies diverses* (Rochefort, 1755).

91. Honoré-Gabriel Riqueti, Comte de Mirabeau, *Le degré des âges du plaisir, ou Jouissances voluptueuses de deux personnes de sexes différents, aux différentes époques de la vie* (Paris, 1798).

92. Diderot, *Pensées,* p. 84.

cessors. The accumulation of useful knowledge, he concluded, would require careful criticism.[93]

. Two works that might be said to summarize Enlightenment views of old age were printed in the first decade of the nineteenth century. J. H. Meister had collaborated with the Baron von Grimm, Diderot, and the abbé Raynal at the end of the ancien régime; his *Etudes sur l'homme, dans le monde et dans la retraite* (1804) and *Lettres sur la vieillesse* (1810) offer a Ciceronian view of the ages of man. They represent an attempt to join the philosophy that had been taught him by Diderot with the religious fervor rekindled in him by J. K. Lavater. Many elderly people in the arts and in society, he remarked in his *Etudes,* manage to retain their youth, "all the freshness of their talent, of their sensations, of their amiability." He pointed to Ninon, Richelieu, Sophocles, and Voltaire. He was willing to accept the sensuality of the aged, observing that because sensuality comes with practice, it is no surprise that older people have difficulty shedding old ways. The old man still believes in his own existence; the narrowing of his focus and the disappearance of certain distractions permit a certain sensual living. And he can still live in the present: "The most decrepit old man can always say to the most vigorous young man:—The present instant belongs equally to me as to you; the instant that follows it belongs no more yet to either the one or the other."[94]

Meister paid homage to Cicero's book but suggested that history had changed the role of the aged; it was now up to such a person as himself to be the modern-day Cicero.[95] He too recommended a semi-retirement, but whereas Cicero's book was intended for officers, Meister's was appropriate for virtually anyone who has a profession and a family. According to his *Lettres,* childhood and old age are the best times of life, and those times commingle as grandparents and grandchildren find time for each other. Such bliss flies in the face of the generational conflict observed by Sénac. But it does recognize the coexistence of three generations, a recognition which—because of either contemporary demographic trends or religious concern for the individual soul—was missing from the earlier Christian literature.

93. M. Bocquet du Hautbosc, "Sur les vieillards . . . ," MS, Académie Royale des Belles-Lettres de Caen, A.D. Calvados, 2D1446.

94. J. H. Meister, *Etudes sur l'homme, dans le monde et dans la retraite* (Paris, 1804), pp. 29, 30, 125, 246.

95. Meister, *Lettres.*

One can detect an evolution within Catholic opinion throughout the eighteenth century.[96] The abbé Trublet, for example, a man of the Church despite his connections with Fontenelle and Montesquieu, was able to offer a compilation of Enlightenment, stoic, and Christian ideas in his *Essais sur divers sujets de littérature et de morale* of 1735. In a chapter devoted to *bonheur* he argued that the aging person needed to avoid boredom. And in a chapter on the similarities between study and life he elucidated some of the sense of aging that would be of interest to both believers and nonbelievers—a far cry from the earlier books of piety. He compared the sense of the passage of time in youth and age, observing that youth can know nothing of the brevity of life. He remarked upon the pains that accompany aging. And although he urged thinking of death in life, doing so was simply a way to achieve a complete view of life in the world. The wisest researcher, he suggested, continues to study "as if he still knows nothing, walks as if he were still taking his first steps."[97]

A book of advice that took to heart much of the devotional literature but used it to recommend ways of growing old within the family was the *Traité de la vieillesse* that the Marquise de Lambert addressed to her daughter. It recommended piety and devotion, an end to life before death, but did so calmly.[98] The domestic nature of the book precluded any of the ranting scare tactics associated with the Counter-Reformation or English Puritan texts. In theme and source the Marquise de Lambert's book is traditional. She repeated familiar prescriptions of retreat and thoughts of death, but her tone provided some originality, for her devotional rigor was mitigated by a sense of family responsibility. Her book was, after all, a guide for her daughter, published for the added benefit of other mothers and daughters. Presenting old age as a time for mutual responsibility within the family was a departure from the alienating texts of retreat.

The Marquise was not alone in joining a Christian sense of piety to an acceptance of economic and emotional attachment to the world. The abbé Fleury's guide to the rights of masters and domestic servants, first

---

96. On the evolution of Catholic ideas, R. R. Palmer, *Catholics and Unbelievers in Eighteenth-Century France* (Princeton, N.J., 1939).

97. L'abbé Trublet, *Essais sur divers sujets de littérature et de morale*, vol. 1 (Paris, 1735), p. 191; vol. 2, pp. 136–139.

98. Anne-Thérèse de Marguenat de Courcelles, Marquise de Lambert, *Traité de la vieillesse*, in *Oeuvres*, 2d ed. (Lausanne, 1748), pp. 145–172.

published in 1688 and reissued throughout the eighteenth century, focused upon a Christian ideal of service; Fleury used the role of Jesus as a model for the service undertaken not only by the servant but also by the master, who offers services of education and support. The life of Jesus could thus be applied in the context of social interaction rather than retreat. Fleury projected a vision of "natural life: that all should work as their strengths permitted, that the young should serve the old and the healthy the sick."[99] Because he recognized the relationship of material conditions to a pious retirement, he urged the master to remember his servants when drawing up his will.

Care of aging servants was analogous to care of any needy member of the household. The "consolation of old age" came more and more to be included among the responsibilities of adult children; it could not be the role simply of a devotional book. The family was evoked time and again in the *drame bourgeois* and the festivals of old age (see Chapter 8). It also came to be considered in such texts as *Les avantages de la vieillesse* of the Prussian J. H. S. Formey, who tried to reconcile philosophy and Christianity. His treatise received a long review in the *Journal Encyclopédique* in 1759. The reviewer, apparently unhindered by the Christian tradition of retreat, assumed a commonsense attitude toward the physical and psychological aspects of aging. He found it paradoxical that the title should announce "advantages": "What advantages, indeed, can man find in that period of his life where he sees his body change, his senses, those wonderful organs of thought, weaken; where his soul, all spiritual as it is, seems to participate in the decrepitude of the frail machine that it animates; where finally he knows his existence only from the feeling of sorrow—sad compensation for the pleasures that he tasted in a less advanced age? Such is the spectacle of old age; at first sight it arouses nothing but dread."[100] Such an approach might have led the pious Christian to seek refuge in his faith, but the reviewer follows along as Formey presents his case for domestic spiritual advantage in old age. Since infirmities are common in all ages, one should not blame the last but should, on the contrary, consider what one has learned over the years.

Formey recounted the loss of two daughters who would have been the support of his declining years, and his memories of them were so

99. L'abbé Fleury, *Devoirs des maistres et des domestiques* (Paris, 1765), p. 8.

100. Review of J. H. S. Formey, *Les avantages de la vieillesse* (Berlin, 1759), in *Journal Encyclopédique,* 4, no. 2 (1759), pp. 3–4.

bittersweet that he imagined the family life of more fortunate elderly people to be positively blissful. He spoke of his "familial sensibility" and his "paternal heart," which induced him to write his book. Still, in old age one has one's soul and an understanding of truth and virtue. Madame Lambert, he said, found more sadness than she ought to have found. Formey found solace in good conscience, in memories of a life of honesty, probity, and virtue.[101] His mixture of philosophy and religion was capable of being used by Christian and philosophe alike, but his focus upon the family directed attention to the earthly and the everyday.

Some ecclesiastical thinkers continued to battle the decline of pious sentiments, however. The abbé Grou, for example, warned against impiety in old age in his *Caractères de la vraie dévotion* of 1788. He used a scientific view to support a traditional Christian idea of the proper remedy: in old age the passions are reduced, the mind loses some of its former clarity, and the senses receive feeble impressions; illness and weakness should combine to alert the aged to the nearness of death, which still, on the eve of the anti-Christian Revolution, deserved some consideration.[102] And right through the war of the Vendée the *curé* of the Angevin town of La Chapelle-du-Genêt, Yves-Michel Marchais, continued to threaten the aged with damnation.[103]

Contradictions between religious or idealist arguments and naturalist ones adopted from the Enlightenment remained unresolved in other books of the period. Madame Necker's *Réflexions sur le divorce* of 1794 used what might have been termed a philosophic conception of a secular old age to argue against the Revolutionary legislation concerning divorce. The family is central to her conception of the good old age and family breakdown the greatest threat to the retirement of the aged. Madame Necker saw marriage as a sacred knot and feared, like conservatives of the nineteenth century, the loss of continuity from generation to generation. She suggested four aims of marriage: the individual happiness of the spouses, the security of the children, the purity of morals, and the consolation of old age. She offered an image of the reciprocal relationship of parents and children: "Filial respect renders to old people all the hopes and nearly all the goods of their youth, like these harvests of violets that grow, in our Alps, beside mountains of ice

---

101. Ibid., pp. 6, 12–14.

102. L'abbé Grou, *Caractères de la vraie dévotion* (Paris, 1788), pp. 63–64.

103. See François Lebrun, *Parole de Dieu et Révolution: Les sermons d'un curé angevin avant et pendant la guerre de Vendée* (Toulouse, 1979).

and which perfume them with their ambrosia." And she praised the interaction of grandparents and grandchildren: "What a picture, that of the old man feeding on nectar meant for his grandchild! what a touching and venerable exchange."[104] Presumably there was enough nectar for both.

Madame Necker's is the most sociable of eighteenth-century visions of old age. The elderly can still "glean something from the field harvested in life," but if the family is broken, old age is miserable: "Solitude is without doubt one of the greatest evils of advanced age."[105] Old age should be spent in the family, with spouses and children. This domestic provision of the Spartans should be adopted, if not their politics or law.

Madame Necker's book can be seen as a pivotal text in the transition to the nineteenth century, when Enlightenment arguments for a sociable, domestic old age could be enlisted in the ranks of conservative ideas. It can be seen as precursor to such documents as the manuscript letter *De la vieillesse* of the abbé Poulle in Avignon. Undated, the text nonetheless makes mention of Chateaubriand and combines a vision of a neoclassical "Temple of Old Age" with an ideal of the "Christian Religion." Poulle accepted Cicero's view but pointed out that his philosophy "stops at the gates of death. If it gives enough strength to endure the inconveniences of old age, it presents no consolation, and the old man needs some." Poulle recognized the importance of social ties in life, of the respect owed to experience, and of considering old age as a season of harvest. But he also observed that social ties begin to break for the aged, and isolation tends to be their common lot.[106]

In the nineteenth century a romantic Christian vision came to characterize texts of spiritual guidance for the aged. The Swiss sectarian César-Henri-Abraham Malan wrote two didactic tales to warn them of the need for religion in their final years. In 1817 he told the tale of the skeptic Henri, who stumbles upon the burial of a young girl, speaks with an old man who gives him a Bible and proves to be the girl's grandfather, and is converted in a scene replete with the romantic imagery of sunset and death.[107] In 1821, he wrote as a pastor who encounters and holds dialogues with two old men. The first is concerned

104. Madame Necker, *Réflexions sur le divorce* (Lausanne, 1794), pp. 40, 44.
105. Ibid., pp. 61, 89.
106. Benoît-Jean-André Poulle, *De la vieillesse: Lettre à Mr. d'Eyragues*, B.M. Avignon *Fonds Requien*, MS 2728.
107. César-Henri-Abraham Malan, *Le vieillard d'Ellacombe* (Paris, 1817).

with this world—a practical, eighteenth-century view that the pastor abhors. The second is a Christian who has suffered great misfortunes and thinks exclusively of heaven: the pastor sees that he alone will be saved.[108] To the eighteenth-century mind, though, the first would have sounded sensible, the second foolish.

The nineteenth century contributed also to the secular library on old age, most notably in medicine (see Chapter 5), but it too tended to see the aged in terms of family life. The Baronne de Maussion translated Cicero and wrote her own *Quatre lettres sur la vieillesse des femmes*, which appeared in 1822. Her thesis was that with the loss of beauty the aging woman could turn her attention to serious matters. Among the Gauls, she argued, mature women made decisions about war and peace; in the past there had generally been greater respect for aging women. Science, she thought, had unmasked the cruelties of nature; simple respect was now found only in the country, and the family was the only refuge from disrespect.[109] Ridicule of the amorous aged found a new audience in the nineteenth century, after an interruption in the second half of the eighteenth. One book on the physiology of bachelorhood railed against the unmarried aged as having cheated nature,[110] but another remarked that while celibacy was unnatural, the marriage of the elderly could be equally unseemly.[111]

Still, many of the themes of the eighteenth-century discourse on old age would be repeated and are still heard today. The secularizing spirit of the eighteenth century permitted a new view even within the religious fold and led to a specialized literature of a living old age. An assault on Christian attitudes toward death had been required to free the subject of age from its grip. That being accomplished, philosophical discussion of old age would not evolve much further; rather, the grounds of debate would become more scientific. Once old age was seen as a time of earthly existence and even happiness, it became appropriate to ask how to live a long life—and for the scientific and medical literature to respond.

108. César-Henri-Abraham Malan, *Les deux vieillards* (Paris, 1821).

109. Baronne de Maussion née Thellusson, *Quatre lettres sur la vieillesse des femmes*, in *Caton l'ancien, ou Dialogue sur la vieillesse, traduit de Cicéron* (Paris, 1822), pp. 46, 69–71.

110. L. Couailhac, *Physiologie du célibataire et de la vieille fille* (Paris, 1841), pp. 8, 111–112, 117.

111. L.-J. Larcher and P. J. Jullien, *Ce qu'on a dit du mariage et du célibat* (Paris, 1858), pp. 200, 212–213, 283.

5 Reaching Old Age: Scientific and Medical Thought

The scientific and medical study of old age is often thought of as a recent phenomenon. If it is not seen as a wholly twentieth-century invention, it is frequently regarded as the product of J.-M. Charcot (1825–93) or, at the earliest, of his predecessors at the Parisian hospital of the Salpêtrière in the first half of the nineteenth century.[1] Others suggest that the origins of the specialty can best be found in the clinical medicine of Xavier Bichat, P. J. G. Cabanis, and others of that Revolutionary cluster studied by Michel Foucault.[2] Nevertheless, French doctors writing in the middle of the eighteenth century had already devoted entire chapters and books to the diseases of the aged. They were still operating in a preclinical context, but such doctors as Jean Astruc and M. J. C. Robert contributed to a new specialization in medical thinking.[3] They responded to the eighteenth-century desire to reach old age and the Enlightenment project of rendering it more comfortable.

Early modern medicine kept alive two variant though by no means mutually exclusive explanations of aging that derived from the ancients.[4] One was the Hippocratic system of humours and their growing

1. Peter N. Stearns, *Old Age in European Society: The Case of France* (New York, 1976), chap. 3.

2. Michel Foucault, *The Birth of the Clinic* (New York, 1973).

3. Jean Astruc, *Traité des maladies des vieillards* (see n. 36); M. J. C. Robert, *De la vieillesse* (Paris, 1777). Developments in scientific thought about the later years of life followed the evolution in ideas about the beginnings of human life, outlined in detail in Jacques Roger, *Les sciences de la vie dans la pensée française du XVIIIe siècle: La génération des animaux de Descartes à l'Encyclopédie* (Paris, 1971).

4. Mirko Drazen Grmek, *On Ageing and Old Age: Basic Problems and Historic Aspects of Gerontology and Geriatrics*, Monographiae Biologicae, no. 5 (The Hague, 1958).

imbalance in the body's metabolism. The other was Galen's theory of a "heat of life" that consumes itself in the course of a lifetime.[5] Even when the ancient wisdom was coupled with, if not quite tested by, observation, the old forms of thought were still considered valid. Early eighteenth-century iatromechanists tried to distance themselves from the believers in innate heat and Aristotelian humours, but variations on the traditional ways of thinking would still enjoy considerable favor among the Montpellier vitalists and leading physiologists at the turn of the nineteenth century.[6]

Popular medicine suggested household remedies for the ailments of the aged. In the early eighteenth century *La médecine et la chirurgie des pauvres* of Dom Nicolas Alexandre offered the following prescription: "Dissolve some peacock dung in a sufficient quantity of eau-de-vie, and have the old man whose head trembles take it on an empty stomach, continuing the next three days in a row." For the prolapsed uterus Alexandre recommended a powder to be added to the daily soup.[7] A seventeenth-century guide held out the promise of *la médecine universelle,* a compound of saltpeter, charcoal, antimony, and alcohol that had undergone considerable beating, heating, exposure to light, and distillation. The author, Claude Comiers, researching the proper balance between humidity and heat, sketched out the battle between those forces in terms of humours. Because moderate diet and vigorous exercise contribute to health, Comiers claimed, peasants outlive gout-ridden aristocrats.[8]

5. Galen too accepted the Hippocratic humours along with the Aristotelian qualities. While Hippocrates and Galen were sometimes opposed—Galen had criticized the Hippocratic texts—they did fit roughly in the same tradition until the Scientific Revolution, when Hippocrates won out as the better clinician. See George Sarton, *Galen of Pergamon* (Lawrence, Kan., 1954), pp. 52–53; Owsei Temkin, *Galenism: Rise and Decline of a Medical Philosophy* (Ithaca, 1973), pp. 103–104, 160–161. As to the heat of life, its historian sees a change in the eighteenth century away from a special internal heat, but the language of the eighteenth century still indicates considerable continuity: Everett Mendelsohn, *Heat and Life: The Development of the Theory of Animal Heat* (Cambridge, Mass., 1964).

6. Sergio Moravia, "From *Homme Machine* to *Homme Sensible:* Changing Eighteenth-Century Models of Man's Image," *Journal of the History of Ideas,* 39 (1978), 45–60; and Martin S. Staum, *Cabanis: Enlightenment and Medical Philosophy in the French Revolution* (Princeton, N.J., 1980).

7. Dom Nicolas Alexandre, *La médecine et la chirurgie des pauvres, qui contiennent des remèdes choisis, faciles à préparer et sans dépense, pour la pluspart des Maladies internes et externes qui attaquent le Corps Humain* (Paris, 1714), pp. 23, 277.

8. Claude Comiers, *La médecine universelle, ou L'art de se conserver en santé, et de prolonger sa vie* (Brussels, 1688), pp. 5–6, 17.

It is often difficult to draw the line between elite and popular medicine, but more and more doctors of the early modern period were doing so.[9] In 1578 Laurens Joubert published a book on popular errors. He denied that the eating of testicles or sleeping with a younger person could rejuvenate the aged, but he did argue that, within limits, one could lengthen the life span. Still, he recognized the inevitable course of events: "Little by little the body dries up. And from there it follows that henceforth such strength is not exercised, and day by day is weakened, so that in the end the body ceases to be able to be sufficiently nourished. And thus as the parts become very dry, the body is drained and diminished, then further it is wrinkled, and this condition is called old age."[10]

In the early modern literature, longevity was considered mainly a question of diet, and anyone who wrote on the subject would have little difficulty in finding the prescriptions of the Venetian Luigi Cornaro, whose *Trattato della vita sobria* was translated into French first among the 1647 *Trois discours nouveaux et curieux* and then independently under two different titles in 1701.[11] Cornaro recommended a strict regimen of twelve ounces of bread and other food, including an egg, and fourteen ounces of fluid. The seriousness with which the prescription was taken is indicated by an anonymous *Anti-Cornaro* of 1702 that recognized the need for a proper diet but questioned the wisdom of this particular one. Moreover, the critic raised the issue of sociability, which certainly loomed large in the eighteenth century. A strict diet, he said, isolates the elderly from the "commerce of the table"; unable "to live with the living, they are constrained to eat apart like lepers, to sequester themselves from company, and to renounce public and private duties of

9. See Jean-Pierre Goubert, "L'art de guérir": "If there is really a separation between these two arts of healing, it is found more, at the end of the eighteenth century, at the level of collective representations than at that of medical knowledge and social practice" (p. 909). See also Matthew Ramsey, "Popular Medicine and Medical Power in France, 1707–1830" (Ph.D. diss., Harvard University, 1979). Ramsey points out that even at the height of the repression of popular medicine in the Revolutionary and Napoleonic periods, medical authorities allowed some popular healers to continue practicing in order to make a living in old age (pp. 594–596). I thank him for permitting me to read the thesis.

10. Laurens Joubert, *Erreurs populaires au fait de la médecine et régime de santé* (Bordeaux, 1578), pp. 26, 30. On popular errors in general, see Natalie Zemon Davis, "Proverbial Wisdom and Popular Errors," in *Society and Culture in Early Modern France* (Stanford, Calif., 1975), pp. 227–267.

11. Luigi Cornaro, *Trois discours nouveaux et curieux* (Paris, 1647), *Conseils pour vivre long-tems* (Paris, 1701), and *De la sobriété et de ses avantages, ou le vray moyen de se conserver dans une santé parfaite jusqu'à l'âge le plus avancé* (Paris, 1701).

civil society. Whosoever will desire such a life, let God grant it to him."[12]

Such considerations became common in the eighteenth century but, as indicated in Chapter 4, departed from most late seventeenth-century French wisdom on aging, which had regarded the desire to prolong life largely as an expression of vanity. Vanity perhaps drove René Descartes and a few others in the seventeenth century to explore ways of prolonging life. Part 6 of Descartes's *Discourse on Method* evokes the possibility that scientific discovery might conquer disease and the debility that came with old age.[13] In fact, his death surprised his colleagues, who believed that he had discovered a regimen for longevity.[14]

The search for long life nevertheless spread among men of science, and fantastic tales of rejuvenation underwent scrutiny. A 1708 essay by a Dr. Begons of the Faculté de Montpellier reported several examples of rejuvenation in the Velay region near le Puy, including the 104-year-old woman who at one hundred had resumed menstruation for the first time in fifty years. Since then she had regained her health, governed her household, and without difficulty eaten foods that had formerly been painful to digest.[15] The reader might infer that there was something peculiarly healthful about the climate of the Velay, but for Begons the explanation lay elsewhere. Aging, he believed, was due essentially to the weakening of the "ferments," which tended to inhibit the workings of bodily organs so that heat escaped. Nature, according to Begons, could reverse the course if it permitted some hidden ferment to act in old age. Moreover, man might help himself by encouraging transpiration through proper baths and balms. What had begun as a discussion of rejuvenation in a particular region ended by shifting its focus from climatic factors to internal natural processes.

With or without explanations, reports of longevity came in a variety of guises: books, academic papers, and popular pamphlets. The 1715 *Histoire des personnes qui ont vécu plusieurs siècles et qui ont rajeûni*

12. *L'anti-Cornaro, ou Remarques critiques sur le Traité de la vie sobre de Louis Cornaro Vénitien* (Paris, 1702), pp. 62–63.

13. René Descartes, *Discours de la méthode* (1637), in *Oeuvres et lettres* (Paris, 1953), p. 169.

14. Mirko Drazen Grmek, "Les idées de Descartes sur le prolongement de la vie et le mécanisme du vieillissement," *Revue d'histoire des sciences*, 21 (1968), 285–302.

15. Begons, *Dissertation physique sur les changemens et mouvemens critiques, survenus à quelques personnes âgées qui ont semblé rajeûnir*, reviewed in *Mémoires de Trévoux*, November 1708, pp. 1933–1958.

of Longeville-Harcouet purported to include the "secret of rejuvenation,"[16] but its collection of classical and modern examples was so
varied that it was not at all clear what the secret was. And explanations
were not always included in the academic papers from England, Germany, Denmark, and Sweden that were translated into French in the
eighteenth century. The tales they contain—of the 152-year-old Shrop-
shire peasant who succumbed to the air and dirt of London and died
"prematurely," and of aged Germans who grew new teeth—may be
fantastic, but they are presented with the utmost objectivity and accompanied by tables of mortality.[17]

With hindsight such a coupling appears bizarre. But at the time a
recognizably modern demographic science was working itself out of the
cluster of concerns that characterized the subject of old age. Even
descriptions that smacked of the magical had to be reported in order to
build up a fund of data. The importance of demographic phenomena to
the strength of nations and their economies was recognized throughout
western Europe in the eighteenth century, and demography permitted a
general view of aging.[18]

The works of Bagard, Beausobre, Moheau, and Butte attempted to
describe aging as it affected parishes and nations,[19] and even those that
borrowed heavily from classic texts used statistics to calculate life expectancies. The title of a 1757 study by Louis de Beausobre of the Royal
Academy of Prussia expressed the multiplicity of concerns: "New considerations on the climacteric years, the length of man's life, the propagation of the human species, and the true power of states."[20] The

16. Longeville-Harcouet, *Histoire des personnes qui ont vécu plusieurs siècles et qui
ont rajeûni: Avec le secret du rajeunissement, tiré d'Arnauld de Villeneuve* (Paris, 1715).

17. Berryat, ed., *Collection académique, composée des mémoires, actes, ou journaux
des plus célèbres académies et sociétés littéraires étrangères . . .*, 13 vols. (Dijon and
Paris, 1755–79), vols. 2, 3.

18. Jean-Claude Perrot and Stuart Woolf, *State and Statistics in France, 1789–1815*
(New York, 1984); Jacques and Michel Dupâquier, *Histoire de la démographie* (Paris,
1985).

19. Bagard, *Recherches et observations sur la durée de la vie de l'homme* (1754),
reviewed in *Mémoires de Trévoux* (November 1754), pp. 2855–2858; Louis de Beausobre, *Nouvelles considérations sur les années climatériques, la longueur de la vie de
l'homme, la propagation du genre humain, et la vraie puissance des Etats, considérée
dans la plus grande population* (1757), reviewed in *Mémoires de Trévoux* (December
1757), pp. 3006–3010; Moheau, *Recherches et considérations sur la population de la
France* (1778; Paris, 1912); Wilhelm Butte, *Echelle physiologique* (Paris, 1822); Butte,
Prolégomènes de l'arithmétique de la vie humaine (Paris, 1812).

20. Beausobre, *Nouvelles considérations,* pp. 3006–3010.

climacteric, the year of crisis, still had some significance, but only as the label for the ages of highest mortality, not some mystical product of sevens and nines.[21] Demographic data would measure the strength of the state but also facilitate the development of old age pensions and annuities.[22]

By the end of the eighteenth century the texts that still addressed the question of the prolongation of human life had begun to occupy a separate sphere from that of medicine.[23] Some notable thinkers, including Condorcet, wrote of rejuvenation in the second half of the century, but they were becoming quite exceptional.[24] The consensus, certainly the general opinion among doctors, was that while diseases might be conquered, age could not, though physicians did think they could ease the transition to old age. In his book on women's medicine Jean Goulin noted the benefits that come to women who survive the menopause: "In a word, what a pleasure for them to give themselves up to comfort in certain circumstances, without fearing the consequences that they could not avoid when they had their period."[25] To menstruate was to be *réglée*, regulated. Old age provided a certain liberation.

Even when a book announced that it held the secret of prolonged life, it did not go so far as to promise actual rejuvenation. Claude Chevalier admitted that the old person would still be old but claimed that proper use of his oil would erase the signs of weakness and age.[26] Writing on the conservation of health, Le Begue de Presle argued that longevity is a good thing, for it permits the fulfillment of duty to other men and to God. In this sense, what had previously been considered vanity became

21. The same can be said for the use of the term "climacteric" in Moheau, *Recherches;* see *âges climatériques,* p. 149, and *mois climatériques,* pp. 163–170.

22. P. J. Richard, *Histoire des institutions d'assurance en France* (Paris, 1956).

23. On the separate field of macrobiotic, Christoph Wilhelm Hufeland, *The Art of Prolonging Life* (London, 1797).

24. Gerald J. Gruman, *A History of Ideas about the Prolongation of Life: The Evolution of Prolongevity Hypotheses to 1800,* Transactions of the American Philosophical Society (Philadelphia, 1966).

25. Jean Goulin, *Le médecin des dames, ou L'art de les conserver en santé* (Paris, 1771), p. 109. Cf. Goulin, *Le médecin des hommes, depuis la puberté jusqu'à l'extrême vieillesse* (Paris, 1772), which considers the ailments of old men: gout, rheumatism, weakened eyesight, weakened legs, catarrh, torpor, apoplexy, heartburn, lethargy, paralysis, diarrhea, scurvy, and the drying-up of seminal fluid and tears (pp. 306–393). On the problem of using eighteenth-century terms, see Jean-Pierre Peter, "Malades et maladies à la fin du XVIIIe siècle," in J.-P. Desaive et al., *Médecins, climat, et épidémies à la fin du XVIIIe siècle* (Paris, 1972), pp. 135–170.

26. Claude Chevalier, *Le triomphe de la vieillesse* (Paris, 1787), pp. viii, 17, 70.

virtue, and the book suggested ways of prolonging life. More compelling, however, were its explanations of why people aged prematurely: "weak constitution received from our parents, bad nourishment in all ages of life, diseases, excessive labor, staying up late, binding food, alcoholic liquids, premature or excessive commerce with women, living in climates very different from that where one was brought up, in places where the air is bad, where one often experiences extremes of cold and heat, of dry and wet, and the rapid passage from one to the other," and so on.[27] Since the full list described the lives of most people in the ancien régime, some premature aging would seem to have been unavoidable. Another book setting forth the proper regimen to retain one's health, however, Anselme Jourdain's *Préceptes de santé* of 1772, took a somewhat more optimistic position, suggesting that old age could yield happiness rather than languor and sadness.[28] Dentists too contributed to the literature on physical preservation.[29]

In addition to texts on the prolongation of life and the conservation of health which addressed geriatric issues, there were medical texts that specifically investigated the problems and needs of the elderly. Those texts, at least in intent and organization if not in scientific discovery, offered a new view and consistently sought to expose the aged to the light of medical scrutiny. Michel Foucault has placed the great change in medical perception at the turn of the eighteenth to the nineteenth century with the clinical work of Cabanis and Bichat (see below),[30] but some doctors and scientists even at midcentury were suggesting clinical observation and sometimes carrying it out. The change in perception had already occurred.[31]

The key text from the middle of the eighteenth century is the chapter on old age and death from Buffon's *Histoire naturelle de l'homme*. The book gave humankind its modest place within the natural world, the

27. Le Begue de Presle, *Le conservateur de la santé, ou Avis sur les dangers qu'il importe à chacun d'éviter, pour se conserver en bonne santé et prolonger sa vie: On y a joint des objets de règlemens de police relatifs à la santé* (Paris, 1763), pp. 384–385.

28. Anselme Jourdain, *Préceptes de santé, ou Introduction au dictionnaire de santé, contenant les moyens de corriger les vices de son tempérament, et de le fortifier par le seul secours du régime et de l'exercice, ou L'art de conserver sa santé et de prévenir les maladies* (Paris, 1772), p. xxi.

29. Claude Jaquier de Géraudly, *L'art de conserver les dents* (Paris, 1737); Henry de Lécluse, *Eclaircissemens essentiels pour parvenir à préserver les dents de la carie, et à les conserver jusqu'à l'extrême vieillesse* (Paris, 1755).

30. Foucault, *Birth of the Clinic*.

31. On this earlier change, see also McManners, *Death and the Enlightenment*.

knowledge of which was expanding with the recent discoveries of travelers and naturalists. Buffon's scope was universal and his presentation of the whole range of natural phenomena encyclopedic. But it is on a smaller point that he is of interest here. In describing purely physical things, he reduced life and death in all their variety to the most basic of principles. Aging, he said, is the interrelationship of the two.[32]

According to Buffon, death begins to work its course from the first moments of life. Destruction inheres within the process of creation and growth; death—not at all otherworldly—is simply the final stage of life. Old age, then, is a part of life that deserves detailed analysis.

> As one advances in age the bones, cartilage, membranes, flesh, skin, and all the fibers of the body become more solid, harder, and drier, all the parts recede and contract, all movements become slower, more difficult, the circulation of fluids is accomplished with less freedom, transpiration diminishes, secretions are altered, the digestion of foods becomes slow and laborious, the nourishing juices are less abundant, and not being able to be received in most fibers that have become too weak, they no longer serve for nutrition; these too solid parts are already dead, for they cease to nourish themselves; thus the body dies little by little and by parts, its movement diminishes by degrees, life extinguishes itself by successive changes, and death is only the last limit of this succession of degrees, the last nuance of life.[33]

Life ends by degrees. It becomes impossible to think of death as a metaphysical principle; it is merely the result of the natural course of life.

Buffon did not bother to dispute the extraordinary cases of longevity reported by European academies; he was more interested in addressing the case of the average person. In general, he believed, people age at about the same rate. Soft women might age more slowly than harder, drier men, and in the distant past the suppler, younger earth might have supported biblical life spans, but in his own day the key factors were elevation and "the quality of the air." People lived longer in the mountains of Scotland, Auvergne, and Switzerland than in the plains of Holland, Flanders, Germany, and Poland. Buffon criticized the demographic sampling done by other students of science. They had ignored migration, which had skewed the data. Even the statistics of Depar-

32. Georges Louis Leclerc, comte de Buffon, "De la vieillesse et de la mort," in *Histoire naturelle de l'homme,* in *Oeuvres complètes,* vol. 4 (Paris, 1774), pp. 338–424.
33. Ibid., pp. 351–352.

cieux, drawn up for the creation of tontines and lifetime annuities, were biased, for who made such arrangements but "men of the elite?" Birth, marriage, and death occurred at all levels and in all varieties of human society. So did aging.[34]

A new specialization in aging was emerging. This is not to say that doctors who treated the aged saw no other patients; it is to say that medical thought recognized the special problems of the aged. And medical thought had consequences beyond the medical profession. The Chevalier Jaucourt's article on old age in Diderot's *Encyclopédie* was a gloss on Buffon's chapter.[35] The diseases of the elderly were discussed in separate chapters of medical texts, even became the subject of whole books. Jean Astruc, doctor at the Collège Royal, gave lectures on the diseases of the aged in 1762; a bound set of notes survives from his *Traité des maladies des vieillards*.[36] The notes present the same view as Buffon's on aging as a process of the hardening of the body and the slowing of "oscillatory" movement. Astruc the geriatrician, though, took a broader view of the gradual hardening and drying of the body and moralized less. He divided old age into three periods—incipient (age 55–65), confirmed (65–80), and decrepit (75–100)—but quickly admitted to varieties in the timing of the process. His lectures discuss a wide variety of symptoms: the graying and loss of hair, the impairment of the senses, problems in respiration, the slowing of the pulse, and such diseases as dysentery and gout. For each symptom he offered a diagnosis, a prognosis, and a cure or palliative. Astruc's work has an impressive range. Though nervous disorders occupy most of the text, all aspects of the body come under scrutiny. In his more famous *Traité des maladies des femmes,* he saw the menopause as clearly bringing on the old age of women, and he urged dignified acceptance of the last stage of life.[37]

Another physician, the revolutionary J.-P. Marat, also put great stock in the hardening and drying processes but was able to focus upon very

34. Ibid., pp. 358, 383. See Antoine Deparcieux, *Essai sur les probabilités de la durée de la vie humaine, d'où l'on déduit la manière de déterminer les rentes viagères, tant simples qu'en tontines: Précédé d'une courte explication sur les rentes à terme, ou annuités; et accompagné d'un grand nombre de tables* (Paris, 1746).

35. Diderot, *Encyclopédie*, vol. 17, pp. 259–260.

36. The notes, taken by H. Coillot, are now in the History of Science Library of Cornell University; I thank Librarian David W. Corson and his staff for their assistance. See also Frederic D. Zeman, "Jean Astruc (1684–1766) on Old Age," *Journal of the History of Medicine and Allied Sciences,* 20 (1965).

37. Jean Astruc, *Traité des maladies des femmes* (Paris, 1761–65).

particular physical mechanisms and extend the analysis to include the mental breakdown of the old person. His materialist conception of old age, an extension of the sensualists' theories of development, permitted a view of both anatomy and senescence. The key, for Marat, was the loss of elasticity in the body, causing a series of changes that included the psychological: "Thus the fibers are stretched and the man can take no repose: until the point where his sensibility is dimmed by age, he is virtually no longer susceptible of any impression of malaise, and finishes his sad existence in inaction and sleep." In agreement with Buffon, Marat wrote, "Man dies in every age."[38] The fetus had become a child and the child an adult by a process of drying, the formation of solid organs from a natural mucus and the compaction of the internal parts. Aging merely continued the development of solidity.

The physiology of aging was treated with more complexity in *De la vieillesse* by Dr. M. J. C. Robert, *docteur-régent* of the Faculté de Paris. Robert praised Cicero for his philosophy of old age but deplored the absence of a rigorous medical analysis of aging. Other doctors, he complained, "have nearly all limited themselves to a few sentences on the etiology of these kinds of diseases, and have barely indicated the sorts of remedies that need to be employed." Robert explored physiology, the stages of life, and the relationship between development and destruction. Once more the general scheme might be summarized as a matter of hardening: "All the parts of a declining body have the air of wanting to convert themselves into a truly bony substance."[39] Robert provided more details about this process of ossification. First of all, there was a liquid substance, mucous tissue, that formed the connective material between all the parts of the body. It was through this tissue that the parts developed and degenerated. Movement through the connective tissue was what constituted life itself. But that movement slowed, and because it was three to four times slower in old age than in childhood, the period of decline was three to four times longer than the period of growth. Even then, when exterior organs lost their ability to act, the interior retained some life. The person turned inward—like Sophocles, still thoughtful and creative—no longer troubled by unwanted passions.

38. J.-P. Marat, *De l'homme, ou Des principes et des loix de l'influence de l'âme sur le corps, et du corps sur l'âme* (Amsterdam, 1775–76), vol. 1, p. 129; vol. 2, p. 275; vol. 3, p. 213.

39. Robert, *De la vieillesse*, pp. xxiii, 20.

Robert proposed a variation on the old outline of age-specific diseases. For him, there was one cause for all diseases—"the repletion of the abdomen." Age determined both the duration of the malady and the body's ability to fight it. "In old age nature is rarely capable of those great efforts which become necessary to heal and destroy the infirmities and incommodities of the aged."[40] Why the body's ability to fight diseases was impaired was not precisely stated, though Robert offered a possible explanation in the degeneration of liquids—again, the theme of drying up.

Robert paid homage to Georg Stahl and the vitalists in his introduction, and the vitalists had suggestions of their own, though they strike one as more poetic than scientific, more metaphorical than analytical. Thus, according to P. J. Barthez, "the constitutional intensity of the radical forces of the vital principle changes according to the diverse ages." In describing the loss of the body's mature tone and the weakening of sensations, appetites, and passions, Barthez wrote, "In old people, the active forces perish at the same time that the radical forces gradually destroy themselves."[41] The death of the aged was not necessarily to be explained by a specific disease, for diseases frequently masked the course of natural death, the extinguishing of the life principle, hardly different from the Galenic "heat of life."

In many ways these doctors were merely repeating the formulations of the ancients, and in many ways those formulations still seemed appropriate. People's senses were weakened; they did slow down; they did require more warmth. Common sense and experience said so. But at the same time the doctors were making a niche for themselves. Their medicine may have been no more reliable than that of the ancients, but they claimed to have at least understood the workings of the body and its aging.

It is a truism to say that the eighteenth century was an age of optimism. But although longevity seemed exceptional and old age inevitable, it was thought that there would be progress if more people reached a healthy old age without being in too much of a hurry. They had not been doing that in large numbers, but in the eighteenth century those numbers grew. Doctors were evidently willing to take credit for this change, and many people were willing to believe them. One such be-

40. Ibid., pp. 94, 108

41. P. J. Barthez, *Nouveaux éléments de la science de l'homme,* 3d ed. (Paris, 1858), vol. 2, pp. 160, 178–179.

liever was Napoleon Bonaparte, who, at age seventeen in 1787, wrote the Swiss doctor S.-A. Tissot about his aged uncle Lucien, who suffered from gout.

Napoleon's letter began with a remark that indicates both the growing fame of French medicine and the primitive state of medicalization in the rural world: "You have passed your days in instructing humanity, and your reputation has penetrated even into the mountains of Corsica, where there are few doctors." After expressing his esteem for Tissot's work, Napoleon went on to describe his uncle's case: "This will be a bad preamble to my consultation, as soon as you know that the patient in question is seventy years old; but, *monsieur,* consider that people live to a hundred years and more, and my uncle, by his constitution, ought to be of the small number of those privileged; of medium height, having engaged in no sort of debauchery; neither too sedentary, nor too active; never having been agitated by these violent passions that derange the animal economy; having had virtually no illness in the whole course of his life."[42] He went on to report that an old gout-ridden Genoese had predicted that the uncle, because of his small hands and feet and large head, would likewise be afflicted with the disease. Napoleon expected that Tissot would call the prediction irrelevant, but he did deem it worthy of mention; thus, he offered a mixture of magic and medicine, to be interpreted by the doctor. There was also some uncertainty on Napoleon's part as to what a doctor could do about his uncle's gout, which had traveled around his body and settled in the knees, making them rigid. If the condition could not be cured, might the gout at least be moved to some other part of the body? Before signing off, he also mentioned his own fever as the reason for a shakiness of the hand. Perhaps he was hoping for some additional advice.

Napoleon's letter expresses some common strains in eighteenth-century French thought on old age. The first is that old age might be a period of vitality, a time of earthly happiness; the second, that doctors might be capable of relieving some pain, albeit in a limited way. Before they could do more than simply treat symptoms, however, they needed to describe the physiology of aging.

The doctor who was most successful in that venture was Xavier Bichat, whose *Recherches physiologiques sur la vie et la mort* was among the most influential texts of the Napoleonic period. Bichat wrote

42. Napoleon Bonaparte, letter to Dr. Tissot of Lausanne, April 1, 1787, in Alexandre Keller, *De Brienne au 13 Vendémiaire* (Paris, n.d.), pp. 54–56. I thank Henri Péquignot for the reference.

grandly of the dialectical principles of life and death and further distinguished between organic life and animal life. The organic, he said, is what all living things have in common—biological being, the processes of assimilation and decomposition, digestion and absorption, circulation, respiration and exhalation, nutrition and secretion; animal life comprises that which requires will or consciousness: the sensations felt by nerves and brain, and the action taken by the will. Aging results from the differential development and deterioration of organic and animal life. The organic begins first in the fetus and infant. The animal develops as the senses develop. In old age the reverse occurs: animal life deteriorates as the senses die. Natural death begins as the outside of the body loses its capacities and the nervous system slows down. Because the animal life ends before the organic, there is no consciousness at the end of life and no capacity for fear of death. In a series of chapters on the death of individual organs, Bichat traced the various pathways by which the body can fail. In this way he analyzed all sorts of premature deaths, sudden deaths in which an internal organ failed before the rest of the body. Most telling, however, is his description of natural death, which "terminates almost entirely the animal life before the organic finishes."[43] Connections with the world disappear. Sociability is lost, and so is consciousness.

The influence of Bichat's method was tremendous. One of his students, P. J. B. Esparron, recalled in his introduction to the *Essai sur les âges de l'homme* the time he spent beside the great man's deathbed. It is in the section devoted to the physiology of the aged that Esparron's debt to Bichat is most evident. He borrowed, almost without modification, the division between organic and animal life. When the animal life begins to fail, he said, the person begins to die in detail. In describing this death, Esparron observed that society had made natural death exceptional and that in primitive societies physiological laws were more commonly carried out without societal intervention. In drawing out the social consequences of physiological decline, however, Esparron went beyond Bichat. For one thing, the old person clings to life, even if it is the life of the past, as physiology breeds habit. Moreover, gradual separation from the world places the old person in a privileged position, one that permits him or her to play an important social role as philosopher and adviser.[44]

43. Xavier Bichat, *Recherches physiologiques sur la vie et la mort* (1800; Verviers, Belgium, 1973), pp. 109–115.

44. P. J. B. Esparron, *Essai sur les âges de l'homme* (Paris, 1803), pp. 114–126.

Esparron's book is most noteworthy for its analysis of the nervous system, and it is exactly in that area that the geriatric physicians of the first half of the nineteenth century made their most important contributions. P. J. G. Cabanis's study of the nervous system enabled him to write a chapter on the influence of age on ideas.[45] Philippe Pinel, best known for his unshackling of the insane, provided a more specialized study on the influence of senility upon acute diseases.[46] For both, the systematic approach to the decline of bodily processes provided a basis for the scientific study of mental processes in the aged. Previously, doctors had discussed bodily functions when addressing physical questions and philosophical themes when addressing the psyche. Cabanis and Pinel were able to make both mind and body the subject of clinical medicine.

Cabanis began where the sensualist philosophers had begun, with sensation. The individual, he said, takes cognizance of the outside world through the movement of sensations from the circumference to the center, and takes action by the subsequent reaction from center to circumference. It all happens because "the nerves are the organs of sensibility."[47] Cabanis likened the workings of the nervous system to the movement of fluids in a canal. Movement within the nerve canals depends upon age, sex, temperament, disease, diet, and climate. The "mind," therefore, undergoes constant mutation.

The physiological changes described by Cabanis sound familiar. Vessels begin to close up. Perceptions are habituated. Life slows and becomes more rhythmical. After the climacteric, there are no further crises. Circulation slows as the arteries harden. Humours move to the extremities, causing gout and rheumatism. As new impressions stop sticking, the individual reverts to old ones that are still vivid and impossible to forget; thus, old age is psychologically like another childhood. But even though his physiological story was the same, Cabanis discussed it in greater detail than had his predecessors, tracing movement along the nerve pathways as it slows and weakens. The distance that a sensation must travel becomes too great for the aged person: "When they [sensations] have reached the point of no longer being able to be

45. P. J. G. Cabanis, *Rapports du physique et du moral de l'homme,* 2d ed. (Paris, 1805).

46. Philippe Pinel, *Considérations sur la constitution sénile et sur son influence dans les maladies aiguës* (1812), in *Mémoires et observations: Archives générales de médecine,* 1, no. 2 (1823).

47. Cabanis, *Rapports,* p. 100.

transmitted from the circumference to the center and from the center to the circumference, the cause of life itself, sensibility, cannot reproduce or maintain itself; the individual no longer exists."[48]

Whereas Cabanis assigned the influence on mental capacity of such factors as age and disease to the operation of the nervous system, Pinel discovered more complex interactions between the phenomena that Cabanis had identified simply as factors. Pinel considered the influence of age upon disease in a paper written in 1812. In his rounds at the Salpêtrière he had noted several complex cases involving disease and age: a seemingly healthy patient who died suddenly, or a very weak one who recovered inexplicably. Physical constitution—dependent (among other factors) upon age—holds some surprises for the clinician, and treatment, he believed, might have to be modified accordingly.

Pinel's paper is less important for its conclusions than for its insistence on further study in the clinic. In publishing it, Pinel's son observed, "It is only in the hospitals devoted to the aged, it is only in this vast theater that one can achieve positive results."[49] In seeming response to the suggestions of father and son, the doctors who worked at the Salpêtrière advanced the medical study of aging to a point that is recognizable by twentieth-century doctors as modern geriatrics.[50]

The hospital did become the site for medical progress in France in the nineteenth century, but that suggests a certain isolation of the aged and their doctors from the mass of the population. As Peter Stearns has observed, the hospital made for progress in science but not in treatment, as most aged Frenchmen did not go to doctors before the twentieth century.[51] It is curious that the hospital system should have been set up because of general interest in old age only to remove the aged from the public eye.

On some issues the late eighteenth-century scientific and medical consideration of aging was in basic agreement with earlier religious and philosophical literature. For the scientist, however, it was the decline of the senses or the deterioration of animal life that forced the aged individual into isolation; retreat or retirement was necessitated by physiology. The similar process of separation from the world described by

48. Ibid., p. 259.

49. Pinel, *Considérations*, pp. 11–12.

50. Guido Geller, *Die Geriatrie an der Salpêtrière von Pinel bis Charcot* (Zurich, 1965); Erwin H. Ackerknecht, *Medicine at the Paris Hospital, 1794–1848* (Baltimore, Md., 1967).

51. Stearns, *Old Age in European Society,* p. 80.

theologians and philosophers required a certain conscious effort. To the religious mind, the decrepit body was a reminder to focus one's attention upon the ageless soul. To the philosophical mind, the weakening of the body was an inconvenience, the maturing of the mind a source of strength and a resource for the living. But either religious retreat or philosophical retirement required a conscious decision on the part of the aged individual. For medical thinkers, conscious decisions became less relevant; they did not separate the aged psyche from the body but treated it as a problem of senescence. Physiology separated the aged individual from the world. It remained for the social scientific literature that emerged in the second half of the eighteenth century to confront that problem. Before addressing that literature, we must do some social history.

6 The Social Context: The Aged in the Rural Family

The Enlightenment, conceived broadly, encouraged the evolution of ideas; in a sense, it *was* that evolution. But ideas do not exist in a vacuum. The discourse on old age whose cultural representations we have examined existed in conjunction with similar discourses about youth, gender, marriage, and death.[1] Culture as a system of meanings bears some relationship to the social world, and a look at society will suggest social historical explanations to complement the cultural ones already explored.

Social historians investigating aging and the aged have used various approaches and a wide range of sources.[2] Here we look more closely at a variety of local sites—rural and urban, north and south—using methods developed in family and local history, the history of charity and welfare, and other specialties to provide a concrete sense of the consequences of demographic and social stresses.

Approximately 85 percent of the French population in the eighteenth century lived outside the cities.[3] There the past "was visible in the shape

1. Jean-Claude Perrot has argued that one must consider the *ensemble* of such topics: "La vieillesse en question," in *Annales de démographie historique 1985* (1986), 145–154.

2. See, e.g., the articles in *Ageing and Society,* 4, no. 4 (1984), and *Annales de démographie historique 1985: Vieillir autrefois* (1986); see also the review articles of Christoph Conrad: "Altwerden und Altsein in historischer Perspektive: Zur neueren Literatur," in *Zeitschrift für Sozialisationsforschung und Erziehungssoziologie,* 2 (1982), 73–90, and "Geschichte des Alterns: Lebensverhältnisse und sozialpolitische Regulierung," ibid., 4 (1984), 143–156; and Louis Roussel and Alain Girard, "Régimes démographiques et âges de la vie," in INED, *Les âges de la vie,* vol. 1, pp. 15–23.

3. Emmanuel Le Roy Ladurie's chapter in Duby and Wallon, eds., *Histoire de la France rurale,* vol. 2 (Paris, 1975), considers the demography of rural life in the period along with a wide range of other aspects of social history.

of white hairs, of ancestry, of physical resemblances, and of inherited deformities and diseases."[4] Village life—family and communal existence—gave individual life its significance, and in the best of circumstances the community acted as a defense against rapid deprivation.

Work often lasted until death, but a gradual disengagement could be arranged. In parts of rural France, when younger workers went on annual treks along traditional routes of transhumance, some of their elders might stay behind and find themselves in positions of continued authority and even some leisure.[5] Others were less fortunate; in villages in the center of France, when younger men migrated to Provence, the aged did the fall planting and, in winter, journeyed to Lyon and Clermont to beg. Elsewhere, the aged too continued to migrate with the seasons, sometimes trying one last time to earn enough for a settled retirement.[6]

Retirement, when it could be afforded at all, required negotiation. Rather than a bureaucratic arrangement between an individual of a prescribed age and an institution, it was a notarized act between, say, a retiring father and his children, who granted his pension. It did not depend solely upon age but upon the person's relations with his or her successors.[7]

Gerontologists have called the forced inactivity of the aged a social death that precedes biological death. If today's social death is characterized by a contradiction between a slower biological aging and a more sudden retirement decided by employer or state rather than family, the older form of withdrawal was characterized by a network of concerns, sometimes adverse, sometimes supportive. The timing of retirement involved the interests of a household: the marriage of children and the transmission of property.[8] In order to understand the process throughout the country, we must look to inheritance law and practice.

As one anonymous Parisian informed the National Assembly in Janu-

4. Richard Cobb, *Paris and Its Provinces, 1792–1802* (London, 1975), p. 30.

5. Emmanuel Le Roy Ladurie, *Les paysans de Languedoc* (Paris, 1966).

6. Hufton, *The Poor of Eighteenth-Century France*, pp. 85, 90.

7. Louis Roussel, *La famille après le mariage des enfants* (Paris, 1976), p. 73; Jean Fourastié, "De la vie traditionnelle à la vie 'tertiaire': Recherches sur le calendrier démographique de l'homme moyen," *Population*, 14, no. 3 (1959); Le Bras, "Parents, grands-parents, *bisaïeux*."

8. On social death, see Anne-Marie Guillemard, *La retraite: Une mort sociale* (Paris, 1972); on old age and the household, Peter Laslett, "The History of Aging and the Aged," in *Family Life and Illicit Love in Earlier Generations* (Cambridge, 1977), and Wall et al., *Family Forms*.

ary of 1791, the old laws of inheritance were equivocal, a mixture of "good and bad." In the ancien régime, children were promised their share of the patrimony in their marriage contracts but forbidden to claim it until their parents' death. The system worked when the parents, after having labored to raise and educate their children, provided them with enough to get started but retained enough to protect themselves in old age. Self-interest had to be exercised by the parents, "because it is only too well-known that the ingratitude of children is so great that if they do not reserve by legal act this food-ration, hardly one of twelve living children will be found to assist them in their distress." Yet parents might err on the side of their own security, leaving their children "reduced to misery." Moreover, if no inventory were taken when the first parent died, the surviving parent might spend the patrimony irresponsibly and deny the children their due.[9]

Thus, a proper balance had to be sought. In the changing demographic circumstances of the eighteenth century, the interests of aged parents and adult children might clash, and the balance between generations might be upset. The impact of demographic stress was mitigated by legal, customary, and familial factors, but results differed by region.

Historians have divided rural France roughly into northern and southern halves in terms of inheritance law,[10] paternal authority, and household structure. Lines between generations were most sharply drawn in the Midi, where Roman law had established patriarchal authority as absolute. The father ruled until death and made provisions for the future—a sort of tyranny of the retired and dead over the living. Parental authority governed marital plans, and parents could in principle even order a child put to death; in practice, however, parental despotism was expressed less lethally.[11] Over the centuries southern

9. "Pétition respectueuse d'un Citoien de Paris à l'Assemblée Nationale: Renvoyé au Comité de Mendicité," January 20, 1791, A.N. F15 2875.

10. Inheritance law was only one aspect of the inheritance system. It has become common to speak of three systems in ancien régime France. See the essays in Jack Goody et al., eds., *Family and Inheritance: Rural Society in Western Europe, 1200–1800* (Cambridge, 1976); and Lutz K. Berkner and Franklin F. Mendels, "Inheritance Systems, Family Structures, and Demographic Patterns in Western Europe, 1700–1900," in Charles Tilly, ed., *Historical Studies of Changing Fertility* (Princeton, N.J., 1978).

11. W. W. Buckland, *A Text-book of Roman Law from Augustus to Justinian* (Cambridge, 1975), p. 101. The elder Mirabeau's use of the *lettre de cachet*, ordering the immediate imprisonment of his son, is perhaps the most famous example of parental absolutism. While in prison at Vincennes the younger Mirabeau wrote his book against despotism, remarking upon the relationship between the political version and the house-

French law had undergone some evolution as various forces fought for jurisidiction—seigniory, Church, and competing monarchies—but despite Parisian hegemony from the sixteenth century on, southern French territory was ruled by Roman law throughout the ancien régime.

The South also went its own way in terms of family type and household structure. Although the Gallic familial communities of ancient and medieval times had disappeared well before the eighteenth century, a variety of remnants could be found. Households were extended vertically in Provence and horizontally in the *frérèches* (adult brothers and their families coresiding) of the sparsely populated Pyrenees, and the aged were said to have ruled.[12] Alain Collomp has proposed a line running from Nantes to Geneva south of which existed a complex family structure. Michel Vovelle has described a general model for the southern family. Clauses in marriage contracts indicate a high rate of coresidence of parents and married children and, hence, the presence of a stem-family system (in which continuity of residence in the household is maintained from generation to generation).[13]

To the north, various customary laws obtained simultaneously. In the western portion, parents had no freedom to favor one child—inheritance was to be egalitarian—while parts of the extreme north practiced a *préciput* system: that is, advantaging one heir above the others (somewhat like the Midi in encouraging inequality). The Paris-Orléans region compromised: there the children previously advantaged at marriage could opt to exchange their portions for new equal shares upon the death of parents. In general, northern elders had less freedom to run

---

hold variety: Honoré-Gabriel Riqueti, comte de Mirabeau, *Essai sur le despotisme* (Paris, 1821), pp. 32–38, 320, and *Des lettres de cachet et des prisons d'état* (Hamburg, 1782).

12. Charles de Ribbe, *Les familles et la société en France avant la révolution d'après des documents originaux* (Paris, 1873); Jean Gaudemet, *Les communautés familiales* (Paris, 1963), p. 181; Peter Laslett, *Household and Family in Past Time* (Cambridge, 1972).

13. Alain Collomp, "Alliance et filiation en Haute Provence au XVIIIe siècle," *Annales: E.S.C.*, 32 (1977), 445–477, and "Ménage et famille: Etudes comparatives sur la dimension et la structure du groupe domestique," *Annales: E.S.C.*, 29 (1974), 777–786; Michel Vovelle, "Y a-t-il un modèle de la famille méridionale?" in *De la cave au grenier* (Quebec, 1980), pp. 39–54. See also Jean-Claude Peyronnet, "Famille élargie ou famille nucléaire? L'exemple du Limousin au début du XIXe siècle," *Revue d'Histoire Moderne et Contemporaine*, 22 (1975), 568–582; E.-G. Léonard, *Mon village sous Louis XV d'après Les mémoires d'un paysan* (Paris, 1941), pp. 137–143; Patrice L.-R. Higonnet, *Pont-de-Montvert: Social Structure and Politics in a French Village, 1700–1914* (Cambridge, Mass., 1971), pp. 21–22, 49.

household affairs from the grave than did their southern counterparts,[14] and their households on earth were smaller. Still, there were ways, even in regions that demanded partibility, of keeping holdings together.[15]

One is tempted to view the South, the land of Roman law before the French Revolution, as a kind of paradise for aged parents. It is not surprising that a recent book on the Provençal family is called *La maison du père*.[16] But as Yves Castan pointed out in his study of eighteenth-century Languedoc, it was necessary for parents to lure children into filial piety, to keep up expectations without giving up power; otherwise, they risked neglect. The aged kept working in order to maintain the facade of authority and independence. When that was no longer possible, disrespect could follow and could lead to separation, violence, even murder. But the taint left on the honor of the family, the "race," would make perpetrators do their best to cover such things up. Castan has found that poisoning was a convenient way of disposing of aged parents; the consumption of rat-poison-tainted food, prepared in kitchen utensils, was easily made to look accidental.[17]

In a society where social continuity was based upon inheritance, a complicated relationship between affection and exploitation lay at the heart of popular attitudes toward family life.[18] How the patrimony was transmitted had important consequences for relations within the family. Once again the distinction between Roman and customary law was key. In regions of Roman law, the patriarch had complete freedom to write his own testament. Under customary law, inheritance practices were supposed to be clearly understood; there was no need for a testament. In one place, one son inherited; in another, all did. In the Pyrenees the

14. Jean Yver, *Egalité entre héritiers et exclusion des enfants dotés: Essai de géographie coutumière* (Paris, 1966). See Emmanuel Le Roy Ladurie's discussion of Yver's work, "Family Structures and Inheritance Customs in Sixteenth-Century France," in Goody et al., *Family and Inheritance*, pp. 37–70.

15. Ralph E. Giesey, "Rules of Inheritance and Strategies of Mobility in Prerevolutionary France," *American Historical Review*, 82 (1977), 271–289.

16. Alain Collomp, *La maison du père: Famille et village en Haute-Provence aux XVIIe et XVIIIe siècles* (Paris, 1983).

17. Yves Castan, *Honnêteté et relations sociales en Languedoc, 1715–1780* (Paris, 1974), p. 231.

18. Hans Medick and David Warren Sabean, "Interest and Emotion in Family and Kinship Studies: A Critique of Social History and Anthropology," in Medick and Sabean, eds., *Interest and Emotion: Essays on the Study of Family and Kinship* (Cambridge, 1984). They make a strong theoretical case for treating interest and emotion together. This poses practical difficulties that most historians working on the family have not yet resolved.

oldest child of either sex inherited. In parts of Normandy, Brittany, and Anjou all children were equal heirs. Parents who had no power to deny a child his or her share in the inheritance could find themselves in a very weak position. Notarized acts of pre-mortem transmission of property and inventories after death suggest that aged Normans were often deprived of their living (by age) and their food and furniture (by children), making old age a time of absolute deprivation.[19]

A good place to explore old age in the rural family is Provence. A land of Roman law, it placed property relations in the hands of the father and his chosen successor.[20] Moreover, the high rate of coresidence of parents and married children provides a precise physical setting for the succession of generations. Much of this chapter is derived from a study of the life of parents after the marriage of their children in the Provençal village of Eguilles in the eighteenth century. A sample population of parents alive at the signing of their children's marriage contracts was traced through the notarial archives until the parents' deaths were announced in the parish register.[21]

The farming *bourg* of Eguilles, perched on a hill surrounded by fields producing grain, grapes, and olives, numbered 2,333 inhabitants in 1765.[22] Despite its proximity to Aix-en-Provence (10 kilometers), where the Boyer d'Eguilles family owned an *hôtel* (now a museum of natural history), the village was socially and economically isolated.[23]

19. Michel de Bouard, *Histoire de la Normandie* (Toulouse, 1970), pp. 360–361.

20. Edouard Baratier, *Histoire de la Provence* (Toulouse, 1969); Roger Aubenas, *Le testament en Provence dans l'ancien droit* (Aix-en-Provence, 1927).

21. The original village study was published as David G. Troyansky, "Old Age in the Rural Family of Enlightened Provence," in Stearns, *Old Age in Preindustrial Society* (New York, 1982), pp. 209–231. Notarial archives for Eguilles, A.D. Aix, 1741–73, Jean-Joseph Carle, 301 E 486–489; cf. 1741–48, Michel-Joseph Séguin, 301 E 494. Parish register: A.M. Eguilles. (Dates are given in the text hereafter.)

22. On the agricultural *bourg,* see Maurice Agulhon, "La notion de village en Basse-Provence vers la fin de l'Ancien Régime," *Actes du 90e congrès national des sociétés savantes, Nice, 1965,* vol. 1 (Paris, 1966), pp. 277–301; for the census, Edouard Baratier, *La démographie provençale du 13e au 16e siècle avec chiffres de comparaison pour le 18e siècle* (Paris, 1961).

23. The Marquis d'Eguilles retired to his château after a conflict in 1763 with the Parlement de Provence, of which he had been *président à mortier:* his brother, the Marquis d'Argens, retired to the village after having served as chamberlain to the king of Prussia and having written epistolary novels of some renown. See Paul Cottin, *Marquis d'Eguilles, un protégé de Bachaumont: Correspondance inédite du Marquis d'Eguilles 1745–1748* (Paris, 1887). Among the works of the Marquis d'Argens, see *Lettres juives* (The Hague, 1736); *Lettres chinoises* (The Hague, 1739–40); and *Lettres cabalistiques* (The Hague, 1741).

Eguiléen married *Eguiléenne* and stayed put, transmitting land or profession from generation to generation. Even the plague that devastated Marseille in 1720 left Eguilles untouched.[24] The only "outside" influence that seems to have affected it was the dechristianization that swept Provence in the eighteenth century. Eguilles too experienced a decline in piety. Inheritance and property arrangements stand out in the secularized testaments, while requests for masses disappear. Concern for earthly reality overrode questions of the soul.[25]

At the beginning of the eighteenth century virtually every testament notarized in Eguilles had opened with the remark that death comes without warning to young and old alike. By the 1740s that sentiment appeared in only 13 percent of the total; then it disappeared completely.[26] Death was still certain, but its hour was becoming more predictable. People of Eguilles had realized that surviving one's childhood enormously improved one's chances of reaching old age. Anyone who lived to acquire property and exercise authority had a good chance of holding on for a long time.

According to Charles de Ribbe, nineteenth-century historian of the family, authority bred respect, and respect guaranteed support in old age. After reading family registers (*livres de raison*) kept by noble and bourgeois fathers, he delightedly reported that chapters were often entitled "memoirs of the births of children that it has pleased God to give to my son"—evidence that the grandfather ran the house.[27] The *livre de raison* is not a likely place to find records of family conflict. It only confirms the legal status of the head of the Provençal family, the *chef de famille*.

In theory a widow could inherit her late husband's role, and the notarial archives include examples of widows wielding considerable power over their children. But such phenomena were exceptions in male-dominated Provence. Aged fathers, and a few mothers, signed contracts along with their adult children. Children under their parents' authority had to be emancipated by notarial act in order to sign for

24. Brigitte Liard, "Les mentalités collectives et les comportements devant la mort d'après les clauses des testaments dans le pays d'Aix-Eguilles 1680–1789," *Mémoire de maîtrise* (Marseille, 1972–73).

25. Vovelle, *Piété baroque.*

26. Ibid., cf. Pierre Chaunu, *La mort à Paris: XVIe, XVIIe, XVIIIe siècles* (Paris, 1978); Bernard Vogler, *Trois mémoires sur les testaments à Strasbourg au 18e siècle* (Strasbourg, 1978).

27. Ribbe, *Les familles,* p. 53; and Charles de Ribbe, *Le livre de famille* (Tours, 1879).

themselves. This relinquishment of parental authority, though relatively uncommon and normally involving sons who left the village, is indicative of power relations; it occurred in the presence of notables and amid considerable feudal pomp.[28] As parental longevity increased, however, emancipation even of adult children staying home became more common.

On November 16, 1745, Jean Reynier emancipated two younger sons, his eldest having died and left four daughters and a son behind. Before the ceremony took place the father convinced the notable witnesses that he had not been "seduced" into the act. The sons knelt before their father, their hands in his; then the father bade them rise, symbolizing their freedom from his authority. In the same document Jean Reynier gave them his house, stable, attic, and cellar along with specified furniture and furnishings, including a bed each and linen. But the father retained the use of a furnished apartment of his choice in the house and the right to storage of his personal effects and goods for the rest of his life.

The role of the community in protecting authority within the family indicates that public status and power were at stake. Indeed, the head of the family had the right to exercise his power outside the household in the municipal council, whose records permit a view of village authority.

An analysis of attendance on annual election days (the council's best attended meetings) for the years 1716–88 yields the names of 203 different persons, of whom only sixty-nine showed up more than four times.[29] Every family head had the right to vote (one of the reasons that nostalgic nineteenth-century historians wrote of a patriarchal village democracy in the ancien régime), but clearly not everyone bothered. The council was not representative of the village household structure; those who attended regularly were the local notables, the large landowners and the surgeons.[30] Though it was in a sense patriarchal, it was not gerontocratic. Of the sixty-nine persons who attended more than four times, the dates of death of forty-one have been recovered; of these only seven participated in an election within a year of their death, and only one elected official actually died in office. An average period of over

28. For the decline in the use of the old formulas, see Raymond Collier, *La vie en Haute-Provence de 1600 à 1850* (Digne, 1973), pp. 129–130; for his remarks on the emancipation, I thank Gérard Delille.

29. A. M. Eguilles, *Délibérations municipales.*

30. On the oligarchical council, see Jean-Pierre Gutton, *La sociabilité villageoise dans l'ancienne France* (Paris, 1979).

seven years passed between last ballot cast and death. There was no institutional framework for retirement; a man just stopped attending and was succeeded by a son or nephew. Thus, local affairs were governed by a council of middle-aged oligarchs, not a council of elders.[31] Class took precedence over age, but even among the local governing elite extreme age brought on a form of public inactivity.

There remained for elderly councilors, however, the possibility of movement to another post upon retirement. In Provence it was said that from the council one moved to the hospital—"Après lou capeiroun, l'Espitau"—either as administrator or as patient. L'Hôpital Notre Dame de la Miséricorde was founded in 1743 by Pierre Giraud, *bourgeois d'Eguilles,* who ordered that the parish priest, current councilors, and specially elected rectors administer it. It has been suggested by one historian of Provence that the role of rector was filled by an aged councilor. But such was not the case in eighteenth-century Eguilles; indeed, old age was the reason for which one rector was relieved of his post.[32]

If the aged did not run the hospital, one might find them as occupants. But the extant records of patients point mainly to orphan girls. Moreover, while a few people may have gone to the hospital to die, those who did not die very shortly after admittance were sent home.[33] The nearest large hospital was the Hôpital Saint-Jacques in Aix, where the aged might find asylum along with orphans, incurables, and beggars.[34]

Most hospital beds, of course, were situated in cities, but even there (see Chapter 7) their number failed to satisfy demand.[35] Small rural hospitals muddled along on the charity of private benefactors, their budgets often as strained as those in the city. In Allanche in the Auvergne, for example, funds were insufficient to keep the Hôtel-Dieu, founded in 1746, going at its full capacity of four inmates. In the 1780s it consisted of "a very bad house where several paupers took refuge in their state of old age, infirmity, or disease." The *seigneur* provided funds

31. But they were probably older than their medieval ancestors; see Marc Bloch, *Feudal Society* (Chicago, 1961), p. 73.

32. Masson, *Les Bouches-du-Rhône,* vol. 3, p. 620; A.M. Eguilles, *Registre des délibérations de l'hôpital,* January 14, 1770.

33. *Registre des délibérations de l'hôpital,* May 13, 1770. An inventory of May 23, 1784, mentions four beds for men and six for women.

34. Nicole Sabatier, "L'hôpital Saint-Jacques d'Aix-en-Provence (1519–1789)" (doctoral diss., Université d'Aix-Marseille, 1964).

35. Muriel Jeorger, "La structure hospitalière de la France sous l'Ancien Régime," *Annales: E.S.C.,* 32 (1977).

for renovations in 1786, but only two years later the administrators appealed to the state for aid.[36]

Elsewhere, private charity was more effective. The Prince de Porrentry paid fifty-seven pensions in the Swiss territory in the Jura mountains that was incorporated into Revolutionary France as the Département du Mont-Terrible. The recipients are known because their pensions were denied during the Revolution:

> Jean Baptiste Decker, former secretary of waters and forest, currently without a position, age 80, deaf and infirm, stripped of all goods, burdened with a wife and a very old sister-in-law, pensioned for no longer being able to fulfill his charge, as much because of his old age as his deafness.
>
> The widow Straub, her husband was *payeur de la cour;* she has obtained a pension, age 67, deaf, infirm, stripped of all goods and burdened with two daughters.
>
> Jacob Gurtlev the elder, former groom, now without occupation, age 70, infirm and without any means, having an old wife and a child to support, pensioned because he was unable to perform his service.
>
> Joseph Maritz, former valet, now unemployed, age 62, afflicted with a hernia, deprived of possessions, charged with an old wife and several children, pensioned because of his infirmities.[37]

For a time there was an old age home in Eguilles, founded by the Marquis d'Eguilles and mentioned in his testament (February 20, 1767); he specified that the poor old men and women in the Hospice Sainte-Catherine at the time of his death should always be provided with the same lodging, clothing, food, and care. In naming his son as heir, he asked that care for the aged poor continue.

Such assistance was an old form of charity that was on the wane. Not generalized welfare, it was clearly not to be counted upon by all the aged of Eguilles.[38] Moreover, medical care, despite the developments discussed in Chapter 5, was not to be trusted either. The rectors of Notre Dame de la Miséricorde reported in their register (October 13, 1771) that people who fell ill avoided the hospital "under the pretext that they had no confidence in the surgeon." One can be sure that it was more

36. A.N. F[15] 231.

37. A.N. D XXVII 1.

38. On the transition from *charité* to *bienfaisance,* see Cissie C. Fairchilds, *Poverty and Charity in Aix-en-Provence, 1640–1789* (Baltimore, Md., 1976); Norberg, *Rich and Poor in Grenoble;* and Colin Jones, *Charity and Bienfaisance: The Treatment of the Poor in the Montpellier Region, 1740–1815* (Cambridge, 1982).

than a pretext, but the language of the administration was charitable toward its staff. And if patients expressed reservations about the surgeon, surgeons in turn expressed reservations about the patients: on May 27, 1776, it was announced that no surgeon wanted to visit them. Consequently, the officers decided to choose for the hospital "Sr. Aubert . . . since he is the oldest surgeon of the place and he offers to perform this service with all the zeal and all the charity of which he is capable." If not trusted by everyone, at least the oldest surgeon in town was respected by his colleagues on the council.

It is often said that in preliterate societies such faith in the wisdom, or at least the memory, of the aged in general—whether doctors or other venerable sages—is of great importance. In semiliterate Eguilles a long memory played a role in court testimony involving customary boundaries and rights of passage through certain fields.[39] Mathieu and Louis Joye claimed in a suit against Mathieu Artaud in 1744 that "since time immemorial man and beast had passed in the land and meadow concerned."[40] They gathered expert witnesses whose ages (in order of testimony) were 85, 82, 80, 73, 73, 85, 57, 60, 58, 48, 46, 43, 41, 38, and 43. Pierre Giraud, "townsman aged about 85 years," remembered practices of the past seventy years, but his competence did not derive solely from age: he was the same influential man who had founded the hospital the previous year. But even if his words constituted the wisdom of the aged, they were only oral testimony. In a village where a clerk took notes at council meetings, where orders from either the monarchy or the Parlement de Provence came in printed form, where the *curé* was dutiful in recording baptisms, marriages, and burials, and where contracts and testaments were carefully written by notaries, little room remained for illiterate memory.

Records of public life yield only glimpses of the aged. The elderly retired from office; they did not go to the hospital in great numbers; only a few went to the *hospice* when granted charity by the *seigneur;* they were called upon only occasionally to remember the past. One must seek them out where most of them remained: in the household.

A census of 1765 counted 2,333 inhabitants of Eguilles living in 397 households. How they were actually distributed is unknown, as no detailed census exists from before 1810. Nevertheless, the 1810 census

39. As to literacy, Eguilles fits the pattern of the region on the eve of the Revolution: 30 percent for men, 10 percent for women. See Liard, "Les mentalités collectives," p. 27.
40. A.D. Aix, VI B 1511, March 31, 1744.

provides an approximation of the eighteenth-century household structure.[41] The ages of all but one (a servant) of the 2,566 residents are given (see Table 6), showing a young population, almost half of it twenty-five years of age or less. Yet it included a high number of survivors for its day: 10.9 percent were sixty and over (see the age pyramid in Figure 2), and the senior group evidently played a significant role in the village economy. Of the 319 persons whose titles and professions are indicated in the census, 68 were at least sixty years old: 15 of 49 large landholders, 27 of 101 small farmers, two of six masons, two of three carders, one of two blacksmiths, one of two priests, and both cloth weavers, plus the builder, lawyer, mayor, rural policeman, tax collector, and plasterer. Whether they were all still actively pursuing their careers in 1810 is unknown; however, they were all identified by profession, whereas their sons were generally not. Such a barrier to professional advancement of the young is more eloquent than the turnover of seats on the ill-attended municipal council.

Conspicuous sexagenarian participation in the work force indicates activity in old age but equally implies a fear of dependence. It was risky to test the respect owed by a generation coming to power. Peasant proverbs certainly made that point: "One father can support one hundred children, but a hundred children wouldn't know how to support one father" was common wisdom in Provence and elsewhere in the Mediterranean world.[42] Central European peasants quoted similar warnings, "To hand over is no longer to live"; "To sit on the children's bench is hard for the old"; "Do not take your clothes off before you go to sleep."[43] But the barrier to the young that protected the aged took a psychological toll, for it undoubtedly tended to estrange the generations.

That barrier was characteristic of the stem-family system.[44] The census lists individuals by block (*isle*), grouped by lines of descent.

<hr>

41. For the 1765 census, Baratier, *La démographie;* for the 1810 census, manuscript in A.M.

42. Michel Vovelle, ed., *Proverbes et dictons provençaux* (Marseille, 1981), pp. 9, 34.

43. Michael Mitterauer and Reinhard Sieder, *The European Family: Patriarchy to Partnership from the Middle Ages to the Present* (Chicago, 1982), p. 167. See also Richard Wall's introduction and David Gaunt, "The Property and Kin Relationships of Retired Farmers in Northern and Central Europe," in Wall et al., *Family Forms.*

44. See Lutz K. Berkner, "The Stem Family," and "Inheritance, Land Tenure, and Peasant Family Structure: A German Regional Comparison," in Jack Goody et al., *Family and Inheritance,* pp. 71–95.

TABLE 6
Eguilles census, by age and sex, 1810

Age	Male	%	Female	%
0–25	629	48.7	639	50.2
26–59	524	40.6	493	38.7
60–91	138	10.7	142	11.1
Total	1,291	100.0	1,274	100.0

Except for the 216 residents of the hamlet of Les Figons (106 of whom were named Alexis), the inhabitants can be grouped in Laslett-type households that necessarily only approximate the actual situation.[45] The number of individuals (type 1) and nonfamilial groups (type 2) is small (see Table 7). Because the census is divided by block rather than house or apartment, the count of nuclear family households (type 3) is probably a maximum and those of the extended and multiple family households (types 4 and 5) minimums (though the total number of all types is undoubtedly high). Though most households were nuclear, a significant 20 percent involved three generations in 1810, a common experience in the developmental cycle of the household.

The consequences of a coresidence clause in a marriage contract can be seen in the situation of the elderly (Table 8). Including those under age sixty, Eguilles had 45 or 46 live-in grandfathers and 60 to 63 live-in grandmothers in 1810. When aunts and uncles and relations outside the household are considered, it becomes clear that the aged were a familiar sight. And widows were a more familiar sight than widowers; more men than women coped with aging by remarrying.[46]

The historical study of the household has often tended to emphasize the continuity of holdings, treating individuals as impediments to the smooth flow of succession. But the very detours that property took obligate the historian of old age to study individuals. The dynamics of the household derived not only from what parents parted with but also from what they retained or demanded. In the household economy, aging

45. For Laslett types, see Laslett, *Household and Family.*
46. On widowhood, see Alain Bideau, "A Demographic and Social Analysis of Widowhood and Remarriage: The Example of the Castellany of Thoissey-en-Dombes, 1670–1840," *Journal of Family History,* 5 (1980), 28–43; and Barbara B. Diefendorf, "Widowhood and Remarriage in Sixteenth-Century Paris," *Journal of Family History,* 7 (1982), 379–395. On remarriage, see Jacques Dupâquier et al., eds., *Marriage and Remarriage in Populations of the Past* (London, 1981).

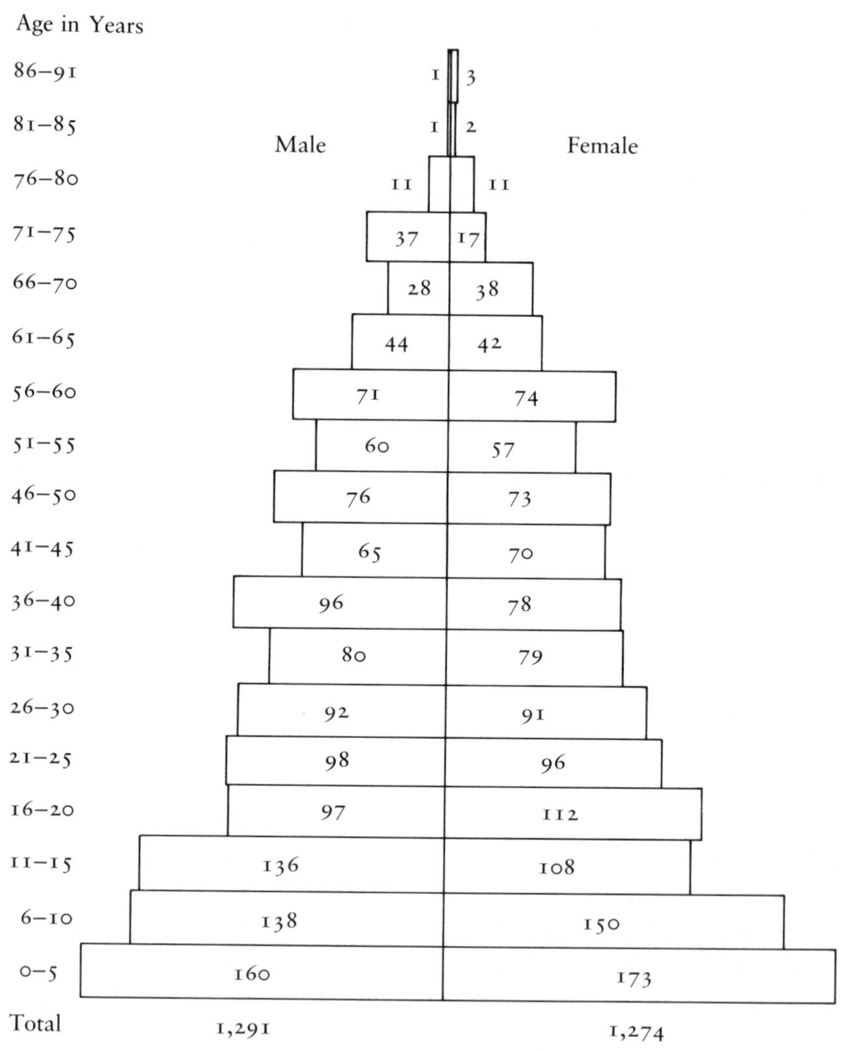

FIGURE 2. Age and sex of the population of Eguilles, 1810

TABLE 7
Household types in Eguilles, 1810

Type	Possible households	Average	%
1	35–68	52	9.4
2	9–19	14	2.5
3	348–397	373	67.7
4	54–74	64	11.6
5	37–58	48	8.7
Total		551	99.9

can be witnessed in various notarized acts—marriage contracts, gifts, testaments—which spelled out responsibilities of individual household members.

Though "old" is not synonymous with "retired," the two states are clearly related. In the village setting, withdrawal from control of the patrimony indicated retreat from the world of adult activity and power. Folkloric sources suggest that it was foolish to pass on property before death, but the family did have to consider its long-term interests. It would have been equally foolish to hold onto power one was incapable of maintaining physically or to withhold authority from adult children eager for their due. Individuals had their demands, but so did household units, and the prospect of a classically restful retirement coupled with a growing belief in the generosity of the family probably induced parents

TABLE 8
Marital status of Eguilles residents aged 60+, 1810

Marital status	Household situation	Male	Female
Never married	living alone	9	5
	with others	7	7
Subtotal		16	12
Married	with spouse	23	20
	with unmarried children	46	25
	with married children	26	24
Subtotal		95	69
Widowed	living alone	1	12
	with unmarried children	5	19
	with married children	19	27
	with others	2	3
Subtotal		27	61
Total		138	142

to overlook some of the evidence of selfishness among their adult children.

The marriage of children normally provided the first opportunity for fathers and mothers to look to their own old age. The marriage contract foreshadowed the future course of the household, making gifts and promising subsequent ones in return for support in retirement. Between 1741 and 1770, 491 marriages were registered in the parish of Eguilles. Not every marriage recorded involved a notarized contract, but most of them did, and the records of the town's two notaries indicate little difference between them. The figures that follow are derived from one, who registered 223 marriages—almost half.[47] The 223 contracts mentioned 522 parents, an average of 2.3 parents per contract; only eleven contracts pertained to marriages where all four parents were dead. As each household was created, it had to coexist with the elders. Sometimes tensions developed—the more readily perhaps when two or more couples resided together, and half of the contracts stipulated coresidence of parents and married children.

Coresidence, of course, did not imply a sudden break in the living situation for all. Since 90 percent of the marriage contracts that stipulated coresidence did so for the husband's parents (see Table 9), the bride's family would have been prepared for the loss of a member and still maintained contact with her; she retained her maiden name in all official dealings. Nor did the contract join two generations that had been living apart; rather, it extended the life of one household beyond a date at which its unity had been threatened. It also introduced a new member, signifying possible shifts in alliance.[48]

The new alliance joined two families of equal status, the wife bringing the dowry and the husband the property. But in the day-to-day fact of coresidence, the husband's family took precedence. Literary sources may suggest that either son or daughter could be the "consolation of old age," and some exceptional daughters did play that role in Eguilles. But in rural Provence, sons served as guarantors of support in old age. Of 111 cases of coresidence, 100, or 90 percent, of families lived with the husband's parents (36 with his father, 19 with his mother, 45 with both); only 11 families (10 percent) lived with the wife's parents (1 with her father, 5 with her mother, 5 with both).

In cases of coresidence the groom's father received the dowry. On

47. Records of Jean-Joseph Carle; see n. 21 above.
48. On the question of lineage and marriage, see Flandrin, *Familles*.

TABLE 9

Parents and coresidence in Eguilles, 1741–70

Living parents	Number of cases	Coresiding	%	Which parents coreside
Hf[a]	8	3	37.5	3 Hf
Hm[b]	4	1	25	1 Hm
Wf[c]	6	0	0	0
Wm[d]	18	3	16.7	3 Wm
Hp[e]	5	3	60	3 Hp
Wp[f]	20	1	5	1 Wp
Hp, Wp	29	25	86	23 Hp, 2 Wp
Hf, Wf	9	4	44	4 Hf
Hf, Wm	19	12	63	11 Hf, 1 Wm
Hf, Wp	27	18	67	18 Hf
Hm, Wf	8	4	50	3 Hm, 1 Wf
Hm, Wm	10	5	50	5 Hm
Hm, Wp	22	12	55	10 Hm, 2 Wp
Hp, Wf	7	4	57	4 Hp
Hp, Wm	20	16	80	15 Hp, 1 Wm

[a]Husband's father. [b]Husband's mother. [c]Wife's father. [d]Wife's mother. [e]Both parents of husband. [f]Both parents of wife.

February 4, 1743, farm laborer Joseph Arquier accepted the dowry of his daughter-in-law Marianne Marroc and gave his son part of an orchard. He housed the married couple, promising to feed and care for them and any children they might have. Arquier literally promised to retire (*retirer*) the couple, thus expressing his control. And when the contract looked ahead to the possibility of a separation of generations, the clause of *insupport*, there was no question of a challenge to patriarchal authority. The dowry would be returned to the departing couple and the father would provide his son with land and vineyard, wheat and wine, a furnished room, clothes, and tools. But the separation clause did not loose all ties. One father would give his son 1,000 *livres*, some land, and the second floor of his house.[49] Others also provided houses.[50]

Most marriage contracts also outlined a future transmission of the patrimony. On August 10, 1761, Jean Baptiste Davin and Marguerite Pelenqui stated the conditions of their son Jean François Davin's marriage to Clère Aillaud. The father agreed to house the couple, and the mother offered a gift (*donation entre vifs*) of a house upon her own and

49. Marriage contract of Joseph Gros and Thérèze Martin, February 3, 1766.
50. Contracts of November 23, 1744, and February 19, 1753.

her husband's death; the only condition was that Jean François house his brother until he too should marry. Antoine Artaud, a maker of pails, took in his son's bride on November 10, 1755, and provided the couple with one room. Upon the parents' death the younger couple would receive two more rooms.

Normally the father promised transmission of most of the patrimony upon his death, reserving some portion for his surviving widow. The contract of Luc Roure's marriage to Catherine Goujet on September 11, 1747, included Luc's father's promise of a house upon his death on condition that Luc provide his widowed mother with a pension of wheat and wine at each harvest, a room in his house or elsewhere, and storage space in the cellar. The same sort of arrangement was often made for a father's second wife—even more urgently, as the son's notion of responsibility might be somewhat weaker for her than for his own mother.[51]

If the groom's mother was a widow, she looked after her own future, usually guided by her husband's testament. When Thomé Jaloux, shepherd of Puyricard, married Marianne Figuière on November 26, 1741, the bride brought a dowry of 350 *livres*. But the contract went into much greater detail about Jaloux's widowed mother, Jeanne Audran, who gave her son some land, a vineyard, and furniture in token of her "friendship" (*amitié*) for him. Thomé promised in return "to feed and care for her in health or sickness as his equal."

When a couple married late—ages at marriage in the ancien régime ranged widely—they looked to their own old age. If widower or widow remarried, the husband set forth his wife's pension in their marriage contract (as in one of January 7, 1770), specifying dates for an annual supply of wheat, wine, oil, and salt. "She will still have the use of the kitchen and a room, both on the ground floor of the house," ran a typical stipulation.

In cases of great longevity three and even four generations entered into negotiations. Ten of the 223 marriages mentioned the presence of at least one grandparent; two involved two grandparents. One included a great-grandmother: on May 2, 1742, Elisabeth Davin received a wedding gift of a house from her great-grandmother Marie Giraud. What made the gift doubly exceptional was that it came from the bride's side. The old woman did reserve the use of the house for herself and her daughter Magdeleine Dumas for the rest of their lives, but that was not

51. Marriage contract of Jean-Baptiste Marroc, April 23, 1758.

long: Magdeleine Dumas died in April, between the first draft of the contract and its completion, and Marie Giraud died on June 2. Meanwhile, the couple, in more traditional fashion, was to be housed by the father of the groom.

Great-grandmothers were rare; the norm was two coexisting adult generations, and even their overlap could be brief. Perhaps the most extreme literary example of the rapid succession of generations occurs in Rétif de la Bretonne's *La Vie de mon père.* Upon the death of Pierre Rétif, his son Edmond is told by his future father-in-law, "You will be my son . . . bless you both! You will be the consolation of my old age." On the morrow, they celebrated the marriage before the body of the dead Pierre.[52]

In similar fashion on April 12, 1770, a marriage contract for Marguerite Gues and her husband (a wool carder from the Dauphiné), who had married without contract three years before, was drawn up before her father's deathbed. The sequence of events was generally not quite so rapid, but whatever the period of time between the marriage of children and the death of parents, it was critical for the household. It was the time of greatest strain, for it forced the aging parents to consider stepping aside, to look ahead to retirement and death.

An average of 10.6 years passed between the marriage contract of children and the death of parents, 9.8 for those involved in coresidence (see Figure 3). During this period aged parents saw fit to ensure support in retirement by a variety of notarized acts. Shepherd Martin Cheiland, married since September 5, 1734, eventually came into control of his father's land, but not until November 15, 1754, did the father, Estienne, hand it over in an act recognizing that Martin had already been in de facto possession of it for several years. Estienne, "finding himself at an advanced age, no longer able to support himself," had Martin promise to pay him an annual pension of thirty-six *livres* in monthly payments of three *livres* as well as five *mierolles* (one *mierolle* = sixty liters) of wine at every harvest.

A notarized gift characteristically expressed gratitude for assistance and expectation that it would continue. On August 9, 1752, François Armieou presented some land to his son-in-law, stipulating that posses-

---

52. Rétif de la Bretonne, *La vie de mon père,* pp. 62–63. Gérard Bouchard (*Le village immobile,* p. 232) finds such timing commonplace in the poor, unhealthy town of Sennely-en-Sologne, where the inventory after parent's death and the adult child's marriage contract were often drawn up on the same day.

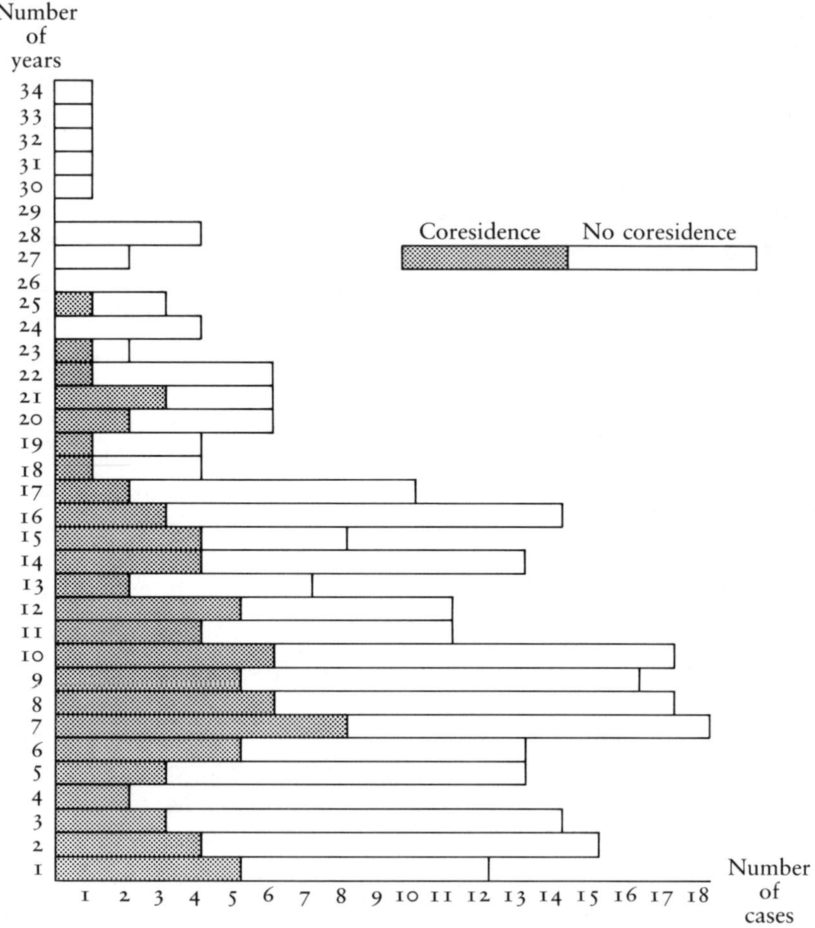

FIGURE 3. Survival of parents beyond marriage of children

sion would be taken "immediately after the death of said Armieou and no sooner." Seven years later his testament mentioned that one daughter and her husband Girard, one widowed daughter, and his wife were all living with him. Three weeks later he was dead. Four years afterward the daughters split their inheritance while reaffirming their obligation to care for their mother.

Retirement in practical terms meant occupation of a particular room in the house; wealth permitting, however, the parent, after welcoming the younger couple, might move to another house. Widowed shepherd Jean Baptiste Armieu housed daughter Marguerite and son-in-law

Louis Aron on May 7, 1742. But on March 26, 1743, he bought part of another house and a barnyard. A transaction of November 9, 1745, shows that he and the couple were no longer living together. Five years later he died at the reported age of seventy-seven.

Though the head of a family in Provence normally chose one principal heir, division of holdings was an option. Division of the patrimony entailed division of the burden of support of aged parents. On April 18, 1758, François Artaud, a large landholder (*ménager*), split his land and houses between two married sons. After taking possession the sons would collect rent from the tenants and pay Artaud 75 *livres* each annually. Payments continued until the father's death on May 6, 1767.[53]

A married son might, after a separation from his parents, return with his own family to live with his widowed mother. In 1739 Antoine Arquier married and left home. On October 23, 1754, Thérèse Bourc declared that her son Antoine had recently come with his wife and family to live with her and had brought with him furniture and other belongings. There followed a two-page list of furniture and utensils. The mother died on January 24, 1757, at the recorded age of eighty-five. The son had returned, no doubt, to help her in old age and perhaps also—though he was not a principal heir—to ensure himself of some share of the inheritance. Even were these and other motivations documented, to sort them out would be very difficult.

Documents did spell out precise financial obligations within the family. On August 25, 1751, widow Rose Salen gave her son Jean Baptiste Artaud a receipt reviewing their recent financial dealings. He owed her a large pension and paid part of it in goods and services. She thought that fifty *livres* should pay for the hospitality he had shown in her first five months of widowhood. Later that year, no longer residing with him, she sent her brother to collect a further installment of the pension. A year and a half later the son made an additional payment and continued to do so until she died nine years later.[54]

Sometimes a grandparent would settle property on a grandchild. Such was the case of Jean Reynier, whose son Jean Estienne had died and who found himself looking after his grandson Joseph (Jean's younger sons had been emancipated a year earlier, as mentioned above). Because the grandfather was too old to work and the grandson too young, the land

53. See receipts of October 18, 1760, and October 31, 1763.
54. See proxy of October 23, 1751, and receipt of March 3, 1753; date of death: June 22, 1762.

that would eventually be passed on to the boy was leased for six years to a local muleteer, Louis Davin, who was obliged to bring part of the harvest of his work to the old man as a pension (May 23, 1746).

The same kind of obligation was undertaken by Louis Girard on September 12, 1761. He was given rights by Thérèse Marroc to land, meadow, vineyard, olive trees, and other trees for two years; the agreement obliged him to deliver to her house half the harvest of "grapes, wine, almonds, and other fruits in their season." Thus, sharecropping for the one was an old age pension for the other. Sharecropping arrangements could involve a house as well as land. On October 11, 1751, Elizabeth Abeille of Aix rented out land and a country house in Puyricard. She would receive in Aix half the yield of the land while maintaining the use of a room and the kitchen in Puyricard.

Divestment within the family might involve travel for the parent. On September 19, 1759, Imbert Perrin wrote the itinerary of his retirement in passing the patrimony down to his sons Antoine and Joseph. Nominally, each would care for him six months of the year, but until Joseph married, Antoine would house him while Joseph contributed thirty *livres* to his support.

Support came in a variety of forms. In a contract that has a modern ring, Agnès Cauvet, widow of Jacques Martin, received a pension when her husband's property was divided between their two sons. She was entitled not only to food, housing, and clothing but also to payment of such medical expenses as she might incur.[55]

Widows who found themselves in a vulnerable position commonly banded together, as did one mother and her daughter-in-law, the widows of a father-son pair of masons in neighboring Ventabren, on June 13, 1755. The elder thanked her daughter-in-law for the care she had shown and offered her the use of the house and the fruits of the land as long as she did not remarry. A young widow might, however, return to her own family, as Magdeleine Salen Goujet did on April 13, 1744. By her late husband's will she received eighty *livres,* including her mourning clothes, from her stepson, whereupon she returned to her father, very likely for the old man's welfare as well as her own.

After the marriage contracts of children and various other donations and arrangements that granted old age pensions, an individual's last opportunity to act on the economy of the household came in his or her

55. *Partage* (division), September 18, 1766.

testament.[56] The mere potential to make a will provided leverage in the family, but the act itself could serve as a support in old age. A public rather than a secret document (not necessarily dictated from a death-bed), it declared conditions for the inheritance, thus providing for the last days of the testator as well as the widowhood of the spouse. A young father would make testamentary provisions for his wife, who promised to raise their children; their upbringing was the condition of her pension. But when the testator was somewhat older, dealing directly with his grown-up children, no conditions were attached to a bequest for his widow except that she not remarry.

In the absence of children, aged siblings usually became involved. The land of the childless mason Mathieu Baume and his wife, Elizabeth Bonnand, came from his family, the house from hers. Upon his death she would have the use of the land until her death, when it would revert to his brothers and sister. The house would be returned immediately to her family, save one room reserved for his sister.[57]

Sometimes the wife, anticipating death, provided for her husband. Magdeleine Arquier requested in her testament of June 6, 1755, that her husband be fed and cared for by their son Lazare Joye. Catherine Honnorat ordered on March 18, 1766, that her son François Anastay care for his father, Jean Baptiste Anastay.

The testament often included recognition of past support. In her will of May 10, 1750, Elizabeth Alexis thanked her son for a pension that he had paid her for the previous two years. And in a very rare act on November 20, 1743, Anne Maurel reduced the pension that her son Louis Marroc was paying her. She would do without half of her promised wheat and some money but would retain the rest of the wheat and three *mierolles* of wine.

The testament also operated outside the family, particularly in the case of aid to servants. Luc Sextius de Boyer, chevalier d'Argens, left thirty *livres* to his mother (a symbolic sum she surely did not need) but, more important, an annual pension of three hundred *livres* to his domestic servant. Jean Baptiste Brun left two hundred *livres* and furniture to his servant Anne Achard but only "in the case that said Achard will be found at his service upon his death."[58]

56. With almost no exceptions, a *testament nuncupatif,* a public document rather than a secret one. See Liard, "Les mentalités collectives," and Aubenas, *Le testament.*

57. Baume's testament, May 4, 1766.

58. Boyer's testament, February 19, 1762; Brun's testament, September 23, 1762.

Such care did not always guarantee a share in the inheritance, as the widow Jeanne Cheiland learned after having taken care of the aged priest Pierre Boyer during his final illness. She was embittered at having received only three articles of worn-out clothing from the priest's nephew. The priest's old age had been cared for, but hers was not.[59]

A more certain form of old age insurance outside the family was the use of *rentes viagères* (lifetime annuities). Some of the *bourgeois d'Eguilles* resorted to this method. And one widow, after being rewarded for care given to Pierre Giraud, lent out her new wealth and collected interest on eight different loans in the last ten years of her life.[60] But such techniques were normally limited to the rich and were not by any means specifically designed for old age. Throughout France, the propertied classes could dispose of wealth in excess of lineal property and the *legitim,* the inalienable portion of their heirs.[61] The purchase of *rentes* freed the buyer from the need to work at any age. But for the vast majority of *Eguiléens* the family was the only source of support.

How reliable was the family? Melchior Gros, a farmer with wealth to distribute, provided a comfortable pension for his second wife, but one clause of his bequest is troubling: "She will be permitted to walk in the vineyards, pick and eat grapes from the vines."[62] Gaspard Marroc, in his testament of January 29, 1746, granted the same right to his wife Jeanne d'Eyme, and the clause also appeared in the contract of Agnès Cauvet mentioned above. Such an act demonstrates the ambiguity of relations between generations in this society. On the one hand, it shows a recognition of the sentimental—as well as biological—attachment of an older person to the land. On the other hand, the need to notarize permission to help oneself to grapes from one's children's field indicates a certain weakness of affective relations.

Care for the aged was a function of family attachments. Yves Castan has suggested a drifting-apart of generations in the late seventeenth and eighteenth centuries in neighboring Languedoc.[63] But in any setting one

59. *Déclaration,* November 10, 1751.

60. Anne Artaud Dumas received payments on April 16 and 18, 1746; October 21 and 28, 1747; November 12, 1748; October 9, November 6 and 13, 1751; and April 15, 1752. She was mentioned in Pierre Giraud's codicil of April 17, 1743; she died January 20, 1757.

61. Roland Mousnier, *The Institutions of France under the Absolute Monarchy, 1598–1789: Society and State* (Chicago, 1979), pp. 66–71.

62. Gros's testament, December 9, 1756.

63. Yves Castan, "Pères et fils en Languedoc à l'époque classique," *XVIIe Siècle,* 102–103 (1974), 31–43; and Castan, *Honnêteté.*

must investigate house to house. And only rarely does a source permit the kind of view of households in conflict given by Roderick Phillips's archives of the revolutionary family tribunals in Rouen.[64]

The seigneurial court of Eguilles heard some cases of battles between households: neighbors feuded at the village fountain, and plaintiffs argued that particular individuals had developed demonic hatreds. Accusations of *vieille masque* (old hag) and *vieille sorcière* (old sorceress) were reminiscent of the days of witchcraft, an activity associated with old women.[65] But the individual household rarely exposed itself to the courts, though in-law problems—occupying a middle ground between family and outsiders—were common. In testimony concerning a nuisance of a mother-in-law who lived above her married daughter and persisted in pouring water through the cracks in her floor to put out the couple's fire, it was said that her sons-in-law had never set foot in her apartment: separate housing was truly separate.[66]

Testimony about an eighty-year-old man and his sons who fought with the man's son-in-law yields conflicting images of the father. On the one hand he is the powerful patriarch, leading his sons into battle and striking the first blow; on the other hand he is the weak old fool, shouting in the middle of the street, "I'll kill him myself," but "get me a stick so that I can stand."[67] Theater may describe one old man as a respectable patriarch, another as a ridiculous graybeard, but in the street the same person could play both roles on the same day. It depended upon who was watching.

If conclusions about individual cases are ambiguous, historical generalizations about affective relations can be problematical. Nevertheless, some tentative conclusions can be drawn. The frequent recourse to contract in Eguilles indicates that although people did retire, there was no harmonious pattern of retirement. Family assistance was not something that was assured without contract, and individual measures resulted from particular attachments and resentments. Eighteenth-century Eguilles was far from being an ideal *Gemeinschaft* (community). Indeed, what is striking about the old person is his or her individuality. Retired from the council and challenged in workplace and household, a

64. Roderick Phillips, *Family Breakdown in Late Eighteenth-Century France: Divorces in Rouen, 1792–1803* (Oxford, 1980).

65. A.D. Aix, VI B 1511, March 3, 1749; Edward Bever, "Old Age and Witchcraft in Early Modern Europe," in Stearns, *Old Age in Preindustrial Society,* pp. 150–190.

66. A.D. Aix, VI B 1512, May 1760.

67. Ibid., 1511, May 3, 1746.

man may have found himself estranged in a supposedly "communal" world. "Community," as Tönnies would have it, existed before there was a need for contracts,[68] but we have seen every detail of household finances spelled out and notarized. In a curious way, the elderly awaited the coming of a national bureaucracy to form a well-defined, albeit segregated, community of the aged.

The first document that presents the aged of Eguilles as a coherent group is a list of the dependents of soldiers of the Revolutionary army.[69] At a meeting of 29 *Ventôse an II,* the Assemblée Générale des Citoyens de la Commune d'Eguilles met to draw up a list of recipients of assistance. Fathers, brothers, and husbands were in the service, but the list accounts most often for sons. Of 148 names of dependents, 139 were parents, 37 aged sixty and older. An additional thirteen were married to sexagenarians, and one was a soldier's father residing with his own seventy-seven-year-old father.

Nearly two years later, administrators of the district of Aix sent an order with further details about such assistance to the citizens of Eguilles. Their letter of 9 *Frimaire an IV* referred to an enclosed printed order from Paris, dated 23 *Brumaire an II,* which prescribed a yearly pension of fifty *livres* for needy parents aged under sixty years and one hundred *livres* for those sixty and up, infirm, or unable to work.[70] The message had taken some time and at least two regimes to make its way from Paris to Eguilles by way of Aix. Even so, of course, it was only a temporary measure; a long-term plan encompassing all aged French men and women would take much longer.[71] Eguilles, like the rest of France, would wait until the twentieth century for a social security system. Even in the first decades of the Third Republic, each village was responsible for the care of its handful of old people.[72]

Care within the family characterized the experience of elderly parents not only in Eguilles but in much of the rest of rural France. To be sure, there were regional differences in family structure and inheritance law as well as in mortality rates throughout the country, so it is absurd to speak of Eguilles as representative of the nation as a whole. However,

68. Ferdinand Tönnies, *Community and Society* (New York, 1963).
69. A.M. Eguilles.
70. Ibid.
71. Stearns, *Old Age in European Society.*
72. Masson, *Les Bouches-du-Rhône,* vol. 15, p. 165. Thirteen people received some assistance in 1911, two in 1931.

the experience of one village does express the range of material and emotional issues involved in the situation of the aged in the French countryside. Family structure and inheritance provisions there are representative of the south. The elderly of the north, like those in England, were more likely to have lived independently, though contact between generations may have remained common.[73] Tensions caused by the increased survival of the aged could occur anywhere in the country.

For purposes of comparison, we need to consider a sample from north of the Nantes-Geneva line, preferably not in a region (such as the western) where heirs received perfectly equal shares of the patrimony, reducing the need for notarized documents (essential for the historian). Notarial records from the village of Picquigny (13 kilometers down the Somme from Amiens) in rural Picardy will suffice.[74] In the *Amiénois* a *préciput* system obtained; parents from the surrounding villages were free to advantage a particular child. Hence, they were more concerned with the immediate *communauté* based upon the conjugal unit than with distant kin,[75] and the stem family—so familiar in the south— made a periodic reappearance. Rates of coresidence, though they do not match southern rates, are significant, 25 percent of marriage contracts in the sample demanding coresidence.[76] Typical is the case of woolen-worker Pierre Martin Gavin and Clotilde Pecquet, whose late father had been a blacksmith.[77] Gavin received some land and produce from his parents, but Pecquet received a house and some land from her widowed mother. In return for the house, the couple agreed to provide her lodging, clothing, lighting, food, laundry, heat, and general support at their table in health and in sickness for the rest of her life, assuming they could all get along. But if they found it impossible to live together, she reserved the use for her lifetime of a room with chimney—to be added to the house at the couple's expense—where she would retire with her own clothes, linen, bed, and furniture.

In the rural Midi such a matrilocal arrangement would have been a

73. Laslett, "The History of Aging." For another southern example, see Abel Poitrineau, "Minimum vital catégoriel et conscience populaire: Les retraites conventionnelles des gens agés dans le pays de Murat au XVIIIe siècle," *French Historical Studies,* 12 (1981), 165–176.

74. A.D. Somme, Picquigny: Etude du Notaire Montigny, E 26.423–26.427 (1771–75). This northern sample, much smaller than the southern one, is intended merely as an indication, not as an exact equivalent of the Eguilles sample.

75. Yver, *Egalité entre héritiers,* pp. 196–202, 221–222.

76. Seventeen of sixty-eight marriage contracts in the 1770s.

77. Marriage contract of September 26, 1773.

rarity, especially as the husband's parents were still alive. But Picardy is not Provence. In the northern sample, twice as many of the coresidence clauses called for matrilocal organization than patrilocal.[78] Custom and culture permitted it. It was more common for aged parents to single out their youngest daughter rather than eldest son to console their old age. In some other northern sites that preference was institutionalized in the *droit de maineté,* the house being reserved for the youngest child.[79] That practice seems to have had its origins among pastoralists who provided animals rather than land or housing to the older children.[80] A greater reliance upon the market and movable wealth as a result of protoindustrialization would also have encouraged such a practice. Only further work over the long term will help separate the variables.

In rural Picardy some workers behaved like their southern counterparts, spelling out details. Marie Madeleine Milloir, widow of a laborer and herself a spinner, sold land, a house, stable, courtyard, and garden to her son, Jean-Baptiste Domart, a woolen worker. But she guarded the usufruct, rent free, of the kitchen and bedroom where she lived, half the garden, and the street entry. The sale price was 450 *livres,* 200 of which would go toward paying off a debt, the balance remaining in the son's hands to be applied, in theory, to the lifelong support of the mother.[81]

Father and son might live and work together until the elder retired: Jacques and Jean Moinet, both weavers, coresided in the village of Yzeux; in appreciation for his son's "respect and friendship," Jacques gave Jean all he owned in return for the usual promise of support.[82] But again, matrilocal arrangements seem to have been more common. Marie Gourguichon, widow of a *journalier* in Argoeuves, made an almost identical donation to her coresiding married daughter in return for a similar promise.[83] And Jean Carton, pit-sawyer, and his wife, Marie Demoyencourt, of Guignemicourt recompensed their unmarried adult daughter, Marie Claire Carton, for "the good and faithful services that she has rendered them until today in helping them subsist for a long time" by giving her a plot of land, "house, room, barn, stable, courtyard

78. Ten matrilineal, five patrilineal, two ambiguous.

79. Le Roy Ladurie mentions this right in Goody, *Family and Inheritance,* p. 67. I thank Liana Vardi for her communication on the subject.

80. See entries on *maîné* and *juveigneur* in Marcel Marion, *Dictionnaire des institutions de la France aux XVIIe et XVIIIe siècles* (Paris, 1923, 1979), pp. 345, 323.

81. *Vente,* March 21, 1773.

82. *Donation entre vifs,* October 24, 1773.

83. *Donation,* April 13, 1772.

and garden . . . furnishings, belongings, livestock," and so on—but only after their deaths. Meanwhile Marie Claire would receive free housing.[84]

Kinship other than that of parent and child often played a role, as in the gift of a house made by the widow of an innkeeper in Fluy to her niece, married to a woolen worker in Breilly. Again, the transaction would be completed only upon the aunt's death, but the niece could reside there rent free and observe her aunt keeping the house in good condition.[85]

In many documents it is implicitly clear that the elders were either feeling their years or planning ahead for a good old age, but some are more explicit about their motives. Madeleine Dieu, the elderly widow of a laborer in the village of La Chaussée-lès-Picquigny—complaining of a long convalescence from an ailment brought on by old age, no longer capable of meeting the increasing demands of this life, and wanting to devote herself to her salvation—promised the inheritance to her son, a woolen worker, and to her daughter and son-in-law, a weaver. She demanded the usual care—to be "sustained, fed, lodged, nursed, tended, and supported"—and to be provided a glass of brandy every morning and evening. The children would house her for alternate months until her death, and she would require eighteen *sous* per week. If her health prevented her moving, she would stay put and be paid the money by the other child.[86]

As in Provence, some individuals in Picardy and elsewhere made arrangements with servants. Testaments typically demanded that the servant serve until the master's death. Antoine Harlé of Crouy promised his servant Ursule Warquins 1,500 *livres* for more than thirty years' service, but in fact he did not have the funds and was only notarizing the promise. The drawing up of the document may reflect the transition from personal to market relations so typical of the period;[87] still, the longevity of the relationship suggests that the money also represented something less crass.

In many ways, personal ties and the "family system" continued to see to the needs of the rural elderly. Family support was hardly automatic,

---

84. *Donation*, July 19, 1772.
85. *Donation*, La Raille, August 21, 1772.
86. *Démission*, January 8, 1774.
87. Cissie C. Fairchilds, *Domestic Enemies: Servants and Their Masters in Old Regime France* (Baltimore, Md., 1984); Sarah C. Maza, *Servants and Masters in Eighteenth-Century France: The Uses of Loyalty* (Princeton, N.J., 1983).

but there were few alternatives. In the late nineteenth century, when the economy of the wine-growing areas of southern France evolved from subsistence agriculture to market-oriented monoculture, the system became even more important as insurance against deprivation.[88] And it exists today alongside the modern, bureaucratic Sécurité Sociale.

For anything new, we must turn to the city, where even in the eighteenth century there were significant differences. In the happiest of rural cases the aged were cared for *en famille;* in the city that possibility was restricted by limitations of space, growing individualism, and dependence upon the market. That restriction lies at the source of much Enlightenment economic literature of the eighteenth century. Without the family to fall back on, the aged were forced to look elsewhere.

88. Laura Levine Frader, "The Poverty of Property: Family and Inheritance in French Rural Society" (paper presented at 1982 meeting of American Historical Association).

7 The Aged, the City, and the Hospital

If the family provides a window on relations between generations in the countryside, the view it provides in the city is considerably narrower. True, aged parents and adult children did sometimes coreside in urban France. In Orange, for example, a city of about 5,000 people, 30 percent of eighteenth-century marriage contracts demanded such arrangements; such was the effect of Roman law and Mediterranean culture on a small city closely integrated with the surrounding countryside.[1] But in northern towns and large cities throughout France, the generations were on their own. Less than 3 percent of the households of Caen, whose population numbered 30,000 to 40,000 in the eighteenth century, included three generations.[2] Samples of marriage contracts from Amiens and Marseille confirm this general impression.[3] Figure 4 contrasts them with the rural samples discussed already.

We would expect a lower rate of coresidence in the north.[4] As we saw in the previous chapter, one-quarter of rural contracts called for such arrangements in Picardy, whereas half did so in Provence. And a mere 6 percent of marriage contracts in the northern city of Amiens stipulated coresidence, usually of people maintaining close ties to the rural econ-

---

1. Vovelle, *De la cave au grenier*, p. 52.

2. Perrot, *Genèse*, p. 314.

3. The Marseille sample covered two years in two of the oldest and largest notarial *études* with very diverse clienteles. The Amiens sample, also chosen for diversity, covers a decade. Dates were chosen to facilitate comparison with previous studies. Marseille: A.D. Marseille, Etude du Notaire François-Joseph-Zacharie Hazard, 351 E 1165–1168 (1757–58); Etude du Notaire Laurent Sard, 361 E 138–139 (1757–58). Amiens: A.D. Somme, Etude du Notaire Louis-François Janvier, 3 E 43–46 (1771–81).

4. Peter Laslett, "The History of Aging"; Collomp, "Ménage et famille."

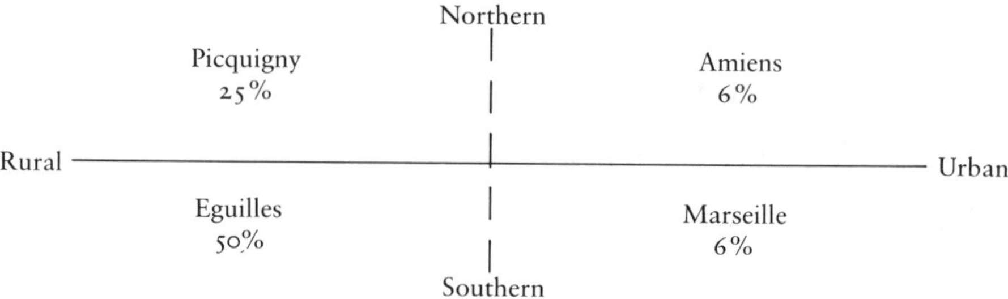

FIGURE 4. Coresidence of parents and married children revealed by marriage contracts

omy.[5] Much more surprising is the identical 6 percent rate in the southern city of Marseille; evidently its urban character transcended its Provençal nature in determining how its population set up house.[6] Further contributing to the low coresidence rate was a high rate of immigration: parents were not in town to house anyone.[7]

What is striking about urban marriage is the relative independence of the new couple with respect to their parents. Less constrained than their rural counterparts by the need for enough land to support a household, individuals amassed sufficient movable wealth (and sometimes real estate) to form new *communautés* of husband and wife. And whereas in rural Provence the parents were mentioned first, before the prospective spouses, in the marriage contract—the elders' gifts and requirements receiving great prominence—in Paris, Amiens, and even Marseille the order was often reversed. The will of the couple was more powerful in the city than in the country, and reciprocal gifts *inter vivos* assured the support of the surviving spouse.

We should not exaggerate the freedom of the urban young. Men were still minors until age thirty, women until twenty-five; even beyond,

5. Marriage contracts are rarer in the north, and the hard figures are only two of thirty-one.

6. Seven of 112 contracts demanded coresidence. The number of contracts per year is higher for these *études* in these years than for the average Marseille *étude* at midcentury; see Mireille Bellenger, "Recherches sur la population marseillaise au milieu du XVIIIe siècle: Structures et relations sociales d'après les contrats de mariage," *Mémoire* (Aix, 1963), p. 47. See also Jean Colonna, "Du contrat de mariage à Marseille de 1680 à la révolution," *Mémoire*, 1953 (A.D. Marseille, VIII F32).

7. On migration to Marseille, see Vovelle, *De la cave au grenier*, pp. 55–131. See also Jean-Pierre Bardet's review of Michel Terrisse, *La population de Marseille et de son terroir de 1694 à 1830*, 3 vols. (Marseille, 1971), in *Annales de démographie historique*, 1973, pp. 353–375.

parental consent was required or sought for many activities.[8] Business-men generally maintained authority over their heirs until death; their wives shared responsibilities and, when widowed, either directed businesses or played important consulting roles.[9] And mature, if not aged, men generally filled key municipal offices.[10] Nevertheless, the urban patriarch wielded less absolute authority than his rural counterpart; older members of the urban elite found reason to retire; and younger people exercised greater freedom as individuals.

Because of the relative independence of the couple, it is impossible to learn the details of relations between generations from the urban marriage contract alone,[11] but other sorts of documents witness the transmission of property, offices, and shops. Testaments and donations reveal a variety of temporary arrangements for dealing with the weakened body and increased longevity. Some disclose the unexpected coresidence of parents and married children or of other kin, co-workers, or friends. But even where coresidence did not occur, there were ties that bound people together and involved the aged, like others, in life-sustaining networks, as examples from notarial archives in Paris, Amiens, and Marseille bear out.[12] Customary practices often obviated the need for contracts or testaments, but those documents that were drawn up indicate a wealth of neighborhood and kinship ties.[13] Urban families sometimes imitated the rural stem family. For example, Parisian Marie Marguerite Montigny, a thrice-widowed manufacturer of chocolate,

8. Jean-Pierre Poussou, "Pour une historie de la vieillesse et des vieillards dans les sociétés européennes," in INED, *Les âges de la vie*, vol. 2, pp. 156–157.

9. Paul Butel, "Comportements familiaux dans le négoce bordelais au XVIIIe siècle," *Annales du Midi*, 88, no. 127 (1976), 139–158. In Marseille as well as Bordeaux, widowed mothers served as *procureurs* for their sons gone off to sea.

10. Garden, *Lyon*, pp. 504–505. Pierre Deyon found municipal officers in seventeenth-century Amiens retiring sooner than businessmen; see *Amiens, capitale provinciale: Etude sur la société urbaine au 17e siècle* (Paris, 1967), p. 260.

11. The contract can yield important data on occupational continuity and mobility, however. See Adeline Daumard and François Furet, *Structures et relations sociales à Paris au XVIIIe siècle* (Paris, 1961).

12. Aside from the *études* in Amiens and Marseille mentioned above, I refer to the randomly selected *étude* XXXVIII, among others, in Paris for the second half of the eighteenth century (A.N., M.C.). Most customary systems permitted retention of usufructory rights to property transferred by gift. See Jean-Marie Ricard, *Traité des donations entre-vifs et testamentaires avec la coutume d'Amiens commentée*, nouvelle édition (Paris, 1734), p. 211.

13. E.g., Arlette Farge has reconstructed the social life of Paris in the eighteenth century from judicial archives, an admittedly partial source: *La vie fragile: Violence, pouvoirs, et solidarités à Paris au XVIIIe siècle* (Paris, 1986).

promised all her equipment and merchandise to whichever daughter housed her; the rest of her wealth would be divided equally among her five children.[14]

Agreements signed in the city of Amiens reveal ways in which the urban middle classes used wealth, occupations, and professions to guarantee retirement. Nicolas Chafart, *bourgeois d'Amiens,* and his wife, Cécile Guilbert, gave her widowed daughter from a first marriage several properties in advance of succession. She received shares in four houses, two *rentes,* two offices, some arable land, furniture, and silver. In return she agreed to feed, clothe, and house her mother and stepfather for the rest of their lives. If the aged couple saw fit to retire to their own house, she would pay them a lifetime *rente* and pension of 800 *livres* per year, reducible to 500 after the death of either one. She would also provide bedding, draperies, and decoration for their room.[15]

Like the farmers who maintained control of their land until death, urban professionals with titles and privileges often avoided passing them on. On July 6, 1759, the *procureur* of the guild of surgeons demanded only a partial retirement: "His great age denying him the facility of enunciating as freely as in the past," he asked to take his son as adjunct to help him as needed, especially in pleading cases. But he kept the title, requesting the guild to approve his son's eventual inheritance of it. The community acceded to both requests, noting the good relationship between father and son.[16] Further down the social scale, Catherine Payan, widow of a farm laborer on the edge of Marseille, finding herself unable to direct her own affairs in very advanced age and anticipating ever greater need in the future, promised her son 300 *livres* of her 500-*livre* dowry and her younger daughter the rest, but she retained its use for life.[17]

Housing arrangements could link grandparents and grandchildren. In Marseille the widow Catherine Barot lived with her grandson, François Clary, a businessman. Bedridden from "infirmities of age," she sat in her room with the garden view on the second floor of his house in the rue Saint-Ferréol and declared her intention of dying *ab intestat.*[18]

Siblings and other kin also managed to care for each other in old age.

---

14. A.N., M.C., XXXVIII 490, *Testament,* September 30, 1762.
15. A.D. Somme, 3 E 45, *Donation,* April 1, 1780.
16. Ibid., E 902, fol. 14.
17. A.D. Marseille, 351 E 1165, *Avancement d'hoirie,* Payan, April 22, 1757.
18. Ibid., 1166, *Déclaration,* December 19, 1757.

On November 23, 1754, Geneviève Lavigne, widow of a master baker, living in the rue du Faubourg Saint-Martin in Paris, promised fifty *livres* of *rentes viagères* to her sister, also a baker's widow, in gratitude for the lodging and food she had provided and would continue to provide until death. She sweetened the deal by promising 300 *livres* to the sister's son, whose own daughter would receive some furniture.[19] Even at the level of domestic servant, the sisters Bouchard of Marseille, both suffering the infirmities of old age (one was going blind, the other deaf), each promised the other the use of her worldly goods and declared as heir their niece in Aix.[20] Aunts, uncles, and godparents thanked kin and godchildren in documents notarized throughout France for a variety of "good services."

As if ratifying the connection drawn by Cicero between old age and friendship, eighteenth-century Frenchmen and -women acknowledged the help of friends as insurance against deprivation in old age. In Paris in the summer of 1792, Pierre Charles Delaulne de Morinval prepared a testament recognizing that for the past twenty-five years he had resided with Monsieur et Madame La Serre *en véritables amis*. They had divided an apartment at 9, quai de Bourbon on the Ile Saint-Louis out of economy and friendship. Delaulne paid half the yearly rent of 1,200 *livres* (plus fifty to the janitor) and agreed that he would fulfill his share of the lease (six or nine years) even after his death. He offered a gift of fifty shares in the *caisse Lafarge* (see Chapter 8) to Madame La Serre and left the remainder to his brother and nephew. What remained was unstated, but several debts in Paris and Languedoc, going as far back as 1754, were recounted in a kind of economic final confession of the old man's past exploits.[21]

In a less wealthy part of town, the widow of a mason in the parish of Saint-Martin-des-Champs lived with an unmarried friend for thirty years.[22] And in the same *quartier* an unmarried ribbonmaker named Anne Claude Laurion, lying in her bed on the fourth floor, dictated a testament providing 200 *livres* to a cousin and 100 *livres*, two dresses, and all her furniture to Jeanne Elizabeth David, also unmarried and independent, who shared quarters with her. That gift was to recognize "all the pains and care that she is taking and will take during her

<hr>

19. A.N., M.C., XXXVIII 424, November 23, 1754.
20. A.D. Marseille, 351 E 1165, *Testaments*, March 12, 1757.
21. A.N., M.C., XXXVIII 490, August 6, 1792.
22. Ibid., 427, November 7, 1755.

[housemate's] illness."[23] Some documents specify what form those "pains and care" will take, from domestic help to sharing a certain number of meals per week.

Servants, more prevalent (and better researched) in the city than in the countryside, often provided those sorts of services and after years of work might imagine themselves their masters' friends and, finally, responsibilities. One Jeanne Catherine Ponthillon was promised a gold watch, a bed with sheets and cover, an armoire, a commode, baskets, plates, brass candlesticks, a silver goblet, other linen, and clothing by her Parisian mistress.[24] But her contemporary, the writer Louis-Sébastian Mercier, was pessimistic about the prospects for most aged servants.[25] Indeed, recent work suggests that relationships between masters and servants were growing less personal and more contractual.[26]

Still, it was difficult for all sorts of eighteenth-century city dwellers to separate the personal and the commercial. Just as professionals with privileges to pass on tried to negotiate satisfactory retirement arrangements with their children, individuals used similar strategies outside the family. Thus, one Lignier, clerk of the first surgeon in Amiens, quit the post on April 21, 1751, but maintained the tax exemption that came with it. His successor, Lendormy, would fill the post for Lignier's lifetime.[27]

It was even more important to benefit from the sale of a lesser post such as measurer and porter of coal for the city of Amiens. Claude Geroux, who had held that position since December 13, 1754, sold it on May 10, 1775, for 2,200 *livres*. But the sum remained in the hands of the purchaser, who agreed to pay Geroux and his wife a weekly pension of six *livres*.[28] In Marseille on August 22, 1758, Louise Cauvin, widow of Mathieu Alies, master carpenter, finding herself unable for reasons of age to operate the shop and anticipating her son's departure for another mastership, conferred power of attorney on another carpenter, Joseph Balthazard Bruno Terris of Cucuron. Terris would run her business; moreover, his father would have permission to work in the shop, providing his own tools and paying an annual rent of ten *livres*.[29]

23. Ibid., 424, March 21, 1754.
24. Ibid., CXVI 562, January 27, 1787.
25. Mercier, *Tableau de Paris*, vol. 7, pp. 162–163.
26. Fairchilds, *Domestic Enemies*; Maza, *Servants and Masters*. Fairchilds and Maza differ on the timing of that transition.
27. A.D. Somme, E 902 fol. 1–2.
28. Ibid., 3 E 44, *Vente d'office*, Geroux, May 10, 1775.
29. A.D. Marseille, 361 E 139, *Procuration*, Cauvin, August 22, 1758.

A protoindustrial workplace might accommodate aged workers, especially as people of all ages were aware of the need to work as long as possible, but the old corporate structures in some ways anticipated modern work discipline.[30] Occasionally, over the course of the seventeenth and eighteenth centuries, textile workers in Amiens asked permission of guild and municipal authorities to work at home for reasons of age and health—if, for example, asthma or some other ailment hindered their ability to keep up the pace of their co-workers.[31] They were trying to avoid full retirement, a difficult and expensive proposition. Authorities who granted permission demonstrated some understanding of the plight of aged workers and of the resentment that younger workers may have felt toward their elders.

In the best of circumstances, guilds saw to the welfare of aging members, and individuals looked after each other as they grew older.[32] An unmarried garment worker in Paris, for example, learned her trade from but evidently also looked after an older single colleague, and an aged landlady even promised her tenants a small sum of money.[33] In the city as in the country, ties of kinship, work, and neighborliness provided both practical help and affection as the privations of old age made survival more and more difficult. Yet as demographic and economic pressure produced tensions in households and in corporate institutions, the urban elderly found themselves increasingly alone.

The aged in the twentieth century are more isolated than ever before.[34] But isolation is neither unprecedented nor necessarily undesirable from their point of view;[35] indeed, it may indicate a kind of

30. For the best introduction to the subject, see Michelle Perrot, "The Three Ages of Industrial Discipline in Nineteenth-Century France," in John M. Merriman, ed., *Consciousness and Class Experience in Nineteenth-Century Europe* (New York, 1979), pp. 149–168. For our period, material in Steven Laurence Kaplan and Cynthia J. Koepp, eds., *Work in France: Representations, Meaning, Organization, and Practice* (Ithaca, 1986), is more particularly appropriate. William Olejniczak's paper presented in 1987 to the Society for French Historical Studies, "Power over the Body: The *Ateliers de Charité* in late Eighteenth-Century Champagne," tries to apply Perrot's ideas (themselves largely borrowed from Michel Foucault) to the eighteenth century.

31. A.M. Amiens, HH 256, *Demandes d'ouvriers d'être autorisés à travailler à domicile,* 1645–1775. I thank Robert Duplessis for drawing this material to my attention.

32. Some of the literature on the origins of social insurance points to the well-intentioned but insufficient work of guilds and provident funds. See Emile Laurent, *Le paupérisme et les associations de prévoyance* (Paris, 1865), 2 vols.; and Richard, *Histoire des institutions d'assurance en France.*

33. A.N., M.C., XXXVIII 427, November 3, 1755.

34. Mitterauer and Sieder, *The European Family,* p. 153.

35. Laslett, "The History of Aging."

independence. Whatever the quality of that independence, however, in the European past it was clearly more common in the city than in the countryside.[36] Moreover, French cities were seeing a significant increase in solitary households in the eighteenth century; in Lyon, for example, the percentage of apartments housing solitary people increased three-fold, to 16.6 percent.[37] The various lists drawn up to deal with the poor of Amiens in the last decades of the ancien régime and during the French Revolution testify to this situation and indicate that women were isolated much more often than men.[38] Moreover, migration to the city had aged urban populations: the birth rate remained high in the countryside while it fell in the city, and Paris had a higher percentage of sexagenarians in the late eighteenth century than it would have throughout the nineteenth.[39]

When all else failed, aged workers might attempt to reestablish ties with relatives in the country. But such attempts, after long separations, were probably in vain. As Richard Cobb has put it for the capital, "The decision whether to stay in Paris or to throw oneself on the uncertainties of family charity was usually a choice between places to die."[40] If family support was not forthcoming, some of the aged might resign themselves to their fate, stay indoors, and starve. Some stole.[41] But vast numbers turned to beggary. When arrested, they were imprisoned or—which often amounted to the same thing—hospitalized.

Early modern French hospitals offered little medical care; they were primarily instruments of social control. Supported by Christian charity, the hospital served to facilitate the giving of alms rather than the healing of the sick. The spiritual salvation of the donor took precedence over

36. Mitterauer and Sieder admit that "old women lived alone in the towns from quite an early period": *The European Family*, p. 162.

37. Emmanuel Le Roy Ladurie, in Georges Duby, ed., *Histoire de la France urbaine*, vol. 3 (Paris, 1981), p. 345, cites the work of Maurice Garden but suggests that the trend can be found throughout urban France.

38. In 1767, 70 percent of the poor living alone in the parish of Saint-Jacques were women, 77 percent in the parish of Saint-Michel: A.M. Amiens, GG 1089–90, *Mendicité*. These documents have been used to good effect in Charles Engrand, "Paupérisme et condition ouvrière dans la seconde moitié du XVIIIe siècle: L'exemple amiénois," *Revue d'Historie Moderne et Contemporaine*, 29 (1982), 376–410. But this is one aspect he overlooks.

39. Bourdelais, "Géographie du vieillissement"; Louis Chevalier, *La formation de la population parisienne au XIXe siècle* (Paris, 1950), p. 263.

40. Richard Cobb, *The Police and the People: French Popular Protest, 1789–1820* (London, 1970), p. 239.

41. Arlette Farge, *Le vol des aliments* (Paris, 1974).

physical relief of the needy. However well-intentioned the individual activity of members of such orders as that of Saint Vincent de Paul or the Sisters of Charity, their motive force came from the religious offensive of the Catholic Reformation: they were spreaders of doctrine first, healers of the sick second. Only in the eighteenth century did a more secular humanitarian philosophy begin to replace the idea of charity with that of welfare. And even then the urgency of a welfare program derived as much from a concern for putting an end to beggary as from a belief in a social debt to the needy.[42]

The institutional structure of public assistance in the eighteenth century bore the mark of its history. Here and there a rural hospice remained from the Middle Ages, when the countryside was dotted with small hospitals.[43] For the most part, however, charity had moved to the cities as war and economic disaster devastated the countryside in the early modern period.[44] But though the hospital had become an urban phenomenon in the two centuries before the French Revolution, the ratio of beds to people was not necessarily higher in the city than in the country. There were simply too many urban poor.

Essays written for a contest sponsored by the academy of Châlons-sur-Marne and published by the abbé Malvaux suggest that a veritable stream of rural beggars, devoid of any hope of retirement, were pouring into the cities to spend their old age in the hospital.[45] Some old people would be cared for by charitable *seigneurs*.[46] But for most working people such charity was not forthcoming; old age brought only abandonment, and the proximity of a hospital destroyed whatever incentive there remained for hard work and savings. The air was filled with a fatalistic chorus of "*J'irai à l'hôpital.*"[47]

There were still those who believed that no structural changes were required. The Archbishop of Paris, finding fault with the distribution of

42. Léon Cahen, "Les idées charitables à Paris au XVIIe et au XVIIIe siècles, d'après les règlements des compagnies paroissiales," *Revue d'Historie Moderne et Contemporaine*, 2 (1900–1901), 5–22; Documentation Française, *Social Security in France* (Paris, n.d.); François Steudler, *Le système hospitalier: Evolution et transformations* (N.p., 1973).

43. Jules Le Glay, "Recherches historiques sur les anciens hospices ruraux du Nord de la France" (Lille, 1858).

44. Jeorger, "La structure hospitalière."

45. L'abbé Malvaux, *Les moyens de détruire la mendicité en France, en rendant les mendians utiles à l'état sans les rendre malheureux* (Châlons-sur-Marne, 1780), p. 93.

46. Ibid., p. 295.

47. Ibid., p. 92.

parish relief in the difficult winter of 1788–89, called simply for additional funds to help reach the frozen poor, but he at least recognized the severity of the problem: "How many poor old men, already frozen by age; how many poor invalids, poor sick people, stretched out on a bed of sorrow, who have only some pitiful rags to cover themselves, and who feel with all their other pains the rigors of the cold, more bitter yet than those of hunger!"[48]

Louis-Sébastien Mercier too expressed skepticism about "political" solutions and called for increased charity. In his *Tableau de Paris,* Mercier reported the death on June 11, 1786, of a 113-year-old Savoyard in Paris. The man had performed the heavy work that was the lot of his fellow immigrants and had survived a fifty-two-foot fall forty years before, but "a second fall of six inches, on the stairs, occasioned his death." Mercier then painted a picture of a city filled with people in dire need of assistance:

> The philanthropic society, in seeking out octogenarians in order to relieve them, has found that there are more of them than would have been imagined. They live in the nooks of the *faubourgs* where they are fed as if by miracle. One has not left a small attic room for eight to ten years and prolongs his life by small gifts that arrive for him from here and there. It is charity (I am happy to repeat) that supports this immense city. Charity does more by itself than the edicts of the sovereign, the decisions of the police, the order of parlement, and all the political virtues put together: this is what is demonstrable and what is demonstrated to my eyes by the result of thirty years of observation.[49]

Hospitalization in the ancien régime normally came under a heavy veneer of religiosity. Funds came most often from religious bequests, and assistance was accorded the worthy; piety had to be coupled with a desire to work.[50] In a world where work, like *retraite,* was a religious

48. "Lettre pastorale de Monseigneur l'Archevêque de Paris: Pour le soulagement des pauvres pendant les rigueurs de cet hiver" (Paris, 1789); see Laurence S. Thompson, *A Bibliography of French Revolutionary Pamphlets on Microfiche* (Troy, N.Y., 1974).

49. Mercier, "L'homme de 113 ans," in *Tableau de Paris,* vol. 12, pp. 63–64.

50. Sometimes the wish of the donor contradicted that of the administration, and a compromise had to be found. A problem arose at the Petites-Maisons in 1745 when Pierre Goudron, clockmaker to the duc d'Orléans, specified in his will of August 18, 1742, that money he left to the home be used in support of the aged. The administrators wanted greater discretionary power and argued that the aged were not necessarily the neediest. The administration appears to have won the battle. B.N., J.F., 1238 fol. 87–100.

act as well as a personal, economic, and social one, the religious and economic aspects of the hospital could not be separated.

Consider the hospital of Oiron, near Thouars in the Poitou and not far from the cities of Poitiers and Niort. Founded in 1704 by Françoise de Rochechouart, Marquise de Montespan, "to retire there up to about one hundred paupers, old people and orphans of either sex," the hospital, housed in a former château, was to be served by "eleven sisters of charity from the community of St. Lazare in Paris." The Marquise herself joined them *en retraite*. Religion was of key importance: "Madame de Montespan, founder, desires that the paupers of this hospital be taught Christian doctrine; to lead an edifying and virtuous life, to occupy themselves in honest labors, to avoid laziness and the vices that derive from it." And discipline would be instilled through labor: "It is necessary to rule them, such that all their days be filled according to their age, their sex, and their strength. Although old people, ordinarily weak and broken, cannot render much service, they will not abandon work, as much to protect them from idleness as to prevent their exiting entirely from the condition to which it has pleased God to reduce them." Religious festivals would be celebrated according to a calendar that expressed a degree of age grading:

> We will be mindful to make the poor feel that all the aid they receive comes only from Providence. . . . We will take for the feast of all the old men St. Joseph; for the old women the feast of St. Anne; for the young boys the circumcision; for the young girls the presentation of the Holy Virgin, and for the twenty-four old men St. John the Evangelist.
>
> All the poor of this hospital will make confession at least once a month, that is one quarter of them each Sunday; and for communion it will be left to the discretion of the chaplain, except for the twenty-four old men, for whom it is necessary to try to have one take communion each day.[51]

The day's schedule was strict. Inmates rose at five in summer, seven in winter. Mass was said at ten. A fifteen-minute break from work preceded the midday meal, at which books of piety were read aloud, and a thirty-minute recreation period followed. The inmates then went back to work until supper at 5:30. After another short period of recreation, more prayers were said, and the old people and children went to sleep.[52]

---

51. *Lettres-patentes du Roi en faveur de l'hôpital de la ville d'Oyron* . . . (Poitiers, 1755), A.N. F[15] 233.

52. The schedule barely differed at the Petites-Maisons; see A.P., F.F., n.s. 61.

The special directions for the twenty-four aged inmates—living reminders of the Revelation of John—indicate that time spent in the hospital was a time of religious retreat. They said prayers specially reserved for them. Their work was all for the church: cleaning the interior, growing grapes for the wine reserved for the mass, and cultivating flowers for the altar. Walks and visits outside the hospital were strictly forbidden. When an inmate was nearing death, a successor would be picked and tested for a year—a kind of novitiate—before being accepted.

That the religious nature of a hospital could conflict with its medical role is indicated in the correspondence of the administrators of the Hôtel-Dieu of Paris in 1787. The prioress of the sisters in charge of the hospital wrote the controller general on October 17, 1787, complaining about a transfer of authority to the surgeons. She appealed to the Neckers and to Loménie de Brienne, arguing that the sisters had been serving for twelve centuries, that their patent dated from the time of Saint Louis, and that further statutes had been accorded by the Parlement de Paris two centuries before. She expressed concern for the poor people, used to the dedicated service of the old sisters, who would now be under the authority of young surgeons. She contrasted their inexperience with the long service of the sisters, "venerable by their age, their experience, attached by ties of religion, of disinterestedness, and of humanity to the fate of these sick paupers."[53]

A similar question of authority was debated at the Petites-Maisons in Paris. Correspondence between the prioress and the office of the attorney general, whose responsibilities included hospitals, indicates that the chain of command was broken at several points. Young sisters would obey only their immediate superiors and not the elders higher up. The sisters hoarded the belongings of dead patients. They failed to call the surgeon when he was needed, and at least one death resulted. When it became obvious to all that a particular sister was beating patients, no one knew how to deal with the problem.[54]

If religion was one priority, work was often another. In one *hospice de charité,* admission was dependent upon it: "The brothers of charity refuse old people who would take a place destined for men more useful to society."[55] In the Hôpital Général de Rouen the aged were admitted

53. A.N. F[15] 233, October 17, 1787.
54. B.N., J.F., 1302 fol. 57, 59, 64–67.
55. A.N. F[15] 397.

if indigent and at least seventy years old, though some exceptions were made for those who were younger but infirm. Proof of poverty and an inability to survive were required, and the administrators investigated these claims personally. Nevertheless, work was expected of "the old men from whom one can still draw some profit."[56]

As the French population increased in the eighteenth century, as the poor migrated to urban centers and charity declined, the hospital system underwent a crisis. Textile workers in Angers might be guaranteed beds in the Hôtel-Dieu in case of illness, and poor residents of Bayeux might generally make their way to the hospital to die. But the aged in France's countryside, where medieval institutions had disappeared, and in the larger cities, where demand was so great, had no such luck.[57]

An analysis of the Hôpital de la Charité of Lyon reveals why certain people were granted places and others not.[58] Those who filled the rolls of the elderly residents were not the poorest of Lyon's poor. The dowries mentioned in their marriage contracts, which were used as proof of age (in principle, the minimum for admission was seventy), while clearly not exorbitant, were certainly not among the smallest. These were artisans who knew a trade and had been able to establish themselves and marry. That Lyon was a textile center suggests why the vast majority of the hospitalized aged were textile workers: it was likely thought dangerous to the local economy to let them leave the city for fear they would spread their expertise elsewhere, thus challenging the Lyonnaise economy with "foreign" competition.

Among the classic roles of the aged in premodern societies has been that of guardian of secret knowledge and practical expertise. The corporate economy of the ancien régime clearly combined those roles in what remained of a feudal guild structure. The technical knowledge acquired along the ladder from apprentice to journeyman to master was ceremoniously shrouded in secrecy. Moreover, the protection provided by regional tariffs would have been threatened by the free movement of poor, retired experts. Thus, what is often seen as a guarantee of security and respect in the premodern world tended in some sectors of eighteenth-century France to lead to a form of confinement. Retired textile

56. A.N. F15 232.
57. C. Tollet, *Les édifices hospitaliers depuis leur origine jusqu'à nos jours* (Paris, 1892), p. 296 n.1; Hufton, *Bayeux*, p. 97.
58. Jean-Pierre Gutton, *La société et les pauvres: L'exemple de la généralité de Lyon, 1534–1789* (Paris, 1970), pp. 29–35, esp. p. 34 n.60. See also Garden, *Lyon*.

workers were not necessarily detained by force, but their privileged position on the waiting list kept them from circulating too freely.

Those who were not members of trades thus privileged waited a long time to enter such hospitals as the Petites-Maisons in Paris. When seventy-three-year-old Marie Anne Morgny reapplied on July 10, 1780, to the Petites-Maisons, where she had been number 308 on the waiting list, the roll stood at 123; there were still 185 people ahead of her.[59] Waiting lists for hospitalization did not end under the Revolution. In January 1793 a woman identifying herself as Luce Négresse wrote Minister of the Interior Joseph Garat asking him to intervene on behalf of a Marie Catherine Dessene, sixty-three, whom she had tended for fourteen years; during the last seven Dessene had been awaiting a place in the Hôpital des Incurables in Paris, where her caretaker had just heard of a vacant bed.[60]

But the hospital crisis in the eighteenth century was not simply one of capacity and finance; it involved also the conditions of residence in such hospitals as there were. In Bayeux, where the aged could go to the hospital to die, they were not particularly happy about eleven-hour workdays: "The old man who broke out and came back drunk was no exception," reports Hufton.[61] One man who had wandered out of curiosity into the Bicêtre Hospital in Paris pleaded with administrators that he would prefer hospitalization anywhere else to the "deadly regimen of Bicêtre, which seems designed only for scoundrels, the bankrupt, and the insane." He would be willing to separate from his wife to die in the Incurables, Quinze-Vingts, or Petites-Maisons.[62] A woman named Lefebvre who had become an inmate of the Hôpital Général of Paris by donating her possessions requested that she be permitted to leave with those objects in July 1791. Her request was refused.[63]

The surgeon and administrator Jacques-René Tenon referred to the Hôtel-Dieu in Paris as "the most murderous of all known hospitals."[64] His remark came as a result of investigations undertaken in the first years of the French Revolution. Turgot and Necker had proposed reforms in public assistance during their terms as royal ministers at the

59. B.N., J.F., 2543 fol. 2, and quoted in Kaplow, *The Names of Kings*, p. 94.
60. A.N. F[15] 244, January 25, 1793.
61. Hufton, *Bayeux*, pp. 91–92.
62. A.N. F[15] 242 no. 655.
63. A.N. F[15] 247 no. 474.
64. Jacques-René Tenon, *Réflexions en faveur des pauvres citoyens malades* (Paris, 1791).

end of the ancien régime. Some experiments in decentralized work-houses (*ateliers de charité*) administered at the provincial level had had some success when regional authorities were responsible administrators, but too many found ways of profiting personally from the workhouses.[65] And when financial difficulties arose, those projects were canceled and replaced by the old punitive *dépôts de mendicité*.[66]

The first step in providing better services under the Revolution was to dismantle the old system—and so the problem was immediately exacerbated. As church and seigneurial properties were nationalized and bought up by individuals, the financial crisis became acute for institutions of public assistance. In a speech to the Comités de Mendicité et de Salubrité on October 14, 1791, Tenon warned that many hospitals would be forced to close at year's end.[67] With the suppression of the urban tariff (the *octroi*), 10 to 29 million *livres* of revenue would be lost. A paper presented by a wholesaler to the Comité de Mendicité in 1790 warned: "For a long time, I have busied myself with ways of destroying beggary in France; but I have never felt so acutely the necessity of eliminating it as during a Revolution that in diminishing the possibility of help, multiplied the number of those who are needy."[68] Such an effect was hardly intentional; "in fact," one historian of French hospitals has said, "financial difficulties alone prevented the realization of the revolutionary projects."[69]

To help care for some of the poor, hospitals in the ancien régime had been happy to admit those wealthy enough to pay their own way (and more).[70] But even when resources were available, they were not always allocated efficiently. As finance minister in the last years before the Revolution, Loménie de Brienne tried to reroute funds in such a way as to provide the best service. He recommended suppressing charitable

65. Jean-Louis Harouel, *Les ateliers de charité dans la province de Haute-Guyenne* (Paris, 1969), p. 101. The view expressed in Olejniczak, "Power over the Body," is more optimistic.

66. Hufton, *Bayeux*, p. 109. See also Robert M. Schwartz, *Policing the Poor in Eighteenth-Century France* (Chapel Hill, N.C., 1988).

67. Jacques-René Tenon, *Opinion . . . sur la réunion des deux comités de mendicité et de salubrité* (Paris, 1791).

68. M. Vollant, *Mémoire sur les moyens de détruire la mendicité en France, et de venir au secours des indigens de toutes les classes* (Paris, 1790), p. 9.

69. Steudler, *Le système hospitalier*, p. 63. More recently, Alan Forrest has blamed bureaucratic incompetence and growing military demands for those financial difficulties; see *The French Revolution and the Poor* (New York, 1981), esp. p. 59.

70. B.N., J.F., 1238 fol. 161.

communities in unpopulated areas and focusing efforts where they were most needed. A report that was sent him concerning a community near Périgueux recommended shifting it to a wealthier and more salubrious community in Bergerac, where it would be perfect for the helpless retired people of the region, all of whom could receive aid.[71]

Under actual conditions, however, for the aged there were not enough places to go around in all of France, and for the ill, ironically, there were fewer. A recommendation for one man aged seventy-nine, seeking a place in a Paris old age home, reported, "He has no infirmities that might exclude him."[72] The head of the *hospice* recommended that one resident be transferred to the Incurables: "He is very infirm and two men alone can hardly turn him in his bed. You know that there are no young men in service in the *hospice* that I direct, but only four women (*citoyennes*) and two serving girls to do what is necessary for more than 100 old people of both sexes."[73]

Often the type of illness was what caused difficulties; the applicant might simply be suffering from the wrong one. A sixty-three-year-old named Lepron, who lived in an attic on the sixth floor of a building in Paris, went to the Hôtel-Dieu complaining of great pain, but he was turned away because the hospital did not take people with his problem. Far from sanguine after that experience, he wrote the mayor for help, prefacing his request with the remark, "You are going to tell me, Monsieur, that the Municipality is too overtaxed."[74] An eighty-six-year-old man was refused admission to the Incurables on August 29, 1792, because "lunacy is not admitted in the hospital of the Incurables; that of the Petites-Maisons receives persons suffering from this malady."[75]

Undaunted by administrative difficulties, people were still clamoring to get into the hospitals. Once in, they would at least be fed. At the Parisian old age home the daily regimen included "a thick soup, 150 grams of cooked, boneless meat, and a tenth of a liter of vegetables." And as if following the peasant proverb that wine is the milk of the old, the daily diet included "a quarter of a liter of wine for men, an eighth for women."[76] Septuagenarians seem to have felt it their due. On March

71. A.N. F[15] 138.

72. A.N. F[15] 257, *16 floréal an III* (May 5, 1795).

73. Ibid., *11 floréal an III* (April 30, 1795).

74. A.N. F[15] 247, no. 505, September 5, 1791.

75. A.N. F[15] 242, no. 730, August 29, 1792.

76. *Règlements des hospices civils de Paris—an 7–13: Cahier des charges pour le service des hospices de Paris, divisé en cinq entreprises. Titre V, Article I.* B.N. 8°Z Le Senne 11269.

18, 1793, a resident of Bicêtre announced that he was seventy years old and demanded "to be given a small portion of wine." The response of the officer in charge reads simply, "Granted."[77] In discussing the budget of the workhouse of Montpellier in 1772, the Estates General of Languedoc mentioned in their deliberations "the wine furnished to the old people as ordered by the doctor."[78] Hospital inmates might also receive clothing from the administrators; again, at the old age home in Paris, "the commission of *hospices* will be able to deliver them clothing that they would not be able to procure themselves, and in disposing in their regard the belongings of the deceased, which it will continue to collect in conformity with custom and regulations."[79] Such arrangements must have been common. Frequently, the price of admission was one's possessions (at the Petites-Maisons, for example, one's furniture) and of exit, one's life.[80]

Those who had contributed to the hospital by their labor might eventually find themselves patients in their former place of work. At first arrangements were informal, the sisters relying on each other: "There are those among the sisters who have performed 28 and 30 years of service in the hospital, . . . are regarded as infirm, but . . . always remain in office and have other sisters relieve them."[81] Supporters of eighty-one-year-old Sister Camus pointed to her thirty-eight years of service and argued: "Her head is still good and quite healthy; but the strength to get through her rounds and to maintain order no longer corresponds to her zeal. Her infirmities demand help."[82] But administrators tried in the 1770s to formalize the process of retirement:

> The person employed . . . is only 60 years old. She has been there for only 6 years and maybe less. She gave a memorandum to the Bureau as soon as she turned 60. She has announced that M. Lamartinière assured her that upon reaching 60 she would be admitted to the Petites-Maisons according to custom. *No one knows this custom, not even M. de Tilière, who has seniority.* The Bureau would regard this usage as an abuse that could facilitate fraud, and indeed if we receive the woman applying today she would be getting a good deal of recompense for little service.

Clearly, whatever they did might set a precedent:

77. A.N. F^{15} 242, no. 828, March 18, 1793.
78. A.N. F^{15} 138.
79. *Règlements, Titre V, Article II.*
80. A.P., F.F. 19.
81. B.N., J.F., 1238 fol. 170.
82. Ibid., fol. 286.

> If she should really quit [her work] . . . to enter the Petites-Maisons, this
> woman could be replaced . . . by another woman who would be aged 58,
> and who, after a year or two, would demand her *entrée* to the Petites-
> Maisons. The administrators have observed that if this usage were estab-
> lished, M. Lamartinière, who is in charge of appointments, could take
> someone of 59 and a half . . . so that it could happen that every year a
> woman would enter the Petites-Maisons . . . without having any right or
> qualification.[83]

None of the employees, in fact, did abuse the system in this way. But
careers were irregular, as a summary of age and tenure in 1790 (Figure
5) suggests.[84]

Eighteenth-century French society was plagued with the problems
involved in changing from a system of personal intervention and irregular work to one of complex bureaucracy and regular careers. Throughout the century, placement in a hospital or old age home seems to have
been accomplished only after several rounds of personal recommendations. These would not guarantee entry, but they were clearly necessary.[85] In soliciting a recommendation from the princesse de Conti, an
aged master tailor wrote that he would like to enter the Petites-Maisons
but could not "without protection."[86] Pierre Leroy, a sixty-six-year-old
native of Amiens, married to a seventy-year-old woman of Paris, wrote
the mayor of Paris reminding him of his promise "given on the steps of
the city [hall]" to help them in their search for hospitalization.[87] In *an
IX* (1800), Napoleon and Lucien Bonaparte were asked to write letters
of recommendation.[88] Requests sent to the mayor of Paris were supported by letters from other mayors, parish priests, local administrators, neighbors, relatives, co-workers, employers, deputies to the
National Assembly, surgeons, and members of the Paris faculty of
medicine.

Successful application required a knowledge of the internal workings
of an institution. An answer to a request might provide, if not entry, at
least some information about entry requirements, documentation, or

83. Ibid., fol. 26.
84. Ibid., 1303 fol. 76.
85. Camille Bloch, *L'assistance et l'état en France à la veille de la révolution (Généralités de Paris, Rouen, Alençon, Orléans, Châlons, Soissons, Amiens) (1764–1790)*
(Paris, 1908), p. 79 n.2.
86. B.N., J.F., 1239 fol. 475.
87. A.N. F[15] 247 no. 436, June 7, 1791.
88. A.N. F[15] 104.

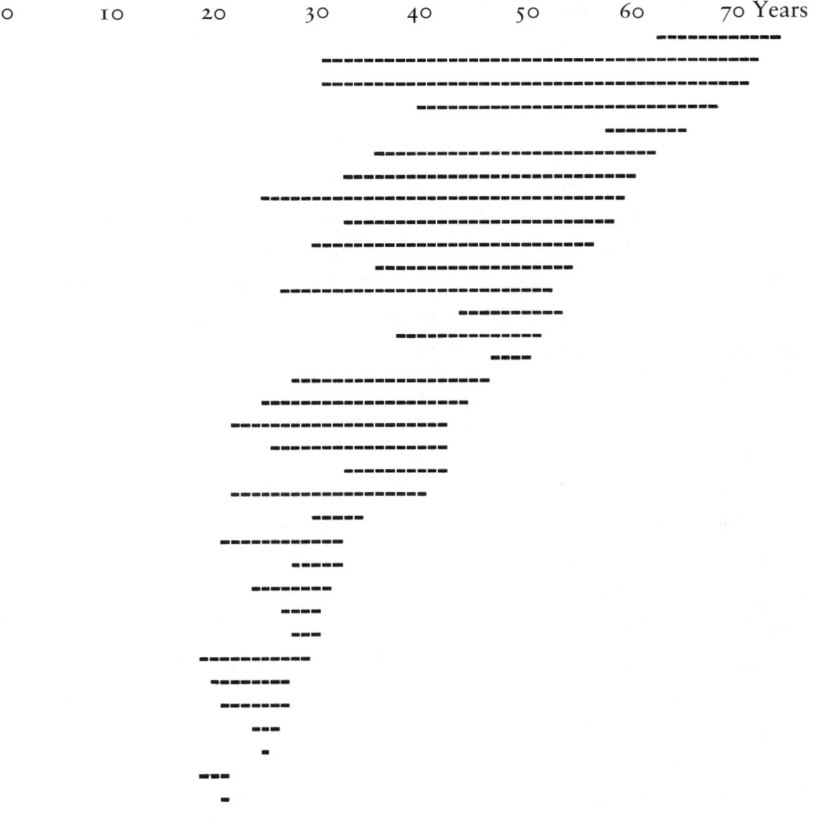

FIGURE 5. Age and tenure of sisters, Petites-Maisons, 1790

the proper procedure for a second request. Petitioners tried to give an impression of familiarity with the institution in question, claiming knowledge of empty beds or underutilized facilities: "Citizen Maugin, aged 83 years, infirm and poor, as well as his wife, having exercised an honest profession, demands a bed at the Incurables or at least a retirement in the Couvent de la Miséricorde which he says is not occupied."[89] The petitioner in this case may well have known more than the administrator who summarized the request.

Sometimes, however, things were not so simply done. On May 27, 1791, two old men named Allardin and Lallemand, employed at the Halle aux Draps, wrote the mayor asking for his help in finding them

89. A.N. F[15] 242.

places in the Incurables. Allardin described himself as seventy-eight years old, "overcome with misery and infirmity"; Lallemand was eighty-six and blind. The mayor's response was a recommendation that places be found.[90] But evidently they failed to materialize, for two months later Lallemand, still blind but having lost two years and gained a wife of sixty-two, applied for entry to the Petites-Maisons. The *curé* of Saint Eustache supported the request. But the mayor's office replied that households were not received at the Hôpital des Petites-Maisons; "the Salpêtrière is the only one that admits them, but the places there are reserved long in advance. We have alerted the *curé* of St. Eustache, who is interested in these two old people."[91] Several days later the request on behalf of Lallemand was renewed by the abbé Quinet, former almoner of the town hall. He argued that the wife was very ill and terribly exhausted from trying for the past two months to find a place in the hospital. She was near death, and if she died, her husband would soon follow.[92] Perhaps the effort did prove too much for both of them. If the following winter intervened, as often happened to the aged, their fate was probably no worse than that of the mayor himself, who was executed on November 12, 1793.

In a society where personal connections counted for so much, one should not be surprised at people's faith in their efficacy. The eighteenth century had witnessed the creation of bureaucratic institutions of conflicting authority—indeed, such was the method by which monarchs had placated commercial classes and, in turn, the various levels of nobility—and the Revolution understandably followed the same pattern. But beneath these layers of authority there remained an abiding belief that the way to achieve something was to gather and present letters of introduction and recommendation.

The philosophical importance of *race et lignage* may have been questioned by the Revolution, and most inquisitively by the Terror, but it created its own hierarchy based upon analogous genetic assumptions. A letter written by the "Provisional administrators of the free city of Mons" on March 19, 1793, requesting a place for an old man in the Incurables of Paris vouched for the applicant's virtue by demonstrating the qualities of his son, a Paris policeman, whose prudence had saved the city from undue carnage and slaughter; the letter made clear that it

90. A.N. F¹⁵ 247 no. 435.
91. Ibid., no. 469.
92. Ibid., no. 472.

was in consideration of the son's laudable conduct that the Parisian authorities should act.[93]

Filial piety would certainly be alluded to in letters seeking assistance. One Florimond Le Roux, deputy to the National Assembly from the city of Amiens, mentioned in a letter of September 7, 1791, that his son had prevailed upon him to recommend their former elderly neighbor in Amiens for a bed at Bicêtre. Although the man could not be accepted, as he was not a resident of Paris, the letter had tried to impress the reader with a vision, albeit in the wrong city, of filial concern and neighborliness.[94] The Enlightenment had prescribed such a vision, and it may well have been broadly shared, especially in the city, where feelings of filial piety were perhaps less sorely tested than on the land. Still, the results were (and are) ambiguous. Placing a father in an institution could have been either a hard-hearted form of parricide or an act of mercy. One wonders what connections were retained through a patient's final stay in the hospital. A rare diary, kept by a pensioner in the Blois hospital, recounts an active social life of entertaining visitors and dining out with friends.[95] But among the poor, of course, family closeness and privacy may have been precluded by a patient's one, two, or even three bedmates (as were encountered in the Hôpital Général de Niort in 1791 by Crussol d'Amboise, deputy from Poitou).[96] But in a world whose sense of privacy differed from ours, it would not be completely absurd to suggest that at least companionship and prospective witnesses for notarial activities were near at hand for hospital inmates.

Moreover, vast numbers of individuals were seeking entry not for their parents but for themselves. The fatalistic chorus of *J'irai à l'hôpital* reflects an expected course of events but certainly does not explain anyone's particular decision. Once again, individual letters provide information lacking in the neatly categorized records of hospitals. How the aged described themselves to administrative authorities informs us not only about institutional requirements but about the applicants' perceptions of themselves.

93. A.N. F[15] 242.
94. Ibid.
95. Isaac Girard's account concerns the years 1722–25. Marie-Claude Dinet-Lecomte, "Vieillir et mourir à l'hôpital de Blois au XVIIIe siècle," *Annales de démographie historique 1985* (Paris, 1986), pp. 85–101, provides additional comments on the document as well as extracts (in the same volume, pp. 311–321: "La vie des personnes âgées à l'hôpital de Blois au XVIIIe siècle").
96. A.N. F[15] 233.

Because proof of age was usually required for entry into hospitals, prominent in the letter would be, say, the figure 70 or the phrase *quatre-vingts environ*. The precise age requirement was often arbitrarily chosen.[97] Hospitals limited their clientele by requiring proof that an applicant had attained the age of seventy (when, biblically, one could expect to be dead) or even, as in the Maisons Philanthropiques de Paris et d'Orléans, eighty.[98] Some petitioners referred more vaguely to "great age" or "indigent old age."[99] One employee of the Salpêtrière argued simply that he was a man whose "great age no longer permits him to continue his job."[100] Administrators were asked to have "special regard" for an "old age of sixty-seven years" or for "advanced age."[101]

The petition for Nicolas Picard of Paris argued that he was prematurely aged in September of 1792: "At 54 he has the grief of seeing himself stricken with practically all the infirmities of old age: deprived of sight, he is in addition affected by two ruptures that deny him the use of his limbs and prevent him from doing any work that can give him subsistence." An infirm fifty-nine-year-old might argue that he was "approaching old age." A curate of the Paris region wrote the administrators of the Petites-Maisons on June 30, 1790: "I have lived 60 years and I am more infirm than many are at 80." Others were, somewhat more poetically, "curved beneath the weight of years."[102]

If it was difficult for an administrator in Paris to verify the ages of all his charges—most of whom probably did not know their own ages anyway—it is virtually impossible for the historian to do so without very sophisticated coding and linkages, which would still miss large numbers of immigrants. Things were not as simple as in the village. Administrators with each year's records before them could easily have added one year to an initially reported age as new lists of the same names were drawn up in each successive year. But they did not bother. Of twenty old beggars in Montreuil receiving assistance in both Germinal, *an IV* (March–April 1796), and Brumaire, *an VI* (October–November 1797)—that is, over some nineteen months—ten remained the same age in the records, eight aged from one to nine years, and two

97. As in England; see Janet Roebuck, "When Does 'Old Age' Begin?: The Evolution of the English Definition," *Journal of Social History,* 12 (1979).

98. C. Bloch, *L'assistance et l'état,* pp. 354–356.

99. A.N. F[15] 242 no. 620.

100. Ibid., no. 804, January 31, 1793.

101. A.N. F[15] 2875 no. 18, May 19, 1791; D XXVII 1 no. 7, *Second état,* 6.

102. A.N. F[15] 242 no. 763; A.N. F[15] 104; B.N., J.F., 1238 fol. 178; A.N. D XXVII 1, Letter of Anne Augustine Louis.

were rejuvenated by three and eight years. The important thing was to be able to identify people. And here the physical signs of age became most important. For names might change (spelling always varied), and addresses might change, but a particular physical infirmity was an important mark of identification. It might be said of someone that she "has no other infirmities but her age," but more often it would be remarked that a person was paralyzed or without fingers; these were marks that officials could see. In the Faubourg du Nord in the 1790s, various aged poor were identified as "infirm in the arm and the left thigh," "suffering from rheumatism," "afflicted with a double inguinal hernia," "suffering from pain in the superior extremities," and the like. The weakness of age was often ascribed to specific infirmities: "cruel pains," "a hernia that is often painful," "frequent attacks of rheumatism," deafness, blindness. One seventy-year-old had "long found himself beset with asthma and violent rheumatism which torment him greatly." Seventy-five-year-old Marie Bargneau complained that she was "infirm, having a paralysis of the tongue." Age and infirmity were independent but mutually punishing forces in the case of a widow whose sons were in military service in *an IX* of the Revolution (1800): "She is aged 76 years, paralyzed throughout her body, and finally overcome with infirmities that her old age and her frailness render ever more painful in augmenting the distress of her position."[103]

Infirmities were to be feared not merely because of the pain that came with them; rarely did the aged complain of pain alone, and exceptional was the individual who described his situation as "a thousand times more painful to me than death." More important, infirmities forced one to stop working. François Joseph Léger, former clerk in the Batimens du Roi, said of himself that "two years ago his sight was so weakened by different illnesses that attacked his eyes that he is unable to work." A seventy-year-old working-class widow had "the honor to tell you that for ten years of widowhood she worked every day in order to make a living, but for the last two her great age and, unfortunately, a cancer that she has on her breast prevent her from continuing her work, denying her all means of subsistence."[104]

It was not only physical handicaps and sense impairments—blindness, deafness, speech impairment, infirmity, inability to walk without a

---

103. A.N. F15 2876; A.N. F16 965; A.N. F15 247 nos. 247, 426, 432, 440, 460, 485; A.N. F15 104, *19 Brumaire an IX* (November 10, 1800).
104. A.N. F15 2875 no. 8; A.N. F15 247 no. 479; A.N. F15 242.

cane[105]—that made work impossible. Sometimes the workplace itself was responsible. Pierre Eustache Courtois, writing to the mayor of Paris on July 15, 1791, to protest the loss of his job as clerk in the Bois à Brûler, mentioned that he was "afflicted with a hernia that threatens his days, which he was unfortunate enough to acquire at the leather market when he worked there as a parceller for 32 years." Charles Bertonnet, a mason employed in construction—and, in the early months of the Revolution, demolition—at the Bastille, blamed his infirmities upon the workplace: "By the force of his labor he has gained a rupture, then a deafness which has absolutely prevented his hearing, that since St. Pierre's day he has been paralyzed." A sixty-eight-year-old former sanitation inspector found himself "by his infirmities unable to fulfill his function by the rheumatism that he gained [at work]." Some workers blamed their bosses; in Poitiers, Jean Bertrand, sixty, lamented his "scrofula gained in service to the king."[106] There had been a time when kings cured that ailment.

When such infirmities struck, there were few jobs the victims could perform. Only younger women could successfully turn to prostitution, though there were such exceptions as sixty-year-old Benoîte Rivière of Lyon. A more likely alternative was begging. Beggars arrested in Paris were found to operate at times in groups or pairs: husband and wife, mother and daughter.[107]

The difficulties of aging—though tending certainly to isolate many with their infirmities—had consequences for whole networks of people. The aged were dependent upon spouses, children, nephews; the young were dependent upon the aged. But there were times when the needs of the individual challenged those of the family. Thus, a son-in-law claimed no longer to be able to support his father-in-law; a former gamekeeper at La Chapelle near Paris lost his job and could no longer aid his seventy-eight-year-old mother, who took refuge in the Salpêtrière. On March 8, 1746, a clockmaker named Pierre Bourdon complained that his aged mother's insanity was interfering with his business; he offered to pay a pension of 200 *livres* if the Petites-Maisons would accept her. Then there were those who unburdened themselves of spouses. A seventy-six-year-old woman from the Ile-Saint-Louis offered

---

105. A.N. F[15] 2876 (Montreuil); A.M. Amiens, GG 1089–90. Engrand, "Paupérisme," p. 400, provides a chart of infirmities of the poor of all ages in 1778 and notes the premature aging of the working class.

106. A.N. F[15] 247 nos. 470, 481, 426; A.N. F[16] 965.

107. A.N. F[15] 2811.

a pension to permit her senile eighty-four-year-old husband to enter the Petites-Maisons. Her curate recommended the husband, saying that the wife was restricted to her room and could not care for him and that before his illness he had been an honest, upright man.[108]

Sometimes the aged were themselves burdened with infirm children. A seventy-two-year-old father wanted to confine his insane daughter, age forty, to the Petites-Maisons and promised to pay her way. An aged couple, worried about what would happen to their blind daughter after their deaths—"The old age of her father and mother is troubled by this sad thought"—applied to the Quinze-Vingts.[109]

The care of two old men was a factor in an appointment to the chaplaincy of the Petites-Maisons. The incumbent resigned his post to seek a less demanding position with a secure income that would help him to support his seventy-year-old father, "to relieve his pains in old age and bear witness to the recognition that right and nature demand of him." He proposed switching positions with a *curé* in the diocese of Bayeux. That *curé* wanted to move to Paris, and his uncle, the abbé de St. Medan, wanted him there too: "At my age of more than ninety years, it would be not a little consoling for me to have him in my vicinity, to enjoy his cares and friendship during the few days that are left me and that it will please God to keep for me."[110] The nephew got the job.

During the Revolution, letters mentioned the problems that arose when sons went into military service, leaving parents helpless in their old age. Such situations occasioned the first national pensions to come to Eguilles and many other places, but frequently, they just meant more deprivation. Laurent Le Beuf, sixty-eight, and his wife, fifty-two, lamented the fact that their five sons were gone to war. A sixty-five-year-old day-laborer, Simon Gros Jean of the rue de Montreuil, wrote that he was unable to work and "burdened with a wife with no job, by a daughter burdened with her own child, whose father is defending the nation"; furthermore he had "a son in the same service, upon whom he used to count to provide him with aid in old age," but the son had been enrolled almost eleven years before, and the father had had no news of him for four years.[111]

Whether as a function of dechristianization or simply secularization, assistance was increasingly seen as a right. A clerk in the Ponts-et-

---

108. A.N. F[15] 247 nos. 443, 493; B.N., J.F., 1238 fol. 57, 62, 64.
109. B.N., J.F., 1239 fol. 464; A.N. F[15] 240, *Quinze-Vingts*.
110. B.N., J.F., 1302 fol. 127, 202.
111. A.N. F[15] 104, *19 frimaire an IX* (December 10, 1800).

Chaussées wrote on 23 Frimaire, *an III* (1794), for his father-in-law, who had worked for thirty-nine or forty years and therefore deserved the retirement "that his great age and seniority of service demand." A worker in Toulon named Serry, suffering for two years from rheumatism, pointed to his fifty-five years of service, forty-four in the Ponts-et-Chaussées.[112] One deserved an earthly reward rather than a heavenly one.

According to twentieth-century gerontologists, a life review is an essential part of aging. The Counter-Reformation too had required a summing-up of one's life as a step toward heavenly salvation. The eighteenth century—especially the period of the French Revolution—required it as an important preparatory act for continued life on earth. Such life reviews fill the letters of request for help in old age. Tales of the workplace, of the weather, of parents and children, and of political events defined each of these aged poor as unique within certain patterns.

First, there were the people whose lives had been ruined by infirmity. Anne Thérèse Faugier, born in Grenoble and residing in the rue Saint-Denis in Paris, wrote the mayor explaining that at the approximate age of seventy she needed help. She had been a linen worker and "lived by the toil of her hands," but she had grown almost entirely blind. Her neighbors had aided her by providing the necessities of life, but her situation endangered those same neighbors, who were "ceaselessly agitated by the fear that she [would] set fire to the place, while blindly cooking and heating" her food. She appealed to the mayor's "paternal tenderness" to find her a place in the *salle Saint-Charles* of the Salpêtrière, as there was "a woman she knows there, who, despite her age, would be able to lead her where her needs would beckon."[113]

Then there were those struck by multiple misfortunes, personal and environmental. Pierre Dominique Leconte, a laborer in Coulogne, and his wife, Marie Antoinette Rohart, presented "the list of the calamities that they would have suffered during the course of their marriage." They had used their money to purchase a farm and raise their children, but for the next twenty years a series of illnesses had struck the family and had killed nineteen horses and eighty cows. Their losses were estimated at 14,000–15,000 *livres;* they were destitute. In addition they were hounded by "barbarous creditors," including a particularly unpleasant Monsieur Drouillard of Dunkirk.[114]

112. A.N. D XXVII 1.
113. A.N. F[15] 247 no. 462, July 10, 1791.
114. A.N. F[15] 2875, May 3, 1791.

Sixty-eight-year-old Monsieur Houdas, from the town of Checy near Orléans, offered a peripatetic history. His latest trouble was the suppression in 1791 of his post as collector of the poor tax, but he had seen previous misfortune as well. In 1758 he had left his native town of Loury-aux-Bois to become an innkeeper. He soon took on the added role of collector, but in 1778 suffered an attack of asthma so severe that he felt it necessary to leave the post to his eldest son and move deeper into the country. Four years later, when his son was killed by "a nasty cow," he returned to town and set up house with his second son, but they eventually found themselves unemployed.[115]

Some postulants argued that a life of hard work deserved a better end. For seventy-year-old Benoist Claude of Créteil, the thirteen-year labor of draining a swamp and making cultivable the plot of land deeded him by the monarchy merited him security in old age, but the municipality had seized the property and deprived him of the "sole resource of his subsistence." Five centuries of labor was the basis of Marin Liberge's claim to the reward of a place in the hospital: at seventy-six he was "native of Coudoux, laborer for 500 years from father to son, living in Paris for forty in the parish of Saint Roch."[116]

If one tactic was to fit one's life into the long-term scheme of things, another was to present it as having begun with promise and personal connections. A grocer named Mouquet, himself a master and therefore a person conscious of corporate responsibilities, wrote to the mayor on behalf of the widow of the writer Godefroi Sellius. Sellius's fellow writers, he said, had promised aid that never materialized. The Duc de Penthièvre had provided some relief, but it had disappeared four years previously. The widow was living on "perpetual bread from her parish (Saint Eustache) and one *écu* per month," but these appeared to be no longer perpetual: "She is again threatened, I say, with losing this bread and therewith her life." She had worked as a laundress until her eyes and hands gave out, but now she could not pay her rent and had no linen and no clothes save the rags on her back. The letter included a personal appeal, as the widow's late husband was a close friend of the mayor's father at whose house in Chaillot the couple was married.[117]

Some applicants presented their lives in terms of a particular contribution to French society. An Irish inventor who identified himself as *Le Citoien Maccarty* claimed that he had improved French manufacturing

115. A.N. F¹⁵ 2875, May 30, 1791.
116. A.N. F¹⁵ 2875; A.N. F¹⁵ 247 no. 518, September 27, 1791.
117. A.N. F¹⁵ 247 no. 478, July 28, 1791.

with his machine for "preparing all materials in silk, wool, and cotton." He had been awarded a pension under the ancien régime, but it had been discontinued. Meanwhile, two of his sons and a son-in-law had died in the French army. As justification for a place in the Incurables, he offered "proof of his good citizenship, of his probity and of the services he [had] rendered the state." Similarly, a sixty-six-year-old inventor named Jacques Faynard, who discovered an "anti-haemorrhagic vulnerary powder" while in England, had brought his product to France and had been promised an allowance by the comte de Vergennes.[118]

Pensions and jobs were lost as regime succeeded regime. Nicolas Philippe Buteux, a sixty-four-year-old clerk in the clockmaking trade, found himself destitute after the suppression of a post he had held for thirty-four years. He recalled the costs of raising his children and caring for his late wife, who had succumbed to a "long and ruinous" malady. He asked to be rescued from "the frightful calamity that he has neither merited nor been able to forsee." He hoped only for the "tranquility in retirement" his life warranted.[119]

More and more individuals spoke the language not of charity but of social debt. The sixty-five-year-old former apothecary, Louis Coulon, who suffered from "two ruptures," had married a widow, raised her eight children, paid her debts, provided for his own five offspring, and, as an apothecary, served "suffering humanity." Humanity now owed him something. As another postulant wrote about his own sad case, "The continually active life merits another conclusion." A sixty-seven-year-old schoolteacher in Saint Pourçain, Claude Causse, describing himself in May 1791 as "abandoned by wife and children and devoted to the bitterest of tears," suggested that his career deserved a proper retirement. He had not only taught reading, writing, and arithmetic for twenty-one years but also worked as a recordkeeper in the town hall for ten. He had served the youth and wider population of his city and *chère patrie*. He hoped to gain from the National Assembly, "the restorers of popular happiness, . . . a retirement that the celestial father will surely crown with the immortal laurel."[120]

The fulfillment of seemingly ordinary roles, the support of family and community, the cultivation of land, and the practice of professions—

118. A.N. F[15] 257, *28 Germinal an III* (April 17, 1795); A.N. F[15] 2875, August 20, 1791.
119. A.N. F[15] no. 620, February 16, 1792.
120. A.N. F[15] 242 no. 758, September 24, 1792; A.N. F[15] 2875, May 19, 1791.

these petitioners believed—warranted state aid. A lifetime of work merited the reward of a suitable retirement. In old age one felt that a life added up to something that could be summarized. The aged poor had undoubtedly recounted similar tales in village squares or urban gathering places, but most of those words are lost to us. In the late eighteenth century they had a new audience, one that wanted their stories in writing.

Of course there were those who were so deprived, or perhaps so ill-equipped to cope with deprivation, that they could not present their lives in summary form; they needed immediate help. If they were foreigners, their problems might well be compounded. One sixty-seven-year-old widow from the Palatinate complained that three different notaries, whose names she had forgotten but whose addresses she remembered, had stolen all her money. A sixty-year-old immigrant from Constantinople, who had fallen victim to the rigors of Parisian life, wrote that she was deprived of the necessities of life and had not paid her rent in six months; she was threatened with eviction, and her laundry was being held by the laundress.[121]

Many others—and by no means exclusively foreigners—were so concerned with extreme poverty that they did not have the leisure to philosophize about their existence; they had to be more succinct. One letter compressed seventy years into a moment: the author described himself as "a septuagenarian born without means."[122]

In the second half of the eighteenth century the literature on poverty was growing. Many of the archival cartons that contain letters demanding assistance also contain plans purporting to solve social problems. Whether called *Caisses d'épargnes* or *Plans pour la répression de la mendicité*, they sought to enable the poor to save. Ways to guarantee retirement funds—not on the basis of particular acts for a particular regime but on the proper wages to permit savings and a stable economy to maintain prices and monetary value at a constant level—became an important topic. It had been common practice for the bourgeoisie to lend money at interest and live on the returns (in the eighteenth century, Church law against the taking of interest was disregarded by municipal authorities, economic theorists, and some churchmen), and savings banks and pension programs were called for in pamphlets before and

121. A.N. F¹⁵ 2875, Anne Catherine Elizabeth Stahl; A.N. D XXVII 1, Geneviève Marie Victoire Zadine.

122. A.N. F¹⁵ 247 no. 475, Maréchal, July 24, 1791.

during the French Revolution.[123] Some plans, such as Condorcet's, were Utopian; others were not. Some came into existence; others never did. Those that did, such as the *caisse Lafarge*, served individuals who had already been lending money individually. Still, it was hoped that such banks would help the poor.[124] Enlightenment ideology was used as the basis for programs well beyond the eighteenth century.

Plans for national old age pensions derived from several traditions of thinking about age, work, and poverty. They also derived from empirical observation. And the pathetic discourse found in letters of ordinary people differed little from that of contemporary social science and politics: both combined old notions of communal and corporate solidarity with new ideas of social debt.[125] The combination was crystallized in French Revolutionary rhetoric, which treated a range of other social and political issues of the era: childhood, gender, the relationship between private and public spheres, and even the Sadean question of pleasure and pain.[126]

It is of course artificial to treat old age in isolation. Revolutionary discourse treated it in the context of remaking all of society, of secularizing the sacred, and of addressing the problem of poverty as it concerned both old and young. The combined pressures of culture and society resulted in new definitions, an awareness of new realities, and a new prescription for social problems. Even when evoking old age, Revolutionaries had grander things in mind, but evoke it they did in a way that set the agenda for our own day.

123. Groethuysen, *The Bourgeois;* Marcel Courdurié, *La dette des collectivités publiques de Marseille au XVIIIe siècle: Du débat sur le prêt à intérêt au financement par l'emprunt* (Marseille, 1974); A.N. F[15] 2875.

124. M.-J.-A.-N Caritat, marquis de Condorcet, *Esquisse d'un tableau historique des progrès de l'esprit humain* (Paris, 1864), and *Sur les caisses d'accumulation,* in *Oeuvres* (Paris, 1847–49); Joachim Lafarge, *Caisse d'épargnes et de bienfaisance du sieur La Farge* (Paris, 1791); *Caisse d'épargnes du C. Lafarge: Liste Générale des numéros . . .* (Paris, an XI [1802–3]); *Projet de bienfaisance* (1789); *Projet de bienfaisance du sieur Lafarge* (Paris, 1790); *Projet de bienfaisance du sieur Lafarge* (Paris, n.d.); *Réflexions utiles et nécessaires aux actionnaires de la caisse d'épargnes et de bienfaisance du citoyen Lafarge* (Paris, an II [1793–94]).

125. Sewell, *Work and Revolution,* is very useful on both continuity and change in the organization of work and popular mentalities.

126. On revolutionary rhetoric, ideology, and mentalities, see Michel Vovelle, *Idéologies et mentalités* (Paris, 1985); *La mentalité révolutionnaire: Société et mentalités sous la révolution française* (Paris, 1985); Bronislaw Baczko, *Lumières de l'utopie* (Paris, 1978); Brian Singer, *Society, Theory, and the French Revolution: Studies in the Revolutionary Imaginary* (New York, 1986); Lynn Hunt, *Politics, Culture, and Class in the French Revolution* (Berkeley, Calif., 1984).

8 A Practical Enlightenment and a Deferential Revolution

Out of a fusion of demographic and economic crisis, scientific activity, and welling sentiment arose a social science that expressed both the critical and the humanitarian strands of Enlightenment thought. It is commonplace to discuss the Enlightenment as that period when the study of human society reached greater heights than had been scaled in the Renaissance and was imbued with an unprecedented belief in progress. As far as the study of aging and the aged is concerned, the eighteenth century indisputably marks a high point, unrivaled until the twentieth century. Such study developed out of a desire for progress but not necessarily a belief in it. Those who proposed assistance for the elderly were reacting to perceptions that life was getting more difficult as it was getting longer; they called for action. Population pressure, urbanization, and a loss of religious faith combined to make aging both a social and an intellectual problem whose solution came to be seen in national political terms.

Such early demographers as Jean-Joseph Expilly, Moheau, Messance, Antoine Deparcieux, and the chevalier des Pommelles extrapolated from parish registers in order to estimate France's population and age composition.[1] But this was hardly demography for its own sake. Deparcieux's *Essai sur les probabilités de la durée de la vie humaine* (1746), a work approved for the Académie Royale des Sciences by François Nicole and Buffon, used contemporary demographic data to demonstrate

1. Abbé Jean-Joseph Expilly, *Tableau de la population de la France* (N.p., 1780); Moheau, *Recherches et considérations;* Messance, *Nouvelles recherches sur la population de la France* (Lyon, 1788); Deparcieux, *Essai;* Chevalier des Pommelles, *Tableau de la population de toutes les provinces de France* (Paris, 1789). See also Jacques and Michel Dupâquier, *Histoire de la démographie,* esp. chaps. 5 and 6.

how lifetime annuities might properly work.[2] Des Pommelles's *Tableau de la population* of 1789 used estimates of age composition to make recommendations for policy concerning military service and exemptions; even the Visigoths, he observed, excused their old men from serving.[3] The *Gazette de France* reported cases of extraordinary longevity as a public service: "It appears to us consoling for humanity to learn that one can prolong one's career beyond a century, and the frequent examples of these men favored by nature inspire the hopes of the rest of society."[4]

A journal that specialized in agricultural and commercial subjects, the *Gazette de l'agriculture, du commerce, et de finance,* turned to demography in 1777 and became a forum for Messance and Moheau, publishing not only their essays and letters but also a considerable quantity of raw demographic data.[5] It compared mortality in hospitals and out, and in Messance's second letter it investigated age-specific death rates—with a separate category for accidental death—in a town between Lyon and Saint-Etienne.[6]

The *Almanach des centenaires* addressed a more popular readership. It began life as the *Almanach de la vieillesse* but, in response to a letter from a reader in Germany, changed its name so as not to displease readers with the word *vieillesse*. Its editors themselves admitted to some doubts as to the benefits of living into old age, remarking that since in Paris someone dies every half-hour, a person who lives to fifty-five must see a million deaths; one who reaches 110, two million. For whatever reason, the almanac itself died within just a few years.[7]

Some authorities carried demographic techniques to extraordinary lengths. Guillaume Daignan wrote that there were fifteen ages of life divided by the onset of fourteen new psychological characteristics—"risk, hope, desire, pleasure, delight, firmness, possession, reflection,

---

2. Deparcieux, *Essai.* See also Abraham de Moivre (Fellow of the Royal Society and member of the Royal Academies of Sciences of Berlin and Paris), *A Treatise of Annuities on Lives,* 2d ed., published with *The Doctrine of Chances; or, A Method of Calculating the Probabilities of Events in Play,* 3d ed. (London, 1756).

3. Des Pommelles, *Tableau* (published with a *Mémoire sur les milices*).

4. *Gazette de France,* 92, p. 422 (Paris, November 16, 1772).

5. J. Lecuir, "*La Gazette de l'Agriculture, du Commerce et de Finance* et le débat sur la population à la fin du XVIIIe siècle," *Annales de démographie historique* (Paris, 1979), pp. 363–441.

6. Demographic portrait of Rivedegier and Châteauneuf, ibid., p. 436.

7. Lottin, *Almanach des centenaires.* This and other almanacs are discussed in John Grand-Carteret, *Les almanachs français* (Paris, 1896).

regret, infirmity, avarice, scorn, indifference, and unconsciousness"—
and constructed a mathematical table of the "varieties of human life" in
which he considered the relationships between age, climate, and en-
vironment.[8] Taking the mathematical view of physiology and geography even further, Wilhelm Butte later outlined a fantastic graphic and
mathematical representation of all human life—in short, "the rapport
that necessarily exists between *the times of man* and *the spaces of the
earth*" and "the influence of the longitudes."[9] Butte's system rests on the
traditional magic of the numbers seven and nine and their multiples—
men live to eighty-one and women to seventy-seven, with "sexual
death" occurring at sixty-three and forty-nine respectively—and the
equally traditional four phases of life, corresponding to the four seasons
as well as to four periods of the day (morning, noon, evening, and
night). But the geographic element is what sets his scheme apart from
others. Northern latitudes are considered masculine, southern feminine.
Degrees of longitude correspond directly to years of age, so the degrees
63 to 81 refer to places of old age, the old world. Life is sketched out in
Kantian schemata (see Figure 6), and the diagrams are read from top to
bottom in Hegelian fashion from unity through opposition to resolu-
tion.[10]

Fanciful as Butte's scheme may be, his justification for it was common
enough: he wanted to measure the relative strengths and weaknesses of
given populations. In this endeavor he came close to the modern notion
of dependency ratios: "The *State* would like to know: what is the
number of its *inhabitants* who find themselves at the age where man is
capable of contributing physically to support it? In order to succeed in
knowing that, it is necessary to subtract from the totality of the population the *young people* and the *old people,* who, in respect to strength,
ought to be considered in a state of *negative quantities.*"[11]

Butte's work was excessively and absurdly quantitative, and it takes
us beyond the eighteenth century, but it does indicate how demography
was developing throughout the early modern period. In the sixteenth
and seventeenth centuries demographic thought was dominated by the

8. Guillaume Daignan, *Tableau des variétés de la vie humaine* (Paris, 1786), quoted
in Mona Ozouf, "Symboles et fonctions des âges dans les fêtes de l'époque révolutionnaire," *Annales historiques de la révolution française,* 42, no. 202. (1970), 576 n. 16;
Daignan, *Echelle de la vie humaine, ou Thermomètre de santé* (Paris, 1811).
  9. Butte, *Prolégomènes,* p. 7, and *Echelle physiologique.*
  10. Butte, *Prolégomènes,* esp. pp. 21–30.
  11. Ibid., pp. 87–89.

Earth

Nature ------- Destiny

Life

Childhood

Puberty ----------Adulthood

Old Age

Phlegmatic

Sanguine --------------Choleric

Melancholic

FIGURE 6. Wilhelm Butte's life diagrams

interest of the prince and the absolutist state. Whether rigidly mercantil-
ist or more libertarian and physiocratic, policies tended to identify
quality with quantity: the more subjects, the greater the state. By the
middle of the eighteenth century, however, there were those who favored virtually Malthusian policies, concerned with both the interest of
the state and the interest of the individual.[12] They were not as extreme
as Malthus was later in demanding moral restraint of the poor, but they
did suggest that overpopulation might become a problem and that
techniques of savings and income distribution should perhaps be studied. Henry de Boulainvilliers recommended a system by which one-fifth
of everyone's wages would be withheld in order to guarantee payment
of taxes and to amass a social insurance fund for the education of
working-class children and the care of the disabled and the elderly.[13]
Joachim Faiguet de Villeneuve similarly proposed the creation of a
government bank to encourage savings by the poorest of Frenchmen,
and Augustin du Beissier de Pizany d'Eden suggested a fund for the
retirement of artists.[14] But those who desired to affect population
trends in France, whether for state reasons or otherwise, believed that
self-interest was not the only factor in decisions about family planning.

12. Antonin Puvilland, "Les doctrines de la population en France au XVIIIe siècle de
1695 à 1776" (doctoral diss., University of Lyon, 1912).

13. Jacqueline Hecht, "Trois précurseurs de la Sécurité sociale au XVIIIe siècle:
Henry de Boulainvilliers, Faiguet de Villeneuve, Du Beissier de Pizany d'Eden," *Popula-
tion*, 14, no. 1 (1959), 73–88; Joseph J. Spengler, *French Predecessors of Malthus: A
Study in Eighteenth-Century Wage and Population Theory* (Durham, N.C., 1942), p. 37.

14. Hecht, "Trois précurseurs."

Particularly when it came to celibacy, moral questions arose. As Moheau observed in discussing both spurs and obstacles to demographic growth, "Reflection and the spirit of calculation would not lead us to propagate the species. Motives above interest, scorn for riches, and abstention from luxury must determine us to support this domestic charge. The attachment of children must also prepare the possibility of happiness for the old age of parents: these sentiments are the result of morals."[15]

One physiocrat who was deeply concerned with the relationship between morals and demographic patterns was the Marquis de Mirabeau, whose *L'ami des hommes, ou Traité de la population* of 1756 encouraged the development of agriculture, reliance on self-help and, where necessary, on private charity, and an avoidance of luxury. He looked back at an idealized past when old gentlemen gathered about the dinner table with wine in hand to dispense justice among their neighbors.[16] Money had destroyed that order and induced disrespect for elders. In a key chapter on luxury Mirabeau warned that the young were gaining positions of cultural hegemony, "maturing" too quickly and ever so falsely, setting styles that were foolishly imitated by their elders. The natural order had to be restored: "The authority of adulthood over youth, and the respect that it has for old age, are natural sentiments, it is true, but dependent upon a certain regime of habit, and of separation of morals from familiarity."[17] When roles are reversed, said Mirabeau, the aged become ridiculous. He did not single them out for reproach; both young and old were debauched, in his view, and French society had reached a critical stage.

In a chapter titled "Age de la France," Mirabeau likened the age of the kingdom to that of an individual. Others may have concluded that a tired France was reaching old age, but he argued that it was just reaching maturity, its youth having ended with the death of Louis XIV. Only the strengthening of monarchy, the love of the people for their sovereign, the reestablishment of the nobility's taste for military affairs, a surge of patriotism, and the exercising of generosity could successfully bring France through its crisis.[18]

15. Moheau, *Recherches et considérations*, vol. 2, p. 99; also quoted in Puvilland, "Les doctrines de la population," pp. 201–202.

16. Marquis de Mirabeau, *L'ami des hommes, ou Traité de la population* (1756; Paris, 1883), p. 84.

17. Ibid., p. 292.

18. Ibid., p. 322.

Central to his reforms was the closing of the hospitals, which, he said, had sapped the strength of the population. The expectation of automatic entry into a public institution (no one has made the hospital appear so cruelly attractive to the aged of the ancien régime as Mirabeau) had caused excessive consumption, debauchery, and dissipation throughout the course of a lifetime. Instead, the French must take responsibility for preparing for old age: "This old drunk who retires peacefully to Bicêtre, having looked forward to it for thirty years, because from there he can still see the towers of Notre-Dame and can even easily come see his friends and the cabaret, would think twice if the route of his retirement were the barge of Montargis, to go from there to take the air of some wild canton of the Hurepoix."[19] He claimed that he did not want to make the poor suffer, only to reduce their numbers.

Mirabeau was one of many who addressed questions of poverty and beggary (*mendicité*) in the second half of the eighteenth century. Others shared his mistrust of the poor and sought ways of employing them. For Turneau de la Morendière, laziness was the "mother of all vices," and work itself would encourage virtue and eliminate robbery, murder, and prostitution. Jobs ought to be created for all.[20] And he meant all, because "however infirm, however crippled they be, there will be few among them unable to work at small tasks that can be performed with one arm, or with one foot, or without feet, and even without arms. It all depends upon the intelligence of the overseers."[21]

In one of the many essays written on beggary in answer to a question posed by a provincial academy, Leclerc de Montlinot also argued in 1779 that hospitals ought to be closed, that they were dehumanizing prisons that only exacerbated France's social problems. The inmate was turned into an automaton, "no longer husband or father, for whom there remains no hope of being consoled in his old age."[22] The work ethic was destroyed by the hospital, and so was the family. Children raised in hospitals grew up to be vagabonds and criminals.[23]

Montlinot too was very much in favor of stimulating work. He

19. Ibid., p. 349.

20. Turneau de la Morendière, *Police sur les mendians, les vagabonds, les joueurs de profession, les intrigans, les filles prostituées, les domestiques hors de maison depuis long-tems, et les gens sans aveu* (Paris, 1764), p. 80.

21. Ibid., p. 45.

22. Leclerc de Montlinot, *Discours qui a remporté le prix à la société royale d'agriculture de Soissons en l'année 1779* (Lille, 1779), p. 24.

23. Ibid., pp. 26–27.

thought that those who were incapable of working, through age or accident, were rare. Too many beggars were thrown into hospitals for the sake of hiding them from public view, and hiding such people only made the rest of the population insensitive.[24] He thought he had hit upon a perfect solution to the problem in a parish relief system (which he claimed was in use in French Flanders) whereby each village took care of its own poor without resorting to a hospital. Every year the poor would be gathered at a public meeting in the cemetery; one by one they would mount a rock and be auctioned off to the lowest bidder, who thereupon agreed to accept that payment from the village to house and feed his charge. A child, he said, went for 75 *livres* per year, an old person for 120.[25] Funds were raised through property taxes. Montlinot suggested transporting this country solution to the city where, he estimated, of a population of 80,000 about one-fifth—some 6,000 men, 4,000 women, and 6,000 children—would need temporary relief for at least three months out of the year, and 1,500 old people, widows, and orphans would require year-round aid.[26]

Seven years later l'abbé de Montlinot's view of work had turned sour. In an essay on beggary which he published in 1789, together with a report dated 1786 on the workhouse of Soissons, Montlinot decided that the very work the poor had to do was what made their lives untenable; the working person was "worn out by painful and murderous labors." In an image foreshadowing those of the worst factories of the nineteenth and twentieth centuries, Montlinot wrote that all crafts, including agriculture, "devour in less than thirty years the living machines of which they take possession."[27]

Surveying the various occupations of eighteenth-century France, Montlinot found them all destructive. Persons employed in cutting precious stones or (Adam Smith to the contrary) making pins lost their eyesight. Quarriers, masons, and carpenters were all wounded by their work. Leather workers gained leaden complexions; metal workers took ill very early. All varieties of farm workers and day laborers contracted chronic illnesses before age fifty: "Society thus consumes the poor." Ninety-five percent of those without wealth died prematurely. In the

---

24. Ibid., pp. 36, 43.
25. Ibid., pp. 49–51.
26. Ibid., p. 57.
27. Leclerc de Montlinot, *Etat àctuel du dépôt de Soissons, précédé d'un essai sur la mendicité* (1786; Soissons, 1789), p. 1.

country, weakness brought death. In the city, skeletons walked the streets.

The rich survived to old age because they did nothing. Montlinot imagined the worker addressing his rich employer: "Born with weak organs, you nevertheless prolong your existence beyond its term . . . and I . . . overwhelmed with incurable ailments at a young age . . . what are you going to offer me after thirty years of toil? . . . perhaps the bread of alms . . . Wretch! I have lived too long." If every man undergoes a crisis around the age of forty-five or fifty, how much worse it must be for the laborer! Yet he must continue to work "because no law exists that requires a boss to feed the servant who has broken a leg in his service, no law that obligates the manufacturer to sustain into old age the workers who have enriched him."[28] Only the apathy that characterizes human nature prevents the poor from revolting.[29] Montlinot's solution was a retirement village in which anyone who had worked for twenty-five years could occupy a cabana, receive medical treatment at home, and be free to breathe the air in liberty.

Still, he distrusted the people whose cause he was upholding. He feared those beggars who banded together in groups: "Nothing . . . would be more likely to inspire terror than those hordes of old men, of mutilated people, who would riotously demand alms and hospitalization." Advising punitive measures for the unworthy, such as the born beggar who refused to work at a job, Montlinot proposed a plan to colonize coastal Africa with such people, encourage them to mix with the native population, and produce a strong race to cultivate America. But such troublemakers, he assured his readers, were in the minority, and the primary goal of the administrator would be to make old age a comfortable time for everyone who reached it.[30]

Enlightenment thinkers who came to administer the finances of the ancien régime in its last years saw further and called for more drastic measures in overhauling the nation's system of assistance. Turgot and Necker attempted to combine workhouses with hospices and provide aid at home within a revised parish-level system, but their legacy would be one of attempting to institute a national system of relief.[31] Such a system would not fully emerge until it had become common to think of

28. Ibid., pp. 2–6.
29. Ibid., p. 14.
30. Ibid., pp. 18–27.
31. C. Bloch, *L'assistance et l'état.*

generational problems in national terms and until charity had given way to social welfare.

Nevertheless, Enlightenment thinkers did suggest a range of solutions to problems of the aged poor. Their prescriptions often concerned wages and savings. Louis-Sébastien Mercier wrote of the aging Parisian worker that his wages could keep him alive only as long as he worked. But, he observed, a working life could not always last an entire life-time.[32] In a discourse on contemporary demography, Elie de Beaumont wrote that traditional practices would have to be changed drastically if artisans were to have a good old age. He proposed a system of lifetime annuities to guarantee aged parents the right to survive.[33] That he referred to *parents* suggests an awareness of the inadequacy of the family alone. Insufficient wages were to be blamed, according to Diderot.[34] The lack of insurance plans or savings banks was at fault, according to Condorcet, who envisaged new institutions.[35] Wages and savings were the key in the view of André-Jean de Larocque, who asserted that the man of the working class

> commonly arrives at old age, attained by fatigue and sweat, only to end his days in misery.
>
> No marginal income is permitted by the meagerness of his salary; and for that reason never does the vision of a happier future, the hope that serves as powerful consoler for the rest of men, come to assuage his fate. Hospitals open to indigence offer only an asylum where humiliation follows: thus the man of this class, condemned since birth to the roughest work, has before his eyes, at the end of his fatigue, only misery and shame.[36]

Larocque presented tables of life expectancy and *rentes viagères* in order to establish the proper workings of a savings bank that would do for the poor in institutional form what wealthy individuals had already been doing for themselves.

Larocque's use of demographic data not only served the practical purpose of refining a solution to the problem of poverty but also pointed

32. Mercier, *Tableau de Paris*, vol. 3, pp. 206–210.

33. Discourse of 1762, quoted in Perrot, *Genèse*, p. 289.

34. Denis Diderot, "Refutation," in *Oeuvres politiques*, p. 473, quoted in Harry C. Payne, *The Philosophes and the People* (New Haven, Conn., 1976), p. 145.

35. Condorcet, *Sur les caisses d'accumulation*, and "Xe époque," in *Esquisse*.

36. André-Jean de Larocque, *Etablissement d'une caisse générale des épargnes du peuple* (Brussels, 1786), p. 3.

out quite simply that longevity itself posed a threat. A long life challenged the resources of the economy; old age was, by definition, a social problem. The mere survival of one generation tightened the reins on the next. In the city, where architecture, economy, and morals all heightened the degree of individualism its population might feel, the problem was exacerbated. Unless one was willing to renounce one's heritage, one had to defer to a patriarchalism that seemed inappropriate and antiquated. The liberty of each younger generation was unduly restricted by the needs and desires of its elders.[37]

Excessive individualism was often blamed for the abandonment of both young and old, yet the communal and corporate limitations on the individual were equally to blame. A new balance between individualism and communalism had to be sought. According to J J. Virey, the two basic needs of human society were reproduction and preservation, the latter demanding particular attention in childhood and old age.[38] The needs of society called for redeeming what Germain Garnier, a translator of Adam Smith, called "this sacred debt with which each generation is charged."[39] Such a debt extended beyond individual families to encompass generations and therefore whole societies. The humanitarian movement of the Enlightenment sought to identify private and public good alike.[40]

The French Revolution permitted further application of the Enlightenment revolution in social thought by which national responsibilities replaced local ones—or, rather, local responsibilities were expressed in national terms. The consequent demand that the broader society pay off its debts to its Belisariuses and Nestors came, moreover, from people other than administrators. *Cahiers de doléances* (grievances prepared for the meeting of the Estates-General) of 1789 suggested national retirement pensions and tax relief for aged workers; priests demanded funds for their old age.[41] As the Revolution moved further and further

37. Sénac de Meilhan, *Considérations*, pp. 307–309.

38. J. J. Virey, *Histoire naturelle du genre humain* (Paris, an IX [1800–1801]), pp. 112–113.

39. Germain Garnier, *Abrégé élémentaire des principes de l'économie politique* (Paris, 1796), *Avertissement*.

40. Cahen, "Les idées charitables"; Shelby T. McCloy, *The Humanitarian Movement in Eighteenth-Century France* (New York, 1972); Walter A. Friedlander, *Individualism and Social Welfare: An Analysis of the System of Social Security and Social Welfare in France* (New York, 1962); Documentation Française, *Social Security in France*; Laurent, *Le paupérisme*; Richard, *Histoire des institutions*.

41. On the *cahiers*, see Jacques Godechot, *Les institutions de la France sous la révolution et l'empire* (Paris, 1968), p. 211; on *cahiers* of the clergy, Timothy Tackett,

to the left, the notion of public responsibility for the aged took precedence over any plans for the revival of private charity. If the Girondins
wanted to limit the role of the state, the Jacobins sought a state monop-
oly on public assistance. Jacobin centralization would allow no inter-
mediary between the aged individual and the income redistribution ap-
paratus of the state. As Robespierre put it: "Society is obliged to provide
for the subsistence of all its members. . . . Aid indispensable to one who
lacks what is necessary is a debt for one who possesses a surplus."[42]

Royal pensions in the ancien régime had been haphazard. They were
awarded in return for services, not necessarily to meet any need, and
only sometimes considered old age pensions. Moreover, while they were
seemingly easy to obtain, they were apparently irregularly paid.[43] Part
of the work of the National Assembly was to reduce their number; by
1787 one-sixth of all royal pensions had already been cut.[44] After more
were eliminated during the Revolution, it was time to begin again the
work of awarding retirement assistance.

Suggestions for old age insurance plans did not all originate in Revolutionary committees. Administrators were recipients of unsolicited
prospectuses as well. One plan that received a lot of attention was the
caisse Lafarge, variously called the *ressource de la vieillesse, projet de
bienfaisance,* or *caisse d'épargnes et de bienfaisance* of Joachim Lafarge.
The author of the plan claimed to have worked on it over the course of
the last ten years of the ancien régime. It surfaced in various versions in
the Estates-General, the Constituent Assembly, and the Convention. It
was studied by Revolutionary committees and the Academy of Sciences
and underwent the scrutiny of those leaders who had proposed their
own plans—such people as Mirabeau and Condorcet—and found
themselves in a position to implement them at the center of political
power.

Lafarge's *Projet de bienfaisance,* addressed in 1789 to the Estates-
General, began with a familiar introduction to the need for a new

---

Priest and Parish in Eighteenth-Century France (Princeton, N.J., 1977), pp. 41–42; and
François Rouvière, *Histoire de la révolution française dans le département du Gard,* vol.
1 (Nîmes, 1887), *Annexes* 3–4.

42. Quoted in Henri Breuil, *L'assistance aux vieillards à Paris de 1789 à 1905* (Paris,
1909), pp. 10–11. See also Fernand Charoy, *L'assistance aux vieillards, infirmes, et
incurables en France de 1789 à 1905* (Paris, 1905).

43. Marion, *Dictionnaire des institutions de la France,* p. 439.

44. François-Alexandre-Frédéric de La Rochefoucauld-Liancourt, *Opinion . . . sur
la motion de M. Camus, relative aux pensions,* in *Assemblée Nationale* (Paris, January 1–15, 1790), p. 2.

approach to the problem of poverty: "I have noticed that most constitutions deal exclusively with the rich, and no one provides for the wretched state of the numerous class of the poor, who, incapable of foresight, have no other perspective, in old age and in illness, than the sad trip to the hospitals. All lifetime loans seem available only to the leisure class; poverty, too disdained, has no recourse other than the perfidious lure of the ruinous gambling of lotteries, a disastrous and forced tax that it pays with its most stringent need." He reprinted a letter of March 28, 1789, from a reader of his prospectus in Lyon calling the plan "this cheerful perspective of a sweet and easy old age." The reader had shown the project to all sorts of people—workers, businessmen, lawyers, and clergymen—who approved of it in general and suggested certain revisions of detail. At that point the plan called for the purchase of shares in a pension fund at ninety *livres* per share, to be deposited in annual installments of six *livres* for fifteen years. Only at the end of that period could a beneficiary withdraw his or her money, plus 5 percent interest, from the *Ressource de la Vieillesse*. The *Projet* included an extract from the Registers of the Conseil d'Etat du Roi, giving the king's approval to the plan: "The king, seriously concerned with the happiness of his subjects, has thought that no means ought to be overlooked for improving the lot of the least fortunate by assuring them, at small sacrifice, of a decent old age."[45]

A version of 1790 indicates an important change. Now the ninety *livres* would be deposited over the course of only ten years, at nine *livres* per annum. An approving letter of September 20, 1790, from the Procureur-Syndic-Adjoint de la Commune, L.-Ch. Mitouflet, was quoted in connection not only with the good the Caisse would do the people but also with the benefit that the government would gain by having so much capital in its coffers.[46] And if that were not enough, the national character, economy, and polity all appeared as beneficiaries of the plan in a 1791 draft:

The spirit of calculation and of finance has made much progress in France in the last several years; but all these schemes, more or less favorable to people rich enough to take part in the establishments which are their object, have most often been dictated by avarice and cupidity and have

45. Lafarge, *Projet de bienfaisance* (1789), p. 1.
46. Lafarge, *Projet de bienfaisance* (1790), p. 9. Revision also in Lafarge, *Projet de bienfaisance* (n.d.).

then become the deadly sources of a speculation that has dried up all the branches of our national industry. Good citizens have made impotent wishes against this political and moral evil, and still seek vainly for a bank that is safe from this scourge, in which the poor and the unfortunate can deposit their savings gathered in the years of strength and of work, to find it again in those of old age and infirmities.[47]

While Lafarge's claims were encompassing more and more territory, his plan was gaining enthusiastic supporters and critical advocates. Approved by the Section du Théâtre Français, the Commune de Paris, the Jacobin Club, and the Club of 1789, it was presented on October 30, 1790, to the National Assembly by the abbé Jean-Louis Gouttes on behalf of the Comité de Mendicité and the Comité des Finances. In his report Gouttes declared: "The unfortunate would find, in a light sacrifice of 6 *deniers* per day, resources for the age of needs and infirmities, old age. . . . Saving, for the poor, by means of an unconscious sacrifice, precious resources for old age, [the plan] could lead, without crisis and without overcharging the people, to the extinction of a very important part of the public debt."[48] This time the pension had undergone further changes, the amount per share being sliced in half to forty-five *livres*. Gouttes urged immediate approval, but Pierre-Louis Roederer and Achille-Pierre Dionis du Séjour convinced the assembly to have the plan studied in committee and by the Academy.[49] Indeed, Condorcet, representing the Academy of Sciences, objected that because ten years would elapse before anyone could benefit from the Caisse, those who were already elderly would hardly benefit at all.[50] But by March 3, 1791, further revisions had been made, and Gouttes presented the plan once more. The comte de Mirabeau followed Gouttes's speech with a supporting harangue against avarice and wastefulness, and estimated that "a pension of 45 *livres* would be a great benefit for the inhabitants of the countryside; this amount is nearly the wages of an entire year's work."[51] He suggested, though, that the fund should always be referred

47. Lafarge, *Caisse d'épargnes et de bienfaisance* (1791), pp. 3–4.
48. Abbé Jean-Louis Gouttes, *Rapport . . .* , ibid., pp. 12–13.
49. Sigismond Lacroix, *Actes de la commune de Paris pendant la Révolution*, vol. 4 (Paris, 1896), pp. 266–268.

50. Condorcet, *Copie de l'extrait des registres de l'Académie des sciences, envoyé au Comité de mendicité le 1er décembre 1790*, in Camille Bloch and Alexandre Tuetey, *Procès-verbaux et rapports du comité de mendicité de la constituante 1790–1791* (Paris, 1911), pp. 210–211.

51. Mirabeau, *Discours . . .* , in Lafarge, *Caisse d'épargnes*, p. 22.

to as a savings bank, never as a *tontine viagère et d'amortissement* (tontine or sinking fund), which sounded more random and less secure.

At this point Mirabeau made a proposal that in an almost comical way exemplifies the unpredictability of Revolutionary politics and led to a setback for the plan. It had appeared headed for passage when he asked his colleagues to contribute five days' salary to the Caisse to be used for the support of poor families. Other deputies agreed, and Jean-François Rewbell went even further, asking that contributions be made from salaries going back to June 1789. At that point Robespierre objected that the new enthusiasm over state assistance was being contaminated by the old spirit of private charity. The salary of a representative of the people, he argued, "is not an individual property; it is a national property, and no one has the right to renounce it."[52] After further debate the entire project was voted down—the original proposal along with the amendments.

Nevertheless, the plan was approved months later and did achieve some degree of success. The Société des Amis de la Constitution of Beauvais opened accounts for four poor young people in that city.[53] By *an II* (1793–94) Lafarge was claiming 5,552 shares for 669 people aged sixty-one to seventy-five; 45,844 for 5,781 aged forty-four to sixty; 116,470 for 25,339 aged thirty to forty-three; 103,578 for 21,824 aged fifteen to twenty-nine; and 111,782 for 21,568 aged one to fourteen.[54] The Caisse, as Condorcet had predicted, was singling out neither the poor nor the elderly, but it did focus attention on their plight.

The activity of French Revolutionary regimes on behalf of the aged poor was not limited to the rather fretful debate over the *caisse Lafarge,* a program whose notoriety exceeded that of other plans perhaps because of its author's superior sense of public relations and simple perseverance. But after the creation of the Comité de Mendicité by a decree of January 21, 1790, care for the aged received high priority in the work of the Constituent Assembly.[55] Presided over by François-Alexandre-Frédéric de La Rochefoucauld-Liancourt, the committee made fourteen reports, half of which were authored by its president. His proposal of

---

52. Robespierre in Archives Parlementaires, *Procès-verbaux de la Convention Nationale* (hereafter Arch. Parl.), vol. 23, pp. 652–656, quoted in Lacroix, *Actes,* pp. 267–268.

53. "Arrêté de la société des amis de la constitution, relatif à la caisse d'épargne de M. Lafarge" (Beauvais, 1791?).

54. Lafarge, *Réflexions utiles,* pp. 7–8. See also Lafarge, *Caisse d'épargnes du C. Lafarge,* and A.N. F22* 801, Société des vieillards.

55. C. Bloch, *L'assistance et l'état,* esp. pp. 428–450.

April 30, 1790, made clear that work for the healthy and assistance for the needy were obligations of society:

> Abundant work for all those who can work, that is what society owes. A healthy and robust man who has only his arms to subsist is poor; but he is not wretched as long as the means of work are furnished to him. If he lacks work, he falls into misery, and from misery to despair is only a step, as from despair to crime.
>
> The duty of society is therefore to seek to prevent misery, to relieve it, to offer work to those for whom work is necessary; to force them if they refuse to work; finally to assist without requirement of work those for whom age or infirmities prevent any means of laboring.[56]

On May 24, 1790, La Rochefoucauld-Liancourt read a *mémoire* on the ways to combat beggary in general. On September 3 he read the third report, assigning individual members of the committee particular topics for investigation. On October 6 M. de Cergy, given the task of studying the aged, reported on the "aid to give old people both at home and in the hospital"; a week later Jacques-Guillaume Thouret presented the results of his work on the number of needy Frenchmen and the amount of support they required. These papers do not survive, but their results were summarized in the fourth and seventh reports of the committee.

Title III, "Secours aux vieillards et infirmes," of the fourth report, read on December 1, 1790, laid out the philosophical bases of Revolutionary assistance to the aged and proposed the most far-reaching reforms ever undertaken in France. It began with the observation, based upon unstated evidence, that respect for old age was a sentiment placed by nature in the human heart. Acting on that sentiment and assisting the needy would contribute greatly to the betterment of mankind in general and the expression of the gratitude of children. Aid provided from public funds would serve not only as replacement for the sort of work that had become physically impossible but also as recognition of society's satisfaction with the contribution of the aged. In seeking a way to express that satisfaction, the committee considered a system of hospitalization and ruled against it not simply on grounds of expense—at least at this point in the paper—but with an eye toward the happiness of the elderly:

56. La Rochefoucauld-Liancourt, *Plan de travail du comité pour l'extinction de la mendicité,* in Bloch and Tuetey, *Procès-verbaux,* p. 317.

Concerned with the means of providing some consolation at this very end of life, we believe we have found it in aid at home; we have seen there the means of maintaining this natural sentiment, this first of all sentiments, this principal of all virtues, affection, filial respect that misery extinguishes with a sort of necessity or at least renders too often ineffectual, and with which the French people, naturally good, gentle, and sensitive, ought to be more imbued than any other; finally, we have seen there, for the relieved old man, more attentive care, more consolation, and the inexpressible sweetness of suffering and dying surrounded by one's children; we have seen there a little more ease for families and thus recompense for their care.[57]

The state, working through children, would serve as consolation in old age. If the children were "monsters" devoid of filial piety, a surrogate family would be sought so that the old person could find "children in friends, relatives, or neighbors," and they would be given the state aid.

It is only at that point that the report makes a claim for the program's financial benefits to the state. Arguing that there is already enough natural discontent in old age and that additional annoyances ought to be avoided, it called for the most convenient combination of aid in kind and in cash. And for those who wished to receive more than the minimum in aid and who preferred to continue to live an active life, work should be made available. Provision for work would be made with an eye toward distraction and happiness rather than punishment. So, too, life in the hospice for those without homes would be more pleasant than in ancien régime institutions. An inmate might take his pension out of the hospice if he chose to live with others, and he could always return at will: "We believed that to compel the old man to live where he would not like to was to upset him unnecessarily; the liberty of following his merest fantasy would provide the only consolation to his natural disquiet."[58] Finally, the furniture of someone who died in a hospice would preferably go to a member of his family. Otherwise, it would be put in a national collection and would not belong to any particular institution.

Perhaps the tone of the report was so optimistic and the contents so generous because the problem was underestimated; that is, the degree to which one could rely upon the family was overestimated. Only three or four old people for every thousand inhabitants of the countryside, it was thought, would need assistance. The seventh report of the committee

57. La Rochefoucauld-Liancourt, *4e rapport du comité de mendicité,* in ibid., p. 421.

58. Ibid., pp. 423–424.

was somewhat more realistic, estimating that between one-eighth and one-ninth of the population (some 120 of every thousand) required aid and that one-quarter of their number were elderly or ill.[59] But the committee stuck by its aims, and governmental plans became, if anything, even more ambitious. In September 1791 it was judged necessary to have three retirement homes as well as a retirement fund in Paris.[60]

The Convention continued this work over the next few years; in fact, through its Comité des Secours Publics, the new regime managed to institute, if only for a very short time, some of the reforms discussed by the Constitutent Assembly.[61] On March 19, 1793, Jean-Baptiste-Jérôme Bo, in the name of the committee, presented a report "on the foundations of the general organization of public assistance." His proposal went further in envisioning aid for

> old age, that daughter of repose, that precursor of eternal rest. Here recognition joins with duty, love with veneration: here, national welfare ought to be as consoling as it is complete. The old man who implores your assistance ought to find in it all that can, in relieving his ailments, slow his steps toward the gates of nothingness. Meanwhile it is not necessary that a man, in the vigor of his age, calculating the perspective that you offer to old age, should forget his duties toward society, neglecting all economic speculation; it is not necessary that sloth be honored as virtue. Your committee thinks that a way of stimulating forethought in the indigent would be the establishment of savings banks based upon public faith, calculated upon probabilities of human life—banks where working men could daily, and without noticeable privation, place a portion of their work.[62]

Three months later, on June 26, 1793, Etienne-Christophe Maignet made a similar report calling for a basic minimum pension to be given at home, with additional funds to be provided according to need.[63] On October 12, 1793 (21 Vendémiaire *an II*), it was Bo's turn again; he proposed a decree to withhold one-quarter of workers' salaries for

59. La Rochefoucauld-Liancourt, *7e rapport . . .*, in ibid., pp. 572–573.

60. Ibid., pp. 764–765.

61. Ferdinand Dreyfus, *L'assistance sous la législative et la convention (1791–1795)* (Paris, 1905); J. Delaitre, *L'assistance aux vieillards* (Paris, 1911).

62. Jean-Baptiste-Jérôme Bo, *Rapport et . . . projet de décret sur les bases de l'organisation générale des secours publics* (March 19, 1793), in Arch. Parl., vol. 60 (Paris, 1901), p. 324.

63. Etienne-Christophe Maignet, *Rapport et . . . projet de décret sur l'organisation des secours à accorder annuellement aux enfants et aux vieillards* (June 26, 1793), in Arch. Parl., vol. 67 (Paris, 1905), pp. 478–489.

public works and savings for illness and old age.[64] Three days later the decree was adopted by the Convention with the provision that all seventy-year-olds without homes would be welcomed by the nearest hospice. Finally, on May 11, 1794 (22 Floréal *an II*), a far-reaching bill, authored by Bertrand Barère, was adopted, calling for pension funds for farmers, artisans, and old women.[65] Subscriptions could be arranged and names inscribed in the *Livre de la bienfaisance nationale* on days of civic festivals. Across the top of the pensioner's receipt was printed: "*La République Française Honore la Vieillesse et le Malheur.*"[66]

In ways other than these pension schemes, too, this most radical of Revolutionary regimes managed to honor and advantage old age. A decree of August 1, 1793, aimed at stamping out counterrevolutionary activity in the Vendée, called for sparing women, children, and the aged, who would be relocated to the interior of the country, their subsistence and safety assured.[67] Carnot's August 23, 1793, *levée en masse* proposed an important role for old warriors: "Old men, taking up again the mission that they had among ancient peoples, will be carried to the public places; there they will inflame the courage of the young warriors; they will promote the hatred of kings and the unity of the Republic."[68] The tax decree of September 3, 1793, allowed exemptions for aged dependents.[69] The public education decree of October 26, 1793, ordered primary school students to spend time seeing to the domestic needs of neighboring old people.[70] An act of November 13, 1793, ordered pensions for elderly and other dependents of the republic's soldiers.[71] And the police act of April 16, 1794, which banished from Paris ex-nobles and nationals of countries at war with France, exempted people seventy years of age and older.[72]

When legislation tended to go in the direction of greater liberty from

64. Bo, *Rapport et projet de décret sur l'extinction de la mendicité* (October 12, 1793), in Arch. Parl., vol. 76 (Paris, 1910).

65. Bertrand Barère, *Premier rapport fait au nom du comité de salut public: Sur le moyen d'extirper la mendicité dans les campagnes et sur les secours que doit accorder la République aux citoyens indigens* (May 11, 1794), in Arch. Parl., vol. 90 (Paris, 1972), pp. 246–259.

66. "The French Republic Honors Old Age and Misfortune"; see Dreyfus, *L'assistance*, p. 75.

67. *Troisième décret*, art. 7–8 (August 1, 1793), in Arch. Parl., vol. 70 (Paris, 1906).

68. *Rapport et décret du 23 août* (1793), in Arch. Parl., vol. 72, (Paris, 1906), p. 677.

69. Arch. Parl., vol. 73 (Paris, 1908).

70. Art. 4 (October 26, 1793), in Arch. Parl., vol. 77 (Paris, 1910), p. 575.

71. See application in Chapter 6.

72. *Décret sur la police générale de a République* (April 16, 1794), art. 7–8, in Arch. Parl., vol. 88 (Paris, 1969), p. 649.

parental power, the needs of the aged were sympathetically debated. Old people would serve as the priesthood of the nation in the local *Temple de la liberté* for the registration of the births of new citizens.[73] Refractory priests over the age of sixty would not suffer deportation, only confinement within the local *maison commune*.[74]

Adoption of the solitary aged was encouraged in several ways. The Constitution of June 24, 1793, provided for citizenship for foreigners who fed the elderly,[75] and people who needed to prove their Revolutionary fervor before various tribunals used similar kindnesses as evidence. The testimony of an old woman who had been supported by Claude-Henri Saint-Simon was enlisted to secure his release from prison.[76] The old age of a prisoner might also be used—not always successfully—in a plea: letters sent to the Committee of Public Safety cited the old age of Saint-Simon's seventy-year-old uncle, Charles-François, but considerations of aristocracy and church office took precedence, and the former Bishop of Agde was executed.[77]

In one of its more sentimental moods, the Committee of Public Safety ordered the Commission de l'Instruction Publique on 13 Floréal *an II* (May 2, 1794) to oversee a contest for the construction of ideal peasant households that would replace "feudal constructions." The new country houses must "offer lessons to childhood, memories to old age," and each room must be suited to its occupant: "Artists, assign to the old man who has grown white in the field a decent apartment, a place where one can surround him with respect, a place where his honorable repose excites the emulation of youth and occupies him in instructing it through the recalling of festivals he has attended, of pains he has suffered and which his patience has surmounted, of virtues he has practiced, of tears he has wiped; that is the past of which it is beautiful for the old man to boast." Appropriate inscriptions should adorn the different apartments—in that of the old man: "Repos honorable après le travail."[78]

Most of this effort, both sentimental and scientific, came to an end

73. Emile Masson, *La puissance paternelle et la famille sous la révolution* (Paris, 1911), p. 127.

74. Marcel Garaud, *La révolution et l'égalité civile* (Paris, 1953), p. 65.

75. Ibid., p. 189.

76. Frank E. Manuel, *The New World of Henri Saint-Simon* (Cambridge, Mass., 1956), p. 31.

77. Ibid., p. 26.

78. *Commission de l'instruction publique, Architecture rurale: Extrait du registre des arrêtés du comité de Salut public de La Convention nationale, du treizième jour du mois Floréal, l'an deuxième de la République française, une et indivisible*, A.N. F[17] 1281, dossier 12, pp. 3, 7, 8; for this reference, I thank Professor James Leith.

with 9 Thermidor. The sentiment alone continued in the *fête de la vieillesse* (see below) throughout the Directory, but the hard work of comprehensive national planning for the old age of French citizens was finished. Government officials still busied themselves with pension programs, but they were not the radical plans for annuities for the poor; rather, they were efforts to restore the *rentes* of returning aristocratic *émigrés*.[79] And while plans for old age homes were bandied about, their authors seemed quite unaware of the Revolutionary attempts to create a national system. Thus, Ricard d'Allauch in 1822 offered a *Plan d'une maison de retraite pour les vieillards, proposé par souscriptions*, claiming that France had never done anything for the elderly and that his proposed home outside Marseille would provide a new beginning—at least for old magistrates, soldiers, churchmen, businessmen, seamen, professors, men of letters, and state officials. Ricard had adopted some of the classical ideas that stimulated the French Revolutionaries—he even made reference to Belisarius—but his vision was clearly contrary to that of the Enlightenment. His model would be the monastery, and his aim would be to isolate the aged from the rest of French society.[80]

Still, though much of the Revolution's work seems to have been forgotten quite easily, some of it survived in the memories of those who had counted on it for a better life. Recollections of the 1790s arose in 1830 and 1848, including proposals of support for the aged. The Revolutionary idea of a social debt to the elderly endured, therefore, but with less urgency. For there were so many other problems to be considered— the right to retire meant little without the right to work[81]—that the aged really had to wait until they became a national issue once more. That would not happen until late in the Third Republic.

The classic question of the connection between Enlightenment thought and Revolutionary action strikes most historians as old-fashioned. Indeed, the kind of history that seeks to lay blame for the Revolution at the doorstep of the philosophes is bankrupt.[82] Some

---

79. *Rentes des émigrés, rentes et pensions, etc. (an 14)*, in *Papiers d'Emmanuel Du Villard*, B.N., MS N.A.F. 20585.

80. Ricard d'Allauch, *Plan d'une maison de retraite pour les vieillards, proposé par souscriptions* (Marseille, 1822). I thank Steve Saba for the reference.

81. Stearns, *Old Age in European Society.*

82. Such was the message of Daniel Mornet, *Les origines intellectuelles de la révolution française (1715–1787)* (Paris, 1933, 1947), which has been further developed in François Furet, ed., *Livre et société;* Vovelle, *Piété baroque;* and Robert Darnton, *The Literary Underground of the Old Regime* (Cambridge, Mass., 1982).

historians argue that the Revolution should be seen as a starting point, the moment of creation of a new political and social discourse.[83] Yet we cannot ignore the roots of that discourse in the old regime.[84] Debates about old age pensions and insurance had begun at midcentury; the Revolution provided an opportunity to apply Enlightenment ideas and foreshadowed debates that would reemerge later in the Western world. Those debates largely concerned issues of social policy, but the contribution of the French Revolution had as much to do with ways of imagining society as with founding particular social institutions.

It is in the rhetoric of the period that one can find and speak of a deferential revolution—the guillotine was hardly deferential and contributed not a whit to longevity—and it is in the language and symbolism of Revolutionary festivals that one finds crystallized an Enlightenment way of thinking. The importance of age as a category and of old age as a social problem is revealed in the protean image of the aged cast by the festivals that marked the great "days" and annual celebrations of the French Revolution. Elders played an important symbolic role as repositories of Revolutionary wisdom and as rulers of an imagined society in which every individual might expect to run the course from dependent child to active adult to respected and honored elder. The aged lent authority to the Revolution, and the Revolution paid its debt with social legislation. For a time, in the mythic present of the 1790s, subject and object, category and problem, were one. But as Mona Ozouf, the historian of the Revolutionary festivals, has so elegantly explained, the biological ordering of humanity as practiced in the festivals—particularly the "moral" festivals of the Directory—tended finally to defuse a Revolutionary situation, to end the Revolution and, we

83. Furet, Jean Starobinski, and Lynn Hunt are among the supporters of this position. See esp. chap. 1 of Hunt, *Politics, Culture, and Class.*

84. Those who have discovered a new form of the intellectual origins in religious, historical, and "constitutional" thought include Dale Van Kley, Keith M. Baker, and Jeffrey Merrick: Van Kley, *The Jansenists and the Expulsion of the Jesuits from France, 1757–1765* (New Haven, Conn., 1975), and *The Damiens Affair and the Unraveling of the Ancien Régime, 1750–1770* (Princeton, N.J., 1984); Baker, "On the Problem of the Ideological Origins of the French Revolution," in Dominick La Capra and Steven L. Kaplan, eds., *Modern European Intellectual History: Reappraisals and New Perspectives* (Ithaca, 1982), pp. 197–219; Merrick, " 'Disputes over Words' and Constitutional Conflict in France, 1730–1732," *French Historical Studies,* 14, no. 4 (1986), 497–520. Alan Forrest and Colin Jones have returned to a concern for Enlightenment origins of Revolutionary ideas about poverty and welfare: Forrest, *The French Revolution and the Poor;* Jones, *Charity and Bienfaisance.*

would add, leave authority where it lay in the public sphere, affirming the rule of the aged only in theory and in private.[85] Discourse survived, but social obligation would not be fulfilled.

Some festivals arose spontaneously in celebration of the great days of the Revolution. One might even argue, with Jules Michelet, that those "days" *were* festivals.[86] But very quickly the festivals were co-opted by the Parisian propaganda machine as a means of public instruction. For François-Antoine, comte de Boissy d'Anglas, they were a way of reaching people more immediately through spectacle and emotion than through word and reason.[87] For Robespierre they provided a means not only of educating the public—"It is a kind of institution which ought to be considered as an essential part of public education"—but also of gaining their adherence to a civil religion: "Have general and more solemn festivals for the whole Republic, have special festivals. . . . Let them all tend to awaken enthusiasm for liberty, love of country, respect for laws."[88] Great productions were mounted in open spaces where the multitudes could gather (those of Jacques-Louis David, on the Champ-de-Mars in Paris, are the most famous) in celebration of the Revolution, its heroes and its ideals.[89]

Old people had a role in most such festivals. A living tableau of David's *Oath of the Horatii* was created by old men and youths at the Fête de l'Etre Suprème; a float honored the aged in the Fête de l'Unité et de l'Indivisibilité of August 10, 1793; a discourse reminiscent of the sentimental tales of the period, *Le bon vieillard,* was offered at a Fête de la Raison et de la Vérité on February 18, 1794; and the aged marched with sticks to be joined together as fasces in the Fête de la Souveraineté du Peuple.[90] Soon old age became a subject in itself for festive treat-

85. Mona Ozouf, "Symboles et fonctions des âges dans les fêtes de l'époque révolutionnaire," *Annales Historiques de la Révolution Française,* 42, no. 202 (1970), 569–593, and *La fête révolutionnaire* (Paris, 1976). See also Michel Vovelle, "La Révolution française: Mutation ou crise des valeurs?" in *Idéologies et mentalités* (Paris, 1985), pp. 295–320.

86. See Ozouf, *La fête révolutionnaire,* chap. 1.

87. Albert Duruy, "Les fêtes nationales pendant la révolution," *Revue de France,* 30 (1878), in Widener, volume on *fêtes:* Fr 1346.27.25.

88. Robespierre, *Rapport fait au nom du Comité de Salut public, sur les rapports des idées religieuse et morale avec les principes républicains et sur les fêtes nationales (18 Floréal an II)* (Paris, an II [1794]), pp. 28–30, quoted in Agnès Villadary, *Fête et vie quotidienne* (Paris, 1968), p. 83.

89. David L. Dowd, *Pageant-Master of the Republic: Jacques-Louis David and the French Revolution* (Lincoln, Neb., 1948).

90. Ibid., pp. 123, 112; le citoyen Dulaurent, *Le bon vieillard: Discours prononcé dans la section des Tuileries, le décadi 30 Pluviôse, à la Fête de la Raison et de la Vérité*

ment. It was not enough that the aged received the respect of the Revolution and the Revolution the approval of the aged. Nor was it enough that the life-cycle terms of Revolutionary discourse expressed a democratic order of things. The age groups would have their own festivals. By act of 18 Floréal *an II* (May 7, 1794), the Convention ordered a series of festivals including the Fête de la Vieillesse; when the number of festivals was cut by order of 3 Brumaire *an IV* (October 25, 1795), the Fête des Vieillards scheduled for 10 Fructidor was among those that survived.[91]

The Fête de la Vieillesse did not require the financial outlays of the larger festivals of the early years, but it still needed the activity of a diverse group of individuals.[92] Composers wrote and musicians and singers performed such songs and hymns as "Le vieillard républicain" (1793), "Romance du vieillard républicain" (1793), "Adieux d'un vieillard à son fils en l'envoyant aux frontières" (1794), "Honorons les vieillards" (1794), "Couplets en l'honneur des vieillards" (1794), "Les vieillards" (1796), "Chant pour le fête de la vieillesse" (1796), and "Hymne pour la fête de la vieillesse" (1799).[93] The need for musical participation by the Garde Nationale in Revolutionary festivals led to the creation of the Conservatoire National.[94] Poets did their part as well. J. F. Ducis contributed "Vers pour une fête à la vieillesse," describing a Swiss festival and so internationalizing the life course of humankind: Nestors of all Switzerland gather in a canton in an Alpine valley, permitting the use of snow-capped, icy mountains as geographic symbols of white-haired, bearded old men.[95] Various government ministers planned festivities, ordering branches, flowers, fruit, and tents, providing transportation for the elderly, and organizing entertainment;

(Paris, *an II*); Albert Maire, "Les fêtes nationales sous la révolution dans le département du Puy-de-Dôme" (Clermont-Ferrand, 1886), in Widener; L. Thiot, "Fêtes nationales pendant la révolution" (Beauvais, 1908), also in Widener.

91. See Arch. Parl. for those dates. The terms *fête de la vieillesse* and *fête des viellards* were interchangeable.

92. See illustration "Fête dédiée à la vieillesse," gravure à l'eau-forte par J. Duplessi-Bertaux (1795) d'après P. A. Wille (1794), in B.N. Estampes, De Vinck. The print is reproduced in Ozouf, *La fête revolutionnaire*, and on p. 208 of this volume. Also see illustration of *fête* at Anvers, August 28, 1796, in Charles Pergameni, "Les fêtes révolutionnaires et l'esprit public bruxellois au début du régime français," *Annales de la Société Royale d'Archéologie de Bruxelles* (1913), in Widener.

93. Constant Pierre, *Les hymnes et chansons de la révolution* (Paris, 1904), nos. 828, 829, 1702, 1193, 1645, 1836; Pierre, *Musique des fêtes et cérémonies de la révolution française* (Paris, 1899), nos. 53, 54.

94. Pierre, *Musique des fêtes,* p. viii.

95. J. F. Ducis, "Vers pour une fête à la Vieillesse," in *Oeuvres,* pp. 321–324.

Festival of Old Age. Duplessi-Berthault print of P. A. Wille painting, 1794. Phot. Bibl. Nat. Paris.

though special new theatrical productions were not always mounted, some appropriate play had to be produced.[96]

The *Patriote français* of 14 Fructidor *an VI* (August 31, 1798) reported: "All the municipalities of Paris celebrated on the tenth the Fête des Vieillards; those among them who had solemnly received the homage due to experience, which is the portion of long years, gathered in the evening and were driven by the municipal officers to the *théâtre des Arts,* where the first boxes had been reserved for them. The sight of these respectable citizens, who appeared crowned with flowers, impressed the public. *Oedipe à Colone* was given."[97] In preparation, the minister of the interior had asked that the theater company "on that day give works where old age and private and civic virtues are honored," and the administrators of the Théâtre de la République et des Arts had replied:

> Citizen Minister,
> Pursuant to your letter of the second of this month, we have looked for the best that the current répertoire, in the difficult circumstances which we find ourselves, might offer for the festival to be celebrated tomorrow. We have ordered that *Oedipe,* a play where the authority of fathers is presented in a very respectable light, be performed; that in the Ballet of *La Rosière,* which would be given next, the crowned young girl would pay homage with her crown to her father; and that this last action be greeted and supported by couplets recalling that it is to the lessons and examples of old people that we owe our talents and our virtues. We have likewise tried to fulfill all your intentions by the measures we have taken to welcome, and seat comfortably, the crowned old people and the magistrates who will accompany them.
>
> *Salut et Respect.*[98]

In *an IV* (1796) a broadsheet advertising the *fête* in Metz began with a philosophical and historical explanation of the event: "The ancient republics put respect for the aged on the same level with the duties of the citizen; the French nation is the only one in which legislators established a public ceremony, a national festival, uniquely devoted to solemnizing old age." The municipal administration next listed the names, ad-

---

96. See correspondence and orders in A.N. F[1C]I 92–102: *Fête de la vieillesse—10 Fructidor—An IV–An VI.*

97. Quoted in Alphonse Aulard, *Paris pendant la réaction thermidorienne et sous le Directoire: Recueil de documents pour l'histoire de l'esprit public à Paris,* vol. 5 (Paris, 1902).

98. Correspondence in A.N. F[1C]I 92–102.

dresses, and ages of four old people to be honored by the city, and then outlined the schedule. At 7:00 A.M. the young people would gather at the city hall and, accompanied by National Guards and National Guard musicians, go to the homes of the four and decorate them with leaves. They would return to the city hall by 8:00 A.M. to be joined by local authorities and all residents of sixty years and older. At 9:00 A.M. a cortège would leave the hall; musicians, youngsters, and old people surrounded by municipal authorities would be escorted by the Guard, *chasseurs,* and *cavalerie* to the four homes to pick up the honorees and help them walk to the Esplanade.[99]

The aged marched with heads covered, the youths with heads bare and in silence. At the Esplanade, the four were helped onto a platform surrounded by the other old and young people of Metz. A local official gave a speech, wreaths were placed on the heads of the honored four, and the young wives of Metz offered them baskets of fruit decorated with flowers. The orchestra entertained with patriotic pieces, and then the old people were taken home. Artillery salvos were fired at noon, 1:00, 2:00, and 3:00 P.M., when the cortège once more picked up the four old people and once more the population gathered at the Esplanade, this time for an athletic event. Children aged ten to fourteen ran races, and the old people conferred prizes on winners and runners-up: swords and caps for the former, branches and honorable mention for the latter. The children then escorted the elders to the "spectacle." The following year a more scholarly event replaced the race, with prizes awarded to the best students in German class at the local *collège.* In *an VI* (1798) the *fête* was still basically the same, though the military was less dominant and more civil authorities took part.[100]

The events were similar in festivals throughout France, though considerable discretion was left to local authorities. The Fête des Vieillards for *an IV* (1796) in Toulon was not held until 1 Vendémiaire *an V,* in conjunction with the Fête de la Fondation de la République Française. Toulon's port added local color with a spectacle of artistically arranged and colorfully decked ships at sea, and news of victory in the Tyrol brought another reason for celebration. But the usual procession, speeches, songs, and dances were performed. In his only specific reference to old age, President Barry of the municipal administration enunciated the Revolutionary desire to unite private and public virtue: "Let us

99. Adam, *Fête des vieillards* (Metz, *an IV*).
100. Ibid. (Metz, *an V, an VI*).

honor old age in private life, as we all honor it together in this august festival, where all the great sentiments of nature and of liberty ought to burst forth."[101]

Revolutionary discourse frequently sought to ally virtues of domesticity and politics. As in colonial America or Confucian China, the family was seen as a little political unit, the nation the sum of such units.[102] One Parisian administrator, in a festival speech delivered immediately after the crowning of the aged and addressed to the young people who were attending, placed republican institutions in the context of all free peoples and of eternal truths from the ancients to the present; he called, in the same sentence, for love of family and of country: "Free peoples have had this imposing characteristic of grandeur, which still today captures our admiration, only because they have put love of country, filial piety, and veneration of young people for old on a par with the first duties of citizens."[103]

An alignment of age and politics in the Fête de la Vieillesse bolstered the argument that a republican regime was natural. One address in Paris argued that the principle of the festival would be found "at the bottom of our hearts, if it did not already exist in our Republican institutions." Respect for the aged was a measure of public and private virtue: "One can judge the legislation of a people, its moral qualities, its domestic virtues, its private and public morals, by the greater or lesser respect that it has for old age." But attitudes toward the elderly were more than a touchstone of national morality: "*It is the wisdom of old men that makes for the strength of States.*" The city had been sapping that strength; urbanization had threatened the position of the aged, who were no longer capable of the physical labor of the city and were left with only a moral authority, which must be restated again and again. Therefore, the *fête* had an important place in republican society as a teacher of the young. In this particular case, the speaker added, a lesson was provided by a 120-year-old freed slavewoman from the Antilles.[104]

101. Etienne Barry, *Précis de la fête de la fondation de la République française, célébrée dans la commune de Toulon, le 1er Vendémiaire an 5e de l'ère républicaine, et à laquelle était jointe celle des Vieillards*, B.N. Lb⁴²1135, p. 11.

102. See, e.g., John Demos, *A Little Commonwealth* (London, 1970), and Marion J. Levy, Jr., *The Family Revolution in Modern China* (Cambridge, Mass., 1949).

103. Laroche, *Discours adressé aux jeunes élèves des deux sexes, assistant à la fête de la vieillesse, immédiatement après le couronnement*, B.H.V.P. 8059, no. 2.

104. *Fête de la Vieillesse, 5e arr.* (Paris, *an VII*), pp. 1, 2, 3, 11. The woman was "La citoyenne Andotte (Jeanne), Américaine, femme de couleur, née aux petites Antilles, Isle Saint-Christophe, en 1676 ou 77, âgée de cent vingt ans passés; voyant parfaitement,

The previous year the aged of the same *arrondissement* had heard that they would survive in their posterity: "You will not die in entirety, you will survive yourselves; the greater society, by a solemn adoption, becomes in some way your family. Your cherished names will be, to those who think of you, a heritage of glory, and they will transmit your example, the memory of your virtues, to their most distant nephews."[105] And in the first *arrondissement* the administrator Moussard celebrated the physical image of the aged: the wrinkles, serene smile, and pure white hair; the image of the judge of past and present and of the seer into the future: "It is with the eye of wisdom and experience that you judge the past; more initiated in the secrets of nature, you embrace the future; this future, you know, is that of peace, of recompense, of immortality. The benefits you will have spread about you, the virtues you will have cultivated, will perpetuate themselves in the hearts of your families, of your friends, of your disciples; you will always live in the recognition of beautiful sentiments; the memory of good never dies." The speech's last paragraphs are pushed along by a cascade of imperatives beginning with the word *vivez* and concludes: "Vive la République où les Vieillards Président!"[106] And the song "A la Vieillesse," sung at that very *fête*, after mistakenly mentioning the possibility of death as a release, once again envisions the continued life and authority of the aged:

> Que dis-je! heureux vieillards, vivez pour notre exemple,
> Présidez les beaux jours de vos nombreux enfans;
> Que vos cheveux blanchis soient les gardiens du temple
> Que la vertu ferme aux méchans.[107]

Throughout the discourses of the 1790s, the authority of the aged as the natural rulers and magistrates of society was given the same strong and uncontradictory emphasis. On the one hand such rhetoric was a plea for an end to artificial distinctions of class and wealth and an

---

entendant de même, lisant sans lunettes, saine de sens et de jugement, et supérieure de beaucoup à son grand âge."

105. *Fête de la vieillesse, 5e arr.* (Paris, *an VI*), p. 14.

106. "Long live the Republic where old men preside"; see Moussard, *Discours prononcé le 10 fructidor, an VI, à la fête de la vieillesse, célébrée par l'administration municipale du premier arrondissement de Paris*, B.H.V.P. 8059, no. 1.

107. "What am I saying? happy elders, live to be our example, / Preside over the fine days of your numerous children; / Let your whitened hair be guardian of the temple / That virtue closes to the wicked." Moussard, "A la Vieillesse," B.H.V.P. 967 963.

affirmation of republican values. But on the other hand it tended to reinforce public authority, whatever the particular order—whether in 1793 or in 1798. The present was often seen as having developed rationally out of the past and as casting a long shadow of continued legitimacy on the future. But the violent and inconsistent course of events could not always admit of such a naive view. And so one official speech, delivered at a district Fête de la Vieillesse in *an VII* (1799), lamented the Terror and wondered what price had to be paid for liberty. In the speaker's view, the aged do not approve of revolutionary change and the rash temerity and impulsive action of youth; rather, they exercise prudence in government and would be remembered for dissociating themselves from the Terror.[108]

Similarly, the moderate J. Dusaulx of the first *arrondissement* in Paris had, two years earlier, expressed relief at having survived "the uncertain course of our terrible revolution." Who would have thought, he mused, that I would be here today? Now it is time to disavow the recent past: "Let us throw a thick veil over so many atrocities, over so many crimes foreign to our former national character." There is patriotism in this address, but the politics have changed: "To honor old age solemnly is in a way to consummate the great work of universal morality; it is to enlarge the spirit, make tender the heart, stir up humanity, make those who are about to quit life taste it again, and consecrate the life of good people; it is finally to sow upon the earth the seed of the most essential social qualities, paternal love, filial love, patriotism, and consequently bravery. When one sincerely loves his family and his country, he is ready to defend them day and night."[109]

Dusaulx's is a patriotism distinct from active politics, expressing a conservative view of the past. As Frédéric Montferrand observed in his *Discours sur la Vieillesse* at Châteauroux in *an VI* (1798): "It is only at the decline of life that man begins to know himself. Thus it is only when he has reached old age that he can give sage counsel and salutary instructions to those who have not yet entered upon a career or have only taken the first steps."[110] The aged voice that had given shrill

108. Mahieu, *Discours prononcé dans le temple décadaire à Deuxponts le dix Fructidor an VII: A la fête de la vieillesse*, B.H.V.P. 28 056.

109. J. Dusaulx, *Discours prononcé par J. Dusaulx: A l'administration municipale du premier arrondissement du canton de Paris, le 10 Fructidor an 5, à l'occasion de la fête de la vieillesse, célébrée en vertu de la loi du 3 Brumaire an 4*, B.H.V.P. 966 264.

110. Frédéric Montferrand, *Discours sur la Vieillesse* (1798), p. 24, MS in B.M. Châteauroux, 38 (B. 206).

support now offers a more considered assessment of things, not a political view of action in universal history but a philosophical view of passivity in current events.

Of course, separating the layers of meaning embedded in these speeches is a delicate operation. Without the disparaging references to Robespierre and the Terror, they would be difficult to distinguish from earlier ones. And there is the additional problem of how they were heard and understood by those in attendance.[111] In his study of Provençal festivals Michel Vovelle claims that the Fête de la Vieillesse never penetrated the Provençal countryside and was celebrated only in Marseille.[112] An earlier historian argued that it succeeded in Nice and failed in Paris. It is difficult to judge. Mona Ozouf's search of police reports throughout France suggests a limited sort of enthusiasm—but how limited, and in what way enthusiastic? Her answer lies in an analysis of the function of the festival. It expressed Revolutionary fervor and taught new ideals. But it also fed upon a long festive tradition.[113]

Traditional festivals, whether official or spontaneous, served as initiation rites aimed at socializing youth. They expressed the social order and symbolically invested young people with their proper roles.[114] They temporarily broke everyday norms of time and space, sometimes fomenting real revolt, but usually managing to return the world to order after having permitted some letting-off of steam.[115] The expression of continuity with an idealized past served to regenerate the present and project a glowing image of the future. The traditional festival explored the boundaries of contemporary norms in order to identify them to the young and recall them to their elders.

A republican festival sought to define new boundaries and to teach political adolescents of all ages the meaning of the new order. But for all its original progressive intent, it managed to take on that old role of

111. This sort of question involves the mentality of the crowd; see George Rudé, *The Crowd in the French Revolution* (Oxford, 1959).

112. Michel Vovelle, *Les métamorphoses de la fête en Provence de 1750 à 1820* (Paris, 1976), p. 196.

113. Joseph Combet, "Les fêtes révolutionnaires à Nice" (1907), pp. 5–6, in Widener; Ozouf, *La fête révolutionnaire.*

114. Abel Poitrineau, "La fête traditionnelle," *Annales Historiques de la Révolution Française,* 47, no. 221 (1975). For the same phenomenon in other terms, S. N. Eisenstadt, *From Generation to Generation* (Glencoe, Ill., 1956).

115. Villadary, *Fête;* Yves-Marie Bercé, *Fête et révolte: Des mentalités populaires du XVIe au XVIIIe siècle* (Paris, 1976); Emmanuel Le Roy Ladurie, *Le carnaval de Romans* (Paris, 1979).

reinforcing traditional ways. The tamed opposition of age and youth resulted in social concord and the reaffirmation of the political status quo.[116] The republican festival, said the Revolutionary Joseph-Marie Lequinio de Kerblay, is "the moral equivalent of a circle in geometry."[117] It never turned the world upside down; it only turned. For this reason, Ozouf prefers a Durkheimian view of the revolutionary festival as a reaffirmation of the social order to a Freudian one of violent release of energy.[118]

Nevertheless, if the festival is finally seen as an instrument of conservatism, it must also be seen as containing the seeds of change, as did the festival of the ancien régime in its periodic switch from make-believe to reality. The speeches and activities of the Fête de la Vieillesse repeated ancient saws and maxims and at times expressed a patriarchal attitude that flew in the face of the Revolutionary preference for individualism. Still, embedded in their texts lay a vision of another world. Beneath the multiplicity of meanings, the memory of traditions, and the infiltration of liberating ideas lay the basis for a definition of distinct political positions about the aged as well as everyone else. As Vovelle has demonstrated, traditional and revolutionary rhetoric were intertwined, but the experience and memory of the French Revolution provided the context for the elaboration of a political culture of opposition.[119]

116. Cf. the feudal relationship described in Georges Duby, *The Three Orders: Feudal Society Imagined* (Chicago, 1980), p. 71.

117. Lequinio, *Des fêtes nationales* (16 Nivôse *an III* [January 5, 1795]), quoted in Ozouf, "Symboles et fonctions," p. 584.

118. Ozouf, *La fête révolutionnaire*, p. 121.

119. Vovelle, *Les métamorphoses de la fête*, p. 284.

Conclusion

Revolutionary discourse looks backward and forward. The history of centuries of attitudes toward the aged lies embedded in the speeches of the Revolutionary festivals. While still repeating a range of traditional views of the ages of man, they provide the philosophical basis for a social view of the aged, a view that led to consideration of very practical political and economic institutions. The basic elements of modern policy concerning the aged were enunciated in the eighteenth century; in that sense, ideas ran ahead of actions then, and the nineteenth and twentieth centuries have been trying to catch up. From time to time, demographic, social, and economic changes have forced a rediscovery of the issues raised in the eighteenth century. Often those issues have been thought unprecedented. By force of numbers and bureaucracy, some are; the welfare state and the medical industry loom large in the twentieth century.[1] But *le troisième âge* existed well before the name. And contemporary ways of viewing "the problem of the elderly," whether in terms of the state or the medicalization of life, have deep roots in the eighteenth century.

Did those roots better prepare France to play its leading role in the aging of Western populations in the contemporary period? Perhaps so, but we need more comparative research on the nineteenth and twentieth centuries in order to draw any firm conclusions. If demographers Louis Roussel and Alain Girard are right in their view of private and public

---

1. For an international perspective, see Anne-Marie Guillemard, ed., *Old Age and the Welfare State* (London, 1983); on Britain, Chris Phillipson, *Capitalism and the Construction of Old Age* (London, 1982); on France, Stearns, *Old Age in European Society*.

age relations, then relations within the family have improved while generational tensions in society have grown.[2] But their assertion is so broad as to be sūggestive for the Western world, not very helpful for France, and next to useless at the local level. Different groups, sexes, classes, and individuals have experienced past and present differently; moreover, their historical memories are selective. As Nietzsche put it, healthy people and cultures forget as much as they remember.[3] There has been a tendency in French culture to forget the socioeconomic problems discovered in the Revolutionary era and to maintain the sentimental view of old age that emerged in the second half of the eighteenth century. Old age again represents something other than itself, often embodying a mythical version of the French past—whether Alphonse Daudet's old Provençal couple abandoned by the rural exodus of the young, the old peasant of *la vieille France* in Gaston Roupnel's meditation on French rural history, or the old man of Claude Berri's film *Le vieil homme et l'enfant*.[4] Serious considerations combine with sentimental evocations. But as eighteenth-century literature demonstrates, sentiment can be serious as well as misleading: it can reveal as well as mask reality.

This book began with a few ideas about the life cycle and the definition of old age and explored the ways in which French culture represented the aged. It considered the aged in art, as images evolved from iconographical representations of metaphysical qualities to depictions of the weak, the widowed, the abandoned, the respected, and the dying. Literature replaced a stereotype of resentment with one of honor and respect. A major movement of secularization downplayed the role of the afterlife, freeing old age from the hands of religion and death and permitting the elaboration of philosophical ideas for coping with longevity. Scientific study focused on the diseases and ailments of the aged as specialization took hold throughout the medical profession; doctors explained the physiological roots of retreat from the world but proposed ways of permitting the elderly to carry on as active members of society. Social science became aware of the plight of the aged along with that of the young, the poor, and the handicapped. Political discourse

2. Roussel and Girard, "Régimes démographiques et âges de la vie."

3. Friedrich Nietzsche, "On the Uses and Disadvantages of History for Life," in *Untimely Meditations* (Cambridge, 1983), p. 63.

4. Alphonse Daudet, "Les vieux," in *Lettres de mon moulin* (Paris, 1925), pp. 143–157; Gaston Roupnel, *Histoire de la campagne française* (Paris, 1932, 1974). The English version of the Berri film was called *The Two of Us*.

inherited this concern, the white-haired Revolutionary symbolizing the political pretensions of men in their thirties and forties.[5]

A philosophical idealist might argue that a description of the evolution of ideas is its own explanation. A historian of *mentalités* can view it only as a beginning. It is an important beginning and one that does provide a partial explanation, but it is only partial. *L'histoire des mentalités* is still part of social history and of the *annaliste* dream of a total history. This does not mean that material conditions alone will provide the entire explanation. *L'histoire des mentalités* is not "vulgar Marxism." In the view of Michel Vovelle, it is horizontal in its exploration of the *longue durée* and vertical in its consideration of all levels of society.[6] I would add a third dimension implicit in Vovelle's own work: the depth that comes from a sympathetic immersion in the sources. Vovelle has written of *mort subie, mort vécue,* and *discours sur la mort.*[7] Incidence, experience, and discourse. I have tried in this book to encompass all three: *vieillesse subie, vieillesse vécue,* and *discours sur la vieillesse. Discours* has come first. This is not to suggest that cultural history takes precedence over social history, nor have I put social history last as a way of explaining at the last minute the story already told. But that order does recognize the drama inherent in the story.

Social history has provided the context for the cultural history and has also permitted further exploration of a demographic and social shift that coincided with the cultural one. People lived longer and experienced a variety of new challenges. We have seen how they confronted those challenges in both rural and urban settings, within the family and without. The family too was evolving, both turning in upon itself and searching for help in a changing world.[8] Far from existing in an unchanging "traditional" society, people of the eighteenth century were pioneers—but, of course, some were more pioneering than others. Some were better placed to scout the future, others more resistant or simply confined in what Fernand Braudel has called *prisons de longue durée.*[9] Eighteenth-century conditions permitted the elite to live longer,

5. Alison Patrick, *The Men of the First French Republic* (Baltimore, Md., 1972), chap. 8 and app. V.

6. Vovelle, "Y a-t-il un inconscient collectif?" in *Idéologies et mentalités,* pp. 85–100.

7. Vovelle, *La mort et l'Occident.*

8. Ariès, *Centuries of Childhood;* Flandrin, *Familles.*

9. Quoted in Vovelle, "Histoire des mentalités, histoire des résistances, ou les prisons de longue durée," in *Idéologies et mentalités,* pp. 236–261.

to retire from work, and to elaborate a new culture of old age. That is another reason for having begun with elite cultural representations. The working classes, though, also played a role, transforming a challenge into a problem and giving voice to it.

This takes us a long way from the central question that guided the first works in the history of old age, the question of whether things got better or worse for the aged.[10] Ideas, images, and roles have evolved, and one need not argue that the situation has improved or declined. Rather, it has changed. People have lived in different material, social, and religious circumstances and have had different expectations of life and, hence, of old age. We need not ascribe the change exclusively to either abstract attitudes or underlying socioeconomic forces.[11] We need both ideas and things. The Enlightenment operated on many levels at once: a philosophical shift toward a worldly and social universe, a scientific interest in clinical observation, a stylistic change toward the natural, and a political movement of great audacity. Simultaneously, France had an early confrontation with demographic and social phenomena that have challenged people with ever growing force.

It is no mere coincidence that so many other changes were occurring at precisely the same time. One need not call it the coming of a "pre-revolutionary sensibility" to recognize that something extraordinary was happening in the middle of the eighteenth century.[12] Many have pointed to it—too many to name—and suggested partial explanations. For students of the period the next step is to determine precisely how those partial explanations fit together.

For gerontologists with an appreciation of the humanities and, indeed, for all of us who seek meaning and value in the aging process, the lessons of the French experience of old age in the eighteenth century are many. We are not the first to have alternatives; even then, people chose

10. John Demos remarked on this development in the historiography of old age in his comments at the "Old Age, Inheritance, and Property in Town and Country" session of the American Historical Association meeting, 1982. For important criticism of a simplistic "before and after" approach, see Jill S. Quadagno, *Aging in Early Industrial Society: Work, Family, and Social Policy in Nineteenth-Century England* (New York, 1982), esp. chap. 8.

11. See the contributions of Brian Gratton, Gerald N. Grob, and Charles E. Rosenberg on the state of the field in David Van Tassel and Peter N. Stearns, eds., *Old Age in a Bureaucratic Society* (Westport, Conn., 1986).

12. Michel Vovelle does call it that in his important article "Le tournant des mentalités en France 1750–1789: La sensibilité pré-révolutionnaire," *Social History*, 5 (1977), 605–629.

from a variety of models for aging. Even then, the elderly prepared for both death and long life, as people juggled ideas of maturation, degradation, and the mere passage of time, and as material circumstances created greater opportunities while continuing to make painful demands. We should not make rash assumptions about families in the past. We should not confuse rhetoric and behavior, nor should we draw simplistic analogies between family and state. Terms like "generational equity" may be new, but aging in the past also had to do with the intersection of private values and public policies. Historical understanding of that intersection is vitally important.

Selected Bibliography

Unpublished Sources, Manuscripts, Prints, and Paintings

Archives

Archives Nationales, Paris (A.N.)

AD XIV 6. Ateliers de charité. Bureaux de Bienfaisance. Caisses d'épargnes. Compagnies d'assurances. Droit des pauvres.

AF I 15. Procès-verbal des séances du Comité de Mendicité et de ses décisions.

D XXVI. Comité de Salubrité.

D XXVII 1. Comité des Secours et de Mendicité. 1 Mai 1789–Brumaire *an IV.*

$F^{1C}I$ 92–102. Esprit public. Fêtes de la république. Jeunessee, Liberté, Reconnaissance, Souveraineté du Peuple, Vieillesse, Victoire. *An IV–An VII.*

F^{15}101. Mémoires sur la Justice et la Finance. Indemnités et Secours. Mendicité. Hôpitaux et Enfants Trouvés. Maison de Secours de Paris. Billets de Confiance. Brevets d'invention. Caisse patriotique. 1777–92 (quelques pièces de l'an II).

F^{15}104. Secours an XI. Hospices an IX.

F^{15}138. Projets sur la Mendicité, les enfants trouvés, les sourds-muets, l'Hôtel-Dieu, la bienfaisance, classés par noms d'auteurs ou par objets. 1775–1808.

F^{15}2282. Haute Vienne. Hôpital-Générale de St.-Aléxis de Limoges-état des vieillards et d'autres.

F^{15}230. Epidémies. Hôpitaux.

F[15]231. Dépôts de Mendicité. Secours à des chirurgiens et à des hôpitaux (1781–89).

F[15]232. Hôpitaux. Bouches-du-Rhône. 1790–*an IV*.

F[15]233. Hôtel-Dieu de Paris. Règlement. 1781–88.
Hospices: Deux-Sèvres. 1791.

F[15]240. Hospice des Quinze-Vingts. 1791–*an III*.
Hospice des Incurables. *An II–An III*.

F[15]242. Département des Etablissements Publics de la Municipalité de Paris. Affaires renvoyées par le Maire. 1792–*an II*.

F[15]243–245. Hôpitaux, Hospices. 1780s–1790s.

F[15]247. Département des Etablissements Publics de la Municipalité de Paris. Affaires Renvoyées par le Maire du 1er janvier au 17 octobre 1791.

F[15]248. Hôpital Général de Poitiers. 1792.

F[15]249. Hospice d'Humanité de Troyes. *An IV*.

F[15]257. Hospices. *An III*. Seine.

F[15]397. Hospices. 1786–87.

F[15]1920. Secours. 1812.

F[15]2811. Police des Moeurs et Mendicité. 1785–*an III*.

F[15]2875. Comité de Mendicité et de Secours de l'Assemblée Constituante. Pétitions. 1790–91.

F[15]2876. Secours aux Mendiants de Paris. *An IV*.

F[16]936. Comité de Mendicité.

F[16]964. Mendicité (1786–*an VIII*).

F[16]965. Mendicité. Dépôts. Comptabilité (1787–90).

F[17]1281, dossier 12. Commission de l'Instruction Publique.

F[22]*688–689. Caisse d'épargnes et de bienfaisance (caisse Lafarge): Procès-verbaux des assemblées générales d'actionnaires. 1791–1888.

F[22]*772–776. Société des Vieillards, Première Société.

F[22]*801. Société des Vieillards, Seconde Société.

A.N., Minutier Central des Notaires Parisiens (M.C.)

XXXVIII. 424. Testaments. 1754.

XXXVIII. 426. Testaments. 1755.

XXXVIII. 427. Testaments. Dons Mutuels. Constitutions Viagères. 1755.

XXXVIII. 490. Testaments de 1761 à l'*an IX*.

LVII. 397. Contrats de Mariage. 1751.

LXVI. 486. Contrats de Mariage. 1751.

CXVI. 562. Testaments. 1787.

Archives de l'Assistance Publique, Paris (A.P.)

Fonds Fosseyeux, MS 19. Histoire des hôpitaux de Paris, première partie du XIXe siècle.

Fonds Fosseyeux, nouvelle série 61. Période révolutionnaire. Grand Bureau des Pauvres et Petites Maisons.

Archives Départementales des Bouches-du-Rhône, Dépôt d'Aix-en-Provence (A.D. Aix)

Notaires d'Eguilles: Jean-Joseph Carle, 301 E 486–489, 1741–1773; Michel-Joseph Séguin, 301 E 494, 1741–1748.

Série VI B. Juridiction d'Eguilles, Procédures civiles et criminelles: 1511–1516, 1741–80.

Archives Départementales des Bouches-du-Rhône, Marseille (A.D. Marseille)

L494. Comité de bienfaisance. Hôpitaux 1790–*an VII*.

L862. Mendicité. 1790–*an II*.

L865. Demandes de secours adressées au District d'Aix par les communes et par les particuliers. 1790–*an IV*.

L866. District d'Aix. Secours aux vieillards. . . . 1791–*an IV*.

351 E 1165–1168. Etude du Notaire Hazard, 1757–58.

361 E 138–139. Etude du Notaire Sard, 1757–58.

Archives Départementales de la Somme, Amiens (A.D. Somme)

3 E 43–46. Etude du Notaire Janvier (Amiens), 1771–81.

E 26.423–26.427. Etude du Notaire Montigny (Picquigny), 1771–75.

Archives Départementales du Calvados, Caen (A.D. Calvados)

D484–499. Palinod de Caen.

D1217–1232. Palinod.

D1233–1262. Recueils des poésies couronnées.

2D1446. Académie Royale des Belles-Lettres de Caen. Discours de M. Bocquet du Hautbosc, "Sur les vieillards qui vantent le passé . . . 1er décembre 1757."

Archives Municipales d'Amiens (A.M. Amiens)

GG781. Hôtel-Dieu, 1634–1790.

GG802. Hôpital Général. 1764–87.

GG813. Hôpital des Incurables, Paris.

GG1087–1100. Mendicité.

HH256. Demandes d'ouvriers d'être autorisés à travailler à domicile, 1645–1775.

2H10 1–4. Secours aux parents des défenseurs de la patrie, 1790–*an II; an III–an IX*; Registre d'inscriptions des parents des défenseurs . . . ayant droit au secours de la république, 1792; 1793–*an II*.

4I3 1. Dépôt de Mendicité.

IQI 1–5. Bureau Général des Pauvres, bureau et comité de secours, 1788–*an III;
  an IV–an VI; an VII–an IX;* Comité de secours (registre) *an II–an
  IV; an IV–an X.*

IQ4 1. Demandes de secours, 1790–91, *an II–an IV.*

3QI 1–3. Hôpitaux, 1790–*an II; an III–V; an VI–IX.*

4QI 1. Caisse d'épargne (Lafarge). 1791.

*Archives Municipales, Hôtel de Ville, Eguilles (A.M.
  Eguilles)*

Registres paroissiaux: baptêmes, mariages et sépultures, 1681–1792 (11 reg.).
Délibérations municipales, 1560–1792 (10 reg.). Lacunes: 1600–22, 1687–90.
Délibérations de l'hôpital, 1743–1827 (1 reg.).
Recensement, 1810.

Archives Municipales, Marseille (A.M. Marseille)

306 fol. 13v, 341 fol. 80v. Annibal Camous.

Libraries

*Bibliothèque Nationale, Paris, Salle des Manuscrits
  (B.N. MS)*

Collection Joly de Fleury (J.F.)

  1238. Hôpitaux de Paris, 29. Petites Maisons, 1.

  1239. Hôpitaux de Paris, 30. Petites Maisons, 2.

  1302. Maisons de Force, II. Petites Maisons.

  1303. Maisons de Force, III. Petites Maisons.

  2543. Papiers d'Espagnac. Affaires de Paris, III.

Papiers d'Emmanuel Duvillard, X. Rentes des Emigrés, Rentes et Pensions, etc.
  N.A.F. 20585.

Treatises

  Cicero. *De Senectute, ou "Livre de viellesse," de "Tulle," traduction de "Lau-
    rent"* (de Premierfait) . . ., F.F. 126.

  "Traitté de la vieillesse." F.F. 4822, Fols. 58–70.

Plays

  A. *Le vieillard supplanté.* F.F. 9248. Soleinne, 7:341–373.

  Beaunoir (Alexandre-Louis-Bertrand Robineau). *La comtoise à Paris, ou Le
    vieillard dupé* (1770, 1783). N.A.F. 2890.

  Bertin d'Antilly, Auguste-Louis, *Bélisaire* (1795). F.F. 9286. Soleinne, 45:92–
    109.

  Cléronome. *Le vieillard coquet* (1786). F.F. 9266.

  Elbée. *Léandre, ou Le bon père.* F.F. 9269.

Laffichard, Thomas. *Le vieillard amoureux.* F.F. 9321.

Lesage, Alain-René, and Fromaget, Nicolas. *Les vieillards rajeunis* (1738). F.F. 9314.

Lesueur, Abraham Nicolas. *Agathe, ou Le vieillard trompé* (1787). F.F. 9278.

Pannard. *Prologue du vieux et du nouveaux* (1742). F.F. 9324.

Ribié, César. *Le vieillard amoureux, ou Les deux Polichinelles* (1788). N.A.F. 3014:190–204.

Les vieux pensionnaires. F.F. 9247. Soleinne, 6:152–167.

Bibliothèque de l'Opéra, Paris (Opéra)

Biancolelli, Joseph Dominique. *Les vieillards dupes de leur amour* (1733). In Gueullette, T.S., *Manuscrit autographe de l'histoire du théâtre italien depuis l'année 1577 jusqu'en 1750 et les années suivantes.* 2 vols., c. 1760. Réserve 625 (2).

Campra, A. *Les âges.* Ballet. A99.

Bibliothèque Municipale d'Avignon, Calvet (B.M. Avignon)

Poulle, Benoît-Jean-André. *De la vieillesse: Lettre à Mr. d'Eyragues.* Fonds Requien, MS 2728.

Bibliothèque, Municipale de Carpentras, Inguebertine (B.M. Carpentras)

Montereul, P. de. *Du bonheur et des avantages de la vieillesse.* MS 254. Fols. 543–548.

Bibliothèque Municipale de Châteauroux (B.M. Châteauroux)

Discours sur les fêtes républicaines, an VI. In *Discours 1798.* 38 (B 206). Includes *fête de la vieillesse* addresses of Pierre Vincent Louis, Frédéric Montferrand, Joseph Talbot.

History of Science Library, Cornell University, Ithaca, N.Y.

Astruc, Jean. *Traité des maladies des vieillards.* Notes of H. Coillot (1762).

Print Collections and Museums

Bibliothèque Nationale, Paris, Cabinet des Estampes (B.N. Estampes)

Collection Deloynes (printed volumes), Ya327: esp. vols. 4–12 (1750–81).

Collection de Vinck, T. 46, fol. 51, no. 6356: "Fête dédiée à la vieillesse," gravure à l'eau-forte par J. Duplessi-Bertaux (1795) d'après P. A. Wille (1794).

B6C. Paris.

Oa 22, 132. France—Moeurs.

226   *Selected Bibliography*

Td 24. T. 1–11. Iconologie. Degrés des Ages.

Musée des Arts et Traditions Populaires, Paris (A.T.P.)
   Iconothèque: Degrés des Ages.

PUBLISHED PRIMARY SOURCES

Adam. *Fête des vieillards.* Metz, *an IV, V, VI* [1796–98].
"Adresse intéressante à tous les bons patriotes français: Par un vieillar de bon sens."
   Paris, 1790?, see Thompson, *Microfiche.*
Alexandre, Dom Nicolas. *La médecine et la chirurgie des pauvres, qui contiennent
   des remèdes choisis, faciles à préparer et sans dépense, pour la pluspart des
   maladies internes et externes qui attaquent le corps humain.* Paris, 1714.
Alix, avocat. *Les quatre âges de l'homme: Poëme.* Paris, 1782.
A.M. *Le vieillard devenue aveugle: Stances.* B.N. Ye 53929.
*L'ami des vieillards, journal dont les bénéfices sont consacrés à former une masse
   destinée aux prêtres non assermentés qui ont atteint l'âge de soixante ans,* 8
   juillet–décembre, 1791. Later published as *Journal de bienfaisance* and *L'ami des
   vieillards infortunés.* B.N. 8°Lc^{2}615–620. Prospectus, *Le cri de l'humanité ou
   l'ami des vieillards,* in Widener Library, Fr. 1328.02.41.
*L'anti-Cornaro, ou Remarques critiques sur le Traité de la vie sobre de Louis
   Cornaro Vénitien.* Paris, 1702.

Bagard. *Recherches et observations sur la durée de la vie de l'homme.* 1754.
   Reviewed in *Mémoires de Trévoux,* November 1754.
Barry, Etienne. *Précis de la fête de la fondation de la République française, célébrée
   dans la commune de Toulon, le 1er Vendémiaire au 5me de l'ère républicaine, et à
   laquelle était jointe celle des Vieillards.* B.N. Lb^{42}1135.
Barry, Paul de. *Pensez-y-bien, ou Réflexions sur les quatres fins dernières.* Paris,
   1737.
Bagard. *Recherches et observations sur la durée de la vie de l'homme.* 1754.
   Reviewed in *Mémoires de Trévoux,* November 1754.
Barry Paul de. *Pensez-y-bien, ou Réflexions sur les quatres fins dernières.* Paris,
   1737.
Barry, Etienne. *Précis de la fête de la fondation de la République française, célébrée
   dans la commune de Toulon, le 1er Vendémiaire au 5me de l'ère républicaine, et à
   laquelle était jointe celle des Vieillards.* B.N. Lb^{42}1135.
Barthez, P. J. *Nouveaux éléments de la science de l'homme.* 3d ed. 2 vols. Paris,
   1858.
Beausobre, Louis de. *Nouvelles considérations sur les années climatériques, la
   longueur de la vie de l'homme, la propagation du genre humain, et la vraie
   puissance des états, considérée dans la plus grande population.* 1757. Reviewed in
   Mémoires de Trévoux, 1757.
Begons. *Dissertation physique sur les changemens et mouvemens critiques, sur-
   venus à quelques personnes âgées qui ont semblé rajeûnir.* 1708. Reviewed in
   Mémoires de Trévoux, November 1708.

Berryat, Jean, ed. *Collection académique, composée des mémoires, actes, ou journaux des plus célèbres académies et sociétés littéraires étrangères, des extraits des meilleurs ouvrages périodiques, des traités particuliers, et des pièces fugitives les plus rares; Concernant l'histoire naturelle et la botanique, la physique expérimentale et la chymie, la médecine et l'anatomie, traduits en François, et mis en ordre par une Société de Gens de Lettres.* 13 vols. Dijon and Paris, 1755–79. 2, Royal Society, London (Dijon, 1755), B.N. R 5603; 3, Germany (Dijon, 1755), B.N. R 5604; 7, Copenhagen (Dijon, 1766), B.N. R 5608; 11, Stockholm (Paris, 1772), B.N. R 5612.

Bertin, Nicolas. *La consolation de la vieillesse.* Paris, 1626.

Bichat, Xavier. *Recherches physiologiques sur la vie et la mort.* Paris, 1800; Verviers, Belgium, 1973.

Blanchard, Antoine. *Nouvel essay d'exhortations pour les états différens des maladies où l'on trouvera un grand nombre d'exhortations pour l'administration du viatique et de l'extrême-onction.* 2 vols. Paris, 1718.

Bloch, Camille, and Alexandre Tuetey. *Procès-verbaux et rapports du comité de mendicité de la Constituante, 1790–1791.* Paris, 1911.

Bonaparte, Napoleon. "Lettre addressée au Docteur Tissot de Lausanne," Ajaccio, Corsica, April 1, 1787. In A. Keller, *De Brienne au 13 Vendémiaire.* Paris, n.d.

Bordelon, Laurent. *Remarques, ou Réflexions critiques, morales et historiques, sur les plus belles et les plus agréables pensées, qui se trouvent dans les ouvrages des auteurs anciens et modernes.* Paris, 1690.

Bossuet, Jacques Bénigne. *Oeuvres.* Paris, 1961.

Bouchardon. *Etudes prises dans le bas peuple, ou Les cris de Paris.* Paris, 1737–42.

Bouilly, J. N., and J. Pain. *La vieillesse de Piron.* Paris, 1810.

Boureau-Deslandes, André-François. *Réflexions sur les grands hommes qui sont morts en plaisantant, avec des poësies diverses.* Rochefort, 1755.

Boyer d'Aguilles, Jean-Baptiste. *Recueil d'estampes d'après les tableaux des peintres les plus célèbres d'Italie, des Pays-Bas et de France, qui sont à Aix dans le cabinet de M. B d'A. gravées par Jacques Coelemans d'Anvers.* Paris, 1744.

Bracciolini, Poggio [Pogge, Florentin]. *Un vieillard doit-il se marier?* Paris, 1877.

Bret, Antoine, and I.V. Guillot de la Chassaigne. *Le calendrier des vieillards.* Paris, 1753.

Buffon, Georges Louis Leclerc, comte de. *Oeuvres complètes.* Paris, 1774.

Butte, Wilhelm. *Echelle physiologique.* Paris, 1822.

———. *Prolégomènes de l'arithmétique de la vie humaine.* Paris, 1812.

Cabanis, P. J. G. *Rapports du physique et du moral de l'homme.* 2d ed. Paris, 1805.

Cahaisse, Henri-Alexis. *Mémoires de Préville.* Paris, 1812.

Campardon, Emile, and Auguste Longnon, eds. *La vieillesse de Scaramouche, 1690–1694.* Paris, 1875.

Camus, Armand-Gaston. *Code des pensions.* Paris, 1792.

Caraccioli, Louis-Antoine de. *Dictionnaire critique, pittoresque, et sentencieux, propre à faire connoître les usages du siècle, ainsi que ses bisarreries.* Lyon, 1768.

Chamfort, Sébastien-Roch-Nicolas. "Epître d'un père à son fils, qui a remporté le prix de l'Académie Françoise en 1764." Paris, 1764.

"Chanson patriotique, à l'autel de la patrie." B.N. Ye Pièce 5525.

Chansonnier des amateurs, ou Choix de chansons des meilleurs auteurs anciens et modernes recueilli par un amateur. Paris, n.d.

Chapelle, Claude Emmanuel Luillier. "Chanson." In *Oeuvres complètes de Voltaire,* vol. 32, p. 533. Paris, 1880.

Chassignet, Jean-Baptiste. *Le mespris de la vie et consolation contre la mort* (1594). Geneva, 1967.

Chevalier, Claude. *Le triomphe de la vieillesse.* Paris, 1787.

Chouvalov, André Pétrovich. *Epître à Ninon L'Enclos.* Geneva, 1774.

Cicero. *Caton l'ancien (De la vieillesse),* ed. P. Wuilleumier. Paris, 1940.

———. *Dialogues de la vieillesse et de l'amitié.* Paris, 1640.

———. *Tusculane . . . sur le mépris de la mort.* Paris, 1732.

Clairon. *Mémoires de Mlle Clairon.* In *Bibliothèque des mémoires relatifs à l'histoire de France pendant le 18e siècle,* vol. 6. Paris, 1846.

Clément, L'abbé. "Réflexions sur la vieillesse." *Mercure de France,* August 1757.

Collin d'Harleville, Jean-François. *Le vieillard et les jeunes gens.* Paris, 1803.

Collot-d'Herbois, Jean-Marie. "Vaudeville de la famille patriote." B.N. 8°Ye Pièce 4473.

Comiers, Claude. *La médecine universelle, ou L'art de se conserver en santé, et de prolonger sa vie.* Brussels, 1688.

Condorcet, Marie-Jean-Antoine-Nicolas Caritat, marquis de. *Esquisse d'un tableau historique des progrès de l'esprit humain.* Paris, 1864.

———. *Sur les caisses d'accumulation.* In *Oeuvres de Condorcet.* Paris, 1847–49.

Conseils d'un vieil auteur à un jeune, ou L'art de parvenir dans la république des lettres. London, 1758.

Cornaro, Luigi. *Conseils pour vivre long-tems.* Paris, 1701.

———. *De la sobriété et de ses avantages, ou Le vray moyen de se conserver dans une santé parfaite jusqu'à l'âge le plus avancé.* Paris, 1701.

———. *Trois discours nouveaux et curieux.* Paris, 1647.

Couailhac, L. *Physiologie du célibataire et de la vieille fille.* Paris, 1841.

"Le cri d'un citoyen sexagénaire, traîné dans les prisons par un abus d'autorité." Paris, 1789? See Thompson, *Microfiche.*

Crillon, Louis-Athanase Des Balbes de Berton, abbé de. *Mémoires philosophiques du Baron de ***.* 2 vols. Vienna, 1777.

Daignan, Guillaume. *Echelle de la vie humaine, ou Thermomètre de santé.* Paris, 1811.

———. *Tableau des variétés de la vie humaine.* Paris, 1786.

D'Alembert, Jean Le Rond. "Lettre à Jean-Jacques Rousseau." In *Oeuvres de D'Alembert,* vol. 4, pp. 432–458. Paris, 1822.

Delavigne, Casimir. *L'école des vieillards* (1823). In *Oeuvres,* vol. 2. Brussels, 1832.

Delisle de Sales, Jean-Baptiste Claude Izouard. *Bélisaire.* In *Recueil des meilleures pièces dramatiques faites en France depuis Rotrou jusqu'à nos jours.* Paris, 1781.

———. *Le vieux de la montagne.* 3 vols. Paris, 1799.

Deparcieux, Antoine. *Essai sur les probabilités de la durée de la vie humaine, d'où l'on déduit la manière de déterminer les rentes viagères, tant simples qu'en tontines: Précédé d'une courte explication sur les rentes à terme, ou annuités, et accompagné d'un grand nombre de tables.* Paris, 1746.

Le discernement de la vraye et de la fausse morale, où L'on fait voir le faux des Offices de Cicéron, et des Livres de l'amitié, de la vieillesse, et des paradoxes. Paris, 1695.

Desfontaines, F. G. Les vieux époux. Paris, an III [1794–95].

Desfontaines, N. M. Bélisaire. Paris, 1641.

Des Pommelles, Chevalier. Tableau de la population. Paris, 1789.

Destouches, Philippe-Néricault. Scènes de l'aimable vieillard (1745). In Oeuvres dramatiques de N. Destouches, vol. 5. Paris, 1811.

Diderot, Denis, ed. Encyclopédie, ou Dictionnaire raisonné des sciences, des arts, et des métiers, par une société de gens de lettres. Neufchastel, 1751–1765.

——. Oeuvres esthétiques. Paris, 1959.

——. Pensées détachées sur la peinture, la sculpture, l'architecture et la poésie, pour servir de suite aux salons. In Oeuvres complètes, vol. 12. Paris, 1876.

——. Salons. 4 vols. Oxford, 1957–1967.

——. Supplément au voyage de Bougainville. Paris, 1935.

Dorat, Claude-Joseph. Anacréon citoyen. Amsterdam, 1774.

Dorvigny, L.-A. L'hospitalité, ou Le bonheur du vieux père. Paris, an III [1794–95].

——. Les noces du Père Duchesne. Paris, 1789.

Douarche, A. Les tribunaux civils de Paris pendant la révolution (1791–1800). 2 vols. Paris, 1905–7.

Dubuisson, Paul Ulric. Le vieux garçon. Paris, 1783.

Ducis, J. F., and M. J. Chénier. Oeuvres de J. F. Ducis suivies des oeuvres de M. J. de Chénier. Paris, 1839.

Dulaurent, Le citoyen. Le bon vieillard: Discours prononcé dans la section des Tuileries, le décadi 30 Pluviôse, à la Fête de la Raison et de la Vérité. Paris, an II [1794].

Dunker, Balthazar-Antoine. Esquisses pour les artistes et amateurs des arts, sur Paris. B.N. V 10496.

Dusaulx, J. Discours prononcé par J. Dusaulx, à l'administration municipale du premier arrondissement du canton de Paris, le 10 Fructidor an 5, à l'occasion de la fête de la vieillesse, célébrée en vertu de la loi du 3 Brumaire an 4. B.H.V.P. 966 264.

Esparron, P. J. B. Essai sur les âges de l'homme. Paris, 1803.

Expilly, Abbé Jean-Joseph. Tableau de la population de la France. N.p., 1780.

Fête de la vieillesse: 5e arrondissement. Paris, an VII, VI [1799, 1798]. B.N. Lb[42] 2481, 618.

Fiaux, Louis. La femme, le mariage, et le divorce: Etude de physiologie et de sociologie. Paris, 1880.

Fleury, L'abbé. Devoirs des maistres et des domestiques. Paris, 1765.

Formey, J. H. S. Les avantages de la vieillesse. Berlin, 1759. Reviewed in Journal encyclopédique, vol. 4. Liège, 1759.

Garnier, Germain. Abrégé élémentaire des principes de l'économie politique. Paris, 1796.

Genlis, Caroline-Stéphanie-F. Ducrest de Mézières, comtesse de. *Mémoires inédits de Madame la comtesse de Genlis, sur le dix-huitième siècle et la révolution française, depuis 1756 jusqu'à nos jours.* 8 vols. Brussels, 1825.
——. *Les souvenirs de Felicie L***.* Paris, 1804.
Geraudly, Claude Jaquier de. *L'art de conserver les dents.* Paris, 1737.
Geronée ou le vieillard rajeuni, drame, sera représenté par les petits pensionnaires du Collège Louis-le-Grand. Paris, 1696. B.N. Réserve Yf 2702–2703.
Gin. *Analyse raisonnée du droit français.* Paris, 1782.
Girard de Villethierry. *La vie des veuves, ou Les devoirs et les obligations des veuves chrétiennes: Nouvelle édition revûë, corrigée, et augmentée de remarques curieuses sur la viduité, tirées des anciens pères grecs et latins.* Paris, 1719.
Gomberville, Marin Le Roy, sieur de. *La doctrine des moeurs, qui représente en cent tableaux la différence des passions, et enseigne la manière de parvenir à la sagesse universelle.* Paris, 1685.
Goulin, Jean. *Lettres à un médecin de province, pour servir à l'histoire de la médecine.* Copenhagen, 1769.
——. *Le médecin des dames, ou L'art de les conserver en santé.* Paris, 1771.
——. *Le médecin des hommes, depuis la puberté jusqu'à l'extrême vieillesse.* Paris, 1772.
——. *Mémoires littéraires, critiques, philologiques, biographiques, et bibliographiques, pour servir à l'histoire ancienne et moderne de la médecine.* Paris, 1777.
——. *Vocabulaire françois, ou Abrégé du dictionnaire de l'Académie Françoise.* 2 vols. Paris, 1771.
Gravelot, Hubert-François Bourguignon, dit, and Charles-Nicolas Cochin. *L'iconologie, ou Traité de la science des allégories à l'usage des artistes en 350 figures, gravées d'après les dessins de MM. Gravelot et Cochin avec les explications relatives à chaque sujet.* Paris, n.d.
Grimm, Baron von, Diderot, Raynal, and Meister. *Correspondance littéraire, philosophique et critique.* 16 vols. Paris, 1877–82.
Grou, L'abbé. *Caractères de la vraie dévotion.* Paris, 1788.
Guillard de Beaurieu, Gaspard. *L'élève de la nature.* 1763.
——. *L'heureux citoyen: Discours à M. Jean-Jacques Rousseau.* Lille, 1759.
——. *L'heureux vieillard, drame pastoral.* Amsterdam, 1768. British Library, 11738.aa.11(1).
——. *Le porte-feuille françois, ou Choix nouveau et intéressant de différentes pièces de prose et de poësie.* Paris, 1765.
Guyot de Merville, Michel. *Le dédit inutile, ou Les vieillards intéressés.* Paris, 1742.
Hayley, William. *Essai satirique et amusant sur les vieilles filles.* Paris, 1788.
Helvétius, Claude-Adrien. *Oeuvres.* Paris, 1793.
Hirzel, Hans Kaspar. *The Rural Socrates; or, An Account of a Celebrated Philosophical Farmer, Lately Living in Switzerland, and Known by the Name of KLIYOGG.* Hallowell, Maine, 1800.
Histoire admirable du juif-errant, lequel depuis l'an 33, jusqu'à l'heure présente, ne fait que marcher: Contenant sa tribu, sa punition, ses avantures admirables qu'il a eu en tous les endroits avant son tems. Rouen, 1751.

Hoffman, F.-B. *La femme de quarante-cinq ans.* Paris, *an VII* [1798–99].

——. *Le jeune sage et le vieux fou.* Paris, *an X* [1801–2].

Holbach, Le baron d'. *Système de la nature, ou Des lois du monde physique et du monde moral: Nouvelle édition, avec des notes et des corrections, par Diderot.* 2 vols. Paris, 1821.

Hufeland, Christoph Wilhelm. *The Art of Prolonging Life.* London, 1797.

Joubert, Laurens. *Erreurs populaires au fait de la médecine et régime de santé.* Bordeaux, 1578.

Jourdain, Anselme. *Préceptes de santé, ou Introduction au dictionnaire de santé, contenant les moyens de corriger les vices de son tempérament, et de le fortifier par le seul secours du régime et de l'exercice, ou L'art de conserver sa santé et de prévenir les maladies.* Paris, 1772.

Jouy, Etienne de. *L'hermite de la Chaussée-d'Antin,* vol. 1. Paris, 1813.

"Le juif errant, tel qu'on l'a vu passer à Bruxelles en Brabant, 22 avril 1774." A.T.P., Photothèque, Ph. 746.362.

La Chaussée, Pierre-Claude Nivelle de. *Le vieillard amoureux.* In *Oeuvres,* vol. 3. Paris, 1777.

La Chétardie, Joachim Trotti de. *Homélie XXVIII pour le dimanche dans l'octave du Saint Sacrement sur la vieillesse.* In *Homélies de M. de S.-Sulpice,* vol. 2. Paris, 1708.

Lacroix, Sigismond. *Actes de la commune de Paris pendant la révolution.* Paris, 1896.

Lafarge, Joachim. *Caisse d'épargnes du C. Lafarge: Liste générale des numéros . . .* Paris, *an XI* [1802–3].

——. *Caisse d'épargnes et de bienfaisance du sieur La Farge.* Paris, 1791.

——. *Projet de bienfaisance.* 1789.

——. *Projet de bienfaisance du sieur Lafarge.* Paris, 1790.

——. *Projet de bienfaisance par le sieur Lafarge.* Paris, n.d.

——. *Réflexions utiles et nécessaires aux actionnaires de la caisse d'épargnes et de bienfaisance du citoyen Lafarge.* Paris, *an II* [1793–94].

Lallemant, Pierre. *Les saints désirs de la mort, ou Recueil de quelques pensées des pères de l'église, pour montrer comment les chrétiens doivent mépriser la vie, et souhaiter la mort* (1673). Brussels, 1713.

Lambert, Anne-Thérèse de Marguenat de Courcelles, marquise de. *Oeuvres.* Lausanne, 1748.

La Mettrie, Julien-Offray de. *L'homme machine.* Paris, 1966.

La Mothe le Vayer, François de. *Opuscules ou petits traictez.* Paris, 1644.

Larcher, L. J., and P. J. Jullien. *Ce qu'on a dit du mariage et du célibat.* Paris, 1858.

Laroche. *Discours adressé aux jeunes élèves des deux sexes, assistant à la fête de la vieillesse, immédiatement après le couronnement.* B.H.V.P. 8059 (2).

La Rochefoucauld-Liancourt, François-Alexandre-Frédéric de. *Opinion . . . sur la motion de M. Camus, relative aux pensions.* In *Assemblée Nationale* (January 1–15, 1790). B.N. 8°Le[29] 415.

Larocque, André Jean de. *Establissement d'une caisse générale des épargnes du peuple.* Brussels, 1786.

Le Begue de Presle. *Le conservateur de la santé, ou Avis sur les dangers qu'il importe à chacun d'éviter, pour se conserver en bonne santé et prolonger sa vie: On y a joint des objets de règlemens de police relatifs à la santé.* Paris, 1763.

Lebrun, François, ed. *Parole de Dieu et Révolution: Les sermons d'un curé angevin (Yves-Michel Marchais) avant et pendant la guerre de Vendée.* Toulouse, 1979.

Leclerc de Montlinot, Charles Antoine Joseph. *Dictionnaire portatif d'histoire naturelle.* Paris, 1763.

——. *Discours qui a remporté le prix à la société royale d'agriculture de Soissons, en l'année 1779, sur la mendicité.* Lille, 1779.

——. *Etat actuel du dépôt de Soissons, précédé d'un essai sur la mendicité (1786).* Soissons, 1789.

Lécluse, Henry de. *Eclaircissemens essentiels pour parvenir à préserver les dents de la carie, et à les conserver jusqu'à l'extrême vieillesse.* Paris, 1755.

Léger, F. P. A., and R. C. Guilbert Pixerécourt. *Le vieux major.* Paris, an IX [1800–1801].

Lemaître de Claville, Charles-François-Nicolas. *Traité du vrai mérite de l'homme considéré dans tous les âges et dans toutes les conditions: Avec des principes d'éducation, propres à former les jeunes gens à la vertu.* Paris, 1734.

Le Pelletier, Claude. *Comes senectutis.* Paris, 1709.

"Lettre d'un vieillard de bon sens aux bonnes gens de Marseille." 1790? See Thompson, *Microfiche.*

Lettre pastorale de Monseigneur l'Archevêque de Paris: Pour le soulagement des pauvres pendant les rigeurs de cet hiver. Paris, 1789.

Linguet, S. N. H. *Plan d'établissemens tendans à l'extinction de la mendicité.* Paris, 1779.

Longeville-Harcouet. *Histoire des personnes qui ont vécu plusieurs siècles et qui ont rajeuni: Avec le secret du rajeunissement, tiré d'Arnauld de Villeneuve.* Paris, 1715.

Lottin, Augustin-Martin. *Almanach des centenaires, ou Durée de la vie humaine au-delà de cent ans, démontrée par des exemples sans nombre, tant anciens que modernes, avec le calendrier de l'année.* 10 vols. Paris, 1764–71.

——. *Recueil de chansons.* Paris, 1781–89.

Mahieu. *Discours prononcé dans le temple décadaire à Deuxponts le dix Fructidor an VII: A la fête de la vieillesse.* B.H.V.P. 28 056.

Malan, César-Henri-Abraham. *Les deux vieillards.* Paris, 1821.

——. *Le vieillard d'Ellacombe.* Paris, 1817.

Malvaux, L'abbé. *Les moyens de détruire la mendicité en France, en rendant les mendians utiles à l'état sans les rendre malheureux; Tirés des mémoires qui ont concouru pour le prix accordé en l'année 1777, par l'Académie des Sciences, Arts, et Belles-Lettres de Châlons-sur-Marne.* Châlons-sur-Marne, 1780.

Mancini-Nivernois, Louis-Jules Barbon Mancini-Mazarini, duc de Nivernois. *Fables.* 2 vols. Paris, 1796–97.

Marat, J.-P. *De l'homme, ou Des principes et des loix de l'influence de l'âme sur le corps, et du corps sur l'âme.* 3 vols. Amsterdam, 1775–76.

Marmontel, Jean-François. *Bélisaire.* Brussels, 1792.

——. *Mémoires d'un père pour servir à l'instruction de ses enfants.* 2 vols. Paris, 1827.

Marmontel, Jean-François, Turgot, and Voltaire. *Pièces relatives à Bélisaire.* Amsterdam, 1767.

Mathon de la Cour, Charles-Joseph. *Almanach des muses, ou Choix des meilleures poésies fugitives qui ont paru en 1765–1768.* Paris, 1766–69.

——. *Lettre à Madame ***, sur les peintures, les sculptures, et les gravures exposées dans le sallon du Louvre cette année.* Paris, 1763.

——. *Lettres à Madame *** . . .* Paris, 1763–65.

——. *Lettres à Monsieur XXX . . . 1765.* Paris, 1765.

——. *Par quelles causes et par quels degrés les loix de Lycurgue se sont altérées chez les Lacédémoniens jusqu'à ce qu'elles ayent été anéanties.* Lyon, 1767.

——. *Seconde lettre à Madame *** . . .* Paris, 1763.

——. *Testament de M. Fortuné Ricard.* 1785.

Matos-Fragoso, Juan de. *Le sage dans sa retraite.* The Hague, 1782.

Maussion, baronne de. *Quatre lettres sur la vieillesse des femmes.* In *Caton l'ancien, ou Dialogue sur la vieillesse, traduit de Cicéron.* Paris, 1822.

Meister, J. H. *Etudes sur l'homme, dans le monde et dans la retraite.* Paris, 1804.

——. *Lettres sur la vieillesse.* Paris, 1810.

——. "Stances d'un vieillard à sa jeune amie." B.N. Ye 52483.

Mercier, Louis-Sébastien. *Contes moraux, ou Les hommes comme il y en a peu.* Paris, 1768.

——. *Du théâtre, ou Nouvel essai sur l'art dramatique.* Amsterdam, 1773.

——. *Tableau de Paris.* 12 vols. Amsterdam, 1783–88.

——. *Le vieillard et ses trois filles.* Paris, 1792.

Messance. *Nouvelles recherches sur la population de la France.* Lyon, 1788.

Mignot, Vincent. *Traités de Cicéron sur l'amitié et la vieillesse.* Paris, 1780.

Mirabeau, Honoré-Gabriel Riqueti, comte de. *Le degré des âges du plaisir, ou Jouissances voluptueuses de deux personnes de sexes différents, aux différentes époques de la vie.* Paris, 1798.

——. *Des lettres de cachet et des prisons d'état.* 2 vols. Hamburg, 1782.

——. *Essai sur le despotisme.* Paris, 1821.

Mirabeau, Victor Riqueti, marquis de. *L'ami des hommes, ou Traité de la population* (1756). Paris, 1883.

——. *Hommes à célébrer.* 2 vols. Paris, 1789.

Moheau. *Recherches et considérations sur la population de la France.* Paris, 1778, 1912.

Moissy, Alexandre Guillaume Mouslier de. *Bélisaire.* Paris, 1769.

——. *Ecole dramatique de l'homme.* 3 vols. Amsterdam, 1769–70.

Moivre, Abraham de. *A Treatise of Annuities on Lives.* 3d ed. London, 1756.

Morellet, abbé André. *Senectutis encomium: La vieillesse.* B.N. 8°Ye Pièce 4438.

Morsollier des Vivetières, Benoît-Joseph. "Le vieillard crédule." *Mercure de France,* April 1772.

Moussard. *A la vieillesse.* B.H.V.P. 967 963.

———. *Discours prononcé le 10 Fructidor, an VI, à la fête de la vieillesse, célébrée par l'administration municipale du premier arrondissement de Paris.* B.H.V.P. 8059 (1).

Necker, Madame. *Réflexions sur le divorce.* Lausanne, 1794.

Nepveu, François. *La manière de se préparer à la mort pendant la vie.* Paris, 1713.

Neveux, N. "Le vieillard amoureux et raisonnable." Paris, *an XI* [1802–3]. B.N. Ye 56375 (449).

Ninon de Lenclos. *Correspondance authentique.* Paris, 1886.

Noüet, Jacques. *Retraite pour se préparer à la mort, prise des dernières paroles et actions de Jésus-Christ, depuis son retour dans la Judée jusques à sa Passion (1679).* Paris, 1694.

Nougaret, Pierre-Jean-Baptiste. *Les passions des différens âges, ou Tableau des folies du siècle.* Utrecht, 1766.

Ozicourt, d'. *Bélisaire.* Paris, 1769.

Pasquier, Etienne. *Oeuvres choisies.* 2 vols. Paris, 1849.

Picard, L.-B. *La vieille tante, ou Les collatéraux.* Paris, 1811.

———. *Le vieux comédien.* In *Fin du répertoire du théâtre français,* vol. 21. Paris, 1824.

Pierre, Constant. *Les hymnes et chansons de la révolution.* Paris, 1904.

———. *Musique des fêtes et cérémonies de la révolution française.* Paris, 1899.

Pierre, G. "Dialogue entre une mère et sa fille." Paris, n.d. B.N. Ye 56375 (460).

———. "Le vieux Richard amoureux d'une bergère." B.N. Ye 55944.

Pinel, Philippe. *Considérations sur la constitution sénile et sur son influence dans les maladies aiguës.* In *Mémoires et observations, Archives Générales de Médecine* (Paris), 1, no. 2 (1823).

Piron, Alexis. *Oeuvres.* Paris, 1758.

Pithou de Loinville, Jean-Joseph. "Vie de Jean Jacob, vieillard du Mont-Jura, âgé de 120 ans." Paris, 1789. See Thompson, *Microfiche.*

Poisson. *Cris de Paris.* Paris, 1774.

Poncet de la Rivière, Pierre. *Considérations sur les avantages de la vieillesse dans la vie chrestienne, politique, civile, économique, et solitaire: Ouvrage du Baron de Prelle, édité par Dominique Bouhours, Jésuite.* Paris, 1677.

Pothier, Robert Joseph. *Traité du contrat de constitution de rente.* Paris, 1774.

Préville, L. de. *Méthode aisée pour conserver sa santé jusqu'à une extrême vieillesse.* Paris, 1752.

Réflexions diverses propres à former l'esprit et le coeur. Paris, 1749.

"Réflexions d'un vieux patriote sur les affairs présentes." 1787. See Thompson, *Microfiche.*

Règlements des hospices civils de Paris. Ans VII–XIII [1798–1805]. B.N. 8°Z Le Senne 11 269.

Regrets d'un vieux soldat avant les glorieuses journées de juillet. Paris, 1830.

"Réponse d'un curé âgé de 97 ans, à Monseigneur le Duc d'Orléans." 1789. See Thompson, *Microfiche.*

Rétif de la Bretonne, Nicolas-Edme. *La vie de mon père* (1779). Paris, 1970.

Ricard, Jean-Marie. *Traité des donations entre-vifs et testamentaires avec la coutume d'Amiens commentée,* 2d ed. Paris, 1734.

Ricard d'Allauch. *Plan d'une maison de retraite pour les vieillards, proposé par souscriptions*. Marseille, 1822. B.M. Marseille, 12.217 (22).

Rilliet de Livron. *Catéchisme sans superstition*. Geneva, 1791.

Robert, M. J. C. *De la vieillesse*. Paris, 1777.

Rotrou, Jean de. *Bélisaire*. In *Recueil des meilleures pièces dramatiques faites en France depuis Rotrou jusqu'à nos jours, ou Théâtre françois*, vol. 7. Lyon, 1781.

Rouault, L. *Les quatres fins de l'homme, avec des réflexions capables de toucher les pécheurs les plus endurcis, et de les ramener dans la voye du salut*. Paris, 1734.

Rousseau, Jean-Jacques. *Oeuvres complètes*. Paris, 1852.

Sabatier de Castres, Antoine. *Dictionnaire des passions, des vertus, et des vices, ou Recueil des meilleurs morceaux de morale pratique, tirés des auteurs anciens et modernes, étrangers et nationaux*. 2 vols. Paris, 1769.

Saurin, Bernard-Joseph. *Epîtres sur la vieillesse et sur la vérité*. Paris, 1772.

Ségur, J. A. *Les vieux fous, ou Plus de peur que de mal*. Paris, 1796.

Sénac de Meilhan, Gabriel. *Considérations sur l'esprit et les moeurs*. London, 1787.

Société des Amis de la Constitution de Beauvais. *Arrêté . . . relatif à la caisse d'épargne de M. Lafarge*. Beauvais, 1791? B.N. Lb[40] 2542.

Le Socrate marseillois, ou Particularités instructives et intéressantes pour l'humanité . . . Marseille, 1773.

Solignac, Le chevalier de. *Eloge historique de M. de Fontenelle prononcé à la séance publique de la société royale des sciences et belles-lettres de Nancy le 8 mai 1757*. Nancy, 1757.

Souvenir joyeux énigmatique, ou Pensée anacréontique, par un vieillard. B.N. Ye Pièce 4449.

"Les souvenirs d'une vieille coquette." B.N. 8°Ye Pièce 4450.

Sue, J.-J. *Essai sur la physiognomie des corps vivans, considérée depuis l'homme jusqu'à la plante*. Paris, 1797.

Tenon, Jacques-René. *Offrande aux vieillards: De quelques moyens pour prolonger leur vie*. Paris, 1813.

——. *Opinion . . . sur la réunion des deux comités de mendicité et de salubrité (séance du 14 oct. 1791)*. Paris, 1791. B.N. 8°Le[33] 3C (15).

——. *Réflexions en faveur des pauvres citoyens malades*. Paris, 1791.

Trublet, L'abbé. *Essais sur divers sujets de littérature et de morale*. 2 vols. Paris, 1735.

Turneau de la Morendière. *Police sur les mendians, les vagabonds, les joueurs de profession, les intrigans, les filles prostituées, les domestiques hors de maison depuis long-tems, et les gens sans aveu*. Paris, 1764.

"Le vieil soldat âgé de cent dix sept ans qui est arrivé ces jours derniers à l'Hôtel Royal des Invalides, qui a fait quatre-vingt campagnes." Paris, 1728. B.N. Ln[27] 28163.

Le vieillard abyssin rencontré par Amlac, empereur d'Ethiopie. London, 1779.

"Le vieillard amoureux, Air." Château-Thierry, 1830. B.N. Ye 55472 (4571).

Le vieillard amoureux: Histoire nouvelle, suivie de plusieurs fables et autres pièces qui n'ont point encore paru. The Hague, 1718.

"Un vieillard à ses compatriotes, Héroide." B.N. Ye 1595.

Le vieillard jaloux tombé en reveries à la louange des Cornes. Avec une expresse d'effence aux femmes de ne plus battre leurs maris . . . etc. Paris, 1618. B.N. Réserve Y² 3579.

La vieille amoureuse: Stances. B.N. Ye 4792.

"La vieille bonne femme de 102 ans, soeur du curé de 97 ans, à Messieurs les Etats-Généraux." 1789. See Thompson, *Microfiche.*

Villiers, L'abbé de. *Dernières stances sur ma vieillesse.* Paris, 1727. B.N. Ye 19974.

Vilorié, de. *Les vieux garçons.* Paris, 1761.

Virey, J. J. *Histoire naturelle du genre humain.* Paris, an IX [1800–1801].

"La vision du vieillard dans la nuit du 12 décembre 1791." 1810? B.N. 8°Ye Pièce 4495.

Vollant, M. *Mémoire sur les moyens de détruire la mendicité en France, et de venir au secours des indigens de toutes les classes.* Paris, 1790.

Voltaire, *Oeuvres complètes.* 52 vols. Paris, 1877–85.

Young, Arthur. *Travels during the Years 1787, 1788, and 1789 . . .* Bury St. Edmund's, 1792.

Yvan, Antoine. *La trompette du ciel, qui réveille les pécheurs, et qui les excite puissamment à se convertir à Dieu.* Rouen, n.d. Musée Arbaud (Aix-en-Provence), MS 595.

Secondary Sources

Achenbaum, W. Andrew, and Peter N. Stearns. "Old Age and Modernization." *Gerontologist,* 18, no. 3 (1978), 307–312.

Ackerknecht, Erwin H. "Hygiene in France, 1815–1848." *Bulletin of the History of Medicine,* 22 (1948), 117–155.

——. *Medicine at the Paris Hospital, 1794–1848.* Baltimore, Md., 1967.

Adhémar, Hélène. *Watteau—sa vie—son oeuvre.* Paris, 1950.

Ageing and Society, 4, no. 4 (1984).

Agulhon, Maurice. *La sociabilité méridionale: Confréries et associations dans la vie collective en Provence orientale à la fin du 18e siècle.* 2 vols. Aix-en-Provence, 1966.

Anderson, George. *The Legend of the Wandering Jew.* Providence, R.I., 1965.

Angers, Julien-Eymard d'. "Stoïcisme et 'libertinage' dans l'oeuvre de François La Mothe Le Vayer." *Revue des Sciences Humaines* (Lille), 75 (1954), 259–284.

Annales de démographie historique 1985: Vieillir autrefois. Paris, 1986.

Ariès, Philippe. *Centuries of Childhood: A Social History of Family Life.* New York, 1962.

——. "Growing Old in America" (review of D. H. Fischer). *New Republic,* July 2, 1977.

——. *Histoire des populations françaises et de leurs attitudes devant la vie depuis le XVIIIe siècle.* Paris, 1948. Rev. ed. Paris, 1971.

——. *L'homme devant la mort.* Paris, 1977.

Arnason, H. H. *The Sculptures of Houdon.* New York, 1975.

Art Institute of Chicago. *Selected Works of 18th Century French Art in the Collection of the Art Institute of Chicago.* Chicago, 1976.

Attinger, Gustave. *L'esprit de la commedia dell'arte dans le théâtre français*. Paris, 1950.

Aubenas, Roger. *Le testament en Provence dans l'ancien droit*. Aix-en-Provence, 1927.

Aubertin, Charles. *L'esprit public au XVIIIe siècle: Etude sur les mémoires et les correspondances politiques des contemporains, 1715 à 1789*. Paris, 1873.

Auguet, Roland. *Le juif errant*. Paris, 1977.

Avalon, Jean. "Les âges de la vie dans l'imagerie populaire." *Passiflora*, 4, no. 10 (1934).

Baehrel, René. *Une croissance: La Basse Provence rurale (fin 15e–1789)*. Paris, 1961.

Baker, Keith Michael. *Condorcet: From Natural Philosophy to Social Mathematics*. Chicago, 1975.

Baratier, Edouard. *La démographie provençale du 13e au 16e siècle avec chiffres de comparaison pour le 18e siècle*. Paris, 1961.

——. *Histoire de la Provence*. Toulouse, 1969.

Barber, Elinor G. *The Bourgeoisie in 18th-Century France*. Princeton, N.J., 1955.

Bardet, Jean-Pierre. *Rouen aux XVIIe et XVIIIe siècles: Les mutations d'un espace social*. Paris, 1983.

Beauvoir, Simone de. *La vieillesse*. Paris, 1970.

Bédier, Joseph. *Les fabliaux: Etudes de littérature populaire et d'histoire littéraire du moyen âge*. Paris, 1964.

Bée, Michel. "La société traditionnelle et la mort." *XVIIe Siècle*, 106–107 (1975), 81–111.

Bellenger, Mireille. "Recherches sur la population marseillaise au milieu du XVIIIe siècle: Structures et relations sociales d'après les contrats de mariage." M.A. thesis, Aix-en-Provence, 1963.

Benoît, Fernand. *La Provence et le Comtat Venaissin: Arts et traditions populaires*. Avignon, 1975.

Bercé, Yves-Marie. *Fête et révolte: Des mentalités populaires du XVIe au XVIIIe siècle*. Paris, 1976.

Berkner, Lutz K. "Inheritance, Land Tenure, and Peasant Family Structure: A German Regional Comparison." In Jack Goody, Joan Thirsk, and E. P. Thompson, *Family and Inheritance*. Cambridge, 1976.

——. "The Stem Family and the Developmental Cycle of the Peasant Household: An Eighteenth-Century Austrian Example." *American Historical Review*, 77 (1972), 398–418.

Bideau, Alain. "A Demographic and Social Analysis of Widowhood and Remarriage: The Example of the Castellany of Thoissey-en-Dombes, 1670–1840." *Journal of Family History*, 5 (1980), 28–43.

Blanc, Charles. *Les peintres des fêtes galantes*. Paris, 1854.

Blayo, Yves. "La mortalité en France de 1740 à 1829." *Population*, 30 (1975), 123–142.

Bloch, Camille. *L'assistance et l'état en France à la veille de la révolution (Généralités de Paris, Rouen, Alençon, Orléans, Châlons, Soissons, Amiens) (1764–1790)*. Paris, 1908.

Bocher, Emmanuel. *Les gravures françaises du XVIIIe siècle*. Paris, 1876.

Bois, Jean-Pierre. "Une politique de la vieillesse: La retraite des vieux soldats, 1762–1790." *Annales de démographie historique 1985*, 7–20.

Bollème, Geneviève. *Les almanachs populaires aux XVIIe et XVIIIe siècles: Essai d'histoire sociale.* Paris, 1969.

——. *La bibliothèque bleue: La littérature populaire en France du XVIe au XIXe siècle.* Paris, 1971.

Bosher, J. F. *French Finances, 1770–1795: From Business to Bureaucracy.* Cambridge, 1970.

Bossy, John. "The Counter-Reformation and the People of Catholic Europe." *Past & Present*, 47 (1970), 51–70.

Bouard, Michel de. *Histoire de la Normandie.* Toulouse, 1970.

Bouchard, Gérard. *Le village immobile: Sennely-en-Sologne au XVIIIe siècle.* Paris, 1972.

Bourdelais, Patrice. "Géographie du vieillissement de la population en France, 1851–1911." In Arthur Imhof et al., eds., *Le vieillissement.* Lyon, 1982.

Braudel, Fernand. "Histoire et sciences sociales: La longue durée." *Annales: E.S.C.*, 13 (1958), 725–753.

Brenner, Clarence D. *A Bibliographical List of Plays in the French Language, 1700–1789.* Berkeley, Calif., 1947.

Breuil, Henri. *L'assistance aux vieillards à Paris de 1789 à 1905.* Paris, 1909.

Brookner, Anita. *Greuze: The Rise and Fall of an Eighteenth-Century Phenomenon.* London, 1972.

——. "Jean-Baptiste Greuze." *Burlington Magazine*, 98 (1956), 157–162, 192–199.

——. *Watteau.* London, 1967.

Bryson, Norman. *Word and Image: French Painting of the Ancien Régime.* Cambridge, 1981.

Burguière, André. "De Malthus à Max Weber: Le mariage tardif et l'esprit d'entreprise." *Annales: E.S.C.*, 27 (1972), 1128–1138.

Cahen, Léon. "Les idées charitables à Paris au XVIIe et au XVIIIe siècles, d'après les règlements des compagnies paroissiales." *Revue d'Histoire Moderne et Contemporaine*, 2 (1900–1901), 5–22.

Cassirer, Ernst. *The Philosophy of the Enlightenment.* Princeton, N.J., 1951.

Castan, Yves. *Honnêteté et relations sociales en Languedoc, 1715–1780.* Paris, 1974.

——. "Pères et fils en Languedoc à l'époque classique." *XVIIe siècle*, 102–103 (1974), 31–43.

Champfleury. *Histoire de l'imagerie populaire.* Paris, 1869.

Charbonneau, Hubert. *Tourouvre au Perche aux XVIIe et XVIIIe siècles: Etude de démographie historique.* Paris, 1970.

Charoy, Fernand. *L'assistance aux vieillards, infirmes, et incurables en France de 1789 à 1905.* Paris, 1905.

Charraud, Alain. "Analyse de la représentation des âges de la vie humaine dans les estampes populaires du XIXe siècle." *Ethnologie française*, 1 (1971), 59–78.

Chartier, Roger. "Les arts de mourir, 1450–1600." *Annales: E.S.C.*, 31 (1976).

Chaunu, Pierre. *La civilisation de l'Europe classique.* Paris, 1966.

——. *La civilisation de l'Europe des lumières.* Paris, 1971.

——. *La mort à Paris: XVIe, XVIIe, XVIIIe siècles.* Paris, 1978.

Chaussinand-Nogaret, Guy. *The French Nobility in the Eighteenth Century: From Feudalism to Enlightenment.* Cambridge, 1985.

Chevalier, Louis. *La formation de la population parisienne au XIXe siècle.* Paris, 1950.

Cioranescu, Alexandre. *Bibliographie de la littérature française du XVIIIe siècle.* 3 vols. Paris, 1969.

Cobb, Richard. *Les armées révolutionnaires.* Paris, 1961.

——. *Death in Paris, 1795–1801.* Oxford, 1978.

——. *Paris and Its Provinces, 1792–1802.* London, 1975.

——. *The Police and the People: French Popular Protest, 1789–1820.* London, 1970.

——. *A Sense of Place.* London, 1975.

Cole, Thomas R., and Mary G. Winkler. "Aging in Western Medicine and Iconography." *Medical Heritage,* 1985, 335–347.

Collier, Raymond. *La vie en Haute-Provence de 1600 à 1850.* Digne, 1973.

Collomp, Alain. "Alliance et filiation en Haute-Provence au XVIIIe siècle." *Annales: E.S.C.,* 32 (1977), 445–477.

——. "Conflicts familiaux et groupes de résidence en Haute-Provence." *Annales: E.S.C.,* 36 (1981), 408–425.

——. "Famille nucléaire et famille élargie en Haute-Provence au XVIIIe siècle (1703–1734)." *Annales: E.S.C.,* 27 (1972), 969–975.

——. *La maison du père: Famille et village en Haute-Provence aux XVIIe et XVIIIe siècles.* Paris, 1983.

——. "Maison, manières d'habiter et famille en Haute Provence aux XVIIe et XVIIIe siècles." *Ethnologie française,* 8 (1978), 301–320.

——. "Ménage et famille: Etudes comparatives sur la dimension et la structure du groupe domestique." *Annales: E.S.C.,* 29 (1974), 777–786.

Combet, Joseph. "Les fêtes révolutionnaires à Nice." Nice, 1907. Widener Fr 1346.27.25.

Conisbee, Philip. *Painting in Eighteenth-Century France.* Ithaca, 1981.

Conrad, Christoph, and Hans-Joachim von Kondratowitz. *Gerontologie and Sozialgeschichte: Wege zu einer historischen Betrachtung des Alters.* Berlin, 1983.

Coornaert, Emile. *Les corporations en France avant 1789.* Paris, 1941.

Corvisier, André. *L'armée française de la fin du XVIIe siècle au ministère de Choiseul: Le soldat.* Paris, 1964.

——. *Les controles de troupes de l'Ancien Régime,* vol. 1, *Une source d'histoire sociale: Guide des recherches.* Paris, 1968.

Coulet, Henri. *Le roman jusqu'à la révolution.* 2 vols. Paris, 1967.

Courboin, François. *Histoire illustrée de la gravure en France.* 4 vols. Paris, 1923–29.

Courdurié, Marcel. *La dette des collectivités publiques de Marseille au XVIIIe siècle: Du débat sur le prêt à intérêt au financement par l'emprunt.* Marseille, 1974.

Cowgill, Donald, and L. D. Holmes. *Aging and Modernization.* New York, 1972.

Crow, Thomas E. *Painters and Public Life in Eighteenth-Century Paris.* New Haven, Conn., 1985.

Curtius, Ernst Robert. *European Literature and the Latin Middle Ages.* Princeton, N.J., 1967.

Darmon, Pierre. *Mythologie de la femme dans l'ancienne France XVIe–XIXe siècles.* Paris, 1983.

——. *Le tribunal de l'impuissance: Virilité et défaillances conjugales dans l'ancienne France.* Paris, 1979.

Darnis, Lucien. *Des tribunaux de famille dans le droit intermédiaire.* Paris, 1903.

Darnton, Robert. *The Literary Underground of the Old Regime.* Cambridge, Mass., 1982.

Daumard, Adeline. *La bourgeoisie parisienne de 1815 à 1848.* Paris, 1963.

Daumard, Adeline, and François Furet. *Structures et relations sociales à Paris au XVIIIe siècle.* Paris, 1961.

Davis, Natalie Zemon. *Society and Culture in Early Modern France.* Stanford, Calif., 1975.

Dejace, André. *Les règles de la dévolution successorale sous la révolution (1789–1794).* Paris, 1957.

Delaitre, J. *L'assistance aux vieillards.* Paris, 1911.

Delumeau, Jean. "Au sujet de la déchristianisation." *Revue d'histoire moderne et contemporaine,* 22 (1975), 52–60.

——. *La peur en occident XIVe–XVIIIe siècles.* Paris, 1978.

Demos, John, and Sarane Spence Boocock. *Turning Points: Historical and Sociological Essays on the Family.* Supplement, *American Journal of Sociology,* 84 (1978).

Deyon, Pierre. *Amiens, capitale provinciale: Etude sur la société urbaine au 17e siècle.* Paris, 1967.

——. "Peinture et charité chrétienne." *Annales: E.S.C.,* 22 (1967), 137–153.

Diefendorf, Barbara G. "Widowhood and Remarriage in Sixteenth-Century Paris." *Journal of Family History,* 7 (1982), 379–395.

Le XVIIe siècle et la famille. XVIIe Siècle, 102–103 (1974).

Documentation Française: Social Security in France. Paris, n.d.

Donzelot, Jacques. *La police des familles.* Paris, 1977.

Dowd, David L. "Art as National Propaganda in the French Revolution." *Public Opinion Quarterly,* 15 (1951), 532–546.

——. "'Jacobinism' and the Fine Arts: The Revolutionary Careers of Bouquier, Sergent, and David." *Art Quarterly,* 16 (1953), 195–214.

——. *Pageant-Master of the Republic: Jacques-Louis David and the French Revolution.* Lincoln, Neb., 1948.

Dreyfus, Ferdinand. *L'assistance sous la législative et la convention (1791–1795).* Paris, 1905.

Dupâquier, Jacques. "Les caractères originaux de l'histoire démographique française au XVIIIe siècle." *Revue d'histoire moderne et contemporaine,* 23 (1976), 182–202.

——. *La population française aux XVIIe et XVIIIe siècles.* Paris, 1979.

——. *La population rurale du bassin parisien à l'époque de Louis XIV.* Paris, 1979.

Dupâquier, Jacques, and Michel Dupâquier. *Histoire de la démographie.* Paris, 1985.

Durand, J. *Le folklore de l'Aube,* vol. 1, *Les âges de la vie.* Troyes, 1962.

Durand, Yves. *Les fermiers généraux au XVIIIe siècle.* Paris, 1971.

——. "L'idéal social en Champagne méridionale du XVIe au XVIIIe siècle." Paris, 1970. B.N. 8°Ll³⁴ 27.

Durry, Marie-Jeanne. *La vieillesse de Chateaubriand, 1830–1848.* Paris, 1933.

Duruy, Albert. "Les fêtes nationales pendant la révolution." *Revue de France,* 30 (1878).

Ehrard, Jean. *L'idée de nature en France à l'aube des lumières.* Paris, 1970.

Eisenstadt, S. N. *From Generation to Generation.* Glencoe, Ill., 1956.

Engrand, Charles. "Paupérisme et condition ouvrière dans la seconde moitié du XVIIIe siècle: L'exemple amiénois." *Revue d'Histoire Moderne et Contemporaine,* 29 (1982), 376–410.

Fairchilds, Cissie C. *Domestic Enemies: Servants and Their Masters in Old Regime France.* Baltimore, Md., 1984.

——. *Poverty and Charity in Aix-en-Provence, 1640–1789.* Baltimore, Md., 1976.

Farge, Arlette. *La vie fragile: Violence, pouvoirs, et solidarités à Paris au XVIIIe siècle.* Paris, 1986.

——. *Le vol des aliments.* Paris, 1974.

Favre, Robert. *La mort dans la littérature et la pensée françaises au siècle des lumières.* Lyon, 1978.

Febvre, Lucien. "Une question mal posée: Les origines de la réforme française et le problème des causes de la réforme." In *Au coeur religieux du XVIe siècle.* Paris, 1968.

Flandrin, Jean-Louis. *Familles: Parenté, maison, sexualité dans l'ancienne société.* Paris, 1976.

Flinn, Michael W. *The European Demographic System, 1500–1820.* Baltimore, Md., 1981.

Fluchère, Henri. "Ploutos, Eros, Molière et les vieillards." In W. D. Howarth and Merlin Thomas, eds., *Molière: Stage and Study.* Oxford. 1973.

Foisil, Madeleine. "Les attitudes devant la mort au XVIIIe siècle: Sépultures et suppressions de sépultures dans le cimetière parisien des Saints-Innocents." *Revue Historique,* 510 (1974), 303–330.

Folts, James D., Jr. "Senescence and Renascence: Petrarch's Thoughts on Growing Old." *Journal of Medieval and Renaissance Studies,* 10, no. 2 (1980), 207–237.

Fontaine, André. *Les doctrines d'art en France—peintres—amateurs—critiques de Poussin à Diderot.* Paris, 1909.

Forcioli, J. *Une institution révolutionnaire: Le tribunal de famille.* D'après les archives du district de Caen. Caen, 1932.

Ford, Franklin L. *Robe and Sword.* Cambridge, Mass., 1953.

Forrest, Alan. *The French Revolution and the Poor.* New York, 1981.

Forster, Robert. *The Nobility of Toulouse in the Eighteenth Century: A Social and Economic Study.* New York, 1971.

Foucault, Michel. *The Birth of the Clinic.* New York, 1973.

——. "The Politics of Health in the Eighteenth Century." From *Power/Knowledge,* reprinted in *The Foucault Reader.* New York, 1984.

Fourastié, Jean. "De la vie traditionnelle à la vie 'tertiaire': Recherches sur le calendrier démographique de l'homme moyen." *Population,* 14 (1959), 417–432.

Frêche, Georges. *Toulouse et la région Midi-Pyrénées au siècle des Lumières.* Paris, 1974.

Fried, Michael. *Absorption and Theatricality: Painting and Beholder in the Age of Diderot.* Berkeley, Calif., 1980.

Friedlander, Walter A. *Individualism and Social Welfare: An Analysis of the System of Social Security and Social Welfare in France.* New York, 1962.

Furet, François, ed. *Livre et société dans la France du XVIIIe siècle.* Paris, 1965.

Gaiffe, Félix. *Le drame en France au XVIIIe siècle.* Paris, 1910, 1971.

Garaud, Marcel. *La révolution et l'égalité civile.* Paris, 1953.

Garden, Maurice. *Lyon et les lyonnais au XVIIIe siècle.* Paris, 1970.

Gaudemet, Jean. *Les communautés familiales.* Paris, 1963.

Gautier, Etienne, and Louis Henry. *La population de Crulai, paroisse normande: Etude historique.* Paris, 1958.

Gay, Peter. *The Enlightenment: An Interpretation.* 2 vols. New York, 1966–69.

Geller, Guido. *Die Geriatrie an der Salpêtrière von Pinel bis Charcot.* Zurich, 1965.

Gerson, Frédérick. *L'amitié au XVIIIe siècle.* Paris, 1974.

Giesey, Ralph E. "Rules of Inheritance and Strategies of Mobility in Prerevolutionary France." *American Historical Review,* 82 (1977), 271–289.

Gilbert, Creighton. "When Did a Man in the Renaissance Grow Old?" *Studies in the Renaissance,* 14 (1967), 7–32.

Glass, D. V., and D. E. C. Eversley, eds. *Population in History: Essays in Historical Demography.* Chicago, 1965.

Godechot, Jacques. *Les institutions de la France sous la révolution et l'empire.* Paris, 1968.

Goncourt, Edmond de, and Jules de Goncourt. *French Eighteenth-Century Painters.* Ithaca, 1981.

——. *Portraits intimes du dix-huitième siècle: Etudes nouvelles d'après les lettres autographes et les documents inédits.* Paris, 1878.

Goody, Jack, Joan Thirsk, and E. P. Thompson, eds. *Family and Inheritance: Rural Society in Western Europe, 1200–1800.* Cambridge, 1976.

Goubert, Jean-Pierre. "L'art de guérir: Médecine savante et médecine populaire dans la France de 1790." *Annales: E.S.C.,* 32 (1977), 908–926.

Goubert, Pierre. *L'ancien régime.* 2 vols. Paris, 1969–73.

——. *Beauvais et le Beauvaisis de 1600 à 1730.* Paris, 1960.

——. "Historical Demography and the Reinterpretation of Early Modern French History: A Research Review." In T. K. Rabb and R. I. Rotberg, *The Family in History: Interdisciplinary Essays.* New York, 1973, 16–27.

Grand-Carteret, John. *Les almanachs français: Bibliographie—iconographie des almanachs—annuaires—calendriers—chansonniers—états—étrennes—publiés à Paris (1600–1895).* Paris, 1896.

Grand Palais. *Les frères Le Nain*. Paris, 1978.

Green, Frederick Charles. *La peinture des moeurs de la bonne société dans le roman français de 1715 à 1761*. Paris, 1924.

Grmek, Mirko Drazen. "Descartes gérontologiste." In *Actes du XIIe congrès international d'histoire des sciences, 1968*, vol. 3, part B, *Science et philosophie, XVIIe et XVIIIe siècles*. Paris, 1971.

———. "Les idées de Descartes sur le prolongement de la vie et le mécanisme du vieillissement." *Revue d'Histoire des Sciences*, 21 (1968), 285–302.

———. *On Ageing and Old Age: Basic Problems and Historic Aspects of Gerontology and Geriatrics*. Monographiae Biologicae, 5. The Hague, 1958.

Groethuysen, Bernard. *The Bourgeois: Catholicism vs. Capitalism in Eighteenth-Century France*. New York, 1968.

Gruman, Gerald J. *A History of Ideas about the Prolongation of Life: The Evolution of Prolongevity Hypotheses to 1800*. Transactions of the American Philosophical Society. Philadelphia, 1966.

Guibert, Louis. *Livres de raison: Registres de famille et journaux individuels limousins et marchois*. Paris, 1888.

Guillemard, Anne-Marie. *La retraite: Une mort sociale*. Paris, 1972.

———, ed. *Old Age and The Welfare State*. London, 1983.

Gutton, Jean-Pierre. *La sociabilité villageoise dans l'ancienne France*. Paris, 1979.

———. *La société et les pauvres: L'exemple de la généralité de Lyon, 1534–1789*. Paris, 1970.

Harouel, Jean-Louis. *Les ateliers de charité dans la province de Haute-Guyenne*. Paris, 1969.

Hatzfeld, Henri. *Du paupérisme à la sécurité sociale: Essai sur les origines de la sécurité sociale en France, 1850–1940*. Paris, 1971.

Hawley, Henry. *Neo-Classicism: Style and Motif*. Cleveland, Ohio, 1964.

Hazard, Paul. *The European Mind, 1680–1715*. New York, 1963.

Hecht, Jacqueline. "Trois précurseurs de la Sécurité Sociale au XVIIIe siècle: Henry de Boulainvilliers, Faiguet de Villeneuve, Du Beissier de Pizany d'Eden." *Population*, 14, no. 1 (1950), 73–88.

Heine, Maurice. "La vieillesse de Rétif de la Bretone (1794–1806)." *Hippocrate: Revue d'humanisme médical*, 1934, 605–633.

Henry, Louis, and Yves Blayo. "La population de la France de 1740 à 1860." *Population*, 30 (1975), 71–122.

Herlihy, David. "Vieillir à Florence au quattrocento," *Annales: E.S.C.*, 24 (1969), 1338–1352.

Higonnet, Patrice L.-R. *Pont-de-Montvert: Social Structure and Politics in a French Village, 1700–1914*. Cambridge, Mass., 1971.

Hoffman, Philip T. *Church and Community in the Diocese of Lyon, 1500–1789*. New Haven, Conn., 1984.

Honour, Hugh. *Neo-classicism*. Harmondsworth, 1968.

Hufton, Olwen H. *Bayeux in the Late Eighteenth Century: A Social Study*. Oxford, 1967.

———. *The Poor of Eighteenth-Century France, 1750–1789*. Oxford, 1974.

Hunt, Lynn. *Politics, Culture, and Class in the French Revolution.* Berkeley, Calif., 1984.

Imbert, J. *Le droit hospitalier de la révolution et de l'empire.* Paris, 1954.

Imhof, Arthur E. "From the Old Mortality Pattern to the Twentieth Century." *Bulletin of the History of Medicine,* 59 (1985), 1–29.

Imhof, Arthur, Jean-Pierre Goubert, Alain Bideau, and Maurice Garden, eds. *Le vieillissement: Implications et conséquences de l'allongement de la vie humaine depuis le XVIIIe siècle.* Lyon, 1982.

Institut National d'Etudes Démographiques (INED). *Les âges de la vie.* 2 vols. Paris, 1982–83.

Jeorger, Muriel. "La structure hospitalière de la France sous l'Ancien Régime." *Annales: E.S.C.,* 32 (1977), 1025–1051.

Jones, Colin. *Charity and Bienfaisance: The Treatment of the Poor in the Montpellier Region, 1740–1815.* Cambridge, 1982.

Jones, S. Paul. *A List of French Prose Fiction from 1700 to 1750.* New York, 1939.

Kafker, Frank. "La vieillesse et la productivité intellectuelle chez les encyclopédistes." *Revue d'Histoire Moderne et Contemporaine,* 28 (1981), 304–327.

Kahn, Léon. *Histoire de la communauté israélite de Paris,* pt. 4, *Les sociétés de secours mutuels philanthropiques et de prévoyance.* Paris, 1887.

Kalnein, Wend Graf, and Michael Levey. *Art and Architecture of the Eighteenth Century in France.* Harmondsworth, 1972.

Kaplan, Steven Laurence, and Cynthia Koepp, eds. *Work in France: Representations, Meaning, Organization, and Practice.* Ithaca, 1986.

Kaplow, Jeffry. *Elbeuf during the Revolutionary Period: History and Social Structure.* Baltimore, Md., 1964.

——. *The Names of Kings.* New York, 1972.

Kelly, George Armstrong. "The History of the New Hero: Eulogy and Its Sources in Eighteenth-Century France." *Eighteenth Century: Theory and Interpretation,* 21, no. 1 (1980), 3–24.

Krantz, Emile. "Sur le *Traité de la vieillesse* de Cicéron." *Annales de l'Est* (Nancy), 1894, pp. 1–31.

La Capra, Dominick, and Steven L. Kaplan, eds. *Modern European Intellectual History: Reappraisals and New Perspectives.* Ithaca, 1982.

Laslett, Peter. "The History of Aging and the Aged." In *Family Life and Illicit Love in Earlier Generations.* Cambridge, 1977.

——. *Household and Family in Past Time.* Cambridge, 1972.

Laurent, Emile. *Le paupérisme et les associations de prévoyance.* Paris, 1865.

Le Bras, Hervé. "Evolution des liens de famille au cours de l'existence: Une comparaison entre la France actuelle et la France du XVIIIe siècle." In INED, *Les âges de la vie,* vol. 1, pp. 27–39. Paris, 1982.

——. "Parents, grands-parents, bisaïeux." *Population,* 28 (1973), 9–38.

Le Bras, Hervé, and Dominique Dinet. "Mortalité des laïcs et mortalité des religieux: Les Bénédictins de St-Maur aux XVIIe et XVIIIe siècles." *Population,* 35 (1980), 347–384.

Lebrun, François. *Les hommes et la mort en Anjou aux XVIIe et XVIIIe siècles.* Paris, 1971.

———. *Se soigner autrefois: Médecins, saints, et sorciers aux 17e et 18e siècles.* Paris, 1983.

Lecuir, J. "La *Gazette de l'Agriculture, du Commerce et de Finance* et le débat sur la population à la fin du XVIIIe siècle." *Annales de démographie historique,* 1979, pp. 363–441.

Lefebvre, Georges. *Les paysans du Nord pendant la révolution française.* Bari, 1959.

Le Glay, Jules. "Recherches historiques sur les anciens hospices ruraux du Nord de la France." Lille, 1858. B.N. Rp 10457.

Leith, James A. *The Idea of Art as Propaganda in France, 1750–1799.* Toronto, 1965.

Léonard, E.-G. *Mon village sous Louis XV d'après Les mémoires d'un paysan.* Paris, 1941.

Le Roy Ladurie, Emmanuel. *L'argent, l'amour, et la mort en pays d'Oc.* Paris, 1980.

Levey, Michael. *Rococo to Revolution: Major Trends in Eighteenth-Century Painting.* New York, 1966.

Liard, Brigitte. "Les mentalités collectives et les comportements devant la mort d'après les clauses des testaments dans le pays d'Aix-Eguilles, 1680–1789." M.A. thesis, Université d'Aix-Marseille, 1972–73.

Lorcin, Marie-Thérèse. "Retraite des veuves et filles au couvent: Quelques aspects de la condition féminine à la fin du moyen âge." *Annales de Démographie Historique,* 1975, pp. 187–204.

Loux, Françoise, and Philippe Richard. *Sagesses du corps: La santé et la maladie dans les proverbes français.* Paris, 1978.

McCloy, Shelby T. *The Humanitarian Movement in Eighteenth-Century France.* New York, 1972.

McManners, John. *Death and the Enlightenment: Changing Attitudes to Death among Christians and Unbelievers in Eighteenth-Century France.* Oxford, 1981.

———. *French Ecclesiastical Society under the Ancien Régime: A Study of Angers in the Eighteenth Century.* Manchester, 1960.

Maigron, Louis. *Fontenelle: L'homme, l'oeuvre, l'influence.* Paris, 1906.

Maire, Albert. "Les fêtes nationales sous la révolution dans le département du Puy-de Dôme." Clermont-Ferrand, 1886, in Widener.

Mâle, Emile. *L'art religieux après le Concile de Trente: Etude sur l'iconographie de la fin du XVIe siècle, du XVIIe, du XVIIIe siècle.* Paris, 1932.

Mandrou, Robert. *De la culture populaire aux XVIIe et XVIIIe siècles: La Bibliothèque Bleue de Troyes.* Paris, 1964.

Manuel, Frank E. *The Eighteenth Century Confronts the Gods.* Cambridge, Mass., 1959.

———. *The New World of Henri Saint-Simon.* Cambridge, Mass., 1956.

———. *The Prophets of Paris.* Cambridge, Mass., 1962.

Marion, Marcel. *Dictionnaire des institutions de la France aux XVIIe et XVIIIe siècles.* Paris, 1923, 1979.

Martin-Ginouvier, F. *Un philanthrope méconnu du XVIIIe siècle: Prairon de Chamousset . . .* Paris, 1905.

Masson, Emile. *La puissance paternelle et la famille sous la révolution.* Paris, 1911.

Masson, Paul. *Les Bouches-du-Rhône: Encyclopédie départementale*. Marseille, 1913–37.

——. *La Provence au XVIIIe siècle*. Paris, 1936.

Mauriange, Edith. *Arts populaires graphiques*. Paris, 1974.

Mauzi, Robert. *L'idée du bonheur dans la littérature et la pensée françaises au XVIIIe siècle*. Paris, 1960.

May, Georges. *Le dilemme du roman au XVIIIe siècle: Etude sur les rapports du roman et de la critique (1715–1761)*. New Haven, Conn., 1963.

Medick, Hans, and David Warren Sabean, eds. *Interest and Emotion: Essays on the Study of Family and Kinship*. Cambridge, 1984.

Mendelsohn, Everett. *Heat and Life: The Development of the Theory of Animal Heat*. Cambridge, Mass., 1964.

Merrick, Jeffrey. " 'Disputes over Words' and Constitutional Conflict in France, 1730–1732." *French Historical Studies*, 14, no. 4 (1986), 497–520.

Merriman, John M., ed. *Consciousness and Class Experience in Nineteenth-Century Europe*. New York, 1979.

Mistler, Jean, François Blaudez, and André Jacquemin. *Epinal et l'imagerie populaire*. Paris, 1961.

Mitterauer, Michael, and Reinhard Sieder. *The European Family: Patriarchy to Partnership from the Middle Ages to the Present*. Chicago, 1982.

Molinier, Alain. *Stagnations et croissance: Le Vivarais aux XVIIe–XVIIIe siècles*. Paris, 1985.

Moravia, Sergio. "From *Homme Machine* to *Homme Sensible:* Changing Eighteenth-Century Models of Man's Image." *Journal of the History of Ideas*, 39 (1978), 45–60.

Morineau, Michel. *Les faux-semblants d'un démarrage économique: Agriculture et démographie en France au XVIIIe siècle*. Paris, 1970.

Mornet, Daniel. *Les origines intellectuelles de la révolution française (1715–1787)*. Paris, 1933, 1947.

Mousnier, Roland. *Les institutions de la France sous la monarchie absolue, 1598–1789*. 2 vols. Paris, 1974–80.

Musée des Beaux Arts de Caen. *L'allégorie dans la peinture: La représentation de la charité au XVIIe siècle*. Caen, 1986.

Musée du Louvre. *François Boucher: Gravures et dessins provenant du Cabinet des Dessins et de la Collection Edmond de Rothschild au Musée du Louvre*. Paris, 1971.

Nahon, Gérard. "Les rapports des communautés judéo-portugaises de France avec celle d'Amsterdam au XVIIe et au XVIIIe siècles." *Studia Rosenthaliana*, 10, no. 1 (1976).

Nicolson, Benedict, and Christopher Wright. *Georges de la Tour*. London, 1974.

Norberg, Kathryn. *Rich and Poor in Grenoble, 1600–1814*. Berkeley, Calif., 1985.

Orangerie des Tuileries. *Georges de la Tour*. Paris, 1972.

Ozouf, Mona. *La fête révolutionnaire*. Paris, 1976.

——. "Symboles et fonctions des âges dans les fêtes de l'époque révolutionnaire." *Annales Historiques de la Révolution Française*, 42, no. 202 (1970), 569–593.

Palmer, R. R. *Catholics and Unbelievers in Eighteenth-Century France*. Princeton, N.J., 1939.

Parker, Harold T. *The Cult of Antiquity and the French Revolution.* Chicago, 1937.

Patrick, Alison. *The Men of the First French Republic.* Baltimore, Md., 1972.

Payne, Harry C. *The Philosophes and the People.* New Haven, Conn., 1976.

Pénélope: Pour l'histoire des femmes, vol. 13, *Vieillesses des femmes.* Paris, 1985.

Pergameni, Charles. "Les fêtes révolutionnaires et l'esprit public bruxellois au début du régime français." *Annales de la Société Royale d'Archéologie de Bruxelles,* 1913.

Peronnet, Michel C. *Les évêques de l'ancienne France.* 2 vols. Lille, 1977.

Perrenoud, Alfred. "Le biologique et l'humain dans le déclin séculaire de la mortalité." *Annales: E.S.C.,* 40 (1985), 113–135.

Perrot, Jean-Claude. *Genèse d'une ville moderne: Caen au XVIIIe siècle.* 2 vols. Paris, 1975.

Perrot, Jean-Claude, and Stuart Woolf. *State and Statistics in France, 1789–1815.* New York, 1984.

Peter, Jean-Pierre. "Malades et maladies à la fin du XVIIIe siècle." In J.-P. Desaive, J.-P. Goubert, E. Le Roy Ladurie, J. Meyer, O. Muller, and J.-P. Peter. *Médecins, climat, et épidémies à la fin du XVIIIe siècle.* Paris, 1972.

Peyronnet, Jean-Claude. "Famille élargie ou famille nucléaire? L'exemple du Limousin au début du XIXe siècle." *Revue d'Histoire Moderne et Contemporaine,* 22 (1975), 568–587.

Philibert, Michel. *Les échelles d'âge dans la philosophie, la science et la société: De leur renversement et des conditions de leur redressement.* Paris, 1968.

Phillips, Roderick. *Family Breakdown in Late Eighteenth-Century France: Divorces in Rouen, 1792–1803.* Oxford, 1980.

——. "Women's Emancipation, the Family, and Social Change in Eighteenth-Century France." *Journal of Social History,* 12, no. 4 (1979), 553–567.

Pigler, A. *Barockthemen: Eine Auswahl von Verzeichnissen zur Ikonographie des 17. und 18. Jahrhunderts.* 3 vols. Budapest, 1974.

Pilon, Edmond. *La vie de famille au XVIIIe siècle.* Paris, 1941.

Pintard, René. *Le libertinage érudit dans la première moitié du XVIIe siècle.* 2 vols. Paris, 1943.

Pitsch, Marguerite. *Essai de catalogue sur l'iconographie de la vie populaire à Paris au XVIIIe siècle.* Paris, 1952.

Poitrineau, Abel. "La fête traditionnelle." *Annales Historiques de la Révolution Française,* 47, no. 221 (1975), 339–355.

——. "Minimum vital catégoriel et conscience populaire: Les retraites conventionnelles des gens âgés dans le pays de Murat au XVIIIe siècle." *French Historical Studies,* 12 (1981), 165–176.

Pressat, Roland. "Evolution générale de la population française." *Population,* 29 (1974), 11–29.

Puvilland, Antonin. "Les doctrines de la population en France au XVIIIe siècle de 1695 à 1776." Doctoral diss., Lyon, 1912.

Quadagno, Jill S. *Aging in Early Industrial Society: Work, Family, and Social Policy in Nineteenth-Century England.* New York, 1982.

Ramsey, Matthew. "Popular Medicine and Medical Power in France, 1707–1830." Ph.D. diss., Harvard University, 1979.

Ranum, Orest. *Paris in the Age of Absolutism.* New York, 1968.

Raphael, Marios. *Pensions and Public Servants: A Study of the Origins of the British System.* Paris, 1964.

Reinhard, Marcel, ed. *Contributions à l'histoire démographique de la révolution française.* 2 vols. Paris, 1962–65.

Réunion des Musées Nationaux, Paris. *French Painting, 1774–1830: The Age of Revolution.* Detroit, Mich., 1975.

Ribbe, Charles de. *Les familles et la société en France avant la révolution d'après des documents originaux.* Paris, 1873.

———. *Le livre de famille.* Tours, 1879.

Richard, P.-J. *Histoire des institutions d'assurance en France.* Paris, 1956.

Rivoire, Jean-Alexis. *Le patriotisme dans le théâtre sérieux de la révolution (1789–1799).* Paris, 1950.

Roberts, Warren. *Morality and Social Class in Eighteenth-Century French Literature and Painting.* Toronto, 1974.

Roche, Daniel. " 'La mémoire de la mort': Recherches sur la place des arts de mourir dans la librairie et la lecture en France aux XVIIe et XVIIIe siècles." *Annales: E.S.C.,* 31 (1976), 76–119.

———. *Le siècle des lumières en province: Académies et académiciens provinciaux.* Paris, 1978.

Roebuck, Janet. "When Does 'Old Age' Begin? The Evolution of the English Definition." *Journal of Social History,* 12 (1979), 416–428.

Roger, Jacques. *Les sciences de la vie dans la pensée française du XVIIIe siècle: La génération des animaux de Descartes à l'Encyclopédie.* Paris, 1971.

Rolland de Villarceaux, H. "Essais d'histoire dramatique: Histoire du barbon (Théâtre antique), I. Théâtre grec; II. Théâtre latin." *Revue Nouvelle,* 5 (1845), 82–113; 7 (1846), 32–76.

Rosen, George. "The Philosophy of Ideology and the Emergence of Modern Medicine in France." *Bulletin of the History of Medicine,* 20 (1946), 328–339.

Rosenberg, Pierre. *The Age of Louis XV: French Painting, 1710–1774.* Toledo, Ohio, 1975.

———. *Chardin, 1699–1779.* Cleveland, Ohio, 1979.

———. *France in the Golden Age: Seventeenth-Century French Paintings in American Collections.* New York, 1982.

———. *French Master Drawings of the 17th and 18th Centuries in North American Collections.* London, 1972.

Rosenblum, Robert. *Transformations in Late Eighteenth Century Art.* Princeton, N.J., 1967.

Roussel, Louis. *La famille après le mariage des enfants.* Paris, 1976.

Rubin, James Henry. "Oedipus, Antigone, and Exiles in Post-Revolutionary French Painting." *Art Quarterly,* 36, no. 3 (1973), 141–171.

Rudé, George. *The Crowd in the French Revolution.* Oxford, 1959.

Sabatier, Nicole. "L'Hôpital Saint-Jacques d'Aix-en-Provence (1519–1789)." Doctoral diss., Université d'Aix-Marseille, 1964.

Saint-Jacob, Pierre de. *Les paysans de la Bourgogne du Nord au dernier siècle de l'Ancien Régime.* Dijon, 1960.

Saisset, Léon, and Frédéric Saisset. "Un type de l'ancienne comédie: Le barbon." *Mercure de France,* 183 (1925).

Sarton, George. *Galen of Pergamon*. Lawrence, Kan., 1954.

Sauvy, Alfred. *La montée des jeunes*. Paris, 1959.

Schalk, Ellery. *From Valor to Pedigree: Ideas of Nobility in France in the Sixteenth and Seventeenth Centuries*, Princeton, N.J., 1986.

Sée, Henri. *La France économique et sociale au XVIIIe siècle*. Paris, 1933.

Seligman, Edmond. *La justice en France pendant la révolution (1789–1792)*. Paris, 1901.

Sewell, William H., Jr. *Work and Revolution in France: The Language of Labor from the Old Regime to 1848*. Cambridge, 1980.

Sheppard, Thomas F. *Lourmarin in the Eighteenth Century: A Study of a French Village*. Baltimore, Md., 1971.

Smith, Martha Kellogg. "Georges de La Tour's 'Old Man' and 'Old Woman' in San Francisco." *Burlington Magazine*, 121 (1979), 288–294.

Soboul, Albert. *La civilisation et la révolution française*. Paris, 1970.

Spanneut, Michel. *Permanence du stoïcisme: De Zénon à Malraux*. Gembloux, Belgium, 1973.

Spengler, Joseph J. *France Faces Depopulation*. Durham, N.C., 1979.

——. *French Predecessors of Malthus: A Study in Eighteenth-Century Wage and Population Theory*. Durham, N.C., 1942.

Spicker, Stuart F., Kathleen M. Woodward, and David Van Tassel, eds. *Aging and the Elderly: Humanistic Perspectives in Gerontology*. Atlantic Highlands, N.J., 1978.

Starobinski, Jean. *L'invention de la liberté*. Geneva, 1964.

——. *1789: The Emblems of Reason*. Charlottesville, Va., 1982.

Staum, Martin S. *Cabanis: Enlightenment and Medical Philosophy in the French Revolution*. Princeton, N.J., 1980.

Stearns, Peter N. *Old Age in European Society: The Case of France*. New York, 1976.

——. "Old Women: Some Historical Observations." *Journal of Family History*, 5 (1980), 44–57.

——, ed. *Old Age in Preindustrial Society*. New York, 1982.

Steiner, George. *The Death of Tragedy*. New York, 1980.

Steudler, François. *Le système hospitalier: Evolution et transformations*. N.p., 1973. B.N. 4L 1875.

Stewart Philip. *Imitation and Illusion in the French Memoir-Novel, 1700–1750: The Art of Make-Believe*. New Haven, Conn., 1969.

Stone, Lawrence. *The Family, Sex, and Marriage in England, 1500–1800*. New York, 1977.

Tackett, Timothy. *Priest and Parish in Eighteenth-Century France*. Princeton, N.J., 1977.

Temkin, Owsei. *Galenism: Rise and Decline of a Medical Philosophy*. Ithaca, 1973.

Thibaux, Louis. "Le faux centenaire marseillais Annibal Camoux (1638!) 1669–1759." *Bulletin de l'Institut Historique de Provence*, 34, no. 2 (1957), 49–50.

Thiot, L. "Fêtes nationales pendant la révolution." Beauvais, 1908. Widener.

Thomas, Keith. *Age and Authority in Early Modern England*. London, 1976.

Thompson, Lawrence S. *A Bibliography of French Revolutionary Pamphlets on Microfiche*. Troy, N.Y., 1974.

Thuillier, Jacques. *Fragonard*. Geneva, 1967.

Tilly, Charles, ed. *Historical Studies of Changing Fertility*. Princeton, N.J., 1978.

Tollet, C. *Les édifices hospitaliers depuis leur origine jusqu'à nos jours*. Paris, 1892.

Tönnies, Ferdinand. *Community and Society*. New York, 1963.

Tourneux, Maurice. *Bibliographie de l'histoire de Paris pendant la révolution française*. Paris, 1900.

Traer, James F. "The French Family Court." *History*, 59 (1974), 211–228.

———. *Marriage and the Family in Eighteenth-Century France*. Ithaca, 1980.

Trésors des Musées du Nord de la France. La peinture française aux XVIIe et XVIIIe siècles. Dunkerque, 1980.

Tuetey, Alexandre. *L'assistance publique à Paris pendant la révolution*. Paris, 1895–97.

———. *Répertoire général des sources manuscrites de l'histoire de Paris pendant la révolution française*. Paris, 1890.

UNESCO. *Revue internationale des sciences sociales*, 15, no. 3 (1963), *Le troisième âge*.

Valmary, Pierre. *Familles paysannes au XVIIIe siècle en Bas-Quercy: Etude démographique*. Paris, 1965.

Van Kley, Dale. *The Damiens Affair and the Unraveling of the Ancien Régime, 1750–1770*. Princeton, N.J., 1984.

———. *The Jansenists and the Expulsion of the Jesuits from France, 1757–1765*. New Haven, Conn., 1975.

Van Tassel, David D., ed. *Aging, Death, and the Completion of Being*. Philadelphia, 1979.

Viard, Paul. "Les tribunaux de famille dans le district de Dijon (1790–1792)." *Nouvelle Revue Historique de Droit Français et Étranger*, 45 (1921).

Villadary, Agnès. *Fête et vie quotidienne*. Paris, 1968.

Vincent, Paul E. "French Demography in the Eighteenth Century." *Population Studies*, 1 (1947).

Vogler, Bernard. "Le testament alsacien en cours au XVIIIe siècle." *Revue d'histoire moderne et contemporaine*, 26 (1979), 439–447.

———. *Trois mémoires sur les testaments à Strasbourg au 18e siècle*. Strasbourg, 1978.

Vovelle, Gaby and Michel Vovelle. *Vision de la mort et de l'au-delà en Provence d'après les autels des âmes du purgatoire XVe–XXe siècles. Cahiers des Annales*, 29 (1970).

Vovelle, Michel. *De la cave au grenier: Un itinéraire en Provence au XVIIIe siècle*. Quebec, 1980.

———. *Idéologies et mentalités*. Paris, 1985.

———. *Les métamorphoses de la fête en Provence de 1750 à 1820*. Paris, 1976.

———. *La mort et l'Occident de 1300 à nos jours*. Paris, 1983.

———. *Mourir autrefois: Attitudes collectives devant la mort aux XVIIe et XVIIIe siècles*. Paris, 1974.

———. *Piété baroque et déchristianisation en Provence au XVIIIe siècle*. Paris, 1973.

———. "Le tournant des mentalités en France, 1750–1789: La sensibilité pré-révolutionnaire." *Social History*, 5 (1977), 605–629.

Wall, Richard, Jean Robin, and Peter Laslett, eds. *Family Forms in Historic Europe.* Cambridge, 1983.

Weber, Eugen. *Peasants into Frenchmen: The Modernization of Rural France, 1870–1914.* Stanford, Calif., 1976.

Wildenstein, Georges. *The Paintings of Fragonard.* Garden City, N.Y., 1960.

Wildenstein, Georges, et al. *Le dessin français dans les collections du XVIIIe siècle.* Paris, 1935.

Wilson, John Montgomery. *The Painting of the Passions in Theory, Practice, and Criticism in Later Eighteenth Century France.* New York, 1981.

Woloch, Isser. *The French Veteran from the Revolution to the Restoration.* Chapel Hill, N.C., 1979.

———. "War-Widows Pensions: Social Policy in Revolutionary and Napoleonic France." *Societas,* 6 (1976), 235–254.

Yver, Jean. *Egalité entre héritiers et exclusion des enfants dotés: Essai de géographie coutumière.* Paris, 1966.

Zeldin, Theodore. *France, 1848–1945.* 2 vols. Oxford, 1973–77.

Zeman, Frederic D. "Jean Astruc (1684–1766) on Old Age." *Journal of the History of Medicine and Allied Sciences,* 20 (1965).

Zonabend, Françoise. "Les morts et les vivants: Le cimetière de Minot en Châtillonnais." *Etudes Rurales,* 52 (1973), 7–23.

Index

Library of Congress Cataloging-in-Publication Data

Troyansky, David G.
    Old age in the old regime.

    Bibliography: p.
    Includes index.
    1. Aged—France—History—18th century.
2. Old age—France—Public opinion—History—
18th century.   3. Public opinion—France—
History—18th century.   4. Old age—France—
History—18th century—Sources. I. Title.
HQ1064.F7T76   1989   305.2'6'0944   88–43286
ISBN 0–8014–2299–X (alk. paper)